Her Cup for Sweet Cacao

The Linda Schele Series in Maya and Pre-Columbian Studies

Her Cup for Sweet Cacao

Food in Ancient Maya Society

EDITED BY TRACI ARDREN

University of Texas Press *Austin*

This series was made possible through the generosity of William C. Nowlin, Jr., and Bettye H. Nowlin, the National Endowment for the Humanities, and various individual donors.

Copyright © 2020 by the University of Texas Press
All rights reserved
Printed in the United States of America
First edition, 2020

Requests for permission to reproduce material from this work should be sent to:
    Permissions
    University of Texas Press
    P.O. Box 7819
    Austin, TX 78713-7819
    utpress.utexas.edu/rp-form

♾ The paper used in this book meets the minimum requirements of ANSI/NISO Z39.48-1992 (R1997) (Permanence of Paper).

Library of Congress Cataloging-in-Publication Data

Names: Ardren, Traci, editor.
Title: Her cup for sweet cacao : food in ancient Maya society / edited by Traci Ardren.
Description: First edition. | Austin : University of Texas Press, 2021. | Includes bibliographical references and index.
Identifiers: LCCN 2020005347 (print) | LCCN 2020005348 (ebook)
ISBN 978-1-4773-2164-5 (cloth)
ISBN 978-1-4773-2165-2 (ebook other)
ISBN 978-1-4773-2166-9 (ebook)
Subjects: LCSH: Mayas—Food. | Mayas—Social life and customs. | Food habits—Central America—History. | Food habits—Mexico—History. | Food—Social aspects—Central America. | Food—Social aspects—Mexico. | Central America—Antiquities. | Mexico—Antiquities.
Classification: LCC F1435.3.F7 H47 2021 (print) | LCC F1435.3.F7 (ebook) | DDC 972.8/01—dc23
LC record available at https://lccn.loc.gov/2020005347
LC ebook record available at https://lccn.loc.gov/2020005348

doi:10.7560/321645

Cover image: An elite woman and seated lord frame a courtier undergoing supernatural transformation. She holds a large ceramic vessel and may have provided the plate of tamales as part of the ritual preparations. Photograph by Justin Kerr, K6059, used with permission.

For Joann Andrews, Maria Transita Varguez Pacheco, and all the women of Quinta MARI who fed my heart and soul

Contents

Preface **ix**
MICHAEL D. COE

1. Introduction **1**
   TRACI ARDREN

2. Potluck: Building Community and Feasting among the Middle Preclassic Maya **25**
   M. KATHRYN BROWN AND CAROLYN FREIWALD

3. A Toast to the Earth: The Social Role of Beverages in Pre-Hispanic Maya Cave Ritual at Pacbitun, Belize **47**
   JON SPENARD, ADAM KING, TERRY G. POWIS, AND NILESH GAIKWAD

4. The Epigraphy of Ancient Maya Food and Drink **87**
   NICHOLAS CARTER AND MALLORY E. MATSUMOTO

5. Plant Foodstuffs of the Ancient Maya: Agents and Matter, Medium and Message **124**
   SHANTI MORELL-HART

6. Food, Friend, or Offering: Exploring the Role of Maya Dogs in the Zooarchaeological Record **161**
   PETRA CUNNINGHAM-SMITH, ASHLEY E. SHARPE, ARIANNE BOILEAU, ERIN KENNEDY THORNTON, AND KITTY F. EMERY

7. Celebrating Sihó: The Role of Food and Foodways in the Construction of Social Identities **188**
   LILIA FERNÁNDEZ SOUZA, MARIO ZIMMERMANN, AND SOCORRO DEL PILAR JIMÉNEZ ÁLVAREZ

8. Cuisine and Feasting in the Copán and Lower Ulúa Valleys in Honduras   219
   JULIA A. HENDON

9. Talking Feasts: Classic Maya Commensal Politics at La Corona   243
   MAXIME LAMOUREUX-ST-HILAIRE

10. Thinking (and Eating) Chichén Itzá: New Food Technology and Creating the Itzá State at Xuenkal   274
    TRACI ARDREN

11. Faunal Foods as Indices of Commoner Wealth (or Poverty) in Rural versus Urban Houselots of the Terminal Classic and Postclassic in Northwest Yucatán   297
    MARILYN A. MASSON, TIMOTHY S. HARE, BRADLEY W. RUSSELL, CARLOS PERAZA LOPE, AND JESSICA L. CAMPBELL

12. Human-Deity Relationships Conveyed through *Balche'* Rituals and Resource Procurement   334
    GABRIELLE VAIL AND MAIA DEDRICK

13. Conclusion: In Maya Food Studies, Who Is Maya? What Is Food?   366
    JEFFREY M. PILCHER

Index   380

Preface

MICHAEL D. COE

A half century ago, it would have made little sense to have a volume of essays wholly dedicated to the study of the foodways of the Classic Maya, since the evidence for such an enterprise barely existed. From key ethnohistoric sources such as Bernal Díaz del Castillo and Fray Bernardino de Sahagún, a great deal is known about Aztec food and drink, markets, and elite feasting. In contrast, for the precontact Maya, we have only meager information on these subjects from Spanish conquistadores and early missionaries in the Maya area. Even our principal sixteenth-century source for the late pre-Conquest Maya—Bishop Diego de Landa—has disappointingly little to say on the subject.

In the decades after 1970, a revolution in Maya research took hold. Epigraphers are now able to read the dedicatory texts painted or carved on Classic Maya vases and bowls, most importantly the glyph for that most prized of elite drinks, cacao—chocolate. The residues of the liquids that once were contained in vessels found in Maya tombs and elsewhere in Classic and Postclassic sites can now be analyzed chemically and identified. The plant foods of ancient Maya cuisine are revealed by microscopic starch grains and phytoliths. And iconographers as well as epigraphers now have at hand the great digital archive of Classic Maya painted or carved vases rolled out by the photographer Justin Kerr—many of which bear vivid witness to feasting, sacrifice, the offering of tribute, and other elite activities in royal courts.

On topics ranging from kitchen areas in Maya palaces to liquids imbibed in cave rituals, to dogs bred for consumption, to the changing access to the meat of game animals in Maya diets, all of these chapters demonstrate how our understanding of ancient Maya society has been enriched by a knowledge of what and how these peoples dined and drank, and with whom. The study of Maya foodways has advanced to maturity.

Her Cup for Sweet Cacao

CHAPTER 1

Introduction

TRACI ARDREN

Growing food requires people to defy the arbitrary catastrophes of nature and create social means of countering them.
DAVID FREIDEL, 2008

In their ruminations on cosmology, food, and the origins of political power, David Freidel and F. Kent Reilly argue that in Mesoamerica, the Olmec invented structural authority and that it rested on a belief in the ability of emergent elites to guarantee sufficient food (Freidel and Reilly 2010). Food and, in particular, the production of maize are at the heart of how power, authority, and destiny were conceptualized in ancient Mesoamerica, and it is hard to find another ancient culture where these linkages are made more explicit than in Classic Maya society. Maya royalty embodied the Maize Deity in ritual theater to assert their vibrancy, their essentialness, their ubiquity in daily life. The divinity of royals was expressly linked to the fertility and life cycle of maize in these rites and in the mythological stories told among the royal court and throughout Classic cities. Classic Maya kings sometimes portrayed themselves as sacred hunters, reenacting mythological scripts later documented in the *Popol Vuh*. Royal Maya women are shown providing highly charged versions of cooked foods to the Maize Deity and other Maya deities in elite art. The ideological responsibility for feeding a city fell squarely on the royal family, and although in reality dietary inequalities were common as well as intentional, the cosmological underpinning of Classic Maya society rested on the social interdependencies that emerge from daily meals.

This volume aims to explore the social aspect of food and foodways in Classic Maya society, to build on the many decades of research into subsistence patterns and dietary habits to reveal the economic, political, religious, and ultimately social aspects of foodways in arenas such as cooking, feasting, ritual, and memory work. These are all rich arenas of ancient lives, filled with choices and sensory experiences that help us as modern scholars blur the artificial boundaries between past and present. Interest in food scholarship has never been stronger, and food studies is an emerging and vibrant transdisciplinary field of investigation. Likewise, public interest in food scholarship is growing as more and more people from different food traditions are drawn together to learn about one another through shared food experiences. A nostalgia for healthier diets from an imagined past, such as the paleo diet fad, is a call to action for archaeologists and others committed to providing accurate information about the richness of ancient lives and the incredibly deep body of knowledge preserved within ancient food traditions (Graff 2017).

The Social Roles of Food and Foodways

In a recent review of archaeological scholarship on cooking and food preparation, Sarah Graff explains that the social practice of cooking has important information to reveal about issues of daily praxis, social life, religious belief, identity formation, and power relations (Graff 2017:2). Turning our attention to these types of practices in ancient lives brings less visible people to light, such as the women and older folks who performed a large share of the culinary labor. It draws our attention to social processes often overlooked because they take place in the domestic setting or in areas of less dramatic social visibility than palaces or pyramids. Culinary practices can reveal difference and heterogeneity in ancient societies by exposing food and preparation choices, such as what foodstuffs were selected and which were avoided or who had preferential access to quality goods. Although of great interest to scholars in other fields, the technology of cooking and food preparation has not received as much attention in archaeology, especially changes in technology that reflect cultural change or contact. Choice and skill are as clearly indicated in how a cook chooses tools to prepare a dish as in how a craftsperson chooses hammer stones to make a lithic blade—in both cases, questions of apprenticeship and learning as well as the impact of repeated actions on identity formation are relevant (Ayora-Diaz 2015; Meyers 2008). Food preparation also facilitates our ability to see the agency of individual chefs, or households, as they make hundreds of choices about provisions, recipes, tools, and service. Changes in foodways rest with choices made by individual cooks, which are often made in response to broader shifts in markets, household economics, and seasonal availability, as well as individual knowledge and memory of culturally specific food systems.

Just as Graff summarized how some scholars have made the economic, political, and religious networks embedded in cooking and food preparation more visible, this volume expands our analyses and understanding of other aspects of Classic Maya foodways such as ritual food use, gardening and agricultural practices, and food marketing. As the authors in this volume show, in nearly every arena of ancient Maya life, the role of food provides a lens through which to explore a fascinating network of social forces and relationships. In a recent monograph quickly becoming a classic reference work, Christine Hastorf explains how food is "a principal medium for social interactions," providing comfort but also reinforcing hidden power dynamics, and that it is part and parcel of reproducing culture (Hastorf 2017:1). Hastorf also reminds us that we cannot unravel the biological aspects of food use and traditions without considering the cultural aspects as well (ibid.). In the case of the ancient Maya, diets were not dominated by corn products simply because it was the most abundant or available food—there were many other less labor-intensive choices. Ideological investments in maize and the role maize cultivation played in the mythological foundations of structural power, coupled with its adaptation to the lowland climate and the deep indigenous knowledge base acquired through generations of investment in this remarkable crop, are all significant components of why most Maya diets were dominated by maize during the Classic period.

Food is a social fact, and it provides a social glue between people who produce, prepare, and consume it together. It is a social fact because all aspects of food, from subsistence methods, to preparation tools, to rituals of consuming, are learned behaviors with social consequences. These are actions children are taught (or they observe) and reproduce as part of the process of becoming "real" members of their society. They are actions that are prescribed by cultural norms yet are capable of influence and modification for a host of reasons, such as scarcity, discovery, or inspiration. Food provides a social glue, a form of connectivity because it nearly always involves social interaction—planting grain, harvesting fruit, grinding corn, cooking stew, fetching water, and eating a meal are activities done communally in most societies today, and certainly in the past when such activities were even more time- and labor-intensive.. This perspective highlights the agency of food in individual and collective life. For example, how many relationships have been formed over cocktails or a holiday meal? What significant gathering does not include the presence of food, often highly scripted to serve the intended outcome of the get-together? We have emotional relationships with food, both constructive and destructive, and we speak of food addictions; there is no reason to suspect that the agency of food was any less complex in ancient times, and in fact there is reason to suspect it was more profound, given the regularity with which ancient lives were impacted by food shortages, inequalities, or seasonal fluctuations. This volume struggles with a theoretical concern in understanding the agency of food: Do foodways reflect social life or do they construct social life? In many cases, the answer is that food and foodways are central to constructing the social experiences that constitute the direct experience of culture, thus they must construct social life.

Foodways play a key role in group identity creation and maintenance. Arjun Appadurai (1988) showed how a national Indian cuisine was created out of a bewildering array of regional traditions through cookbooks that organized foods into standard categories and elevated certain dishes that had significant ideological or historical importance. A number of modern studies have followed, which explore the creation of national cuisines in newly independent countries like Belize (Wilk 2006) or places where a unified national identity is under reconstruction (Ichijo and Ranta 2016; James 1997; Pite 2013). Naming certain dishes as representative of the nation or of a highly diverse population that shares tenuous connections across thousands of miles is as powerful a tool in nation building as standardizing language or currency. Often this process involves the nomination of what Hastorf (2017:262) calls a "signature food," one substance among many that the state selects for inclusion in every meal or for enhanced ideological emphasis. When Japan was unified in the sixteenth century, early emperors used shared harvest rituals as a metaphor for unified political control, and thus the rice harvest, and rice as a signature food, was embedded in ideological mechanisms of the Japanese state. It is easy to see a similar process at work within Mesoamerica, where elite power was tied to the life cycle of corn, and agricultural success was appropriated as a metaphor for the power of the state.

Like all people of Mesoamerica, Maya people identify with corn and the myriad ways in which its dietary importance structures many aspects of their lives. Scholars have written about the emotional reactions Mexicans have to GMO drift from North America and the value of perpetuating genetic and culinary variation in corn, and of course corn continues to be a signature food in Mexican diets today (Castellanos and Bergstresser 2014; Good Eshelman and Corona de la Peña 2011). These sorts of deep emotional connections to common foodstuffs are easily manipulated by political forces, and Classic period art demonstrates an emphasis on the ideological centrality of corn. In fact, the ubiquity of the Maize Deity and other aspects of corn agriculture are features that link art made across the Maya region in the Classic period. We should explore how this single component of a diverse subsistence system came to be used so strategically by elites concerned with maintaining group identity as well as their own privileged positions of power. Other foodstuffs such as venison and cacao were also ascribed heightened social significance, but our scholarly understanding of these processes has been obscured by a repetitive focus on the rather obvious question of how Mayaness equals corn.

The social aspect of foodways is particularly visible when the spatial component of food production and consumption is considered. Feasting at centrally located platforms is a well-documented component in the emergence of early elites in the Maya area (and elsewhere). In such rituals of inclusion, we know people of different social experiences were brought together for a short time to share a meal and perhaps some entertainment or political theater (Brown 2008; Brown and Freiwald, this volume; Clark and Blake 1994; Hayden and Gargett 1990; Hendon 2003; Rosenswig 2007). Bonds were formed over a shared culinary experience that then implicated the participants in an ongoing set of social obligations and relationships. The feasting debris found in excavations is often not only located in a central gathering spot but conspicuous, abundant, and unusual. Maya feasts were communal by definition but also often opportunities for the public display of resources, and the remains of the feast may have festered for days following the event. The places feasts took place were marked in this way, not only by the event itself but by the preparations for the feast, the debris left behind, and the memories participants shared with one another that reinforced their experiences.

Likewise, kitchens are ideologically charged locations where many social relationships come into play that require the negotiation of gendered and age-based expectations for interaction. In kitchens, we can see material evidence of apprenticeship as new family members learn methods of preparation and of the tools used by those who exert authority in this socially charged space. Broken water jars may be evidence of an inept or careless assistant; new tools are evidence of learning taking place. Kitchens are also a nexus for economic, political, and religious forces that act upon those who prepare food and those who consume it. What ingredients are available, which ones are allowed, what is prohibited, and what is desired—these are all daily considerations in the kitchen that reflect on broader social forces such as trade or tribute requirements, long-distance exchange networks, or taboo and sacramental foods. Those people who moved through a kitchen came under the influence of these societal forces, and those who tended the garden or agricultural fields were subject to different but related considerations. It is widely understood that in Classic Maya cities, infield gardens were tightly controlled by household groups, and agricultural land located in rural areas was less tightly controlled. People who spent time producing food in either of these contexts negotiated the political systems of a hierarchical state and economic systems that relied on significant tribute demands. These types of food-production spaces were just as highly charged with ideological significance to the state as palace feasting rooms, and it is likely that the majority of the rural and urban population experienced these arenas of the food landscape as far from neutral places.

Even a seemingly simple topic like meals, which have long been of interest to archaeologists primarily in terms of calories consumed rather than as a setting for highly scripted and repetitive social behaviors, is worth returning to with an eye to exploring in greater depth the various social networks that converge in this one setting (Atalay and Hastorf 2006; Hastorf 2017; Weismantel 1988). Meals are embedded in long histories of food consumption, they express values and can be a venue for debates around authenticity, and they can even have moral consequences. A meal is a microcosm of all the social forces that surround cultural foodways, with the potential for heightened emotional content. Who participates? How often are meals served and under what conditions? What foods are considered appropriate to eat together or at different times of the day? These are basic questions for which we have no definitive answers in terms of Classic Maya society despite centuries of research. Inspiration can be drawn from ethnographic analogy to modern Maya meal habits, but we have not explored the material record of the past for confirmation of such continuities. Historic documents are hardly more revealing, as the mealtime habits of the bulk of the population were not of interest to most of the literate population. It is the task of archaeologists and other students of ancient cultures to recover the delicious minutiae of co-eating, the recipes and choices of a family or a household, and how eating structured the rhythms of daily circulations. Household debris such as broken pottery or fruit seeds may seem a fragile basis on which to reconstruct ideas about who should eat with whom and when, but we must ask the question to find the data. Archaeologists have been very successful in reconstructing the most elaborate forms of meals, such as feasts (Dietler and Hayden 2001;

Klarich 2010). Just as we turned from exploring only tombs of kings to a consideration of the living spaces of a majority of the population, we can pivot from examining the remains of a royal feast to exploring the daily food habits of the 99 percent.

What We Already Know about Food in Ancient Maya Social Life

Bishop Diego de Landa was perhaps the first outsider to show an interest in documenting Maya foodways, and his sixteenth-century memoir, *Relación de las cosas de Yucatán*, includes an entire section on "food and drink" that explains in great detail the essential Maya technique of corn processing known as nixtamalization. Like so many later commentators, Landa focuses on products made from maize and the centrality of these to Maya diets. He describes the balls of corn dough that were made and transported into the fields or in the bundles of travelers as well as a host of drinkable forms of maize that were consumed throughout the day. Landa describes foods that were eaten three times a day, with the largest meal of vegetable "ragouts" in the evening, and he even captured the cultural practice of consuming warm drinks in the morning and cool drinks during the day. In a later section, he describes what to his eyes appeared to be raucous feasts fueled by large jars of honey-wine and dancing. Roast fowl and cacao accompany the honey-wine, and he mentions that feasts were both elaborate and expensive events when celebrated by "leading men" or intimate events among kinsfolk to commemorate a marriage or birth (Gates [Landa] 1937:35).

John Lloyd Stephens recorded cooking practices during his nineteenth-century journeys through the Maya area that inform us about the persistence of indigenous culinary traditions (Stephens 1963 [1843], 1969 [1854]). When visiting the ruins of Uxmal, Stephens's caravan employs a local woman to prepare eggs, which she does in a manner they have never seen before. Later they witnessed the venerable Maya tradition of roasting a pig in an underground oven, better known as *pibil* (Stephens 1963 [1843]:149). Despite occasional descriptions of breakfast, it is clear that food culture was not an interest of Stephens, and even subsistence systems like maize agriculture and fishing receive very little attention in his work.

The beginning of modern scholarly interest in Maya foodways could be attributed to the work of Ralph L. Roys, a member of both the Carnegie Institution of Washington and Tulane Middle American Research Institute expeditions and an ethnohistorian. Many of the ceremonies and texts Roys studied include the mention of ritually significant foods. Maya colonial documents, such as the *Book of Chilam Balam of Chumayel* (Roys 1933) or the *Ritual of the Bacabs* (Roys 1965), both of which Roys translated, include gastronomic offerings to deities. But his first significant publication, *The Ethno-botany of the Maya* (Roys 1931), is perhaps the most significant in terms of how later scholars would understand Maya foodways. Filled with medicinal and culinary information, Roys's work catalogued the vast knowledge of plants, trees, and herbs that existed in early twentieth-century Yucatán. As he states in the first sentence of his publication, "The study and observation of plants have always been considered of high importance by the Maya Indians of Yucatan; indeed this branch of their ancient culture is the one which has suffered least from several centuries of European domination" (Roys 1931:v).

Foodways were not a topic of substantial interest within Maya studies for many decades following the work of Roys, but individual scholars interested in trade and dietary patterns began to investigate these topics in the 1980s. Anthony P. Andrews's (1983) early work on salt production in the Maya area is a good example of how food practices are part of a network of many other social systems and can be approached from a variety of intellectual directions. Andrews was interested in the role of trade in Maya history and chose to work on recovering information about pre-Hispanic salt production due to the importance of this commodity and the absence of prior scholarship on it. Vital to the human body, salt played a larger role in Maya long-distance trade systems than it did in many other places in the world, given the relative absence of salt in the Maya plant-based diet of corn and beans, which lacked natural sources of sodium from animal protein. Salt extraction and exchange has since grown into a significant area of research, with many scholars looking into the variety of ways salt was made available within the Maya area (Hutson 2017; McKillop 2008; Nance 1992).

In the 1970s, Elizabeth S. Wing published some of the earliest faunal analyses in the Maya area (1974, 1975), and in the 1980s, Mary Pohl began publishing the results of her early zooarchaeological studies into Maya dietary patterns, following the completion of her dissertation on Maya ethnozoology at five ancient Maya sites. In a long and prolific career, Pohl has published on many aspects of Maya subsistence, but of particular relevance here is her work on ritual fauna, hunting, deer consumption, and the gendered components of the subsistence economy (Pohl 1983, 1985, 1990, etc.; Pohl and Feldman 1982). Nancy Hamblin published a book-length zooarchaeological study in 1984, which explored how animals were understood on ancient Cozumel, using all the faunal remains from the Harvard project. From this very large and diverse collection, which included species that rarely preserve at Maya sites, such as fish and amphibians, Hamblin (1984:165) built on an observation by Pohl that Maya diets favored fat-rich mammals such as peccary, dog, opossum, and paca. Many other zooarchaeologists followed Wing's and Pohl's early contributions, and today faunal studies continue to expand as a number of the chapters in this volume demonstrate (Emery 2004; Götz 2014).

The recovery of dietary information from plant remains arrived in Maya studies in the late 1980s, primarily under the influence of the paleoethnobotanist David L. Lentz. Like Pohl, Lentz remains an active scholar today and has mentored a growing number of younger scholars who continue his work with plant remains (Morehart and Morell-Hart 2015). In a series of highly influential articles, Lentz showed that contrary to the expectations of earlier generations, plant materials could preserve in tropical environments, and that with the right recovery techniques, sophisticated data were recoverable. Lentz applied insights from both macro and micro botanical remains to key problems within ancient Mesoamerica, such as the domestication of maize; agricultural practices; and the uniquely Mesoamerican dietary miracle of corn, beans, and squash (Lentz 1991, 1999; Lentz et al. 1996). It is not an exaggeration to say that Lentz's scholarship changed how Maya archaeology was conducted, as paleobotanical analysis is now considered a standard part of every excavation project and a powerful way to recover unique data on diet and food practices.

A landmark in the study of ancient Maya foodways was the publication in 1994 of *America's First Cuisines*, by the food historian Sophie D. Coe. Extremely accessible to scholars and interested foodies alike, this book was widely read by those curious about ancient food in the New World, and it is still in print today. Coe introduced the nonspecialist (and Mayanists, too!) to the rich world of Maya food and drink, including the fruits, greens, and meats often used in feasting that appear in Maya art. She compiled so much information on chocolate that she began another book, *The True History of Chocolate* (1996), completed by her partner, Michael D. Coe, after her untimely death in 1994. These two books treated Maya foodways as serious traditions worthy of scholarly study and placed New World culinary innovations within a broader worldwide context of food scholarship. *The True History of Chocolate* opened the door for a huge wave of scholarship on chocolate, both in the Maya area and throughout the New World. Today we know more about how chocolate was grown, traded, prepared, and consumed than we know about any other Maya foodstuff (Dreiss 2008; Gómez-Pompa, Salvador Flores, and Aliphat Fernández 1990; Henderson et al. 2007; LeCount 2001; McAnany et al. 2002; McNeil 2006; Ruz 2016).

Bone isotope studies was another major methodological innovation within Maya studies of diet. Starting in the 1990s, Christine D. White introduced the use of trace elements, stable isotopes, and nutritional and dental pathologies as tools for recovering information about ancient nutrition and diet (1997, 1999, 2005; White et al. 2004; White, Longstaffe, and Schwarcz 2009). Her edited volume *Reconstructing Ancient Maya Diet* (1999) brought together specialists in faunal, botanical, paleopathological, and bone chemical analyses in a comprehensive assessment of what was known at the time about nutrition and health within Classic Maya society. This volume made important contributions to our understanding of the gendered nature of Maya foodways, to how status impacted access to food and thus health, and to our knowledge of the regional variability of Maya diets.

In the 2000s, many more scholars engaged with questions of diet, subsistence, and even food culture of the ancient Maya. Using the methodological tools mentioned above, scholars expanded our understanding of what faunal and plant remains were found, based on a shift in excavation strategy that prioritized middens and other domestic debris often overlooked in earlier investigations. It would be unwise to try to list all the publications on this topic since 2000, but many of the scholars included in this volume have been investigating questions of food culture since that time. Recently, scholars engaged in the food studies literature have included the Maya area in broader studies that address questions of memory, power, technology, and nationhood that are at the heart of this emergent transdisciplinary field. *Pre-Columbian Foodways*, edited by John E. Staller and Michael D. Carrasco (2010), included chapters on epigraphic references to Maya beverages on elite ceramic vessels, feasting events, and the role of food in Maya cosmological origin myths, among other topics. The paleoethnobotanist and longtime Andean food scholar Christine Hastorf includes discussion of Maya foodways in her introduction to the role of food in archaeological research, *The Social Archaeology of Food* (2017). Hastorf points out many important aspects of what she calls the "Maya culinary tradition," especially the creation of group identities through culinary boundaries and daily habitus.

Two unique archaeological discoveries also pushed the study of Maya foodways forward in unexpected ways—one was the excavation in the

1980s of the ancient site of Joya de Cerén, where a volcanic eruption covered and instantly preserved the domestic gardens and associated fields of a Classic village. Cerén has provided us more information on ancient house gardens and the economically useful plants grown in them than perhaps any other source, or at least the quality of the data is unique and particularly significant. The paleoethnobotanical and archaeological analyses from Cerén, which (for example) identified the first manioc grown in the Maya area and vessels filled with achiote seeds, have been extraordinary (Farahani et al. 2017; Lentz et al. 1996; Sheets 2002). The second find, the Chiik Nahb murals discovered at Calakmul in 2004, could not be more different from the extraordinary data preserved at Cerén, but these murals have also profoundly changed our understanding of ancient Maya food culture. A series of food vendors are shown in a marketplace, selling or exchanging a variety of foods named in small glyphic captions (Boucher and Quiñones 2007). One has brought a huge pot of atole to serve with a ladle, another is described as the "tamale person," and so on (Carrasco Vargas, Vázquez López, and Martin 2009). The presence of food vendors is well attested in later Aztec marketplaces seen by Spanish chroniclers, but the Chiik Nahb murals are the first and most substantial evidence for marketplace exchange of foodstuffs in the Maya area. These are neither nobles nor commoners; they are well-to-do merchants likely trading surplus comestibles made in their homes. Analysis of these murals has moved the study of foodways out of the domestic realm, or the palace, and into economic venues never before considered. It is an exciting time to study Maya cooking, cuisine, and sustenance.

Food and Memory Work

My objective with this volume is not only to explore the social roles foodways played in Classic Maya culture but to do so in a manner that contributes to how we understand the role of memory in cultural reproduction and identity construction. Attention to memory is implicit in much of the current scholarship on food, especially in contemporary ethnographies of immigrant or diasporic communities as well as popular literature on the history of foodways (Ayora-Diaz 2012; Brulotte and Di Giovine 2014; Holtzman 2006; Sutton 2001). There is no question that the slippery notions of nostalgia and imagination both figure prominently in modern food studies, but memory, too, is often in the background, providing a quiet foundation for the more imaginative and dynamic processes by which food traditions are reinvented or remembered. Memory work, or the many social practices that create meaning (Mills and Walker 2008), has been carefully considered in a variety of archaeological contexts, although with less attention to foodways than to other forms of social remembering (Hendon 2010; Mills and Walker 2008; Stanton and Magnoni 2008; Van Dyke and Alcock 2003; cf. LeCount 2010). The useful term "memory work" encompasses attention to practices such as recalling, inventing, or forgetting memories but also to understanding the materiality of those practices—how objects or substances are used to concretize such experiences (Mills and Walker 2008:4). Here we explicitly consider the ways food is deployed to intensify or ritualize an experience that will be remembered as a touchstone, to mediate the introduction of new ideas or practices, or simply to show how the skills of food preparation contributed to the bodily memories that often constitute a key component of subjectivity. In the schema provided by Susan Gillespie (2010:402) for the major foci of memory studies within archaeology, this volume speaks to "how social memory reproduces or transforms society and its constituent groups," or what can be called the "work" of memory work.

The bodily memory of food preparation and consumption is a powerful vehicle for the creation of a shared social imaginary or shared social experiences that create bonds of enduring emotional significance (Connerton 1989; Sutton 2001). In agricultural societies like that of the Classic Maya, learning how to tend plants and animals was a crucial component of growing to adulthood. While skills such as planting corn or butchering ducks became routine for the majority of the population, they likely retained a highly charged emotional content, given the importance of these skills to meeting daily subsistence needs. The memory of how to perform such tasks correctly was not incidental but rather the result of deliberate and methodical repetition of bodily movements, social interactions, and memory in which each step recalls part of the whole experience (Douglas 1971; Douglas and Gross 1981). Likewise, learning to prepare food in a certain manner was another highly charged activity during which resources had to be carefully marshaled and transformed from wild and raw to cultured and cooked. In food studies, the kitchen has emerged as a particularly significant space for the transference of knowledge along identity-based lines, be those gendered, age based, or familial—this was no less true for ancient societies where resources were even more limited. Isotopic analyses from across the ancient Maya Lowlands show clear and repetitive patterns of food scarcity in the human skeletal record, and gustatory memories were not always pleasant or nurturing but included the memory of deprivation—climatic and intentional—that was intrinsic to the operation of ancient states (Dine et al. 2019).

Jon D. Holtzman (2006) and other scholars in the emergent field of food studies have explored why food is such a powerful vehicle for memory work. Certainly archaeologists have identified other common activities that also provided a venue for the creation of shared memories, such as the construction and abandonment of monumental architecture, crafting, boundary maintenance, the maintenance of sacred sites, and others. As a topic of study, the experience of food has the advantage of universal participation, cross-cutting all social distinctions while simultaneously reinforcing them, and of providing a "language" for social meaning and memories that all members of society experience. The study of how food and memory work together holds the promise of new insights into questions that have long been at the heart of the anthropological cannon—ritual, exchange, nostalgia, embodiment. Food is highly sensual, and shared sensory memories take on a heightened recall ability, which means that foodways that engage multiple senses, such as sight, taste, aroma, and even sound, generate particularly durable recollections. An anthropology attentive to the senses challenges a purely "symbolic" reading of food and can reveal a lot about the power of food memories and food traditions (Sutton 2001:161).

Ritual is a key site where food and memory come together. The consumption of daily foods in a ritualized context where they assume new meanings, such as during feasting associated with weddings or funerals, adds texture and ambiguity to the memory of that particular food and thus to the "meaning" of the food. In most societies, certain foods are only consumed in ritual settings, and they occupy a special place in the culinary repertoire for that reason. The memory of the ritual will be constituted in part by the memory of consuming an unusual food. For ancient Maya emerging elites, the consumption of rare and prestigious foods in formal feasting contexts was a ritual of intensification that solidified their alliances and obligations to dynastic powers (Brown 2008; Brown and Freiwald, this volume; Clark and Blake 1994; Hayden and Gargett 1990; Hendon 2003; Rosenswig 2007). Often situated in highly charged elite architectural arenas such as palaces or acropolises, these feasts brought together the royal family with visiting dignitaries and lower-ranking members of the court and polity. Remnants of these feasts have been found across the Maya Lowlands, and though the specific foods that were served vary from site to site, the ritualized nature of the feast is clear. Excessive consumption of high-status food and drink followed by conspicuous disposal in a restricted location were social practices that contributed to the Classic Maya feast as a key component of memory creation and the reproduction of asymmetrical social relations. Funerary rituals were also places where memories were created and solidified via food—whether through consumption of a funerary feast by mourners, which is challenging to see in the Maya material record, or via the ubiquitous food offerings left with the departed, which are extremely visible at all social levels, since food was an integral component of the funerary experience. These social encounters, where heightened emotions were combined with a variety of sensory experiences, were mediated and facilitated through shared foodways (Hamilakis 1998).

An examination of food-centered remembering likewise requires us to consider food-centered forgetting as a social process with similarly profound implications. Food not only cements social bonds; it can also be used to dissolve them. Scholars have argued that funerary food offerings are integral to the re-membering of the departed, which requires the forgetting of the living family member in order to create an ancestor (Conklin 1995; Munn 1986; Sutton 2001). The ethnographer Nancy Munn (1986: 177) argues that food exchanges between kin relations at a mortuary feast are a way of closing paths of exchange and interdependence. The use of food in funerary ritual intentionally invokes the emotional ambivalences of food to mediate the forgetting of a royal dynast or a beloved family member. Classic Maya royal tombs are often filled with tens of ceramic vessels that retain evidence of the elite cuisine they contained when the tomb was sealed, and even the most modest burial in a residential context often contained multiple serving vessels alongside the deceased. This durable residue of the central role food played in ancestral memory creation suggests that forgetting was deeply intertwined with remembrance, practice, and sensation.

Food can also be a powerful tool in other forms of forgetting—during processes of cultural transformation, earlier foodways are often left behind. When immigrants leave their homeland, they may cling ferociously to the food traditions of their home, locked in to the time of their departure, or they may deliberately forget these tastes in order to manage the experience of living elsewhere (Alfonso 2014; Marte 2012; Singer 1984). Political shifts also frequently employ an ability to forget the foodways or tastes of subjugated or oppositional cultures, while the conversion experience can employ new food prohibitions (i.e., the forgetting of prior foodways) as a form of identity construction. Eliot Singer (1984) demonstrates how new converts to American Hinduism use food taboos to intentionally forget and erase earlier personal histories, and Ivan Alonso (2014) explains how Cubans in London gradually come to see "Cuban" food as unhealthy while incorporating English foods into their diets.

The uses of food, the ways in which it encapsulates cultural values and is a medium for social change, and the power of its sensory nature to enhance other social interactions and experiences all signal that food is a potent tool for understanding the social imaginary. An imagined community is implied in shared food traditions—the knowledge that others all across a large Classic Maya urban center are consuming maize tamales or tortillas, that they understand the heightened social value of corn-based food products, and that despite differences of personality or means they choose to eat this food over and over again—is a fundamental component of shared culture. Sutton (2001:84) writes about the "embodied knowledge that others are eating the same food" as an underappreciated component of the social imaginary, which is just as influential as the daily newspaper was to an emerging national consciousness in nineteenth-century India. Daily food traditions kept identity near the surface, familiar and present (Anderson 1991; Palmer 1998). While the chapters that follow differ in the details of the food traditions they present, there are powerful connections of practice that constitute a shared social imaginary of Mayaness.

Contributions of This Volume

Readers will notice that the chapters of *Her Cup for Sweet Cacao* do not embrace a single theoretical perspective, nor do they utilize the same methodologies or exactly the same chronological frameworks. The diversity of approaches represented in this volume is deliberate—my objective was to advance the discussion and analysis of Maya foodways as a social fact through the presentation of new data and new voices. In many ways, this volume is a reflection of the nascent stage of research in ancient Maya foodways, when compared to food studies literature from other regions and times. Were I to have limited the authors to those scholars who share a single theoretical, geographical, or methodological perspective, *Her Cup* would not contain the wonderful multiplicity of new data the current volume brings to bear on the topic of the social uses of food. Interest in ancient Maya foodways is growing, and this volume aims to inspire a larger field of scholars to engage in similar questions. This was not the moment to narrow our focus or our conversation. Chapters are arranged chronologically, meaning we begin with the Middle Preclassic and conclude with discussion of the Postclassic and Colonial periods. Although this organizing principle is customary in volumes such as this, certainly other choices could have been made in terms of how to structure the volume—to cluster the chapters on feasts or individual foods, for example. Instead, I invite readers to allow those connections to be made organically as you consume the rich and diverse material presented.

We begin the case studies of Maya foodways in chapter 2 with an exploration of a chronologically very early example of that quintessential social food experience, the feast. M. Kathryn Brown and Carolyn Freiwald present data from ceramic, faunal, and botanical analyses of a Middle Preclassic deposit at the site of Blackman Eddy, Belize. The authors argue that these very early deposits were the result of highly ritualized experiences that brought the community together and simultaneously established social hierarchies. Feasting has played a large role in our explanatory frameworks for the emergence of social complexity in the Maya area, and this chapter shows that even at smaller sites, which may have organized what are known as "potluck" feasts, expressions of power are central. In chapter 3, Jon Spenard, Adam King, Terry G. Powis, and Nilesh Gaikwad share fascinating new data recovered from residue analyses of ceramic vessels found in the caves near Pacbitun, Belize. Although scholars recognize caves as places of tremendous ritual significance in Maya culture, there are few published studies on the role of food offerings in these special contexts. Using absorbed residues from liquids held in containers, Spenard and colleagues have identified a number of new substances that expand our understanding of what foods were used in ceremonial contexts.

Chapter 4 presents a detailed introduction to what Maya hieroglyphic inscriptions have to say about royal foods, especially those served in elaborate painted ceramic pots well known for their depictions of palace life. Nicholas Carter and Mallory Matsumoto focus particular attention on three foods that played enormously important roles in elite Maya cuisine—maize, cacao, and pulque. Carter and Matsumoto explain how each of these three foods anchored a cluster of mythic narratives, social values, and practices of production and consumption. Hieroglyphic statements not only describe important beverages and foods, they also help us understand something about the cultural and linguistic classes of food, drink, and some of the implements used to consume them, as well as the social norms and religious concepts connected with those categories. In chapter 5, Shanti Morell-Hart provides an overview of the special position of botanical foodstuffs in ancient Maya society. Utilizing paleoethnobotanical data from a variety of her projects, as well as other published studies from the Maya area, Morell-Hart explores how plant foods operated simultaneously as icons, indices, and symbols, often independent of human intention and sometimes in opposition to it. Chapter 6 is a comprehensive review of existing and new chronological and spatial evidence of dog remains in different archaeological sites and contexts throughout the Maya region. Petra Cunningham-Smith, Ashley E. Sharpe, Arianne Boileau, Erin Kennedy Thornton, and Kitty F. Emery use detailed fauna analysis coupled with ethnohistoric and artistic data to explore the possible role of dogs as food and the complex interactions of food, ceremony, and symbol. Dogs have long been known to be a source of sustenance in the Maya region, but as Cunningham-Smith and colleagues show, dogs had a diverse set of uses across time and space that went far beyond purely culinary ones, including their use as sacred offerings.

Moving from studies of specific food groups, chapter 7 explores the foodways of Classic period Sihó in Yucatán, Mexico. Lilia Fernández Souza, Mario Zimmerman, and Socorro del Pilar Jiménez Álvarez utilize a suite of technologies, including chemical and starch grain analyses, to explore the role of food technology in cementing shared social identities. Sihó was particularly rich in ground-stone tools, and it presents a unique opportunity to examine how the processing of a "signature food" like maize both brought the community together and reinforced social hierarchies. In chapter 8, Julia Hendon also examines the role of food in social group negotiation, comparing data from the Copán and Ulúa valleys in Honduras. Hendon explores commensality, or the act of eating together, and cuisine, or the specialized knowledge of how food is prepared, to suggest that the ways basic foodstuffs such as maize or root crops were transformed into dishes reflected local identities, created distinction, and fostered commensal relations. Many of these themes continue in chapter 9, in which Maxime Lamoureux-St-Hilaire addresses the communicational functions of feasting practices at Classic Maya royal courts, using new data from La Corona, Guatemala. During the end of the Late Classic and Terminal Classic periods, when environmental stress and food insecurity were constant features of daily life, hosting an elaborate royal feast took on heightened significance and brought legitimate risks. Lamoureux-St-Hilaire explores these risks, as well as associated issues of storage technology and the consequences of disappointing subordinate vassals.

The final chapters address commensality as well, but also the more explicitly ideological components of changes in food technologies, differential access to food, and ceremonial offerings. My contribution (chapter 10) on the arrival of new cooking technologies during the Terminal Classic period at the site of Xuenkal, in Yucatán, Mexico, examines how regional elites were drawn into the sociopolitical influence of a new regional power centered at Chichén Itzá. Along with the many ways leaders of Chichén Itzá reinvented the Maya tradition of urbanism, new foodways were shared with local elites in highly charged feasting events. New cooking technology fostered new foods, which helped solidify new identities and new loyalties. In chapter 11, Marilyn A. Masson, Timothy S. Hare, Bradley W. Russell, Carlos Peraza Lope, and Jessica L. Campbell also explore the way food remains inform us about social stratification. By looking at faunal scarcity in humble rural houselots of the Terminal Classic and Postclassic periods at Mayapán, Yucatán, Mexico, Masson and colleagues argue that at this time, animals were absorbed into political economies to a degree not seen earlier in Maya history. With careful attention to attendant methodological issues, Masson and colleagues show how the study of foodways can reveal new subtleties and inequalities within commoner populations. Gabrielle Vail and Maia Dedrick present an overview and summary of ethnohistoric, historic, and contemporary evidence for the manufacture and use of fermented honey-wine, known in the Maya area as *balche'*. Focusing on two key ceremonies in which honey plays a significant role, the feeding of the bees and the replenishment of god pots, Vail and Dedrick explore human-deity relationships in the Postclassic Maya codices, in particular those related to beekeeping and harvest rituals that utilize food as payments to deity protectors. Finally, the food historian Jeffrey Pilcher draws connections between the ideas presented in the previous chapters on ancient Maya foodways and parallel trends within historical studies of Latin American foodways. Pilcher notes the importance of continuing to deconstruct Maya cuisine, which was never a unified or solitary practice, to identify the specific influences of gender, class, or region on the ideological structures surrounding Maya foodways. He also encourages archaeologists to expand their use of embodied perspectives to better grasp the experiences of ancient kitchens, feasts, and food rituals, and to explore mobility studies, or the notion that although the movements of people, goods, and ideas are often studied in isolation, they are in fact connected and can only be understood in relationship to one another.

This volume would not have been possible without the decades of research by earlier scholars who led the way in understanding ancient Maya food culture. It is our hope that the time is right to move beyond recovering data on calories, species, and vessel forms, valid and essential though those efforts may be. *Her Cup for Sweet Cacao* aims to bring rich new data from the archaeological, epigraphic, and artistic record left by the ancient Maya to ongoing conversations happening within the transdisciplinary space of food studies. As one of the New World cultures that cherishes its highly sophisticated culinary history, the Maya world deserves thoughtful attention to its gastronomic accomplishments. This work is intended for both modern Mayan-speaking people who are curious about their ancestral traditions and scholars interested in the specific achievements of this unique tropical culture, so we invite you to find a cup of hot chocolate and read on.

References

Alfonso, Ivan Darias. 2014. "We Are What We Now Eat: Food and Identity in the Cuban Diaspora." *Canadian Journal of Latin American and Caribbean Studies* 37 (74):173–206.

Anderson, Benedict. 1991. *Imagined Communities: Reflections on the Origin and Spread of Nationalism*. London: Verso.

Andrews, Anthony P. 1983. *Maya Salt Production and Trade*. Tucson: University of Arizona Press.

Appadurai, Arjun. 1988. "How to Make a National Cuisine: Cookbooks in Contemporary India." *Comparative Studies in Society and History* 30(1):3–24.

Atalay, Sonya, and Christine A. Hastorf. 2006. "Food, Meals, and Daily Activities: Food Habitus at Neolithic Çatalhöyük." *American Antiquity* 71(2):283–319.

Ayora-Diaz, Steffan Igor. 2012. *Foodscapes, Foodfields, and Identities in Yucatán*. New York: Berghan Books.

———. 2015. *Cooking Technology: Transformations in Culinary Practice in Mexico and Latin America*. New York: Bloomsbury Academic.

Boucher, Sylviane, and Lucía Quiñones. 2007. "Between Markets, Fairs, and Feasts: The Murals of Chiik Nahb Sub 1–4, Calakmul." *Mayab* 19:47.

Brown, M. Kathryn. 2008. "Establishing Hierarchies in the Middle Preclassic Belize River Valley." *Research Reports in Belizean Archaeology* 5:175–184.

Brulotte, Ronda L., and Michael A. Di Giovine, eds. 2014. *Edible Identities: Food as Cultural Heritage*. Burlington, VT: Ashgate.

Carrasco Vargas, Ramón, Verónica A. Vázquez López, and Simon Martin. 2009. "Daily Life of the Ancient Maya Recorded on Murals at Calakmul, Mexico." *Proceedings of the National Academy of Sciences*, November 17, 2009, 106(46):19245–19249.

Castellanos, Erick, and Sarah Bergstresser. 2014. "The Mexican and Transnational Lives of Corn: Technological, Political, Edible Object." In *Edible Identities: Food as Cultural Heritage*, ed. Ronda L. Brulotte and Michael A. Di Giovine, 201–218. Burlington, VT: Ashgate.

Clark, John E., and Michael Blake. 1994. "The Power of Prestige: Competitive Generosity and the Emergence of Rank Societies in Lowland Mesoamerica." In *Factional Competition and Competitive Development in the New World*, ed. Elizabeth Brumfiel and John W. Fox, 17–30. Cambridge: Cambridge University Press.

Coe, Sophie D. 1994. *America's First Cuisines*. Austin: University of Texas Press, 1994.
Coe, Sophie D., and Michael D. Coe. 1996. *The True History of Chocolate*. New York: Thames and Hudson.
Conklin, Beth. 1995. "'Thus are Our Bodies, Thus was Our Custom': Mortuary Cannibalism in an Amazonian Society." *American Ethnologist* 22:75–101.
Connerton, Paul. 1989. *How Societies Remember*. Cambridge: Cambridge University Press.
Dietler, Michael, and Bryan Hayden, eds. 2001. *Feasts: Archaeological and Ethnographic Perspectives on Food, Politics, and Power*. Washington, DC: Smithsonian Institution Press.
Dine, Harper, Traci Ardren, Grace Bascopé, and Celso Gutiérrez Báez. 2019. "Famine Foods and Food Security in the Northern Maya Lowlands: Modern Lessons for Ancient Reconstructions." *Ancient Mesoamerica* 30:517–534.
Douglas, Mary. 1971. "Deciphering a Meal." In *Myth, Symbol, and Culture*, ed. Clifford Geertz, 61–82. New York: W. W. Norton.
Douglas, Mary, and Jonathan Gross. 1981. "Food and Culture: Measuring the Intricacy of Rule Systems." *Social Science Information* 20(1):1–35.
Dreiss, Meredith L. 2008. *Chocolate: Pathway to the Gods*. Tucson: University of Arizona Press.
Emery, Kitty F., ed. 2004. *Maya Zooarchaeology: New Directions in Method and Theory*. Los Angeles: Cotsen Institute of Archaeology at UCLA.
Farahani, Alan, Katherine Chiou, Rob Q. Cuthrell, Anna Harkey, Shanti Morell-Hart, Christine Hastorf, and Payson Sheets. 2017. "Exploring Culinary Practices through GIS Modeling at Joya de Cerén, El Salvador." In *Social Perspectives on Ancient Lives from Paleoethnobotanical Data*, ed. Matthew P. Sayne and Maria C. Bruno, 101–120. New York: Springer.
Freidel, David. 2008. "Olmec: the Origins of Ancient Mexican Civilization." Paper presented at the Lozano Long Institute for Latin American Studies annual conference, Austin, Texas.
Freidel, David, and F. Kent Reilly III. 2010. "The Flesh of God: Cosmology, Food, and the Origins of Political Power in Ancient Southeastern Mesoamerica." In *Pre-Columbian Foodways*, ed. John. E. Staller and Michael D. Carrasco, 635–680. New York: Springer.
Gillespie, Susan D. 2010. "Maya Memory Work." *Ancient Mesoamerica* 21(2):401–414.
Gómez-Pompa, Arturo, José Salvador Flores, and Mario Aliphat Fernández. 1990. "The Sacred Cacao Groves of the Maya." *Latin American Antiquity* 1(3):247–257.
Good Eshelman, Catharine, and Laura Elena Corona de la Peña, eds. 2011. *Comida, cultura y modernidad en México*. Mexico City: Instituto Nacional de Antropología e Historia.
Götz, Christopher M. 2014. "La alimentación de los mayas prehispánicos vista desde la zooarqueología." *Anales de Antropología* 48(1):167–199.
Graff, Sarah R. 2017. "Archaeological Studies of Cooking and Food Preparation." *Journal of Archaeological Research* 26(3):1–47.
Hamblin, Nancy L. 1984. *Animal Use by the Cozumel Maya*. Tucson: University of Arizona Press.
Hamilakis, Yannis. 1998. "Eating the Dead: Mortuary Feasting and the Politics of Memory in the Aegean Bronze Age Societies." In *Cemetery and Society in the*

Aegean Bronze Age, ed. K. Branigan, 115–132. Sheffield, UK: Sheffield Academic Press.

Hastorf, Christine A. 2017. *The Social Archaeology of Food: Thinking about Eating from Prehistory to the Present*. New York: Cambridge University Press.

Hayden, Brian, and Robert Gargett. 1990. "Big Man, Big Heart? A Mesoamerican View of the Emergence of Complex Society." *Ancient Mesoamerica* 1(1):3–20.

Henderson, John S., Rosemary A. Joyce, Gretchen R. Hall, W. Jeffrey Hurst, and Patrick E. McGovern. 2007. "Chemical and Archaeological Evidence for the Earliest Cacao Beverages." *Proceedings of the National Academy of Sciences of the United States of America* 104(48):18937–18940.

Hendon, Julia A. 2003. "Feasting at Home: Community and House Solidarity among the Maya of Southeastern Mesoamerica." In *The Archaeology and Politics of Food and Feasting in Early States and Empires*, ed. Tamara L. Bray, 203–233. New York: Kluwer Academic/Plenum.

———. 2010. *Houses in a Landscape: Memory and Everyday Life in Mesoamerica*. Durham, NC: Duke University Press.

Holtzman, Jon D. 2006. "Food and Memory." *Annual Review of Anthropology* 35:361–378.

Hutson, Scott, ed. 2017. *Ancient Maya Commerce: Multidisciplinary Research at Chunchucmil*. Boulder: University Press of Colorado.

Ichijo, Atsuko, and Ronald Ranta. 2016. *Food, National Identity and Nationalism: From Everyday to Global Politics*. London: Palgrave Macmillan.

James, Alison. 1997. "How British Is British Food?" In *Food, Health and Identity*, ed. Pat Caplin, 71–86. London: Routledge.

Klarich, Elizabeth A., ed. 2010. *Inside Ancient Kitchens: New Directions in the Study of Daily Meals and Feasts*. Boulder: University Press of Colorado.

Landa, Diego de. 1937. *Yucatan Before and After the Conquest* (translation of *Relación de las cosas de Yucatán*). Trans. William Gates. New York: Dover.

LeCount, Lisa J. 2001. "Like Water for Chocolate: Feasting and Political Ritual among the Late Classic Maya at Xunantunich, Belize." *American Anthropologist* 103(4):935–953.

———. 2010. "Maya Palace Kitchens: Suprahousehold Food Preparation at the Late and Terminal Classic Site of Xunantunich, Belize." In *Inside Ancient Kitchens: New Directions in the Study of Daily Meals and Feasts*, ed. Elizabeth A. Klarich, 133–160. Boulder: University Press of Colorado.

Lentz, David L. 1991. "Maya Diets of the Rich and Poor: Paleoethnobotanical Evidence from Copan." *Latin American Antiquity* 2(3):269–287.

———. 1999. "Plant Resources of the Ancient Maya: The Paleoethnobotanical Evidence." In *Reconstructing Ancient Maya Diet*, ed. Christine D. White, 3–18. Salt Lake City: University of Utah Press.

Lentz, David L., Marilyn P. Beaudry-Corbett, Maria Luisa Reyna de Aguilar, and Lawrence Kaplan. 1996. "Foodstuffs, Forests, Fields, and Shelter: A Paleoethnobotanical Analysis of Vessel Contents from the Ceren Site, El Salvador." *Latin American Antiquity* 7(3):247–262.

Marte, Lidia. 2012. "Dominican Migrant Cooking: Food Struggles, Gendered Labor, and Memory-Work in New York City." *Food and Foodways* 20(3–4):279–306.

McAnany, Patricia, Ben S. Thomas, Steven Morandi, Polly A. Peterson, and Eleanor

Harrison. 2002. "Praise the Ahaw and Pass the Kakaw: Xibun Maya and the Political Economy of Cacao." In *Ancient Maya Political Economies*, ed. Marilyn Masson and David Freidel, 123–139. Walnut Creek, CA: Altamira Press.

McKillop, Heather. 2008. *Salt: White Gold of the Ancient Maya*. Gainesville: University Press of Florida.

McNeil, Cameron L. 2006, ed. *Chocolate in Mesoamerica: A Cultural History of Cacao*. Salt Lake City: University of Utah Press.

Meyers, Carol L. 2008. "Grinding to a Halt: Gender and the Changing Technology of Flour Production in Roman Galilee." In *Engendering Social Dynamics: The Archaeology of Maintenance Activities*, ed. S. Montón-Subías and M. Sánchez-Romero, 65–74. BAR International Series 1862. Oxford: Archaeopress.

Mills, Barbara J., and William H. Walker, eds. 2008. *Memory Work: Archaeologies of Material Practices*. Santa Fe, NM: SAR Press.

Morehart, Christopher T., and Shanti Morell-Hart. 2015. "Beyond the Ecofact: Toward a Social Paleoethnobotany in Mesoamerica." *Journal of Archaeological Method and Theory* 22(2):483–511.

Munn, Nancy D. 1986. *The Fame of Gawa: A Symbolic Study of Value Transformation in a Massim Society*. Cambridge: Cambridge University Press.

Nance, C. Roger. 1992. "Guzmán Mound: A Late Preclassic Salt Works on the South Coast of Guatemala." *Ancient Mesoamerica* 3(1):27–46.

Palmer, Catherine. 1998. "From Theory to Practice: Experiencing the Nation in Everyday Life." *Journal of Material Culture* 3(2):175–199.

Pite, Rebekah E. 2013. *Creating a Common Table in Twentieth-Century Argentina: Doña Petrona, Women, and Food*. Chapel Hill: University of North Carolina Press.

Pohl, Mary. 1983. "Maya Ritual Faunas: Vertebrate Remains from Burials, Caches, Caves, and Cenotes in the Maya Lowlands." In *Civilization in the Ancient Americas*, ed. Richard M. Leventhal and Alan L. Kolata, 55–104. Albuquerque: University of New Mexico Press.

———. 1985. "Privileges of Maya Elites: Prehistoric Vertebrate Fauna from Seibal." In *Prehistoric Lowland Maya Environment and Subsistence Economy*, ed. Mary Pohl, 133–146. Papers of the Peabody Museum of Archaeology and Ethnology 77. Cambridge, MA: Peabody Museum at Harvard University.

———. 1990. "Ethnozoology of the Maya: Faunal Remains from Five Sites in the Petén, Guatemala." In *Excavations at Seibal, Department of Peten, Guatemala*, ed. Gordon R. Willey, *Peabody Museum of Archaeology and Ethnology Memoirs* 17(3): 143–174.

Pohl, Mary, and Lawrence Feldman. 1982. "The Traditional Role of Women and Animals in Lowland Maya Economy." In *Maya Subsistence: Studies in Memory of Dennis E. Puleston*, ed. Kent V. Flannery, 295–312. New York: Academic Press.

Rosenswig, Robert. 2007. "Beyond Identifying Elites: Feasting as a Means to Understand Early Middle Formative Society on the Pacific Coast of Mexico." *Journal of Anthropological Archaeology* 26(1):1–27.

Roys, Ralph L. 1931. *The Ethno-botany of the Maya*. Middle American Research Series Publication Number 2. New Orleans: Tulane University.

———. 1933. *The Book of Chilam Balam of Chumayel*. Carnegie Institution of Washington Publication 438. Washington, DC: Carnegie Institution.

———, ed. and trans. 1965. *Ritual of the Bacabs*. Norman: University of Oklahoma Press.
Ruz, Mario Humberto, ed. 2016. *Kakaw, oro aromado: De las cortes mayas a las europeas*. Mexico City: Universidad Nacional Autónoma de México, Instituto de Investigaciones Filológicas.
Sheets, Payson, ed. 2002. *Before the Volcano Erupted: The Ancient Cerén Village in Central America*. Austin: University of Texas Press.
Singer, Eliot A. 1984. "Conversion through Foodways Enculturation: The Meaning of Eating in an American Hindu Sect." In *Ethnic and Regional Foodways in the United States: The Performance of Group Identity*, ed. Linda Keller Brown and Kay Mussell, 195–214. Knoxville: University of Tennessee Press.
Staller, John E., and Michael D. Carrasco, eds. 2010. *Pre-Columbian Foodways: Interdisciplinary Approaches to Food, Culture, and Markets in Ancient Mesoamerica*. New York: Springer.
Stanton, Travis, and Aline Magnoni, eds. 2008. *Ruins of the Past: The Use and Perception of Abandoned Structures in the Maya Lowlands*. Boulder: University Press of Colorado.
Stephens, John Lloyd. 1963 [1843]. *Incidents of Travel in Yucatan*. New York: Dover.
———. 1969 [1854]. *Incidents of Travel in Central America, Chiapas, and Yucatan*. New York: Dover.
Stuart, David. 2006. "The Language of Cacao: References to Cacao on Classic Maya Drinking Vessels." In *Chocolate in Mesoamerica: A Cultural History of Cacao*, ed. Cameron L. McNeil, 184–201. Gainesville: University Press of Florida.
Sutton, David E. 2001. *Remembrance of Repasts: An Anthropology of Food and Memory*. London: Berg.
Van Dyke, Ruth M., and Susan E. Alcock. 2003. *Archaeologies of Memory*. New York: Blackwell.
Weismantel, Mary J. 1988. *Food, Gender, and Poverty in the Ecuadorian Andes*. Prospect Heights, IL: Waveland Press.
White, Christine D. 1997. "Ancient Diet at Lamanai and Pacbitun: Implications for the Ecological Model of Collapse." In *Bones of the Maya: Studies of Ancient Skeletons*, ed. Stephen L. Whittington and David M. Reed, 171–180. Washington, DC: Smithsonian Institution Press.
———, ed. 1999. *Reconstructing Ancient Maya Diet*. Salt Lake City: University of Utah Press.
———. 2005. "Gendered Food Behaviour among the Maya: Time, Place, Status and Ritual." *Journal of Social Archaeology* 5(3):356–382.
White, Christine D., Fred J. Longstaffe, and Henry P. Schwarcz. 2009. "Social Directions in the Isotopic Anthropology of Maize in the Maya Region." In *Histories of Maize: Multidisciplinary Approaches to the Prehistory, Linguistics, Biogeography, Domestication, and Evolution of Maize*, ed. John E. Staller, Robert H. Tykot, and Bruce F. Benz, 143–159. Walnut Creek, CA: Left Coast Press.
White, Christine D., Mary D. Pohl, Henry P. Schwarcz, and Fred J. Longstaffe. 2004. "Feast, Field, and Forest: Deer and Dog Diets at Lagartero, Tikal, and Copán." In *Maya Zooarchaeology: New Directions in Method and Theory*, ed. Kitty F. Emery, 141–158. Los Angeles: Cotsen Institute of Archaeology at UCLA.

Wilk, Richard. 2006. *Home Cooking in the Global Village: Caribbean Food from Buccaneers to Ecotourists*. New York: Berg.

Wing, Elizabeth S. 1974. "Vertebrate Faunal Remains." In *Excavation of an Early Shell Midden on Isla Cancun, Quintana Roo, Mexico*, ed. E. Wyllys Andrews IV et al., 186–188. Middle American Research Institute Publication Number 21. New Orleans: Tulane University.

———. 1975. "Animal Remains from Lubaantun." In *Lubaantun, a Classic Maya Realm*, ed. Norman Hammond, 379–383. Cambridge, MA: Peabody Museum Monograph No. 2, Harvard University.

CHAPTER 2

Potluck: Building Community and Feasting among the Middle Preclassic Maya

M. KATHRYN BROWN AND CAROLYN FREIWALD

Introduction

Communal meals serve numerous purposes in societies both past and present. Feasts accompanied many important events in ancient societies and drew people together to reinforce social norms and create a sense of community (Dabney, Halstead, and Thomas 2004:213; Klarich 2010a; Twiss 2012) but also emphasized social affiliations and status differences (Joyce 2010). Communal meals at the suprahousehold level were associated with distinctive milestones such as weddings, funerals, and other rites of passage, as well as political events, and with the ongoing production of crafts and community-building projects (Hastorf 2017; Klarich 2010b). The distinct components of these events, from planning the menu and acquiring the foods, to their display and consumption, to the discard of the remains, all provide a window into the social interactions that took place (Hastorf 2017). As Potter (2010:241) states, "Feasting and all of its attendant public behaviors—exchange, display, ritual competitive consumption—have been a source of fascination for anthropologists and, later, archaeologists for more than a century." This "fascination" with studying feasts in archaeology has led to an explicit theoretical discourse surrounding this topic and the production of a substantial body of empirical data. Feasting figures prominently in approaches to understanding the establishment of social hierarchies and the rise of social and political complexity worldwide (Clark and Blake 1994; Dietler and Hayden 2001; Hayden and Gargett 1990; Rathje 2002), including within the ancient Maya civilization. Food can also act as an agent that connects people to one another and to their gods (see Morell-Hart, this volume). Feasts, especially those that celebrated and honored the gods—important parts of communal ceremonies—may have provided avenues for emergent elites to become important leaders within the community.

Dietler (2001:67) defines feasts as "a form of public ritual activity centered around the communal consumption of food and drink." For the purpose of this chapter, we favor this definition of feasting, as we believe that feasts were highly ritualized practices within ancient Maya society. Although there is a strong ritualized nature to the suprahousehold sharing of food and drink, feasts are also political events (Dietler 2001). As Hastorf (2017:195) states, "Feasts are the material manifestation of political action." In both modern and ancient societies alike, social and political negotiations are conducted at communal feasts regardless of the nature and size of the event. "Food and drink are the media that embody hospitality, largesse, and society as they harness real goods and labor, with the material control of decision making lurking throughout the event" (Hastorf 2017:195).

While feasts are both ritual and political in nature, they vary in scale and type, depending on the goals that are to be accomplished through the suprahousehold event. Although there exists a broad spectrum of feast types, Hastorf (2017:199) classifies feasts into four main categories: celebratory feasts, potluck feasts, alliance-building feasts, and competitive feasts. While these categories provide a useful framework for studying feasts, broad overlap between these types occurs in the archaeological record. In many instances, feasts are communal in nature and are a strategy used by early leaders to create obligations and indebtedness with followers, debt they could then utilize to help elevate their status. In spite of the collective nature of the event, including feasts that would fall within the categories of celebratory and potluck feasts, the host of the ritual feast created obligations of reciprocity with his or her participants, which, over time, could have led to unequal social relationships. Small-scale feasts like those that likely took place within the earliest Maya communities were probably intimate in nature and emphasized sacred implements and highly valued food resources, such as maize, cacao, and animal protein sources. The communal character of these celebrations would have allowed participants to both contribute to and participate in community rituals. As the case study we present in this chapter illustrates, even within a "potluck"-style feast where participants would contribute food and drink, a host could emphasize the sacred component in the ceremony by holding the feast at a ceremonial/public venue, overseeing particular ritual aspects of the event, and displaying powerful symbols. Furthermore, participants have expressed aspects of their identity through the types of foods they contributed to these feasts, as well as through the serving implements used. Therefore, we should expect variability in foods and serving vessels within assemblages that represent even small-scale communal feasts.

The display of symbols, through performance, dress, and body ornamentation, as well as food presentation and icons exhibited on material objects, is a component of feasting events. Although much of the spectacle involved in feasting is lost to archaeologists, some material remains can give us insight into aspects of these ceremonies. For example, some of the earliest ceramics in the Belize River valley, Cunil- and Kanocha- phase serving vessels from Cahal Pech (Awe 1992) and Blackman Eddy (Garber et al. 2004), have important ideological symbols incised on them that would have been seen and shared among the ritual participants of early feasts. Furthermore, the ceramic serving vessels, including plainwares, used in the feasts themselves likely had symbolic meanings as portals (Brown 2007). Ceramic bowls with or without incised symbols contained sacred foods, fluids, and materials that were offered to the gods and shared among feast participants. Through repeated display, use, and ritual disposal, pots, especially bowls, became a central component of ritualized feasts, and the vessels themselves took on a sacred meaning. This is apparent, as ceramic pots, predominately serving vessels, are often found smashed or broken in ancient Maya ritual contexts beginning in the early Middle Preclassic period. The ritual breaking of vessels may be linked to renewal ceremonies and associated with certain types of feasting activities, including activities associated with building projects.

Faunal remains are often used to distinguish between the remains of everyday meals and special ones. The evidence includes the types of animals utilized and where they were acquired, the cuts of meat, and how the remains were discarded (Twiss 2012). However, very few direct comparisons of faunal use in early Maya feasting deposits have been published, despite the recent increase in research on Preclassic animal use (Bauer 2005; Clutton-Brock and Hammond 1994; Emery et al. 2013; Sharpe 2015, 2016; Sharpe, Saturno, and Emery 2014; Thornton and Emery 2016). Moreover, in the Maya region, the remains of similar animal species may be present in both ritual and residential deposits (e.g., Freiwald forthcoming; Lentz 1991; Shiratori 2019), though larger or more diverse faunal assemblages have been found in association with wealthier residences (e.g., Rice et al. 2018; Yaeger 2000:1209).

This, however, is not surprising, as foods that are consumed in everyday meals are also included in feasts as well, albeit in higher quantity and often prepared with special recipes. As has been noted (Joyce 2010), everyday foods can be transformed into special ones by the manner of preparation, by where they are served, or by what they are served in. For example, in the country of Belize today, an everyday chicken soup, called *chilmole*, or black soup, can be transformed into a special event soup (*relleno negro*) through the addition of certain spices, beef meatballs, and the occasional use of raisins and olives. Adding these additional ingredients enhances this traditional dish, making it special. Another relevant example from modern Belize is that an everyday meal may include chicken tamales, but a feast may include not only chicken tamales but also tamales made with other meat or *chaya*, a leafy green harvested from a perennial shrub.

As we have suggested above, ancient Maya feasting practices are highly ritualized. Suprahousehold feasts were typically held in or near ceremonial buildings (Hayden and Gargett 1990). Feasting activities may have been a part of Preclassic communal building projects in the Maya lowlands, as feasting debris is associated with several early public structures in the Belize River valley (Brown 2008). The link between the power of early leaders and the ability to mobilize labor has been noted in other societies (Junker and Niziolek 2010), and inequalities created in the construction of public spaces might have extended to unequal access to them.

Yet our understanding of early feasting practices remains limited due to the challenges scholars face when investigating the Preclassic period in the Maya lowlands. Early deposits and buildings are often deeply buried by Classic period constructions. When penetrating excavations are conducted, the limited exposure or visibility of Preclassic deposits may not allow a full understanding of context or full recovery of cultural materials. In this chapter, we present data from a Middle Preclassic special deposit associated with an early public platform complex at the site of Blackman Eddy, Belize (Figures 2.1 and 2.2). Detailed analysis of the ceramic and faunal data supports the interpretation that this deposit represents the remains of a feast. Moreover, due to the diversity of animals present within the fauna assemblage, we argue that this event was communal in nature and that participants may have contributed food and offerings.

Communal feasts, including potluck feasts, can also be both ritual and political in nature, allowing avenues for both hosts and participants to elevate their status. These feasting events may have included food sharing that was typical of small-scale feasts such as potlucks, yet we argue that even small-scale events have underlying aspects of competitive feasting as seen through food choices, object display, and ritualized consumption and discard. In addition, we suggest that the early public platforms at Blackman Eddy were constructed as communal building projects and that feast-

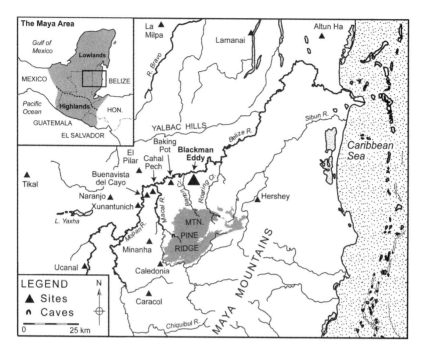

Figure 2.1. Map of Maya Lowlands showing location of Blackman Eddy

ing and ceremonial discard of feasting debris was part of the ritual sanctification of the building location prior to construction events. Although we focus on the final stage of the feasting event—the ritualized discard of the feasting debris—we also describe where some of the food was acquired. This case study from Blackman Eddy provides a glimpse into the types of rituals that were conducted at early public buildings in the Maya lowlands, shedding light on early practices that may have provided pathways for aspiring elites to advance themselves socially and politically.

Background

The site of Blackman Eddy is a small- to medium-sized ceremonial center located on a ridgetop above the Belize River floodplain. The relatively small site had a north-south configuration with two main plazas, an E-Group, and a ball court (Figure 2.2). Fourteen years of investigation by the Belize Valley Archaeological Project (BVAP), directed by James F. Garber, documented a long history of occupation spanning the early Middle Preclassic (ca. 1000 BCE) to the Terminal Classic (ca. 900 CE) periods. This

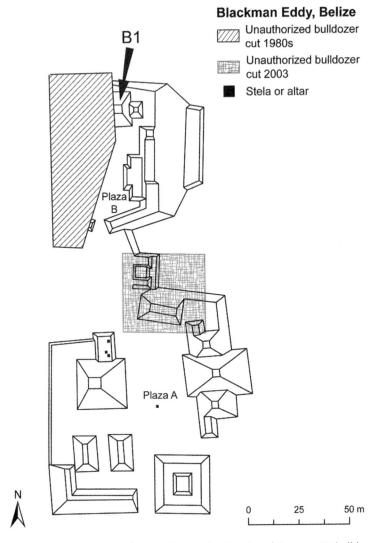

Figure 2.2. Site map of Blackman Eddy showing location of Structure B1, bulldozer cut

chapter focuses on the northernmost pyramid, Structure B1, a mound with thirteen documented construction phases and approximately eighteen hundred years of use and rebuilding programs. Because this mound was partially destroyed by bulldozing activity in the 1980s, the Structure B1 sequence presented a unique research opportunity. The remaining intact half of the mound was excavated in a horizontal fashion, allowing a thorough exposure of the different construction phases and associated deposits and features. We briefly highlight the architectural history of Structure B1 below, as this has been presented in more detail elsewhere (Brown 2003; Brown and Garber 2008; Garber et al. 2004). This introduction to the construction sequence is followed by a more in-depth discussion of a special deposit that we believe represents ritual feasting debris associated with an early construction project that resulted in the platform complex designated Structure B1-5th.

The earliest architectural phases of Structure B1 were relatively small, apsidal domestic platforms dating to the early Middle Preclassic, ca. 1000 BCE (Kanocha phase) to ca. 700 BCE (early facet Jenney Creek phase). Slightly later in the Middle Preclassic (ca. 700–600 BCE), the Blackman Eddy inhabitants constructed a series of low, rectangular platforms at this location. Due to the increased size and change in form, we believe these early rectangular platforms served a public and ceremonial function within the community. Long-distance trade objects, such as jade, marine shell, and obsidian, and ceramic objects that include figurines, ocarinas, and roller seals were associated with these platforms, further supporting a ceremonial function (Garber et al. 2004). As we discuss in more detail below, several problematic deposits containing fauna, broken ceramics, and exotic items suggest that these early platforms were venues for ritual feasts. Through the late Middle Preclassic (ca. 600–300 BCE), the constructions became more elaborate and culminated in the pyramidal form by the Late Preclassic period (300 BCE–200 CE; Brown 2003). Data from excavations in the ball court complex and E-Group architectural assemblage suggest that these other important ceremonial architectural features were also in use by the Late Preclassic. By the end of the Late Preclassic, the inhabitants completely rebuilt their northern temple (Structure B1) and decorated it with elaborate stucco deity masks flanking the central staircase. Although the preservation of the mask façade was poor, the lower, eastern mask displayed a large deity emerging from a bowl in profile, most probably the Maize Deity (Garber et al. 2004). As discussed in the introduction, this iconographic program emphasized the importance of the bowl as a sacred container and portal. Further, this construction phase, Structure B1-2nd, was identical in form to that of the famous pyramid, Structure 5C-2nd, at the site of Cerros, Belize (Freidel and Schele 1988), suggesting that by this time, the rulers of Blackman Eddy were utilizing visual symbolism to display power in a way similar to early Cerros kings. The Structure B1 temple was remodeled extensively at some time during the Early Classic period, but then was left exposed and not refurbished, quite possibly abandoned, for several centuries. However, large

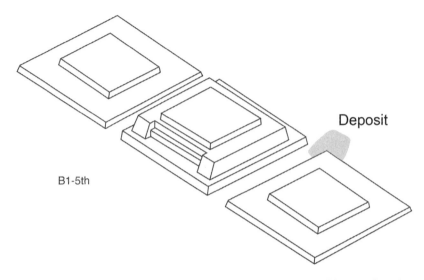

Figure 2.3. Isometric drawing of Structure B1-5th showing location of feasting deposit

deposits of Late and Terminal Classic smashed ceramics dumped on the side of the temple suggest that this sacred temple was the venue for later ritual feasting activities. During this time, the Blackman Eddy inhabitants rebuilt their sacred northern temple and buried an important ancestor at the summit. No additional rebuilding episodes were documented at this location, but early Postclassic ceramics were found on the surface, indicating ritual visitation, which suggests that this abandoned temple remained a sacred place on the landscape (Brown 2011).

As this brief architectural sketch suggests, Structure B1 had a long and complicated construction history and was an important ceremonial building beginning in the Middle Preclassic. Since the topic of this chapter is food consumption and ritual feasting activities at Preclassic public/ceremonial venues, we focus the remainder of our discussion on a Middle Preclassic platform complex found buried within the core of the mound. BVAP's excavations of the Middle Preclassic public platform complex encountered a primary deposit that we believe has all the components of ritual feasting debris. Our discussion will detail the cultural materials found within this deposit.

Dating to the Middle Preclassic (ca. 600 BCE), Structure B1-5th appears to have actually been three platforms placed in an in-line triadic form (Figure 2.3). The central platform was taller, approximately 1.5 m in height, and was a four-stepped platform. The eastern platform, and presumably the western platform (destroyed by the bulldozer), was two-tiered, only about 50 cm in height, and did not exhibit a perishable superstructure (Garber et al. 2004). This multilevel, open platform space may have served different functions within the community, such as a performance space and an elevated gathering place for ceremonial and communal activities and events.

Clearing excavations revealed a rich and dense deposit located beneath Structure B1-5th, extending to the north and downslope. This deposit directly covered the remains of an earlier small circular building (3 m in diameter) that appears to have been a special-function structure no longer in use by the time Structure B1-5th was built. Contextual analysis of the deposit suggests that it represents the remains of a ritual that involved communal feasting (Brown 2008; Brown, Awe, and Garber 2018). The deposit consisted of a concentration of broken ceramics, faunal remains, carbon, and long-distance trade objects such as obsidian and marine shell. The ceramic assemblage included sherds from the Jocote and Savana Groups, suggesting that the deposit dates to the transition between early and late facet Jenney Creek phase (ca. 700–600 BCE), and two AMS radiocarbon dates of 2400+/-40 BP and 2380+/-40 BP support this assertion.

Ten partial vessels were recovered, all of which were serving vessels (Brown 2007), similar to ceramic assemblages interpreted as feasting deposits (Dabney, Halstead, and Thomas 2004; LeCount 2001; also see LeCount 2010). The partial vessels included a chocolate pot (Reforma Incised: Mucnal Variety), three Savana Orange bowls, an unusual Savana Orange stirrup spout, a Jocote Orange-Brown jar, one volcanic ash–tempered Joventud bowl, and two unusual red-slipped volcanic ash–tempered bowls (Brown 2007; Garber et al. 2004). Both of these ash-tempered bowls exhibited a horizontal finger punctate decoration encircling the outer surface. The red slip extended from the lip to just above the punctate design. One of these vessels appears to be an unidentified type within the Savana Group due to paste color and texture, while the other has more affinities to the Joventud Group and most likely represents a new type (Brown 2007). The assemblage includes numerous other sherd refits, and therefore we believe that several other whole or partial vessels may be present within the unexcavated portion of this deposit.

Several lines of evidence support the ritual nature of the deposit. One of the vessels, a Savana Orange: Rejolla Variety bowl, was placed above nine chert flakes, a number that seems unlikely to be coincidence, as it also refers to the nine layers of the underworld. Furthermore, several of the partial vessels were intentionally halved and quartered. In fact, as

Figure 2.4. Three halved vessels from feasting deposit

Brown has noted elsewhere (Brown 2007; Brown, Awe, and Garber 2018), the unusual breakage pattern on three vessels with straight and regular edges strongly suggests that they were cut in half, possibly by a string saw (Figure 2.4). We believe that the vessels were ritually broken as part of this feasting event to evoke the partitioning of the universe into quarters at the beginning of time.

Several lines of evidence suggest that the deposit was part of an event associated with the initiation of the construction of the Structure B1-5th in-line triadic platform complex. First, the deposit did not appear to have been transposed to this location, suggesting that it was not a secondary midden or part of the construction fill of Structure B1-5th. Second, the excellent preservation of the faunal remains, coupled with the large angular breakage pattern of the ceramic sherds, suggests that the deposit was not trampled or left exposed for long; it seems to have been covered rapidly. Third, the construction fill of Structure B1-5th directly overlaid the deposit. Therefore, we believe this deposit represents ceremonial trash *sensu* Walker (1995), buried in order to animate the building (Duncan 2011). The intentional breakage of the serving vessels, coupled with the placement of one of these vessels above nine small chert flakes, suggests a highly ritualized event. Furthermore, the association of an assemblage dominated by serving vessels and rich plant and animal remains strongly suggests the ritually deposited remnants of a feast.

The plants recovered in a particular deposit may also reflect the nature of the activities that led to the deposit, although many species are found in both domestic and ritual contexts in the Maya region (Goldstein and Hageman 2010; but see Lentz 1991). Phytolith analysis found maize (*Zea mays*) and nondomesticated plants in two samples from vessels in the deposit (Bozarth 2007). The first of these samples comes from the bottom of a large olla with charred material on the interior. Interestingly, no domesticated plants were found within this burned sample (Bozarth 2007). It seems probable that certain nondomesticated plants were ritually burned to produce smoke and fragrance, suggesting that the bottom half of this olla functioned as an open *incensario*, or incense burner.

The second phytolith sample came from a Savana Orange stirrup spout that was broken off from the vessel body and deposited alone. Stirrup-spouted vessels are an unusual form in the Maya lowlands, with only a few examples documented in the Belize River valley to date. A more complete partial stirrup-spouted vessel, discussed in more detail below, was found at Blackman Eddy in a slightly later ritual deposit, indicating that this rare form was used by the Middle Preclassic inhabitants of the site. This Savana Orange stirrup-spouted vessel has a body in the form of an incurving bowl with the stirrup spout extending upward from the side of the vessel. Similar to the spouted vessels colloquially called "chocolate pots," stirrup-spouted vessels were most likely used to serve liquid. Chemical analyses of Middle Preclassic chocolate pots have shown the presence of cacao (Powis et al. 2002; also see McNeil 2010). The phytolith sample from the stirrup spout, however, exhibited maize. This suggests that the liquid served from this vessel was maize-based, possibly maize beer. Chemical analysis has not been conducted on this particular stirrup spout, so we do not know at this time if cacao was also present. However, it seems possible that the liquid may also have contained cacao. Serving fermented beverages such as frothy maize beer or cacao in front of participants would add a performance element to a feast (Joyce and Henderson 2007; also see Green 2010). Furthermore, as many scholars have noted (Dietler 2001; Joyce 2010), alcoholic beverages often have a prominent role in ritual feasts.

In addition to the phytoliths scraped from the stirrup-spouted vessel's interior surface, sediment from within the spout suggests the presence of maize kernels as well as some chaff, leading Bozarth (2007) to suggest that offerings of maize may also have been present.

The vertebrate faunal remains found within this deposit were analyzed at the University of Wisconsin-Madison Zoological Museum using standard zooarchaeological quantitative and qualitative methods (e.g., Gilbert 1990; Lyman 1994; Reitz and Wing 1999). Analysis of the 197 fauna specimens demonstrates a diversity of animal species, with a minimum of fifteen distinct mammals, reptiles, amphibians, and fish, along with one invertebrate crab analyzed as part of this assemblage (Table 2.1). Preservation of the faunal material was excellent: 30 percent of the bone fragments were identified to species, although 25 percent of the assemblage was only identified as vertebrate due to a lack of diagnostic features. None of the terrestrial animals that could be identified are exotic species; all could have been obtained in the vicinity of the site. This represents a minimum number of nine individuals (MNI=9). The animals were distributed across the deposit in ten clusters, with armadillo, fish, rabbit, and deer remains found in multiple places.

In addition to the faunal remains in Table 2.1, small numbers of riverine species of *jute* snails (*Pachychilus* spp.) and freshwater clams (*Nephronaias* sp.) were found scattered throughout the deposit. Remains of these riverine species were commonly found within Preclassic contexts at Blackman Eddy, suggesting that they were an important part of the Preclassic diet. On the other hand, fifty-three marine shell pieces were also recovered within the assemblage. Cochran (2009) identified eight worked pieces of marine shell, two tinklers and six shell beads, along with forty-five fragments interpreted as debitage from the production of objects such as beads, pendants, or *adornos*. Both the broken pieces of marine shell and the shell beads were from small-to-medium conch species, predominately *Strombus pugilis* (Cochran 2009:25). Since most of these fragments appear to have been debris from marine shell crafting activities, it seems likely that these do not represent the remains of food.

People understand the food served at special events in light of what they eat on a day-to-day basis (Graff 2018). In general, Early and Middle Preclassic deposits indicate a diet that reflects the diversity of animals in the Maya region (Masson 2004). In this regard, it is interesting to note that the species found within the Blackman Eddy deposit are similar to those found in midden and construction fill contexts across the Maya lowlands, which have been interpreted as everyday food choices (Emery 2004;

Table 2.1. Blackman Eddy, Belize, faunal remains analyzed from the Operation 20i deposit. MNI is the minimum number of individuals, and NISP is the number of identified specimens.

Fauna Identified	MNI	NISP	Weight in grams
Crab (Decapoda)	1	1	0.1
Brocket deer (*Mazama* sp.)	1	1	0.8
Opossum (*Didelphus virginianus*)	1	1	1.1
Cane toad (*Bufo marinus*)	1	1	0.1
Medium carnivore (Carnivora)	1	2	0.9
Agouti (*Dasyprocta punctata*)	1	3	0.4
Iguana (cf. *Ctenosaura similis*)	1	4	1.2
Turtle (Testudines)	1	5	6.1
Rabbit (*Sylvilagus* sp.)	1	6	2.7
Armadillo (*Dasypus novemcinctus*)	1	23	2.2
Whitetail deer (*Odocoileus virginianus*)	2	21	56
Fish (Osteichthyes)	3	17	4.3
Medium mammal	—	21	10.4
Large mammal	—	36	28.5
Mammal	—	4	1.7
Vertebrate	—	49	10.4
Totals	15	195	126.9

Twiss 2012). The assemblage did not indicate a clear preference for a single species, but rather an emphasis on a variety of species. For example, dog remains have been reported in other special Preclassic deposits elsewhere in the Maya lowlands, including some that may have been purposefully fed (White et al. 2001; also see Cunningham-Smith et al., this volume; Emery et al. 2013; Thornton and Emery 2016), although none were recovered in this deposit.

The species and diversity in the deposit are generally comparable with remains found at other sites in the region. For example, Middle Preclassic fauna from the Tolok Group at Cahal Pech suggest a subsistence strategy based on medium-to-large mammals, including whitetail and brocket deer, opossum, rabbit, dog, and agouti and other rodents, as well as turkey and currasow, turtle, and iguana (Powis et al. 1999:367). Also important were reef fish and shellfish and the "freshwater mollusk triad" of the Preclassic (*sensu* Stanchly and Burke 2018:96), which includes riverine and lake gastropods of the *Pachychilus*, *Pomacea*, and *Nephronaias* genera.

At the site of Pacbitun, whitetail deer were the most common animal in late Middle Preclassic deposits, but there were also carnivores, rodents, artiodactyls, and a smaller number of reptiles and fish (Boileau 2014). The variation among faunal assemblages at Blackman Eddy, Tolok, and Pacbitun may reflect the microenvironments near each site, with different suites of animals reported elsewhere in the lowlands, depending on the local environment (Pohl 1994; Stanchly 1999).

The animals likely were available in catchments near the site or along the Belize River valley floodplain. $^{87}Sr/^{86}Sr$ variability reflects a combination of geology and soil formation processes, which are reflected in the plants and animals living in the region (see Bentley 2006; Freiwald 2018; Price et al. 2008; Thornton 2011). Three modern faunal samples collected within ten kilometers of Blackman Eddy returned an average value of 0.70843 $^{87}Sr/^{86}Sr$ (Freiwald 2011:218), providing a baseline for the local signature. Samples from three deer specimens (whitetail and brocket) from the Preclassic deposit returned $^{87}Sr/^{86}Sr$ values within the range of Belize River valley baseline fauna (0.7082 to 0.7090 $^{87}Sr/^{86}Sr$ in Freiwald 2011; Freiwald et al. 2014), suggesting that attendees or sponsors used local animals (Table 2.2). Two additional whitetail deer samples and one ocelot (*Felis pardalis*) sample from other Preclassic deposits at the site also exhibit signatures local to the Belize River floodplain (Table 2.2). The local whitetail and brocket deer, as well as the ocelot, suggest a preference for local catchments in the Preclassic landscape in the Belize River valley. Oxygen ($\delta^{18}O$) and carbon ($\delta^{13}C$) isotope values, which are not discussed in detail, show similar water and browse sources for three of the animals. In contrast, most Classic period assemblages across the Maya region include nonlocal deer, peccary, and even tapir (Thornton 2011; Yaeger and Freiwald 2009), suggesting differences in animal acquisition and resource use.

Only partial animals are represented in this deposit, which suggests to us that the animals had been butchered and consumed. Whole or nearly complete animal skeletons often reflect animal offerings, such as the complete bird skeletons in a Preclassic deposit underneath the El Castillo acropolis at the nearby site of Xunantunich (Freiwald 2010). Furthermore, all of the animals represented in the deposit were known food sources for the ancient Maya. The likely exceptions were the conch shell fragments and beads, which we believe reflect materials that added symbolic value to the deposit.

Human modification of faunal remains can shed light on whether animals were processed for consumption and, in some cases, how they were

Table 2.2. Isotope values from Blackman Eddy, Belize, fauna in Operation 20 and other archaeological contexts (samples were prepared at the University of Wisconsin-Madison and processed at the University of North Carolina at Chapel Hill [$^{87}Sr/^{86}Sr$] and the University of Arizona [$\delta^{18}O$ and $\delta^{13}C$]; procedures are outlined in Freiwald 2011; Price, Burton, and Bentley 2002)

Sample number	Species detail	Tooth	$^{87}Sr/^{86}Sr$	$^{18}O/^{16}O$	$^{13}C/^{12}C$
F4501 20i9	Whitetail deer, subadult	upper left 4th premolar	0.708022	−0.52	−13.78
F4221 20i9	Whitetail deer (~1 year)	upper left 3rd molar	0.708126	−0.92	−12.85
F4222 20i6	Brocket deer (<1 year)	deciduous right lower premolar	0.708490	−1.26	−13.69
F5281 15n74	Whitetail deer (>3 years) (same as F5282)	lower left 1st molar	0.708628	—	—
F5282 15n74	Whitetail deer (3–4 years) (same as F5281)	lower left 2nd molar	0.708665	—	—
F5283 15n118	Ocelot	lower right 1st molar	0.708564	—	—
F5277	Toad (Bufonidae)	bone	0.708527	—	—
F1751	Opossum (Didelphidae)	tooth enamel	0.708397	—	—
F5274	Rat snake (*Spilotes pullatus*)	bone	0.708380	—	—

processed. The fragmentation of the bones within this Middle Preclassic deposit exhibits evidence of human modification that is consistent with animal processing for consumption. For example, thirty-two limb bones exhibit possible spiral fracture patterns associated with butchering, and one limb bone has a possible chop mark. Two bone fragments exhibited evidence of exposure to fire, and one was a fragment of an awl-type implement, one of three worked-bone fragments. Thus, it seems likely that much of the meat was butchered and removed prior to cooking, or the cuts of meat were processed in ways that did not expose them to direct flame, such as stewing, roasting in an earth oven, or steaming in tamales. It is interesting to note that none of the bones exhibited signs of gnaw marks or other animal damage, further supporting the notion that this deposit was covered quickly. The small assemblage also included three fragments of worked-bone objects that do not directly reflect food use, including fragments of one perforator, one polished bone, and another with a hole drilled into it.

Twenty-two percent of the animal remains present (NISP) were immature animals, including four of the individual animals (MNI). A high proportion of immature animals may be representative of animal management (e.g., deFrance and Hanson 2008; Hamblin 1984; Masson and Peraza Lope 2008), consumption choices, or ritual activities (Pohl 1990). One immature animal was a whitetail deer that probably was a subadult who was sexually mature but not fully grown, and another was a brocket deer whose dental age suggests that it was a juvenile. The other animals, however, were not identified to species. Although the sample size is small, the presence of immature animals may perhaps reflect a preference for younger animals for feasting.

Conclusion

Feasting accompanied many important events in ancient societies and served both to maintain group cohesion and to build a sense of communal identity. At the same time, feasts allowed participants to negotiate relationships within social and political realms. Dietler (2001:66) argues that "feasts are inherently political and that they constitute a fundamental instrument and theater of political relations." Many scholars have noted (see Ardren, this volume) that feasts were also used by sponsors to create uneven social relations with other participants, and thus they likely played an important role in establishing social hierarchies in many societies, including that of the ancient Maya. As Potter (2010:242) states, feasting is "often seen as a strategy used by leaders and potential leaders to actively transform structure through the opportunities created by building a following, placing followers in debt, and out-competing other aspiring leaders and using the resultant power differential to political advantage." Feasting activities may also have been an important component of public building programs in the Maya lowlands. As Dietler and Herbich (2001: 240) argue, "The use of feasts to mobilize collective labor has been a widespread and fundamental economic practice of societies around the world."

In this chapter, we present a case study from Blackman Eddy, Belize, of an early feasting event that occurred prior to the construction of a Middle Preclassic public platform, Structure B1-5th. The ceramic, botanical, and faunal data all support the interpretation of this deposit as the remains of a feast, one that was highly ritualized in nature. The ritual component of the feasting debris reflects sanctification themes that reference ancient Maya cosmology. Evidence of these themes includes: (1) the intentional partitioning of ceramic vessels into halves and quarters, (2) the placement of one vessel above nine chert flakes that likely reference the nine layers of the underworld, (3) the presence of an *incensario*, and (4) the presence of marine shell fragments and objects that reference the watery underworld. Furthermore, the deposit was left in place, forming a basal layer for the construction of Structure B1-5th. Phytolith data from a very rare stirrup-spouted vessel suggest that the feast included special maize-based beverages.

While multiple lines of evidence indicate that this deposit was the remains of a feast, the faunal data are especially interesting, given the great variety of animal species represented in the deposit, the butchery patterns on the bones, and the local origins of the animals. It is interesting to note that the oft-cited *cuch* renewal ceremony described by Pohl (1994) included a variety of animal species as well as a possible preference for immature animals.

Taken together, we believe that the material and contextual analysis of this deposit is consistent with an early communal feasting event in which the host and participants brought a variety of dishes for consumption, a "potluck" of sorts. While we think it likely that multiple participants brought food to this feast, we do not completely agree with Hastorf's (2017:198) assessment that "[p]otluck meals are truly a feast among equals in which each participant brings a dish to share, in an ambience of equality." Rather, we suggest that communal feasting practices—even small-scale events like this one at Blackman Eddy—had subtle ritual and political dimensions that created the possibility for social positioning and provided opportunities for key participants to gain status and create debts that could lead to their political advantage.

References

Awe, Jaime J. 1992. "Dawn in the Land between the Rivers: Formative Occupation at Cahal Pech, Belize, and Its Implications for Preclassic Development in the Maya Lowlands." PhD diss., University of London.

Bauer, Jeremy R. 2005. "Between Heaven and Earth: The Cival Cache and the Creation of the Mesoamerican Cosmos." In *Lords of Creation: The Origins of Sacred Maya Kingship*, ed. Virginia M. Fields and Dorie Reents-Budet, 28–29. Los Angeles: Los Angeles County Museum of Art.

Bentley, R. Alexander. 2006. "Strontium Isotopes from the Earth to the Archaeological Skeleton: A Review." *Journal of Archaeological Method and Theory* 13(3):135–187.

Boileau, Arianne. 2014. "Maya Exploitation of Animal Resources during the Middle Preclassic Period: An Archeozoological Analysis from Pacbitun, Belize." Master's thesis, Trent University, Peterborough, Ontario, Canada.

Bozarth, Steven. 2007. "Phytolith Analysis at Blackman Eddy, Belize." Manuscript on file at the University of Texas at San Antonio.

Brown, M. Kathryn. 2003. "Emerging Complexity in the Maya Lowlands: A View from Blackman Eddy, Belize." PhD diss., Southern Methodist University.

———. 2007. "Ritual Ceramic Use in the Early and Middle Preclassic at the Sites of Blackman Eddy and Cahal Pech, Belize." Accessed September 20, 2018. famsi.org/reports/02066/index.html.

———. 2008. "Establishing Hierarchies in the Belize River Valley." *Research Reports in Belizean Archaeology* 5:175–184.

———. 2011. "Postclassic Veneration at Xunantunich, Belize." *Mexicon* 33(5):126–132.

Brown, M. Kathryn, Jaime Awe, and James F. Garber. 2018. "The Role of Ideology, Religion, and Ritual in the Foundation of Social Complexity in the Belize River Valley." In *Pathways to Complexity: A View from the Maya Lowlands*, ed. M. Kathryn Brown and George J. Bey III, 87–116. Gainesville: University Press of Florida.

Brown, M. Kathryn, and James F. Garber. 2008. "Establishing and Re-using Sacred Space: A Diachronic Perspective from Blackman Eddy, Belize." In *Ruins of the Past: The Use and Perception of Abandoned Structures in the Maya Lowlands*, ed. Travis W. Stanton and Aline Magnoni, 147–170. Boulder: University Press of Colorado.

Clark, John E., and Michael Blake. 1994. "The Power of Prestige: Competitive Generosity and the Emergence of Rank Societies in Lowland Mesoamerica." In *Factional Competition and Political Development in the New World*, ed. Elizabeth M. Brumfiel and John W. Fox, 17–30. Cambridge: Cambridge University Press.

Clutton-Brock, Juliet, and Norman Hammond. 1994. "Hot Dogs: Comestible Canids in Preclassic Maya Culture at Cuello, Belize." *Journal of Archaeological Science* 21(6):819–826.

Cochran, Jennifer. 2009. "A Diachronic Perspective of Marine Shell Use from Structure B1 at Blackman Eddy, Belize." Master's thesis, University of Texas at Arlington.

Dabney, Mary K., Paul Halstead, and Patrick Thomas. 2004. "Mycenaean Feasting on Tsoungiza at Ancient Nemea." *Hesperia* 73(2):197–215.

deFrance, Susan D., and Craig A. Hanson. 2008. "Labor, Population Movement, and Food in the Sixteenth-Century Ek Balam, Yucatán." *Latin American Antiquity* 19 (3):299–316.

Dietler, Michael. 2001. "Theorizing the Feast: Rituals of Consumption, Commensal Politics, and Power in African Contexts." In *Feasts: Archaeological and Ethnographic Perspectives on Food, Politics, and Power*, ed. Michael Dietler and Brian Hayden, 65–114. Washington, DC: Smithsonian Institution Press.

Dietler, Michael, and Brian Hayden. 2001. "Digesting the Feast: Good to Eat, Good to Drink, Good to Think: An Introduction." In *Feasts: Archaeological and Ethnographic Perspectives on Food, Politics, and Power*, ed. Michael Dietler and Brian Hayden, 1–20. Washington, DC: Smithsonian Institution Press.

Dietler, Michael, and Ingrid Herbich. 2001. "Feasts and Labor Mobilization: Dissecting a Fundamental Economic Practice." In *Feasts: Archaeological and Ethnographic Perspectives on Food, Politics, and Power*, ed. Michael Dietler and Brian Hayden, 240–266. Washington, DC: Smithsonian Institution Press.

Duncan, William N. 2011. "A Bioarchaeological Analysis of Sacrificial Victims from a Postclassic Maya Temple from Ixlú, el Petén, Guatemala." *Latin American Antiquity* 22(4):549–572.

Emery, Kitty F., ed. 2004. *Maya Zooarchaeology: New Directions in Method and Theory*. Los Angeles: Cotsen Institute of Archaeology at UCLA.

Emery, Kitty F., Erin K. Thornton, Nicole R. Cannarozzi, Stephen Houston, and Héctor Escobedo. 2013. "Archaeological Animals of the Southern Maya Highlands: Zooarchaeology of Kaminaljuyu." In *The Archaeology of Mesoamerican Animals*, ed. Christopher M. Götz and Kitty F. Emery, 381–416. Atlanta: Lockwood Press.

Freidel, David A., and Linda Schele. 1988. "Kingship in the Late Preclassic Maya Lowlands: The Instruments and Places of Ritual Power." *American Anthropologist* 90(3):547–567.

Freiwald, Carolyn. 2010. "Dietary Diversity in the Upper Belize River Valley: A Zooarchaeological and Isotopic Perspective." In *Pre-Columbian Foodways: Interdisciplinary Approaches to Food, Culture, and Markets in Ancient Mesoamerica*, ed. John E. Staller and Michael D. Carrasco, 399–420. New York: Springer.

———. 2011. "Maya Migration Networks: Reconstructing Population Movement in the Belize River Valley during the Late and Terminal Classic." PhD diss., University of Wisconsin-Madison.

———. 2018. *Mobility and Diet in the Belize River Valley: A Resource Guide*. Report submitted to the Belize Valley Archaeological Reconnaissance Project, ed. Claire Ebert and Julie Hoggarth, 357–386.

———. Forthcoming. "Changes and Continuity in Animal Use in Early Colonial Households at San Bernabé, Tayasal, Guatemala." In *Colonialism at Tayasal, Petén, Guatemala*, ed. Timothy Pugh. Boulder: University Press of Colorado.

Freiwald, Carolyn, Jason Yaeger, Jaime Awe, and Jennifer Piehl. 2014. "Isotopic Insights into Mortuary Treatment and Origin at Xunantunich, Belize." In *The Bioarchaeology of Space and Place*, ed. Gabe D. Worbel, 107–139. New York: Springer.

Fridberg, Diane. 2015. "Case Studies in Ancient Maya Human-Animal Relations: El Perú, La Corona, and Commensal Mammals." PhD diss., Washington University.

Garber, James F., M. Kathryn Brown, Jaime J. Awe, and Christopher J. Hartman. 2004. "Middle Formative Prehistory of the Central Belize Valley: An Examination of Architecture, Material Culture, and Sociopolitical Change at Blackman Eddy." In *The Ancient Maya of the Belize Valley: Half a Century of Archaeological Research*, ed. James F. Garber, 25–47. Gainesville: University Press of Florida.

Gilbert, B. Miles. 1990. *Mammalian Osteology*. Columbia: Missouri Archaeological Society.

Goldstein, David J., and Jon B. Hageman. 2010. "Power Plants: Paleobotanical Evidence of Rural Feasting in Late Classic Belize." In *Pre-Columbian Foodways: Interdisciplinary Approaches to Food, Culture, and Markets in Ancient Mesoamerica*, ed. John E. Staller and Michael D. Carrasco, 421–440. New York: Springer.

Graff, Sarah R. 2018. "Archaeological Studies of Cooking and Food Preparation." *Journal of Archaeological Research* 26(3):1–47.

Green, Judith Strupp. 2010. "Feasting with Foam: Ceremonial Drinks of Cacao, Maize, and Pataxte Cacao." In *Pre-Columbian Foodways: Interdisciplinary Approaches to Food, Culture, and Markets in Ancient Mesoamerica*, ed. John E. Staller and Michael D. Carrasco, 315–343. New York: Springer.

Hamblin, Nancy. 1984. *Animal Use by the Cozumel Maya*. Tucson: University of Arizona Press.

Hastorf, Christine A. 2017. *The Social Archaeology of Food: Thinking about Eating from Prehistory to the Present*. New York: Cambridge University Press.

Hayden, Brian, and Robert Gargett. 1990. "Big Man, Big Heart? A Mesoamerican View of the Emergence of Complex Society." *Ancient Mesoamerica* 1(1):3–20.

Joyce, Arthur A. 2010. "Expanding the Feast: Food Preparation, Feasting, and the Social Negotiation of Gender and Power." In *Inside Ancient Kitchens: New Directions in the Study of Daily Meals and Feasts*, ed. Elizabeth A. Klarich, 221–239. Boulder: University Press of Colorado.

Joyce, Rosemary A., and John S. Henderson. 2007. "From Feasting to Cuisine: Implications of Archaeological Research in an Early Honduran Village." *American Anthropologist* 109(4):642–653.

Junker, Laura Lee, and Lisa Niziolek. 2010. "Food Preparation and Feasting in the Household and Political Economy of Pre-Hispanic Philippine Chiefdoms." In *Inside Ancient Kitchens: New Directions in the Study of Daily Meals and Feasts*, ed. Elizabeth A. Klarich, 17–54. Boulder: University Press of Colorado.

Klarich, Elizabeth A. 2010a. "Behind the Scenes and into the Kitchen." In *Inside Ancient Kitchens: New Directions in the Study of Daily Meals and Feasts*, ed. Elizabeth A. Klarich, 1–16. Boulder: University Press of Colorado.

———, ed. 2010b. *Inside Ancient Kitchens: New Directions in the Study of Daily Meals and Feasts*. Boulder: University Press of Colorado.

LeCount, Lisa J. 2001. "Like Water for Chocolate: Feasting and Political Ritual among the Late Classic Maya at Xunantunich, Belize." *American Anthropologist* 103(4):935–953.

———. 2010. "Maya Palace Kitchens: Suprahousehold Food Preparation at the Late and Terminal Classic Site of Xunantunich, Belize." In *Inside Ancient Kitchens: New Directions in the Study of Daily Meals and Feasts*, ed. Elizabeth A. Klarich, 133–160. Boulder: University Press of Colorado.

Lentz, David L. 1991. "Maya Diets of the Rich and Poor: Paleoethnobotanical Evidence from Copan." *Latin American Antiquity* 2(3):269–287.
Lyman, Lee. 1994. *Vertebrate Taphonomy*. Cambridge: Cambridge University Press.
Masson, Marilyn A. 2004. "Fauna Exploitation from the Preclassic to the Postclassic Periods at Four Maya Settlements in Northern Belize." In *Maya Zooarchaeology: New Directions in Method and Theory*, ed. Kitty F. Emery, 97–122. Los Angeles: Cotsen Institute of Archaeology at UCLA.
Masson, Marilyn A., and Carlos Peraza Lope. 2008. "Animal Use at the Postclassic Maya Center of Mayapán." *Quaternary International* 191(1):170–183.
McNeil, Cameron L. 2010. "Death and Chocolate: The Significance of Cacao Offerings in Ancient Maya Tombs and Caches at Copan, Honduras." In *Pre-Columbian Foodways: Interdisciplinary Approaches to Food, Culture, and Markets in Ancient Mesoamerica*, ed. John E. Staller and Michael D. Carrasco, 293–314. New York: Springer.
Pohl, Mary. 1990. "The Ethnozoology of the Maya: Faunal Remains from Five Sites in the Petén, Guatemala." In *Excavations at Seibal, Guatemala*, ed. Gordon R. Willey, 144–174. Peabody Museum Monographs, Vol. 18, No. 3. Cambridge, MA: Harvard University Press.
———. 1994. "The Economics and Politics of Maya Meat Eating." In *The Economic Anthropology of the State*, ed. Elizabeth Brumfiel, 119–147. Lanham, MD: University Press of America.
Potter, James M. 2010. "Making Meals (Matter)." In *Inside Ancient Kitchens: New Directions in the Study of Daily Meals and Feasts*, ed. Elizabeth A. Klarich, 241–252. Boulder: University Press of Colorado.
Powis, Terry G., Norbert Stanchly, Christine D. White, and Paul F. Healy. 1999. "A Reconstruction of Middle Preclassic Maya Subsistence Economy at Cahal Pech, Belize." *Antiquity* 73(280):364–376.
Powis, Terry G., Fred Valdez Jr., Thomas R. Hester, W. Jeffrey Hurst, and Stanley M. Tarka Jr. 2002. "Spouted Vessels and Cacao Use among the Preclassic Maya." *Latin American Antiquity* 13(1):85–106.
Price, T. Douglas, James H. Burton, and R. Alexander Bentley. 2002. "The Characterization of Biologically Available Strontium Isotope Ratios for the Study of Prehistoric Migration." *Archaeometry* 44(1):117–135.
Price, T. Douglas, James H. Burton, Paul D. Fullagar, Lori E. Wright, Jane E. Buikstra, and Vera Tiesler. 2008. "Strontium Isotopes and the Study of Human Mobility in Ancient Mesoamerica." *Latin American Antiquity* 19(2):167–180.
Rathje, William L. 2002. "The Nouveau Elite Potlatch: One Scenario for the Monumental Rise of Early Civilizations." In *Ancient Maya Political Economies*, ed. Marilyn A. Masson and David A. Freidel, 31–40. Walnut Creek, CA: Altamira Press.
Reitz, Elizabeth, and Elizabeth S. Wing. 1999. *Zooarchaeology*. Cambridge: Cambridge University Press.
Rice, Prudence M., Arianne Boileau, Leslie G. Cecil, Susan D. deFrance, Carolyn Freiwald, Nathan J. Meissner, and Matthew P. Yacubic. 2018. "Zacpeten Structure 719: Activities at a Contact Period Popol Nah before Rapid Abandonment." *Ancient Mesoamerica* 29(1):137–155.
Sharpe, Ashley E. 2015. "Los animales en la economía emergente de Ceibal Pre-

clásico." In *XXIX Simposio de Investigaciones Arqueológicas en Guatemala*, ed. Bárbara Arroyo and Héctor Escobedo, 1–19. Guatemala City: Asociación Tikal.

———. 2016. "Un análisis isotópico de la ganadería y comercio de los animales en Ceibal." In *XXX Simposio de Investigaciones Arqueológicas en Guatemala*, ed. Bárbara Arroyo, Luis Méndez Salinas, and Gloria Ajú Álvarez, 1–19. Guatemala City: Asociación Tikal.

Sharpe, Ashley E., William A. Saturno, and Kitty F. Emery. 2014. "Shifting Patterns of Maya Social Complexity through Time: Preliminary Zooarchaeological Results from San Bartolo, Guatemala." In *Animals and Inequality in the Ancient World*, ed. Sue Ann McCarty and Benjamin Arbuckle, 85–105. Boulder: University Press of Colorado.

Shaw, Leslie C. 1991. "The Articulation of Social Inequality and Faunal Resource Use in the Preclassic Community of Colha, Northern Belize." PhD diss., University of Massachusetts.

———. 1999. "Social and Ecological Aspects of Preclassic Maya Meat Consumption at Colha, Belize." In *Reconstructing Ancient Maya Diet*, ed. Christine D. White, 83–100. Salt Lake City: University of Utah Press.

Shiratori, Yuko. 2019. "Constructing Social Identity through the Past: The Itza Maya Community Identity through the Late Postclassic Period (1250–1525 CE)." PhD diss., The Graduate Center, City University of New York.

Stanchly, Norbert. 1999. "Preliminary Report on the Preclassic Faunal Remains from Pacbitun, Belize: 1995 and 1996 Field Seasons." In *Belize Valley Preclassic Maya Project: Report on the 1996 and 1997 Field Seasons*, ed. Paul F. Healy, 41–52. Report submitted to the Belize Institute of Archaeology.

Stanchly, Norbert, and Chrissina Coleen Burke. 2018. "Preclassic Animal Resource Use and the Origins of Ancient Maya Lifeways and Society: Contributions from Belize Zooarchaeology." *Research Reports in Belizean Archaeology* 15:93–104.

Thornton, Erin K. 2011. "Reconstructing Ancient Maya Animal Trade through Strontium Isotope ($^{87}Sr/^{86}Sr$) Analysis." *Journal of Archaeological Science* 38(12): 3254–3263.

Thornton, Erin K., and Kitty F. Emery. 2016. "Patterns of Ancient Animal Use at El Mirador: Evidence for Subsistence, Ceremony and Exchange." *Archaeofauna* 25: 233–264.

Twiss, Katheryn. 2012. "The Archaeology of Food and Social Diversity." *Journal of Archaeological Research* 20(4):357–395.

Walker, William H. 1995. "Ritual Prehistory: A Pueblo Case Study." PhD diss., University of Arizona.

White, Christine D., Mary Pohl, Henry P. Schwarcz, and Fred J. Longstaffe. 2001. "Isotopic Evidence for Maya Patterns of Deer and Dog Use at Preclassic Colha." *Journal of Archaeological Science* 28(1):89–107.

Yaeger, Jason. 2000. "Changing Patterns of Social Organization: The Late and Terminal Classic Communities at San Lorenzo, Cayo District, Belize." PhD diss., University of Pennsylvania.

Yaeger, Jason, and Carolyn Freiwald. 2009. "Complex Ecologies: Human and Animal Responses to Ancient Landscape Change in Central Belize." *Research Reports in Belizean Archaeology* 6:83–92.

CHAPTER 3

A Toast to the Earth: The Social Role of Beverages in Pre-Hispanic Maya Cave Ritual at Pacbitun, Belize

JON SPENARD, ADAM KING, TERRY G. POWIS, AND NILESH GAIKWAD

Introduction

The study of food and foodstuffs in pre-Hispanic Maya ritual practice is often limited to discussions of feasting, whether it be a local practice promoting social cohesion or the political maneuverings of the elite (Clark and Blake 1994; Hayden and Gargett 1990; Hendon 2003; LeCount 1999, 2001; Montero-López 2009; Reents-Budet 2000; Staller and Carrasco 2010). Yet extensive ethnographic accounts suggest food was likely used in a much wider range of ceremonial venues in the pre-Hispanic past (Astor-Aguilera 2010; Chinchilla Mazariegos 2017; Christenson 2010:578; Dreiss and Greenhill 2008; Kintz 1990:128; Love 2004; McGee 1990; Nash 1970: 208; Taube 1989; Vogt 1976). Among the more prominent of those other ceremonial venues are geographic landmarks, including caverns, rock shelters, other cave-like features, bodies of water, and mountain and hill tops where Maya people ritually communicate, petition, and interact with ancestors, earth forces, and other nonhuman people (Astor-Aguilera 2010; Christenson 2010; Kufer and Heinrich 2006; Scott 2009). Undoubtedly, pre-Hispanic Maya people used caves for ritual purposes, foodstuffs were involved at times, and in one known instance, a hieroglyphic text on the wall of a cave in Chiapas, Mexico, mentions an actual feast in association with a calendrical ceremony held there (Bassie-Sweet 1991, 1996, 2008; Bassie-Sweet et al. 2015:102; Brady and Prufer 2005; Brown 2005, 2009; Brown and Emery 2008; Emery 2002; Moyes et al. 2009; Prufer and Brady 2005; Stone 1995). Collectively, these ethnographic and archaeological data suggest foodstuffs should have been common components of pre-Hispanic Maya cave ritual practice, yet few researchers have sought out such information (cf. Morehart 2005, 2011; Morehart and Butler 2010;

Morehart, Lentz, and Prufer 2005; Parker 2014). The limited studies available, primarily of macrofaunal remains, have revealed that plants, particularly domesticated plant foods and tree species, were a major component of pre-Hispanic Maya ritual activity (Morehart 2005; Morehart, Lentz, and Prufer 2005; Parker 2014). The significance of our findings presented here is threefold: (1) the data presented in this chapter add to that small body of literature on ritual plant use in the eastern Maya region; (2) the plant foods identified in the study help us understand better the function and purposes of rituals; and (3) the data demonstrate that the identity of the social actors who may have participated in rituals is more complex than the common belief that participants were only men.

Microfloral studies of starch grains from soils and residues recovered from cave ceramics have also proven to be a useful avenue for determining the types of plants used in rituals (Morehart 2011). As found in macrofloral studies, many of the identified plants are domesticates. Our research employs another form of residue analysis focused on absorbed residues from liquids held in containers. Our aim is to capture the remains of things once held in low-fired ceramic and bone containers. Both of these materials are sufficiently porous that some parts of the liquids they once held are absorbed into their matrices' rough surfaces. If those residues can be captured (recovered in a physical sample) and identified (detected chemically), they can help us understand how particular containers were used and also when, where, and how particular foods or other concoctions were made.

Caves are excellent venues for the study of ritual plant use in the Maya Lowlands for symbolic and archaeologically practical reasons. As discussed in further detail below, underground places were of utmost importance in Maya ceremonial life because they were prime locations where nonhuman people, including environmental forces, could be contacted (Astor-Aguilera 2010; Chinchilla Mazariegos 2017:69; Prufer and Brady 2005; Stone 1995, 2005). On the other hand, because of their stable microenvironments, caves allow much greater artifact preservation than is possible in the hot, humid tropical forests outside them. Broken ceramics, and occasionally whole pots, are ubiquitous in caverns throughout the pre-Hispanic Maya region. Unslipped jars are typically the most common forms encountered. Bowls, dishes, and plates, some incised, gouged, or carved and ranging in decoration from monochromes to elaborate polychrome slipped wares, make up the majority of most assemblages. In other words, the forms of cave ceramic assemblages closely reflect those found in surface sites, though they were used for different purposes. In addition to ceramics, perishable artifacts of shell, wood, and human and animal bone are encountered regularly in subterranean contexts (Anya H., Guenter, and Mathews 2001; Brady 1989; Brown 2005; Emery 2002; Morehart 2005, 2011; Spenard 2006, 2014; Spenard and Mirro 2017; Stuart 1999).

For this preliminary study, we sampled pottery vessels and bone tubes from four cave sites near the medium-sized pre-Hispanic Maya city of Pacbitun, Belize (Figure 3.1). That settlement is located on the southern rim of the western Belize River valley, and about one kilometer north of the first foothills of the Maya Mountains in central western Belize. The caves—Actun Lak, Slate Cave, Tzul's Cave, and Actun Hayach Naj—vary in distance from Pacbitun, from 1.5 km to 5.5 km, and in size and geomorphic complexity from one another, yet they represent just four of the seventy known and likely hundreds of caves in the region. Elsewhere, Spenard (2014) has suggested that Actun Lak was a Late Preclassic through Early Classic period community rain shrine for Pacbitun, which was transformed in the mid-ninth century into a space restricted to all except royalty and the highest-level elites from that site. Slate and Tzul's Caves are about one hundred meters apart, on opposite sides of a valley at the head of which is an isolated hill on top of which sits the secondary center of Sak Pol Pak (Conlon 1999; Spenard, Mai, and Mai 2012). That small settlement holds the tallest pyramidal structure (11 m) anywhere in the region except for Pacbitun's Structure 1 (13 m), located in the site core. Late Classic period Pacbitun Maya people constructed a *sacbe* (causeway) from the site core directly to the head of the valley where Sak Pol Pak and Slate and Tzul's Caves are located (Weber 2011). Considering the direct tie to Pacbitun's site core, and the presence of the largest ceremonial architecture in its periphery, these data suggest that Pacbitun's elite were performing rituals at those sites. The fourth cave in this study, Actun Hayach Naj, sits just across a perennial stream from the Mountain Pine Ridge, 5.5 km from Pacbitun but two hundred meters from two unexplored minor plaza groups.

What do the results of this residue study tell us about who was performing rituals in the caves? Do they confirm elite and royal use of the caves, or do they show other people were using them? Why were these rituals performed? As we discuss below, our data offer a more nuanced understanding of the social uses of these spaces than we previously held, but they ultimately result in more questions about the social use of caves in this part of the Maya Lowlands than they provide definitive answers.

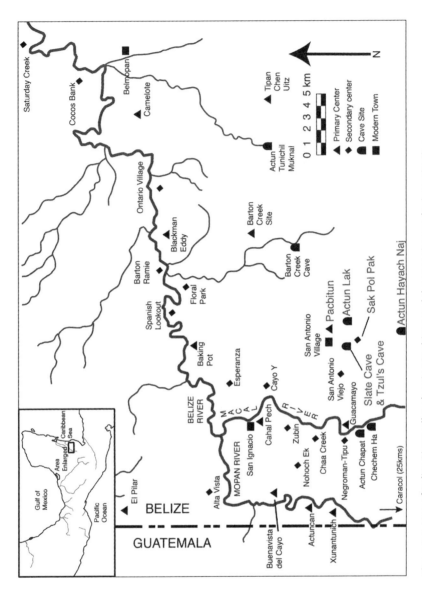

Figure 3.1. Map of Belize River valley showing Pacbitun and the cave sites under investigation. Map redrawn by Jon Spenard from Chase and Garber 2004, Map 1.

Caves in Mesoamerican Worldview

Multidisciplinary studies conducted throughout Mesoamerica have documented a close relationship between caves and cave-like features and ancestors, human origins, Earth forces, and other nonhuman beings (Astor-Aguilera 2010; Boone 1997:409; Brady and Prufer 2005; Chinchilla Mazariegos 2017; Durán 1994; Holland 1964:302; Miller and Taube 1997: 60; Monaghan 1995:202; Rincón Mautner 2005; Saturno et al. 2005; Taube et al. 2010; Tedlock 1996; Vogt and Stuart 2005). Such underground places and the mountains housing them are the heart of community identity (García-Zambrano 1994; Wilson 1993, 1995). In Classic period Mayan, the couplet *chan ch'een* (sky-cave) was a general referent to population centers (Martin 2001:178). In Nahuatl, the term for community is *altepetl*, translated literally as "water-mountain" (Lockhart 1992). Additionally, Mayan place-names for sites often incorporated significant cave-like features (Stuart and Houston 1994; Vogt and Stuart 2005). The importance of these underground places to polity identity is further hinted at by the fact that they were targeted for desecration during warfare events (Brady and Colas 2005; Stuart and Houston 1994:13).

Mountains, caves, and water were conceptually related in pre-Hispanic Mesoamerican thought (Brady 1997:604; Brady and Ashmore 1999). Mountains were thought of as animate water receptacles, and their breath, symbolized by snakes exhaled from their zoomorphic cave maws, carried the liquid out of the underworld and into the sky, creating clouds of rain (Broda 1991:84; Schaafsma 1999; Schaafsma and Taube 2006; Taube 2001:104). Carrying and lifting water-filled jugs, a metaphor for rain, was common to pre-Hispanic Mesoamerican thought (Schaafsma 1999). For example, Late Classic period Quiriguá Zoomorph P depicts flying Chaks (rain beings) pouring water from jars (Schaafsma and Taube 2006:249). Late Preclassic period Izapa Stela 1 depicts the being with a jar strapped to his back from which flow torrents of water, producing a stream in which he fishes (Norman 1973). Thus, jars deposited in caves likely indicate rain rituals performed inside of mountains.

Dripstone cave formations, stalagmites, stalactites, and particularly columns, the physical joining of the former two, were favored foci for rain-related rituals in the Mesoamerican past and present (Bassie-Sweet 1991: 152; Brady 1999:63; Fitzsimmons 2005; Josserand and Hopkins 2007; Moyes et al. 2009; Navarrete and Martínez 1977; Seler 1901:163–169). For example, a high percentage of pre-Hispanic and contemporary stone effigies of the Rain Deity, both carved and unmodified, were made from cave formations (Brady 1999:65–66; Graham 1997; Navarrete and Martínez 1977; Stone 2005). In Quintana Roo, speleothems were regular components of offerings at rain shrines (Lorenzen 1999:102). Moreover, faces were frequently carved near sources of water, particularly in cenotes, suggesting connections to the Rain Deity (Rissolo 2005:363; Strecker 1985: 20). Similarly, censers decorated with the visage of the Central Mexican Rain Deity, Tlaloc, were placed around a large stalagmitic column deep within Balankanche Cave in Yucatán (Andrews 1970).

For contemporary Maya people in Chichicastenango, Guatemala, stone effigies, possibly speleothems, are associated with wind and tempests, the destructive aspects of rain (Brady 1999:65; Bunzel 1952:268). Lacandón Maya people place into censers called god pots small stones taken from the sacred abodes of deities (McGee 1990:52; Soustelle 1961; Tozzer 1907: 87). The stones are variably referred to as mediums or thrones for the deity whose residence they were taken from, and they allow the Lacandón to communicate with those beings (McGee 1990:52). Day of the Cross rituals at the Jolja' Caves performed by Ch'ol Maya of Chiapas, Mexico, incorporate drip water collected from the back of one of the caverns, and candles are placed on or adjacent to stalagmites (Bassie-Sweet et al. 2015: 160–161; Halperin and Spenard 2015:77). That ritual functions to convince the Earth Lord, Don Juan, to release the rains (Bassie-Sweet et al. 2015:159). Speleothems are one of a group of common items used in agricultural rituals for the Maya of Yucatán (Astor-Aguilera 2010:171). The Mixtec of Oaxaca similarly present cave formations with offerings for rain, believing them to be the Rain Deity (Monaghan 1995:106–108; Ravicz and Romney 1969:394).

Mountains and caves are also commonly noted in ethnographic and ethnohistoric accounts, as well as in pre-Hispanic iconography, as being places of ancestral emergence and where the ancestors reside throughout pre- and post-contact Mesoamerica (Durán 1994; García-Zambrano 1994; Monaghan 1995; Saturno et al. 2005; Tedlock 1996; Vogt 1969). Nevertheless, this well-documented aspect of the social importance of caves has been an infrequent aspect of Mesoamerican, and particularly Maya, cave archaeology (Aguilar et al. 2005; Heyden, 1973, 1975, 1981; Spenard 2006). Instead, researchers have focused on the environmental associations of caverns discussed above.

Site Descriptions

Actun Lak "Pottery Cave"

Of the four caves in this study, Actun Lak is geographically the closest to Pacbitun. Its name, translated as "Pottery Cave," comes from the thick carpet of ceramic sherds lying over the entire floor of the cavern and on most of its low-lying ledges. Its entrance, a horizontal, mouthlike hole, is halfway up a hillside, at the bottom of which is another massive cavern that receives vast quantities of water from the surrounding landscape during the rainy season. Actun Lak is a horizontal cave 43 m long with variable ceiling height ranging from 1 m to 11 m. The cavern is composed of a highly modified entrance passage and three main chambers, labeled 1 through 3, from the entrance to the rear of the cave. The modifications to the entrance area are part of a massive single-phase construction project dating to the Terminal Classic period (800–900 CE), which included constructing a set of stairs on the hillside down to the entrance of the other cavern (Spenard 2014). Just outside of Actun Lak, the stairs terminate at a buried, stone-faced earthen platform measuring 5 × 8 m. The platform terminates at the dripline of the cave, but the contemporary floor was artificially raised by up to 3 m over the entire 8 horizontal meters of the entrance area.

Chamber 1 is dominated by a series of broken stalagmitic formations rising up from the cave floor, between which past Maya people placed an artificial pavement of river and limestone cobbles carried into the cave. During periods of continuous rain, the thousands of stalactites hanging from the ceiling in the chamber drip heavily, creating a rainy environment. The antiquity of the cobble pavement is demonstrated by the thick coat of calcium carbonate cementing together the imported rocks. Hundreds of ceramic sherds cover the cobble pavement and the matrix adjacent to it. Stylistically, they date from the Late Preclassic (300–100 BCE) through the early Postclassic period (900–1000 CE), although most date to the Terminal Preclassic (100 BCE–300 CE) through the first two centuries of the Early Classic period (300–550 CE). Horizontal excavations beneath a small alcove in the cave wall adjacent to the cobble pavement revealed a two-vessel cache of Hewlett Bank Unslipped type bowls (Gifford 1976: 190–191), labeled Feature 1 (Figure 3.2). The vessels were stacked offset on top of one another with the base of the upper bowl touching the lip of the lower.

As Chamber 1 is the focus of our study, we only note that the front portion of Chamber 2 from floor to ceiling is heavily burned due to an inten-

Figure 3.2. Actun Lak Feature 1, in situ Hewlett Bank Unslipped bowls sampled for this study. Photo by Jon Spenard.

sive fire or series of fires associated with an altar created from cave formations. A radiocarbon assay (770–940 cal CE) from a partially burned wood fragment suggests the activities at the altar were contemporaneous with the modifications made to the cave entrance (Spenard 2014:416). Chamber 3 is a small room with a high ceiling and a steeply sloping floor that turns into a naturally restricted passage that abruptly ends after a 180-degree turn. Heavy concentrations of ceramic sherds cover the floor of this part of the cave (Spenard 2012).

Slate Cave

Slate Cave is a 55 m long, undulating, low-ceilinged passage uphill from the western bank of a seasonally active stream. That waterway flows into a massive cave opening in the base of an isolated hill at the juncture of two ranges of foothills on the rim of the Maya Mountains, 2.5 km from Pacbitun. The larger cave is the entrance to the most extensive network of underground passages known in the Pacbitun region, all of which make up a massive drainage system for that portion of the Maya Mountains.

On top of the hill is the Late Classic period secondary center, Sak Pol Pak, which contains the tallest pyramidal structure in the region outside of the main plaza at Pacbitun (Conlon 1999; Spenard, Mai, and Mai 2012).

Slate Cave was named in reference to the ubiquity of slate rocks throughout the cave, imported by human agents and occasionally by major flooding in the waterway below (Spenard and Mirro 2017). With a bell-shaped entrance spanning 8 m wide at its base and 4 m tall, the cave penetrates an exposed portion of bedrock on the side of a gently sloping hillside. There are two main areas of the cave, naturally separated by a bedrock wall with a small hole at its base 30 m into the cave. The hole is just large enough for a person to squeeze through. The front section of the cave, and the focus of our discussion in this chapter, is relatively open with smooth walls, but the walls of the back half are craggy and filled with dissolution holes. Artifacts were recorded on the surface in both areas of the cave, although they occur in much higher quantities in the front portion. Based on ceramic styles, this cave was first used in the Early Classic period and continued through the Terminal Classic period.

The pattern of use of Slate Cave is unique in the Pacbitun region because it is the only one known to contain rock art, which in this case is a carved petroglyph panel on a seasonally active globular cave formation. The panel consists of six simple faces (round eyes and bar mouth), geometric shapes, and a full-figure anthropomorphic character, which may be either a spider monkey or a boxer character.

The feature of note in this cave for the current study is located at the farthest extent of the light zone. It is a burial or cache with human remains placed in an excavated and infilled pit below an alcove in the cave wall. The alcove containing the burial runs north–south and is just over 2 m long, although the last half meter is beneath a low-hanging ceiling no more than 30 cm high. In this cramped space, Maya people excavated an ovular-shaped pit approximately 2 m long by 1 m wide and 0.25 m deep, in the bottom of which they excavated a smaller hole 1.5 m long by 0.5 m wide and an additional 0.25 m deep. Few artifacts were recovered in the larger pit, but a flowstone block and a slate cobble pavement covered the lower hole, and on the northern end of the pavement was a single undecorated ceramic jar body sherd.

The southern side of the lower pit beneath the pavement was empty of cultural material, although several sequential linear stains were noted at the very bottom that may be the remains of a wooden bier. Soil samples from the stains were collected and await further analysis to determine their composition. The cobbles in the southern half of the pit were in gen-

Figure 3.3. Slate Cave Feature 1, human cranium surrounded by bone tubes sampled in this study. Photo by Jon Spenard.

eral disarray when uncovered, with few lying close to horizontally flat; several others were standing nearly upright. This contrasts strongly with the northern side of the pit, where the cobbles are orderly and remain mostly horizontally flat. These varying conditions suggest that the southern side of the pit was excavated in the past, and whatever objects originally deposited in there were removed. Nevertheless, it seems this was done with care, as the pit was refilled, the cobbles were laid back down close to their original depth, and the entire pavement was reburied.

The northern side of the pit contained a wide variety of artifacts. Almost directly below where the jar fragment was placed was a human cranium and mandible surrounded by at least six mammal bone tubes (likely deer), and other bone objects too fragmented and deteriorated to identify (Figure 3.3). The cranium was laid facing west, in a position halfway between facedown and on its side. The bone tubes were clustered around the face and chin area of the skull, with another two located at the base of the occipital bone. Four had been incised with either a horizontal line encircling the tubes or X-shaped designs, and the two others were uncarved. The tube with the X-shaped incisions was standing nearly upright when first uncovered, and the top of it was capped with a large chert flake, one of the few nonbone artifacts recovered in the smaller pit. Spenard and Mirro (2017:130) have proposed that these bone objects may have been used as delivery tubes for entheogenic enemas.

Tzul's Cave

On first impression, Tzul's Cave appears to be a small, restricted grotto of three horizontal tubelike passages connected to one another by vertical drops; however, through a labor-intensive, single-phase construction effort at the end of the Late Classic period, Pacbitun Maya people buried a tight, winding passage opening into a much larger chamber that has yet to be fully explored. The known entrance to Tzul's Cave is located just inside a small alcove that penetrates a bedrock outcrop jutting up from a natural bench on a gently sloping hillside. The area of the cave that has been explored consists of six chambers of varying size and complexity. To understand why we sampled the vessels from this cave and to gain more clarity on the social use of caverns in the Pacbitun region, we offer a more comprehensive description of this underground site than the others in this chapter.

Immediately inside the entrance alcove, the floor drops 4 m into the largest known room in the cave, Room A, a chamber measuring 10 m long, with an average ceiling height of 4 m, but it is narrow, measuring no more than 3 m wide. The floor is bedrock, and no evidence of Maya use of that part of the cave has been recovered, save for systematically harvested stalactites. Nevertheless, water actively drips from the ceiling in accordance with the weather outside, at times covering the floor of the chamber in a shallow pool of water, and thus any artifacts left there in the past may have been washed away. The cave continues to Room B, a 2.5 m long, 1 m tall by 1 m wide passage that had been artificially restricted in the past by a cobble wall, which had been torn down prior to our investigations. Passing through Room B, one arrives in Room C, a 3 m long by 1.5 m wide chamber with a 1.5 m tall ceiling. In both rooms, the cave walls skirting the outer edges of the bedrock outcrop into which the cave penetrates are pockmarked with dissolution holes that the Pacbitun Maya filled with rocks. In addition to infilling the natural windows, the Maya also leveled and raised the floor of the cave by as much as 1 m, using a mix of large imported limestone cobbles and dirt. A small alcove holding a cluster of Late to Terminal Classic period broken jar rims and large pieces of slate intermixed with limestone cobbles is present along the western wall of the room. At the

Figure 3.4. Ceramic vessels in Tzul's Cave Room D sampled for this study. Photo by Terry Powis.

far end of that artifact concentration, the floor leveling stops abruptly, leaving a glaring hole in the cave floor that had been covered over in the past by a slate block plastered into place.

The slate plug capped a vertical drop of 3 m that provided access to Rooms D, E, and F. Room D is the largest known in the lower level of the cave, and it is aligned north to south, while Room E is a small alcove at its northern end. Room F, described in further detail below, branches from the southwest corner of Room D. Together, Rooms D and E measure only 6.5 m long and average 1.5 m wide. Few artifacts are present directly below the drop and in the main accessway of the room, but an alcove beneath the entrance ledge connecting with Room E contains several whole and partial vessels, including the remains of approximately fifteen jars and fewer than six bowls/dishes. Identified ceramic types in Rooms D and E include Alexanders Unslipped, Cayo Unslipped, Belize Red Incised, Dolphin Head Red, Garbutt Creek Red, Mount Maloney Black (bowls and globular jars), and Puhui-zibal Composite types (Gifford 1976:266), all dating to the last two centuries of the Classic period (Figure 3.4).

A test excavation into the elevated floor near the junction with Room F revealed that at least 20 cm of dirt had been imported into the chamber to level the floor. Beneath the dirt was cobble fill, indicating that the leveling process began with importing hundreds of rocks into the chamber through the confined upper portions of the cave. Ceramic sherds recovered from that excavation were identified in the field as Mount Maloney Black and Cayo Unslipped type jars (Gifford 1976), both stylistically dating to the Late to Terminal Classic periods.

Room F is the most restricted space known in the cave. It is simply a downward-sloping fingerlike passage extending from the southwest corner of Room D. It measures 4 m long and 0.5 m wide and tall. The Maya blocked its entrance with a triangular-shaped slate plug that reportedly had been plastered into place similar to the other plug from Room C. It is entered by way of a 0.5 m deep hole in the floor of Room D. Looking back up to Room D, one can see that the walls of the hole are actually cobble fill used to artificially raise and level the floor of Room D, as with the floor in Room C. The recovery of Mount Maloney Black globular jar sherds in the excavation unit and the presence of purely Spanish Lookout phase ceramics in Room D date these modifications and the use of the cave to the last two centuries of the Late Classic period (Gifford 1976:243). Ledges are present on either side of Room F and are filled with large Cayo Unslipped, Dolphin Head Red, and Mount Maloney Black type ceramic sherds, all stylistically dated to the Late and Terminal Classic periods.

The cave appears to terminate at the back of Room F, at a point where the ceiling slopes downward to meet the slightly inclined floor. At that point, a partially buried pile of three large cobbles suggested the end of the cave, yet through them blew a slight breeze, indicating that the cave continued beyond that point. Excavations at that terminus revealed that the Maya intentionally blocked a highly restricted winding passage opening up to a much larger chamber beyond. That the passage was intentionally blocked is unquestionable. The ceiling and walls of the rooms of the entire known portions of the cave are smooth and geologically stable, which indicates that any cobbles found there arrived by human agency. Thus, the three stacked cobbles are manuports purposefully carried to that part of the cave. More significantly, during excavation we removed 20 cm of soil matrix over a 2 m by 0.5 m area underlain and intermixed with several hundred more cobbles. Additionally, approximately 15 cm below the surface at the rear of Room F, we uncovered a stack of Mount Maloney Black globular jar body sherds topped with a large Cayo Unslipped type disc, as well as charcoal providing definitive evidence that the fill was cultural. Unfortunately, technical climbing gear was necessary to explore the new portion of the cave, and none was available at the time of excavation. Nonetheless, no artifacts were seen in the small landing on the other side of the passage, nor were any footprints present on the muddy floor there, indicating the Pacbitun Maya may never have accessed that part of the cave.

When considering the cave as a whole, one can see that significant labor was expended to modify it. Thousands of cobbles and several tons of dirt were carried bit by bit through the cave's cramped passages and multiple levels. At times, navigating the cave for our work required taking off our backpacks and pushing or pulling them through the restricted areas. Thus, moving the quantity of dirt and rocks necessary to complete the constructions in the cave was certainly a herculean task. We mention this difficulty of navigating tight passages because, as expanded on below, Tzul's Cave is far from unique in the Pacbitun area in terms of energy-expended modification. In fact, our project has documented over seventy caves and cave-like landmarks around Pacbitun, most within a few kilometers of one another, and in the first range of foothills in the Maya Mountains. Each of the caves had architectural constructions similar to those in Tzul's Cave. There are probably hundreds, if not thousands, of caves in the greater Pacbitun region, all of which are likely to have been modified in a manner similar to Tzul's Cave.

Actun Hayach Naj

The subject of one day of reconnaissance, Actun Hayach Naj Cave is the least understood of the four within this study. Nevertheless, we include it here because its artifact assemblage is unusual for the Pacbitun region, and because the residues found in the vessel are, to date, unique in our study. At 5.5 km from Pacbitun, either it may represent a pilgrimage cave, or it was used by local populations from the two nearby settlements mentioned above, or both.

The entrance to the cave is a wide, shallow sinkhole at the bottom of a cliff face opening onto a steeply declining alluvium-covered slope. At the bottom of the sinkhole is a sloping passage of collapse debris that leads to a single ovicular-shaped room measuring approximately 25 m at its longest point. The center of the chamber is dominated by a large block of ceiling collapse, and small ledges, a few low crawls, and short passages extending from the outer bounds of the chamber quickly lead to dead ends. Ceramic sherds with strong affiliations to Pacbitun and the Belize Valley abound on the cave floor, and most date to the Classic period. The Aguila Orange tripod sampled in the current study and chert flakes were recovered from a cobble-filled niche in the cave floor abutting the block of ceiling collapse in the center of the cave. In addition to ceramics, at least fifty granite mano preforms were noted throughout the cave. While these are not uncommon artifacts to find in caves, the quantity noted is highly unusual for the Pacbitun region. No more than three had been found in any other cavern investigated.

Absorbed Residue Study

In this study, we attempt to add to our understanding of pre-Hispanic Maya use of caves by exploring absorbed resides found in pottery vessels and bone tubes. We used mass spectrometry and applied the biomarker method to accomplish this task (Evershed 2008). With that method, chemical compounds (biomarkers) found exclusively in the suspected contents of containers are identified. For example, cacao beans and drinks made from them contain three key alkaloids (among other compounds): theobromine, theophylline, and caffeine, which have long been used in absorbed residue studies as biomarkers whose presence in ancient pottery is used to identify cacao residues (Powis et al. 2008). Most often, the chemical compounds used as biomarkers are identified using mass spectrometry. For this approach, the choice of biomarkers is critical. The compound or suite of compounds selected as biomarkers must be found exclusively in the suspected contents of ancient containers. If the biomarkers chosen are found in many different plants or animals, they will not be useful in identifying residues created by specific foods, drinks, or other concoctions held in containers.

This early-stage pilot study is aimed at exploring the usefulness of absorbed residues for understanding activities once carried out in caves. Based on existing ethnographic and archaeological information, there could have been a wide variety of plants and other concoctions used in those settings. In exploring this method, we have chosen to focus on a small number of plants and their associated biomarkers (Table 3.1).

The Sample

From the four cave sites described above, we sampled ten pottery vessels and six bone tubes made from deer long bones (Table 3.2). Sampled vessels were selected to represent the variety of forms and types found in the entire cave assemblage, rather than particular decorative elements or slip colors. Bone tubes were chosen for sampling based on their degree of preservation. Those tubes that could not withstand the sampling process

Table 3.1. Plants and biomarkers

Plant	Scientific Name	Biomarker
Chile	*Capsicum* sp.	Dihydrocapsaicin, Capsaicin
Vanilla	*Vanilla planifolia*	Vanillin, Vanillic Acid
Willow	*Salix* sp.	Salicylic acid
Cacao	*Theobroma cacao*	Theobromine, Theophylline, Caffeine

were eliminated from consideration, even though they were all recovered in the same context.

The pottery samples were collected from vessels found in three caves, Actun Lak, Actun Hayach Naj, and Tzul's Cave. In Actun Lak, we sampled the two Hewlett Bank Unslipped type bowls from Feature 1. At Actun Hayach Naj Cave, we sampled the Early Classic period Aguila Orange tripod plate found in the artificially enclosed alcove beneath the cave floor in Chamber 1. In Tzul's Cave, seven of the pottery vessels from Room D were sampled. Each of the vessels dates to the Terminal Classic period, with three of the pots identified as Mount Maloney Black globular ollas. All six of the bone tubes sampled were found in Late Classic period Feature 1 in Slate Cave (Spenard and Mirro 2017).

In absorbed residue studies, contamination presents a significant potential bias (King et al. 2017; Washburn et al. 2014). By contamination, we mean the introduction of the biomarkers of interest (see Table 3.1) into samples through sources other than the ancient uses of containers. For example, compounds may become airborne or be introduced into water systems because of industrial production and common consumer usage. People may also introduce biomarkers during artifact collection and sampling. A finger splashed with morning coffee can later add caffeine to containers and residue samples if allowed to touch containers sampled or sampling instruments. Finally, contamination may happen as remnants of a sample from one container are mixed with a sample from a different container (cross-contamination).

Our sample collection methods were designed to minimize both cross-contamination (multiple samples were collected) and contamination introduced by the individual collecting the samples (Figure 3.5). To reduce the risk of contamination, a mask was worn during sampling, and each sample was collected with a new pair of nitrile exam gloves. We used a metal Dremel bit to grind a portion of the interior surface of each vessel and bone tube. The resulting powdered residues were collected on a clean

Table 3.2. Samples from Belize River valley caves analyzed (samples 8, 9, 11, 12, 16, 17 are not part of this study)

Sample	Material	Cave	Context	Object
1	Bone	Slate	Feature 1	Tube 8
2	Bone	Slate	Feature 1	Tube 13
3	Bone	Slate	Feature 1	Tube 4
4	Bone	Slate	Feature 1	Tube 12
5	Bone	Slate	Feature 1	Tube 3
6	Bone	Slate	Feature 1	Tube 2
7	Soil	Slate	Bone Tube 2, Feature 1	
10	Paper			JD Copy-Rite copier paper
13	Ceramic	Actun Lak	Chamber 1, Unit 8/9, Level 2, Feature 1	Vessel 1 Hewlett Bank Unslipped bowl
14	Ceramic	Actun Lak	Chamber 1, Unit 8/9, Level 2, Feature 1	Vessel 2 Hewlett Bank Unslipped bowl
15	Ceramic	Actun Hayach Naj	Chamber 1, Surface	Aguila Orange tripod plate
18	Ceramic	Tzul's		Small black slipped jar
19	Soil	Tzul's	Chamber 1, Group 1	Under large Mt. Maloney olla sherd
20	Water			RYO Demineralized Water
21	Ceramic	Tzul's	Chamber 1, Group 1	Red slipped dish with legs snapped off
22	Ceramic	Tzul's	Chamber 1, Group 1	Large Mt. Maloney olla with narrow orifice
23	Ceramic	Tzul's	Chamber 1, Group 1	Large Mt. Maloney olla with narrow orifice
24	Ceramic	Tzul's	Chamber 1, Group 1	Large red slipped dish with ring base
25	Ceramic	Tzul's	Chamber 1, Group 1	Small red slipped bowl with pseudo glyphs
26	Ceramic	Tzul's	Chamber 1, Group 1	Black slipped bowl with rolled rim
27	Water			RYO Demineralized Water

Figure 3.5. Junior author Terry Powis collecting a sample from a bowl in Tzul's Cave Room D. Photo by George J. Micheletti.

piece of white copier paper before being transferred into an unused vial that had been cleaned with demineralized water. The drill bit was cleaned with demineralized water after each sample was collected.

Analytical Methods

A total of sixteen samples were extracted using the following procedure. For the burr samples, 90 to 200 mg of burr from each sample was added to a 0.25 ml water-methanol mixture (1:1). Samples were vortexed and incubated at 80°C for thirty minutes. After incubation, samples were sonicated (1 min.), vortexed (1 min.), and centrifuged (3 min.). The resulting precipitate from each sample was removed, and the supernatant was filtered with 5 kD membrane filters. Water-based samples obtained by sonicator were freeze-dried completely. A 0.25 ml water-methanol mixture (1:1) was added, and the samples were sonicated (1 min.), vortexed (1 min.), and centrifuged (3 min.). The supernatant was filtered with 5 kD membrane filters. The filtrates from both extraction methods were transferred to vials for Ultra Performance Liquid Chromatography (UPLC)/MS-MS analysis.

A Xevo-TQ triple quadrupole mass spectrometer (Waters, Milford, MA, USA) was used to record MS and MS-MS spectra using Electro Spray Ionization (ESI) in positive ion (PI) mode, capillary voltage of 3.0 kV, an extractor cone voltage of 3 V, and a detector voltage of 500 V. Cone gas flow was set at 50 L/h, and desolvation gas flow was maintained at 600 L/h. Source temperature and desolvation temperature were set to 150°C and 350°C, respectively. The collision energy was varied from six to thirteen to optimize four different daughter ions. The acquisition range was 20–350 D. Pure standards (atropine and scopalamine) were introduced to the source at a flow rate of 10 μl/min by using a methanol, water (1:1) and 0.1 percent formic acid mixture as the carrier solution to develop the multiple reaction monitoring (MRM) method for UPLC/MS-MS operation.

UPLC/MS-MS analyses of all the samples were carried out with a Waters Acquity UPLC system connected with a Xevo-TQ triple quadruple mass spectrometer. Analytical separations on the UPLC system were conducted using an Acquity UPLC C18 1.7 μm column (1 × 150 mm) at a flow rate of 0.15 ml/min. The gradient started with 100 percent A (0.1% formic acid in H_2O) and 0 percent B (0.1% formic acid in CH_3CN), changed to 50 percent A over 3 minutes, followed by a 4-minute linear gradient to 10 percent A, resulting in a total separation time of 7 minutes. The elutions from the UPLC column were introduced to the mass spectrometer, and resulting data were analyzed and processed using MassLynx 4.2 software. Pure standard mixture was used to optimize the UPLC conditions prior to analysis.

Impacts of Contamination

In conducting absorbed residue studies, modern contamination of the objects or samples is always a concern (King et al. 2017; Washburn et al. 2014). Artifacts can be exposed to modern contamination at a variety of points in their life. One point comes before the artifacts are recovered. It is also possible that the containers sampled in our study were contaminated by water or even air as they rested in the caves. A wide variety of chemicals and compounds are ubiquitous both in the air and in our water systems, especially near major population and manufacturing centers. We have assumed that the risk of contamination from these sources is relatively low, given their location within caves in a relatively rural portion of Belize. The general validity of this assumption was confirmed when we analyzed samples of soil from two caves (see Tables 3.2 and 3.3) and detected none of the biomarkers of interest (Table 3.1).

Artifacts may also be exposed to modern contamination as they are removed from their archaeological context, processed, and analyzed. The greatest risk of exposure comes from contact with people, laboratory surfaces, and tools. Because the vessels from Tzul's Cave were sampled directly in the cave, these sources of contamination likely had little impact on our results. The risk of contamination is greater for the objects sampled from Actun Lak, Actun Hayach Naj, and Slate Cave because they were removed from the caves and brought to the lab, where they received some cleaning and handling. For the vessels from Actun Lak and the bone tubes from Slate Cave, postrecovery processing involved the removal of soil accumulated in the interior. The single vessel from Actun Hayach Naj was cleaned with a dry brush to remove a powdery calcium carbonate deposit. As we discuss later, the actual impact of contamination from these sources is best assessed using the residue analysis results.

Storage materials and location can also play a role in exposure to modern contamination. It has been shown that objects stored in the open on shelves are exposed to a variety of airborne contaminants most likely introduced through air circulation systems (Washburn et al. 2014). In this study, that potential has been minimized because all of the objects removed from the caves were stored in sealed plastic containers.

Finally, it is possible for sampling methods and materials to intro-

Table 3.3. Mass spectrometry results (samples 8, 9, 11, 12, 16, 17 are not part of this study)

Sample	Material	Cave	Dihydro-capsaicin ng/g	Capsaicin ng/g	Atropine ng/g	Vanillin ng/g	Vanillic Acid ng/g	Salicylic Acid ng/g	Theobromine ng/g	Theophylline ng/g	Caffeine ng/g
1	Bone	Slate	0	0	0	0	12.5	0	0	0	0
2	Bone	Slate	0	0	0	0	0	0	0	0	0
3	Bone	Slate	0	0	0	0	0	0	0	0	0
4	Bone	Slate	0	0	0	0	0	0	0	0	0
5	Bone	Slate	0	0	0	0	0	19.6	0	0	0
6	Bone	Slate	0	0	0	0	0	23.5	0	0	0
7	Soil	Slate	0	0	0	0	0	0	0	0	0
10	Paper		0	0	0	0	33.5	0	0	0	76.1
13	Ceramic	Actun Lak	0	0	0	0	0	1,407.6	0	0	0.739
14	Ceramic	Actun Lak	0	0	0	0	0	458.9	0	0	0
15	Ceramic	Actun Hayach Naj	0	0	0.016	0	0	876.5	2.69	0.25	2.48
18	Ceramic	Tzul's	0	0	0.024	0	0	0	0	0	0
19	Soil	Tzul's	0	0	0	0	0	0	0	0	0
20	Water*		0	0	0	0	0	0	0	0	0
21	Ceramic	Tzul's	0	0	0	0	0	0	0	0	0
22	Ceramic	Tzul's	0	0	0	0	0	0	0	0	43.3
23	Ceramic	Tzul's	0	0	0	405.5	0	0	0	0	20.5
24	Ceramic	Tzul's	0	0	0	0	0	0	0	0	19.6
25	Ceramic	Tzul's	0	0	0	0	0	0	0	0	0
26	Ceramic	Tzul's	0	0	0	0	0	62.8	0	0	0
27	Water*		0	0	0	0	0	1.16	0	0	0

*ng/l

duce contaminants into residue samples collected. As discussed above, our sampling protocol was specifically designed to minimize the potential for cross-contamination, as multiple samples were collected, and for the sampler to introduce contaminants. To assess the possibility that our sampling materials contaminated our results, we tested the demineralized water and a sheet of white copier paper used to collect the samples (Tables 3.2 and 3.3). One of the water samples analyzed contained none of our biomarkers, but in a second sample, a small amount of salicylic acid was detected. The sample taken from a sheet of our collection paper showed the presence of small amounts of caffeine and vanillic acid. Using these results, we considered any other positive samples with amounts of salicylic acid, caffeine, or vanillic acid below those found in the paper and water to be potentially contaminated.

Results

Half of the samples analyzed (eight out of sixteen) tested positive for at least one of our biomarkers of interest (see Tables 3.3 and 3.4). Surprisingly, the most frequently detected biomarker was *Salix*, or salicylic acid, which was present in three-quarters of the positive samples. Salicylic acid, which is found naturally in various parts of willow trees, is a common constituent in airborne and waterborne contamination because of its widespread use as an analgesic. This leaves open the possibility that its presence, and prevalence, in our samples is the result of some form of contamination. Given that salicylic acid was not detected in soils from two of the caves, we do not think its presence is the result of contamination in the caverns. The fact that five of the six samples that tested positive for salicylic acid were collected from objects processed and stored in the lab suggests that our lab treatment could be a source. The one piece of evidence arguing against modern contamination as the source of the salicylic acid in our samples is the fact that we detected it in one of the vessels sampled within Tzul's Cave. For the moment, we will treat the presence of salicylic acid as a real result and not the product of modern contamination.

Two samples contained *Datura*, and one had residues indicative of vanilla. Cacao was also found in only one sample, the tripod plate from Actun Hayach Naj, but that vessel is the only one of our samples to be positive for more than one biomarker. It also had residues from *Datura* and salicylic acid. No residues were found containing the biomarkers for chile. Historical information documents the addition of chile to elite beverages like cacao, and also to ritual beverages like *balche'* (see Vail and Dedrick, this

Table 3.4. Samples positive for plants of interest

Sample	Material	Cave	Datura	Vanilla	Willow	Cacao
1	Bone	Slate				
2	Bone	Slate				
3	Bone	Slate				
4	Bone	Slate				
5	Bone	Slate			X	
6	Bone	Slate			X	
7	Soil	Slate				
13	Ceramic	Actun Lak			X	
14	Ceramic	Actun Lak			X	
15	Ceramic	Actun Hayach Naj	X		X	X
18	Ceramic	Tzul's	X			
19	Soil	Tzul's				
21	Ceramic	Tzul's				
22	Ceramic	Tzul's				
23	Ceramic	Tzul's		X		
24	Ceramic	Tzul's				
25	Ceramic	Tzul's				
26	Ceramic	Tzul's			X	

volume). Its absence from our samples may indicate that it was not part of ritual practice in caves, or its absence may be the result of sampling error.

Discussion and Conclusion

Salix

Very little has been written about the use of *Salix* sp. in the ethnographic and ethnohistoric literature on Mesoamerica. Among the Tzotzil Maya of Zinacantan, it has a few utilitarian uses, including making shade and growing into living fences (Breedlove and Laughlin 1993:201). It also has minor medicinal uses, for treating muscle pain and tonsillitis. Symbolically, it is believed to be the origin of water, thus it is regularly planted near water holes. Perhaps the most significant use of this plant for the present study is that it is one of the ingredients used to make gunpowder in community rituals, including the Holy Cross ceremony. Certainly, we are not proposing that the pre-Hispanic Maya invented gunpowder; instead, it is interesting to note that *Salix* is used in conjunction with the Holy Cross ceremony. Holy Cross or Day of the Cross is a ritual celebrated at the beginning of May to ensure the rains come, among other goals. Huastec Maya use *Salix* as a medicinal plant to treat nausea and as a stimulant to prevent tiredness (Alcorn 1984:780). Bernardino de Sahagún (1963:110) simply describes the tree in his review of "earthly things" in Aztec Mexico without ascribing any uses to it, as he does for many other plants in that inventory, yet there is some evidence that *Salix* had symbolic significance for the Aztec. Pillars shaped from willow trees were used for foundation posts in the Templo Mayor in Tenochtitlan (López Luján, Torres, and Montúfar López 2003:153). More significantly, willow leaves were included in the many offerings placed throughout that same temple. Unfortunately, the symbolic significance of these leaves has yet to be determined.

A review of two online ethnobotany databases, "Dr. Duke's Phytochemical and Ethnobotanical Databases," hosted by the US Department of Agriculture (USDA 2018), and the "Native American Ethnobotany Database" (Moerman 2008) provides some insight into how *Salix* may have been used ritually. Just as in Mesoamerica, various species of *Salix* have been used for medicinal purposes throughout North America, to treat ailments ranging from gastrointestinal issues to fever and warts (USDA 2018). More significantly for our purposes, various parts of the tree, including bark and leaves, are often burned and the ashes added to tobacco and snuff (Moerman 2008). Although we did not test for tobacco, cigars and other types of cigarillos are known in Maya art, where various gods are shown smoking them (Taube 1992). The presence of a tobacco person on the Chiik Nab market murals at Calakmul suggests that the use of tobacco was common among the Maya (Martin 2012).

Due to a paucity of literature on the ritual use of *Salix* in pre-Hispanic and contemporary Mesoamerica, interpreting its appearance in the Actun Lak and Actun Hayach Naj bowls and Slate Cave bone tubes is difficult, but we can offer some tentative hypotheses. As mentioned earlier, Spenard (2014) has proposed that Actun Lak was used as a community rain shrine in the Late Preclassic through Early Classic periods. Although the presence of *Salix* in the bowls cannot currently provide evidence of the social standing of the people performing the rituals within the cave, its symbolic and physical closeness to water, discussed above, does support the proposal of rain rituals performed in the cave. The presence of *Salix* in the vessel sampled from Actun Hayach Naj is more difficult to interpret, in part because that cavern has been only a minor focus of our larger studies to this point. We will return to this cave again in the following discussion, but note for now that when considering the ethnographic literature on the medicinal qualities of the genus, its presence may indicate that the vessel was used during a healing ritual. Considering the medicinal properties of *Salix*, its appearance in the bone tubes from Slate Cave suggest that they may have been used at some point for administering medicine, although why they were buried in a pit around the neck area of a possibly severed cranium remains unclear. Perhaps the individual was a shaman or healer, and the bone tubes were part of their tool kit in life.

Cacao

Cacao has long been discussed as a tightly controlled elite foodstuff, and the plant's beans were used as a form of currency by Maya during the Late Postclassic and Colonial periods (Coe and Coe 2007; Dreiss and Greenhill 2008; Gasco 1987; McNeil 2006a; Tozzer 1941). Moreover, elite polychrome feasting and drinking cups regularly contained hieroglyphic texts just below their exterior lips labeling the contents as "so-and-so's [adverb(s)/ingredient(s)] chocolate drinking cup" (see the introduction to this volume; Colas et al. 2002; Grube 1991; Houston and Taube 1987; LeCount 2001, 2010; Reents-Budet 1994, 2000). Yet recent research indicates cacao was available to most people in the pre-Hispanic Maya area—in limited quantities—where it was used during important ritual events and lineage feasts (LeCount 2001; McNeil 2006b:18). In areas where cacao was grown, such as the western Belize Valley, broad social access seems to have been the norm (McAnany and Murata 2006:446; McNeil 2006b:18). We return to this discussion below.

Martin (2006) discusses the strong symbolic overlap between corn and cacao in pre-Hispanic Mesoamerican art. For example, on a blackware vessel known as the Berlin Vase, anthropomorphic cacao and *guanábana* (soursop) trees and a vine sprout from the skeletal remains of the deceased Maize Deity. A similar scene occurs on the sarcophagus of Pakal from Palenque, where the deceased king is dressed as the Maize Deity. Images of his ancestors as saplings of fruit trees emerging from cracks line the sides of his sarcophagus. His mother, who appears twice, is portrayed as a cacao tree (Martin 2006:160–161).

Kufer and Heinrich (2006) note strong symbolic similarities between cacao and corn among the Ch'orti' Maya of eastern Guatemala of today. In short, the plants are binary complements of one another and likened to a married couple bound in a mutually dependent relationship (Kufer and Heinrich 2006:402). Cacao is dark and considered in the humoral classification system to be a cool plant, perfectly suited to counter the high heat produced during rituals (Kufer and Heinrich 2006). This opposition also resembles the environments in which the plants prefer to grow, which in turn structures symbolic views of them. Maize prefers the bright, direct sun and is symbolically tied to daytime. Cacao, on the other hand, can only grow in the shade, and as such is tied to darkness, the night, and caves, and it is also the same color as rain clouds. Moreover, maize is associated with men, and cacao with women (Kufer and Heinrich 2006:404). The Ch'orti' employ these complementary plants together when conducting Day of the Cross rain rituals at the beginning of the rainy season. The association between cacao and women has roots in the pre-Hispanic past in Mesoamerica. McNeil (2006b:15) notes that although cacao appears with both women and men in Mesoamerican art, it is more commonly depicted with the former.

What does the above discussion of cacao tell us about the social use of Actun Hayach Naj and Tzul's Cave, where the residues were found? Ironically, it can be seen to both support and challenge the elite, androcentric view of Maya ritual cave use. If we take the common (and well-supported) position that cacao beverages were largely restricted to elite consumption, then we can see how these two caves could be understood as elite spaces. Moreover, some ethnographic and ethnohistoric literature suggests women were largely restricted from entering caves and participating in the rituals performed within them (Adams and Brady 2005; Thompson 1975:xxi–xxii). Thus, we see how these two caves could be considered ritual places for elite men. Yet some ethnographic accounts report the opposite. For example, at the Day of the Cross ceremony performed at the Jolja' caves, all members of the community, including children, women, and men, participate in the ceremonial activities (Bassie-Sweet et al. 2015). In Tojolobal communities, women participate in cave rituals with men, although their participation is said to lead to infidelity (Whittaker and Warkentin 1965:81–85). During his study of caves near Cancuén, Guatemala, Spenard (2006:152) was informed that women were responsible for preparing the meal for rituals performed in caves, and that they could go if they wanted, but most choose to stay at home because they do not like to travel at night when the ceremony takes place. These data collectively indicate that taboos against women participating in cave rituals vary by community in the ethnographic present, and thus whether they were involved in underground rituals in the past remains unclear.

When we consider specific details about Pacbitun and the caves, we can see how our data challenge the elite male usage interpretation. As noted, Pacbitun is located in one of the prime regions of cacao production in the pre-Hispanic past; thus, cacao was likely more widely available for the people there than it was for others elsewhere in the Maya Lowlands. Moreover, the symbolic ties between cacao and women seen in the ethnographic literature and on pre-Hispanic art do suggest women may have been ritual participants in cave ceremonies. Overall, we interpret our data on the gendered use of caves as equivocal.

Even if we place the two caves into their broader settlement contexts, the picture of who used them remains cloudy. As we discussed earlier, Actun Hayach Naj is only a few hundred meters away from two formal patio groups, one of which may have a small pyramidal structure affiliated with it, but all three are about 5.5 km from Pacbitun (Spenard, Mai, and Mai 2012). Many such patio groups have been recorded closer to Pacbitun, and they appear to indicate some kind of local communities, perhaps acting as lineages, neighborhoods, or district shrines (Spenard and Powis 2014). The people or lineages from the nearby settlements were most likely the ones using Actun Hayach Naj, although we cannot rule out long-distance pilgrimage as a factor, nor can we make a definitive statement about the social status of occupants until the settlements have been studied further.

Regarding Tzul's Cave, as noted above, some people affiliated with Pacbitun spent a great deal of time and energy modifying the cave by dragging thousands of kilograms of dirt and rocks through its restricted passages. These actions alone suggest it was a special place. Given that the elite from Pacbitun commissioned a 2.5 km long road between the site core and the valley, elite use of the cave seems likely. When adding cacao to the mix, the argument for elite use becomes even stronger. Yet, as we noted above, all of the architecture and modifications made to the cave are common in the Pacbitun region. Of the seventy cave and cave-like features we have investigated in the region, almost all have been heavily modified. In fact, given the size and length of Tzul's Cave in front of the blocked passage, the modifications would have been energetically cheaper to make than those in many of the other larger and more complex cave systems. Given the hundreds of caves in the Pacbitun region, it is likely that most, if not all, were heavily modified like Tzul's Cave, and would also show regular use from the Early Classic through Late Classic periods. Simply stated, it would be impossible for only elites to have made all the modifications and performed all of the ceremonies in all of the caves, known and unknown to archaeology, in the region, even if that is all they did every day of their lives. Consequently, it seems highly unlikely that cave rituals in Tzul's Cave were only performed by elites, even if a causeway ran directly by it. Undoubtedly, Maya of all social classes were performing cave rituals at Pacbitun.

Vanilla

Currently, we are unable to say much about the appearance of vanilla in our samples, as it was only recovered from one vessel, a jar from Tzul's Cave, but with none of our other targeted biomarkers. In Belize today, vanilla is combined with skunk urine and a popular brand of perfume to brew love charms for preventing wayward loved ones from leaving (Balick and Arvigo 2015:151–152). At the turn of the twentieth century in Belize and adjacent parts of Mexico, Maya peoples used leaves from *chiohle*, a particular species of vanilla, to flavor smoking tobacco (Gann 1918:30). Yet, overall, its most common role is as a flavoring for cacao beverages (Horwich and Lyon 1990; Lundell 1938; Rätsch 2005:500). Perhaps most significant for the current study is that Lacandón Maya people use the plant to flavor *balche'*, a mild intoxicant, but not an entheogen, consumed in ritual contexts (Rätsch 2005:724). Thus, the most likely scenario is that the vanilla residue recovered from the Tzul's Cave jar was used for flavoring for some kind of noncacao-based beverage, possibly *balche'*.

Datura

People worldwide, and especially in the Americas, have used ritual and ceremonial entheogens made from plants and other sources for millennia (Furst 1972; Moore 2014; Schultes 1972). For example, iconography at Chavín de Huantar in Peru depicts priests in various stages of shamanic transformations caused by the ingestion of mind-altering plants (Burger 2011). Such art has also been described at later Huari and Tiahuanaco sites (Knobloch 2000; Torres and Repke 2006). Similarly, archaeologists have long reported the presence of "snuff spoons" from Olmec sites, which may have been used for ingesting ground entheogens for assisting in shamanic transformation (Reilly 1989).

Datura is a genus of flowering plants in the Solanaceae family whose leaves, seeds, and flowers contain tropane alkaloids like atropine, scopolamine, and hyoscamine (Lester, Nee, and Estrada 1991). These alkaloids produce psychotropic effects and can be toxic when consumed in high enough doses. Ethnographic evidence suggests that the pre-Hispanic Maya may have added *Datura* to fermented drinks as a means to induce a mindaltering state (Stross and Kerr 1990:355). Similarly, Tarahumara medicine men add *Datura* to a fermented maize drink, and use the roots, leaves, and seeds of the plant to make psychotropic beverages used to diagnose disease. Litzinger (1994:134) proposes that *Datura* may have been used by pre-Hispanic Maya people, noting that the plant is associated with death, war, directional symbolism, and transformation among the Yucatec and Lacandón Maya of today. He proposes that those attributes are at the core of pre-Hispanic Maya religious thought and thus may have had a ceremonial significance.

In our study, we recorded one instance of *Datura* possibly being mixed with salicylic acid and cacao. In another instance, it is the only compound found in the vessel. As mentioned above, the pre-Hispanic Maya may have added *Datura* to ferment drinks as a means to induce a mind-altering state. In two cases, we have *Datura* in two pottery vessels from two different cave sites from two different time periods (Early Classic and Terminal Classic). If it was used to produce psychotropic effects, then how was this done, especially in a cave setting?

Enema scenes are commonly depicted on Maya pottery and in iconography. For example, a vase housed in the Princeton Art Museum depicts an elaborate scene where the central figure receives an enema poured from a large jar or gourd with the help of an assistant (K1550). Behind these individuals is a third person dipping more liquid from a cloth-wrapped jar with a gourd (Stross and Kerr 1990:349). Several other vessels depicting enema scenes have been recovered from sites throughout the Maya area, many of which show the liquid being served in a gourd-like bowl similar to those found in Actun Lak. At the site of San Diego, Yucatán, a series of carved relief sculptures depict people self-administering enemas with gourd-like objects and performing ceremonies while under the influence of the ingested drink (Barrera Rubio and Taube 1987). The figures are depicted dancing, hunched over, pulling their hair, and transferring liquids between vessels. Archaeologists working outside the Maya area in Veracruz, Mexico, have uncovered ceramic figurines with ecstatic facial expressions and bodies in reclining positions with legs spread and propped in the air, a position similar to that seen on the Princeton Art Museum vase (Furst and Coe 1997). What such representations and others like them have in common is that the enema liquid was held in gourd-like objects, and it was administered with a hollow bone tube (Hellmuth 1985, Figure 30). In fact, these types of artifacts, including hollow bone tube syringes, often made from deer bone femurs, have been found throughout Mesoamerica (Barrera Rubio and Taube 1987, Figure 20).

Thus, could mind-altering enemas have been performed in caves in the periphery of Pacbitun during the Classic period? Although the pots indicate that this is a possibility, the bone tubes we tested do not, as none contained the biomarkers for *Datura*. This may be the result of the sample size being too small. It is equally plausible that the atropine was put into some sort of concoction and consumed as a ritual beverage. We feel safe in arguing that *Datura* was used as part of rituals associated with caves and that caves were identified with rain, water, and fertility. We do not understand much about those rituals, but at least now we know *Datura* was part of them.

Concluding Remarks

What has our study taught us about the social use of caves by the Pacbitun Maya? In short, we have learned that understanding who was performing rituals in caverns is far from straightforward. Was all cave use restricted to elites? It appears unlikely, although our plant data are equivocal. Cacao is considered an elite foodstuff, but it was regularly available to all social classes in areas where it was grown, including in the Belize Valley where Pacbitun is located. Were only men performing rituals in caves? Again, it appears unlikely, although our data are equivocal. We return to cacao, which has strong symbolic connections with women in the present and pre-Hispanic past; thus, finding cacao residue in the Pacbitun caves may also be interpreted to demonstrate the presence of women. Did some rituals include ingesting mind-altering beverages? In some instances, yes, but the practice appears to have been infrequent. Were rain rituals performed in the Pacbitun caves? Yes, and they appear to have included willow trees in some form.

What, then, can we say about the social use of caves in the Maya area? We answer that question with a note and a call for future research that perhaps cave archaeologists need to broaden and complicate the scope of who was using caves beyond social class and gender, to also ask about occupation. Ethnographic data reveal that major rituals related to rain, agricultural fertility, ancestors, and health are seldom performed by individuals; instead, a person or group seeks out ritual specialists who contact and interact with the appropriate nonhuman persons on their client's behalf (Bassie-Sweet et al. 2015:155; Freidel, Schele, and Parker 1993; Hopkins, Bassie-Sweet, and Laughlin 2015:42–43; Love 2004; Redfield and Villa Rojas 1934:74–77; Scott 2009; Vogt 1969:416–476). The social status and opinions about such ritual specialists vary; some are held in the highest esteem as community elders, whereas others are met with suspicion and considered lechers, and sometimes the same person is considered to be both by members of the community (Arvigo, Epstein, and Yaquinto 1994:7; Bassie-Sweet et al. 2015:155). The ubiquity of such practitioners throughout the Maya area today suggests that similar people were present in the pre-Hispanic past. In fact, research in caves in the southern Maya Mountains in Belize has revealed several instances of specialized ritual practitioners using and, in one case, being interred in a cave (Prufer 2005; Prufer and Dunham 2009). Moreover, Zender (2004) finds hieroglyphic and iconographic evidence of an elite priestly class with a hierarchically organized set of offices that included both men and women among the Late Classic through Late Postclassic period Maya. Drawing on these data, we wonder if each social group, lineage, or neighborhood had its own ritual specialists to perform major cave ceremonies on their behalf, whether it be to heal a sick person, to bring the rain, or to communicate with the ancestors.

Lastly, archaeologists commonly assume the rituals performed in caves were benevolent, as we have largely done in this chapter. Nevertheless, sorcery performed with the intent of harming individuals is practiced among the Maya today, and it is often performed in the same caves and landmarks where beneficial ceremonies are performed (Bassie-Sweet et al. 2015:155; Lucero and Gibbs 2007; Scott 2009). Thus, we cannot discount the possibility that some rituals, and thus some of the residues we identified, especially *Datura* and possibly *Salix* as a medicinal plant, were used in the past for similarly harmful purposes. In the end, although our data remain largely equivocal about identifying who was performing rituals in caves, that uncertainty hints at a much more complex pattern of use by a much broader spectrum of social actors than previously recognized.

References

Adams, Abigail, and James E. Brady. 2005. "Ethnographic Notes on Maya Q'eqchi' Cave Rites: Implications for Archaeological Interpretation." In *In the Maw of the Earth Monster: Mesoamerican Ritual Cave Use*, ed. James E. Brady and Keith M. Prufer, 301–327. Austin: University of Texas Press.

Aguilar, Manuel, Miguel Medina Jaen, Tim M. Tucker, and James E. Brady. 2005. "Constructing Mythic Space: The Significance of a Chicomoztoc Complex at Acatzingo Viejo." In *In The Maw of the Earth Monster: Mesoamerican Ritual Cave Use*, ed. James E. Brady and Keith M. Prufer, 69–87. Austin: University of Texas Press.

Alcorn, Janis B. 1984. *Huastec Mayan Ethnobotany*. Austin: University of Texas Press.

Andrews, E. Wyllys, IV. 1970. *Balankanche, Throne of the Tiger Priest*. Middle American Research Institute Publication 32. New Orleans: Tulane University.

Anya H., Armando, Stanley Guenter, and Peter Mathews. 2001. "An Inscribed Wooden Box from Tabasco, Mexico." Accessed February 16, 2014. http://www.mesoweb.com/reports/box/.

Arvigo, Rosita, Nadine Epstein, and Marilyn Yaquinto. 1994. *Sastun: My Apprenticeship with a Maya Healer*. 1st ed. San Francisco: HarperSanFrancisco.

Astor-Aguilera, Miguel Angel. 2010. *The Maya World of Communicating Objects: Quadripartite Crosses, Trees, and Stones*. Albuquerque: University of New Mexico Press.

Balick, Michael J., and Rosita Arvigo. 2015. *Messages from the Gods: A Guide to the Useful Plants of Belize*. Oxford: Oxford University Press.

Barrera Rubio, Alfredo, and Karl A. Taube. 1987. "Los relieves de San Diego: Una nueva perspectiva." *Boletín de la Escuela de Ciencias Antropológicas de la Universidad de Yucatán* 83:3–18.

Bassie-Sweet, Karen. 1991. *From the Mouth of the Dark Cave: Commemorative Sculpture of the Late Classic Maya*. Norman: University of Oklahoma Press.

———. 1996. *At the Edge of the World: Caves and Late Classic Maya World View*. Norman: University of Oklahoma Press.

———. 2008. *Maya Sacred Geography and the Creator Deities*. Norman: University of Oklahoma Press.

Bassie-Sweet, Karen, Nicholas A. Hopkins, Robert M. Laughlin, and Alejandro Sheseña. 2015. "Contemporary Mountain, Thunderbolt, and Meteor Deities." In *The Ch'ol Maya of Chiapas*, ed. Karen Bassie-Sweet, 145–170. Norman: University of Oklahoma Press.

Bassie-Sweet, Karen, Marc Zender, Jorge Pérez de Lara, and Stanley Guenter. 2015. "The Paintings of Joljá Cave 1." In *The Ch'ol Maya of Chiapas*, ed. Karen Bassie-Sweet, 86–104. Norman: University of Oklahoma Press.

Boone, Elizabeth Hill. 1997. "Prominent Scenes and Pivotal Events in the Mexican Pictorial Histories." In *Códices y documentos sobre México: Segundo simposio*, ed. Salvador Rueda Smithers, Constanza Vega Sosa, and Rodrigo Martínez Baracs, 407–424. Mexico City: Instituto Nacional de Antropología e Historia.

Brady, James E. 1989. "An Investigation of Maya Ritual Cave Use with Specific Reference to Naj Tunich, Petén, Guatemala." PhD diss., University of California, Los Angeles.

———. 1997. "Settlement Configuration and Cosmology: The Role of Caves at Dos Pilas." *American Anthropologist*, n.s., 99(3):602–618.

———. 1999. "The Gruta de Jobonche: An Analysis of Speleothem Rock Art." In *Land of the Turkey and the Deer: Recent Research in Yucatan*, ed. Ruth Gubler, 57–68. Lancaster, CA: Labyrinthos Press.

Brady, James E., and Wendy Ashmore. 1999. "Mountains, Caves, Water: Ideational Landscapes of the Ancient Maya." In *Archaeologies of Landscape: Contemporary Perspectives*, ed. Wendy Ashmore and A. Bernard Knapp, 124–145. Oxford: Blackwell.

Brady, James E., and Pierre Robert Colas. 2005. "Nikte Mo' Scattered Fire in the Cave of K'ab Chante': Epigraphic and Archaeological Evidence for Cave Desecration in Ancient Maya Warfare." In *Stone Houses and Earth Lords: Maya Religion in the Cave Context*, ed. Keith M. Prufer and James E. Brady, 149–166. Boulder: University Press of Colorado.

Brady, James E., and Keith M. Prufer, eds. 2005. *In the Maw of the Earth Monster: Mesoamerican Ritual Cave Use*. Austin: University of Texas Press.

Breedlove, Dennis E., and Robert M. Laughlin. 1993. *The Flowering of Man: A Tzotzil Botany of Zinacantán*. 2 vols. Vol. 1, Smithsonian Contributions to Anthropology No. 35. Washington, DC: Smithsonian Institution Press.

Broda, Johanna. 1991. "The Sacred Landscape of Aztec Calendar Festivals: Myth, Nature, and Society." In *To Change Place: Aztec Ceremonial Landscapes*, ed. David Carrasco, 74–120. Boulder: University Press of Colorado.

Brown, Linda A. 2005. "Planting the Bones: Hunting Ceremonialism at Contemporary and Nineteenth-Century Shrines in the Guatemalan Highlands." *Latin American Antiquity* 16(2):131–146.

———. 2009. "Communal and Personal Hunting Shrines around Lake Atitlán, Guatemala." In *Maya Archaeology 1*, ed. Charles Golden, Stephen D. Houston, and Joel Skidmore, 36–59. San Francisco, CA: Precolumbia Mesoweb Press.

Brown, Linda A., and Kitty F. Emery. 2008. "Negotiations with the Animate Forest: Hunting Shrines in the Guatemalan Highlands." *Journal of Archaeological Method and Theory* 15:300–337.

Bunzel, Ruth. 1952. *Chichicastenango: A Guatemalan Village*. Seattle: University of Washington Press.

Burger, Richard L. 2011. "What Kind of Hallucinogenic Snuff Was Used at Chavín de Huántar?" *Ñawpa Pacha, Journal of Andean Archaeology* 31(2):123–140.

Chase, Arlen F., and James F. Garber 2004. "The Archaeology of the Belize Valley in Historical Perspective." In *The Ancient Maya of the Belize Valley: Half a Century of Archaeological Research*, ed. James F. Garber, 1–14. Gainesville: University Press of Florida.

Chinchilla Mazariegos, Oswaldo. 2017. *Art and Myth of the Ancient Maya*. New Haven: Yale University Press.

Christenson, Allen J. 2010. "Maize Was Their Flesh: Ritual Feasting in the Maya Highlands." In *Pre-Columbian Foodways: Interdisciplinary Approaches to Food, Culture, and Markets in Ancient Mesoamerica*, ed. John E. Staller and Michael D. Carrasco, 577–600. New York: Springer.

Clark, John E., and Michael Blake. 1994. "The Power of Prestige: Competitive Generosity and the Emergence of Rank Societies in Lowland Mesoamerica." In *Factional Competition and Political Development in the New World*, ed. Elizabeth M. Brumfiel and John W. Fox, 17–30. Cambridge: Cambridge University Press.

Coe, Sophie, and Michael D. Coe. 2007. *The True History of Chocolate*. 2nd ed. New York: Thames and Hudson.

Colas, Pierre Robert, Christophe G. B. Helmke, Jaime J. Awe, and Terry G. Powis. 2002. "Epigraphic and Ceramic Analyses of Two Early Classic Maya Vessels from Baking Pot, Belize." *Mexicon* 24(2):33–39.

Conlon, James M. 1999. "Preliminary Reconnaissance at the Minor Centre of Pol Sak Pak, Near Pacbitun, Belize." In *Belize Valley Preclassic Maya Project: Report on the 1996 and 1997 Field Seasons*, ed. Paul F. Healy, 31–40. Peterborough, Ontario, Canada: Trent University.

Dreiss, Meredith L., and Sharon Edgar Greenhill. 2008. *Chocolate, Pathway to the Gods: The Sacred Realm of Chocolate in Mesoamerica*. Tucson: University of Arizona Press.

Durán, Fray Diego. 1994. *The Histories of The Indies of New Spain*. Trans. Doris Heyden. Norman: University of Oklahoma Press.

Emery, Kitty F. 2002. "Animals from the Maya Underworld: Reconstructing Elite Maya Ritual at the Cueva de los Quetzales, Guatemala." In *Behaviour Behind Bones: The Zooarchaeology of Ritual, Religion, Status and Identity*, ed. Sharon Jones O'Day, Wim Van Near, and Anton Ervynck, 101–113. Oxford: Oxford Books.

Evershed, Richard P. 2008. "Organic Residue Analysis in Archaeology: The Archaeological Biomarker Revolution." *Archaeometry* 50(6):895–924.

Fitzsimmons, Jeanne M. 2005. "Pre-Hispanic Rain Ceremonies in Blade Cave, Sierra Mazateca, Oaxaca, Mexico." In *In The Maw of the Earth Monster: Mesoamerican Ritual Cave Use*, ed. James E. Brady and Keith M. Prufer, 91–116. Austin: University of Texas Press.

Freidel, David A., Linda Schele, and Joy Parker. 1993. *Maya Cosmos: Three Thousand Years on the Shaman's Path*. New York: W. Morrow.

Furst, Peter T., ed. 1972. *Flesh of the Gods: The Ritual Use of Hallucinogens*. London: Allen and Unwin.

Furst, Peter T., and Michael Coe. 1997. "Ritual Enemas." In *Magic, Witchcraft, and Religion: An Anthropological Study of the Supernatural*, ed. Arthur C. Lehmann and James E. Myers, 118–121. Mountain View, CA: Mayfield.

Gann, Thomas. 1918. "The Maya Indians of Southern Yucatan and Northern British Honduras." *Bureau of American Ethnology, Bulletin* 64:1–146.

García-Zambrano, Ángel Julián. 1994. "Early Colonial Evidence of Pre-Hispanic Rituals of Foundation." In *Seventh Palenque Round Table, 1989*, ed. Merle Greene Robertson and Virginia M. Fields, 217–227. San Francisco: Pre-Columbian Art Research Institute.

Gasco, Janine L. 1987. "Cacao and the Economic Integration of Native Society in Colonial Soconusco, New Spain." PhD diss., University of California, Santa Barbara.

Gifford, James C. 1976. *Prehistoric Pottery Analysis and the Ceramics of Barton Ramie in the Belize Valley*. Memoirs of the Peabody Museum of Archaeology and Ethnology, Vol. 18. Cambridge, MA: Harvard University Press.

Graham, Ian. 1997. "Discovery of a Maya Ritual Cave in Peten, Guatemala." *Symbols* (Spring): 28–31.

Grube, Nikolai. 1991. "An Investigation of the Primary Standard Sequence on Classic Maya Ceramics." In *Sixth Palenque Round Table, 1986*, ed. Merle Greene Robertson and Virginia M. Fields, 223–232. Norman: University of Oklahoma Press.

Halperin, Christina T., and Jon Spenard. 2015. "Archaeological Survey of the Joljá and Nuevo México Caves." In *The Ch'ol Maya of Chiapas*, ed. Karen Bassie-Sweet, 68–85. Norman: University of Oklahoma Press.

Hayden, Brian, and Rob Gargett. 1990. "Big Man, Big Heart? A Mesoamerican View of the Emergence of Complex Society." *Ancient Mesoamerica* 1(1):3–20.

Hellmuth, Nicholas M. 1985. "Appendix B: Principal Diagnostic Accessories of Maya Enema Scenes." In Peter A. G. M. de Smet, *Ritual Enemas and Snuffs in the Americas*, 137–148. Amsterdam: Centro de Estudios y Documentación Latinomericanos.

Hendon, Julia A. 2003. "Feasting at Home: Community and Household Solidarity among the Maya of Southeastern Mesoamerica." In *The Archaeology and Politics of Food and Feasting in Early States and Empires*, ed. Tamara Bray, 203–233. New York: Kluwer Academic/Plenum.

Heyden, Doris. 1973. "¿Un Chicomóztoc en Teotihuacan? La cueva bajo la Pirámide del Sol." *Boletín del Instituto Nacional de Antropología e Historia* 6 (Julio-Septiembre):3–18.

———. 1975. "An Interpretation of the Cave Underneath the Pyramid of the Sun in Teotihuacan, Mexico." *American Antiquity* 40(2):131–147.

———. 1981. "Caves, Gods, and Myths: World-View and Planning in Teotihuacan." In *Mesoamerican Sites and World Views*, ed. Elizabeth P. Benson, 1–39. Washington, DC: Dumbarton Oaks Research Library and Collection.

Holland, William R. 1964. "Contemporary Tzotzil Cosmological Concepts as a Basis for Interpreting Prehistoric Maya Civilization." *American Antiquity* 29(3):301–306.

Hopkins, Nicholas A., Karen Bassie-Sweet, and Robert M. Laughlin. 2015. "The Colonial to Twentieth-Century Period in the Ch'ol Region." In *The Ch'ol Maya of Chiapas*, ed. Karen Bassie-Sweet, 29–43. Norman: University of Oklahoma Press.

Horwich, Robert H., and Jonathan Lyon. 1990. *A Belizean Rainforest: The Community Baboon Sanctuary*. Gays Mills, WI: Orangutan Press.

Houston, Stephen D., and Karl A. Taube. 1987. "'Name Tagging' in Classic Mayan Script: Implications for Native Classifications of Ceramics and Jade Ornaments." *Mexicon* 9:38–41.

Josserand, J. Kathryn, and Nicholas A. Hopkins. 2007. "Tila y su cristo negro: Historia, peregrinación y devoción en Chiapas, México." *Mesoamerica* 28(49):82–113.

King, Adam, Terry G. Powis, Kong F. Cheong, and Nilesh W. Gaikwad. 2017. "Cautionary Tales on the Identification of Caffeinated Beverages in North America." *Journal of Archaeological Science* 85:30–40.

Kintz, Ellen R. 1990. *Life Under the Tropical Canopy: Tradition and Change among the Yucatec Maya*. Case Studies in Cultural Anthropology, eds. George Spindler and Louise Spindler. San Francisco: Holt, Rinehart, and Winston.

Knobloch, Patricia J. 2000. "Wari Ritual Power at Conchopata: An Interpretation of Anadenanthera Colubrina Iconography." *Latin American Antiquity* 11(4):387–402.

Kufer, Johanna, and Michael Heinrich. 2006. "Food for the Rain Gods: Cacao in Ch'orti' Ritual." In *Chocolate in Mesoamerica: A Cultural History of Cacao*, ed. Cameron L. McNeil, 384–407. Gainesville: University Press of Florida.

LeCount, Lisa J. 1999. "Polychrome Pottery and Political Strategies in Late and Terminal Classic Lowland Maya Society." *Latin American Antiquity* 10(3):239–258.

———. 2001. "Like Water for Chocolate: Feasting and Political Ritual among the Late Classic Maya at Xunantunich, Belize." *American Anthropologist* 103(4):935–953.

———. 2010. "Ka'kaw Pots and Common Containers: Creating Histories and Collective Memories among the Classic Maya of Xunantunich, Belize." *Ancient Mesoamerica* 21(2):341–351.

Lester, R. N., M. Nee, and N. Estrada. 1991. "Solanaceae III—Taxonomy, Chemistry, Evolution." In *Proceedings of the Third International Conference on Solanaceae*, ed. John G. Hawkes, 197–210. Kew, Richmond, Surrey, UK: Royal Botanic Gardens.

Litzinger, W. J. 1994. "Yucateco and Lacandon Maya Knowledge of Datura (Solanaceae)." *Journal of Ethnopharmacology* 42(2):133–134.

Lockhart, James. 1992. *The Nahuas after the Conquest: A Social and Cultural History of the Indians of Central Mexico, Sixteenth through Eighteenth Centuries*. Stanford, CA: Stanford University Press.

López Luján, Leonardo, Jaime Torres, and Aurora Montúfar López. 2003. "Los materiales constructivos del Templo Mayor de Tenochtitlan." *Estudios de Cultura Náhuatl* 34:137–168.

Lorenzen, Karl. 1999. "New Discoveries at Tumben-Naranjál: Late Postclassic Reuse and the Ritual Recycling of Cultural Geography." *Mexicon* 21(5):98–107.

Love, Bruce. 2004. *Maya Shamanism Today: Connecting with the Cosmos in Rural Yucatan*. Lancaster, CA: Labyrinthos Press.

Lucero, Lisa J., and Sherry Gibbs. 2007. "The Creation and Sacrifice of Witches in Classic Maya Society." In *New Perspectives on Human Sacrifice and Ritual Body Treatments in Ancient Maya Society*, ed. Vera Tiesler and Andrea Cucina, 45–73. New York: Springer.

Lundell, Cyrus L. 1938. "Plants Probably Utilized by the Old Empire Maya of Petén and Adjacent Lowlands." *Papers of the Michigan Academy of Science, Arts, and Letters* 24:37–56.

Martin, Simon. 2001. "Under a Deadly Star: Warfare among the Classic Maya." In *Maya: Divine Kings of the Rainforest*, ed. Nikolai Grube, 174–185. Cologne, Germany: Könemann.

———. 2006. "Cacao in Ancient Maya Religion: First Fruit from the Maize Tree and Other Tales from the Underworld." In *Chocolate in Mesoamerica: A Cultural History of Cacao*, ed. Cameron L. McNeil, 154–183. Gainesville: University Press of Florida.

———. 2012. "Hieroglyphs from the Painted Pyramid: The Epigraphy of Chiik Nahb Structure Sub 1-4, Calakmul, Mexico." In *Maya Archaeology 2*, ed. Charles Golden, Stephen Houston, and Joel Skidmore, 60–81. San Francisco: Precolumbia Mesoweb Press.

McAnany, Patricia A., and Satoru Murata. 2006. "From Chocolate Pots to Maya Gold: Belizean Cacao Farmers through the Ages." In *Chocolate in Mesoamerica: A Cultural History of Cacao*, ed. Cameron L. McNeil, 429–450. Gainesville: University Press of America.

McGee, R. Jon. 1990. *Life, Ritual, and Religion among the Lacandon Maya*. Belmont, CA: Wadsworth.

McNeil, Cameron L., ed. 2006a. *Chocolate in Mesoamerica: A Cultural History of Cacao*. Gainesville: University Press of Florida.

———. 2006b. "Introduction: The Biology, Antiquity, and Modern Uses of the Chocolate Tree (*Theobroma cacao* L.)." In *Chocolate in Mesoamerica: A Cultural History of Cacao*, ed. Cameron L. McNeil, 1–28. Gainesville: University Press of Florida.

Miller, Mary E., and Karl A. Taube. 1997. *An Illustrated Dictionary of the Gods and Symbols of Ancient Mexico and the Maya*. New York: Thames and Hudson.

Moerman, Dan. 2008. "Native American Ethnobotany: A Database of Foods, Drugs, Dyes and Fibers of Native American Peoples, Derived from Plants." Accessed August 15, 2018. http://naeb.brit.org.

Monaghan, John. 1995. *The Covenants with Earth and Rain: Exchange, Sacrifice, and Revelation in Mixtec Sociality*. Norman: University of Oklahoma Press.

Montero-López, Coral. 2009. "Sacrifice and Feasting among the Classic Maya Elite and the Importance of White-Tailed Deer: Is There a Regional Pattern?" *Journal of Historical and European Studies* 2:53–68.

Moore, Jerry D. 2014. *A Prehistory of South America: Ancient Cultural Diversity on the Least Known Continent*. Boulder: University Press of Colorado.

Morehart, Christopher T. 2005. "Plants and Caves in Ancient Maya Society." In *Stone Houses and Earth Lords: Maya Religion in the Cave Context*, ed. Keith M. Prufer and James E. Brady, 167–185. Boulder: University Press of Colorado.

———. 2011. *Food, Fire, and Fragrance: A Paleoethnobotanical Perspective on Classic Maya Cave Rituals*. Oxford: BAR International Series 2186.

Morehart, Christopher T., and Noah Butler. 2010. "Ritual Exchange and the Fourth Obligation: Ancient Maya Food Offering and the Flexible Materiality of Ritual." *Journal of the Royal Anthropological Institute* 16(3):588–608.

Morehart, Christopher T., David L. Lentz, and Keith M. Prufer. 2005. "Wood of the Gods: The Ritual Use of Pine (*Pinus* spp.) by the Ancient Lowland Maya." *Latin American Antiquity* 16(3):255–274.

Moyes, Holley, Jaime J. Awe, George A. Brook, and James W. Webster. 2009. "The Ancient Maya Drought Cult: Late Classic Cave Use in Belize." *Latin American Antiquity* 20(1):175–206.

Nash, June. 1970. *In the Eyes of the Ancestors: Belief and Behavior in a Mayan Community*. New Haven, CT: Yale University Press.

Navarrete, Carlos, and Eduardo E. Martínez. 1977. *Exploraciones arqueológicas en la Cueva de los Andasolos, Chiapas*. Mexico City: Universidad Autónoma de Chiapas.

Norman, V. Garth. 1973. *Izapa Sculpture Part 1: Album*. Papers of the New World Archaeological Foundation No. 30. Provo, UT: New World Archaeological Foundation, Brigham Young University.

Parker, Megan. 2014. "A Paleoethnobotanical Perspective on Late Classic Maya Cave Ritual at the Site of Pacbitun, Belize." Master's thesis, Georgia State University.

Powis, Terry G., W. Jeffrey Hurst, María del Carmen Rodríguez, Ponciano Ortiz C., Michael Blake, David Cheetham, Michael D. Coe, and John G. Hodgson. 2008. "The Origins of Cacao Use in Mesoamerica." *Mexicon* 30(2):35–38.

Prufer, Keith M. 2005. "Shamans, Caves, and the Roles of Ritual Specialists in Maya Society." In *In the Maw of the Earth Monster: Mesoamerican Ritual Cave Use*, ed. James E. Brady and Keith M. Prufer, 186–222. Austin: University of Texas Press.

Prufer, Keith M., and James E. Brady, eds. 2005. *Stone Houses and Earth Lords: Maya Religion in the Cave Context*. Boulder: University Press of Colorado.

Prufer, Keith M., and Peter S. Dunham. 2009. "A Shaman's Burial from an Early Classic Cave in the Maya Mountains of Belize, Central America." *World Archaeology* 41(2):295–320.

Rätsch, Christian. 2005. *The Encyclopedia of Psychoactive Plants: Ethnopharmacology and Its Applications*. Rochester, VT: Park Street Press.

Ravicz, Robert, and A. Kimball Romney. 1969. "The Mixtec." In *Handbook of Middle American Indians*. Vols. 7 and 8, *Ethnology Pt. 1*, ed. Evon Z. Vogt, 367–399. Austin: University of Texas Press.

Redfield, Robert, and Alfonso Villa Rojas. 1934. *Chan Kom: A Maya Village*. Chicago: University of Chicago Press. Original edition, 1934.

Reents-Budet, Dorie J. 1994. *Painting the Maya Universe: Royal Ceramics of the Classic Period*. Durham, NC: Duke University Press.

———. 2000. "Feasting among the Classic Maya: Evidence from the Pictorial Ceramics." In *The Maya Vase Book: A Corpus of Rollout Photographs of Maya Vases*, ed. Barbara Kerr and Justin Kerr, 6:1022–1037. New York: Kerr Associates.

Reilly, F. Kent, III. 1989. "The Shaman in Transformation Pose: A Study of the

Theme of Rulership in Olmec Art." *Record of the Art Museum, Princeton University* 48(2):4–21.

Rincón Mautner, Carlos. 2005. "Sacred Caves and Rituals from the Northern Mixteca of Oaxaca, Mexico: New Revelations." In *In the Maw of the Earth Monster: Mesoamerican Ritual Cave Use*, ed. James E. Brady and Keith M. Prufer, 117–152. Austin: University of Texas Press.

Rissolo, Dominique. 2005. "Beneath the Yalahau: Emerging Patterns of Ancient Maya Ritual Cave Use from Northern Quintana Roo, Mexico." In *In the Maw of the Earth Monster: Mesoamerican Ritual Cave Use*, ed. James E. Brady and Keith M. Prufer, 342–372. Austin: University of Texas Press.

Sahagún, Bernardino de. 1963. *Florentine Codex: General History of the Things of New Spain, Book 11: Earthly Things*. Monographs of the School of American Research No. 14, Part XII. Salt Lake City: University of Utah Press.

Saturno, William A., Karl A. Taube, David S. Stuart, and Heather Hurst. 2005. *The Murals of San Bartolo, El Petén, Guatemala, Part 1: The North Wall*. Ancient America No. 7. Barnardsville, NC: Boundary End Archaeological Research Center.

Schaafsma, Polly. 1999. "Tlalocs, Kachinas, Sacred Bundles, and Related Symbolism in the Southwest and Mesoamerica." In *The Casas Grandes World*, ed. Curtis F. Schaafsma and Carroll L. Riley, 164–192. Salt Lake City: University of Utah Press.

Schaafsma, Polly, and Karl A. Taube. 2006. "Bringing the Rain: An Ideology of Rain Making in the Pueblo Southwest and Mesoamerica." In *A Pre-Columbian World*, ed. Jeffrey Quilter and Mary E. Miller, 231–285. Washington, DC: Dumbarton Oaks Research Library and Collection.

Schultes, Richard Evans. 1972. "An Overview of Hallucinogens in the Western Hemisphere." In *Flesh of the Gods*, ed. Peter Furst, 3–54. New York: Praeger.

Scott, Ann M. 2009. "Communicating with the Sacred Earthscape: An Ethnoarchaeological Investigation of Kaqchikel Maya Ceremonies in Highland Guatemala." PhD diss., University of Texas at Austin.

Seler, Edward. 1901. *Die alten Ansiedelungen von Chacula im Distrikte Nenton des Departements Huehuetanango der Republik Guatemala*. Berlin: Verlag von Dietrich Reimer.

Soustelle, Georgette. 1961. "Observaciones sobre la religión de los lacandones de México meridional." *Guatemala Indígena* 1(1):31–105.

Spenard, Jon. 2006. "The Gift in the Cave for the Gift of the World: An Economic Approach to Ancient Maya Cave Ritual in the San Francisco Hill-Caves, Cancuen Region, Guatemala." Master's thesis, Florida State University.

———. 2012. "Defining Community Ch'een: A Report on the 2011 Archaeological Cave and Karst Landscape. Investigations around Pacbitun, Cayo District, Belize." In *Pacbitun Regional Archaeological Project (PRAP): Report on the 2011 Field Season*, ed. Terry G. Powis, 144–188. Report submitted to the Institute of Archaeology National Institute of Culture and History, Belmopan, Belize.

———. 2014. "Underground Identity, Memory, and Political Spaces: A Study of the Classic Period Maya Ceremonial Karstscape in the Pacbitun Region, Cayo District, Belize." PhD diss., University of California, Riverside.

Spenard, Jon, Javier Mai, and Oscar Mai. 2012. "They Lived Where?!: A Report on the 2011 Settlement Reconnaissance around Pacbitun, Cayo District, Belize." In *Pacbitun Regional Archaeological Project (PRAP): Report on the 2011 Field Season*, ed. Terry G. Powis, 125–143. Report submitted to the Institute of Archaeology National Institute of Culture and History, Belmopan, Belize.

Spenard, Jon, and Michael J. Mirro. 2017. "Report on the Phase II Karstscape Investigations at Pacbitun, Cayo District, Belize: The 2016 Field Season." In *Pacbitun Regional Archaeological Project (PRAP): Report on the 2016 Field Season*, ed. Terry G. Powis, 104–150. Report submitted to the Institute of Archaeology National Institute of Culture and History, Belmopan, Belize.

Spenard, Jon, and Terry G. Powis. 2014. "Karstic Communities: A Study of Cave Ritual, Community Organization, and Memory Making in the Classic Period Maya Polity of Pacbitun, Cayo District, Belize." In *Climates of Change: The Shifting Environments of Archaeology: Proceedings of the 44th Annual Chacmool Conference*, ed. Shelia Kulyk, Cara G. Tremain, and Madeline Sawyer, 227–237. Calgary: Chacmool Archaeology Association, University of Calgary.

Staller, John E., and Michael D. Carrasco, eds. 2010. *Pre-Columbian Foodways: Interdisciplinary Approaches to Food, Culture, and Markets in Ancient Mesoamerica*. New York: Springer.

Stone, Andrea J. 1995. *Images from the Underworld: Naj Tunich and the Tradition of Maya Cave Painting*. Austin: University of Texas Press.

———. 2005. "Divine Stalagmites: Modified Speleothems in Maya Caves and Aesthetic Variation in Classic Maya Art." In *Aesthetics and Rock Art*, ed. Thomas Heyd and John Clegg, 215–233. Hampshire, England: Ashgate.

Strecker, Matthias. 1985. "Cuevas mayas en el municipio de Oxkutzcab (II): Cuevas Ehbis, Xcosmil y Cahum." *Boletín de la Escuela de Ciencias Antropológicas de la Universidad de Yucatán* 70:16–21.

Stross, Brian, and Justin Kerr. 1990. "Notes on the Maya Vision Quest through Enema." In *The Maya Vase Book: A Corpus of Rollout Photographs of Maya Vases*, ed. Barbara Kerr and Justin Kerr, 2:349–361. New York: Kerr Associates.

Stuart, David, and Stephen D. Houston. 1994. *Classic Maya Place Names*. Studies in Pre-Columbian Art and Archaeology, No. 33. Washington, DC: Dumbarton Oaks Research Library and Collection.

Stuart, George E. 1999. *A Maya Wooden Figure from Belize*. Research Reports on Ancient Maya Writing No. 42. Barnardsville, NC: Boundary End Archaeological Research Center.

Taube, Karl A. 1989. "The Maize Tamale in Classic Maya Diet, Epigraphy, and Art." *American Antiquity* 54(1):31–51.

———. 1992. *The Major Gods of Ancient Yucatan*. Studies in Pre-Columbian Art and Archaeology, No. 32. Washington, DC: Dumbarton Oaks Research Library and Collection.

———. 2001. "The Breath of Life: The Symbolism of Wind in Mesoamerica and the American Southwest." In *The Road to Aztlan: Art from a Mythic Homeland*, ed. Virginia M. Fields and Victor Zamudio-Taylor, 102–123. Los Angeles: Los Angeles County Museum of Art.

Taube, Karl A., William A. Saturno, David Stuart, and Heather Hurst. 2010. *The Murals of San Bartolo, El Petén, Guatemala, Part 2: The West Wall*. Ancient America 10. Barnardsville, NC: Boundary End Archaeological Research Center.

Tedlock, Dennis. 1996. *Popol Vuh: The Mayan Book of the Dawn of Life*. New York: Simon and Schuster.

Thompson, J. Eric S. 1975. "Introduction." In *The Hill-Caves of Yucatan: A Search for Evidence of Man's Antiquity in the Caverns of Central America*, ed. Henry Mercer, vii–xliv. Norman: University of Oklahoma Press.

Torres, Constantino Manuel, and David B. Repke. 2006. *Anadenanthera: Visionary Plant of Ancient South America*. Binghamton, NY: Haworth Press.

Tozzer, Alfred A. 1907. *A Comparative Study of the Mayas and the Lacandones*. Report of the Fellow in American Archaeology 1902–1905. New York, NY: Macmillan.

———. 1941. *Landa's Relación de las Cosas de Yucatan: A Translation*. Papers of the Peabody Museum of American Archaeology and Ethnology, Vol. 18. Cambridge, MA: Peabody Museum at Harvard University.

USDA. 2018. "Dr. Duke's Phytochemical and Ethnobotanical Databases." Accessed August 21, 2018. phytochem.nal.usda.gov/phytochem/help/index/about.

Vogt, Evon Z. 1969. *Zinacantan: A Maya Community in the Highlands of Chiapas*. Cambridge, MA: Harvard University Press.

———. 1976. *Tortillas for the Gods: A Symbolic Analysis of Zinacanteco Rituals*. Cambridge, MA: Harvard University Press.

Vogt, Evon Z., and David Stuart. 2005. "Some Notes on Ritual Caves among the Ancient and Modern Maya." In *In The Maw of the Earth Monster: Mesoamerican Ritual Cave Use*, ed. James E. Brady and Keith M. Prufer, 155–185. Austin: University of Texas Press.

Washburn, Dorothy K., William N. Washburn, Petia A. Shipkova, and Mary Ann Pelleymounter. 2014. "Chemical Analysis of Cacao Residues in Archaeological Ceramics from North America: Considerations of Contamination, Sample Size, and Systematic Controls." *Journal of Archaeological Science* 50(1):191–207.

Weber, Jennifer U. 2011. "Investigating the Ancient Maya Landscape: A Settlement Survey in the Periphery of Pacbitun." Master's thesis, Georgia State University.

Whittaker, Arabelle, and Viola Warkentin. 1965. *Chol Texts on the Supernatural*. Norman, OK: Summer Institute of Linguistics.

Wilson, Richard. 1993. "Anchored Communities: Identity and History of the Maya-Q'eqchi'." *Man* 28(1):121–138.

———. 1995. *Maya Resurgence in Guatemala: Q'eqchi' Experiences*. Norman: University of Oklahoma Press.

Zender, Marc. 2004. "A Study of Classic Maya Priesthood." PhD diss., University of Calgary.

CHAPTER 4

The Epigraphy of Ancient Maya Food and Drink

NICHOLAS CARTER AND MALLORY E. MATSUMOTO

The anthropological value of epigraphic decipherment to Mayanist archaeologists lies in the access it grants scholars to how ancient Maya elites—the authors and readers of all known Classic texts—thought about their world. In the case of food and drink, the hieroglyphs make it possible to say something about what ancient Maya people ate; what their cultural and linguistic classes of food and drink were, along with some of the implements they used to consume them; and what the social norms and religious concepts connected with those categories were. However, epigraphic interpretation is far from straightforward, and, as specialists know well, archaeological data limit such interpretation in some ways while opening up new possibilities in others. As we suggest, epigraphers may need to consider possible alternative readings of terms and phrases widely understood as describing the ingredients of chocolate drinks and the purposes of certain kinds of vessels in light of recent evidence that challenges literal or long-standing interpretations.

The most ample data on Classic Maya culinary practices come from ceramic vessels painted, molded, or incised with standardized dedicatory texts, which were first recognized as a genre and dubbed the Primary Standard Sequence by Michael Coe (1973:18–22). Primary Standard Sequences were initially interpreted as funerary texts, until a series of decipherments revealed that they record the dedication of painted (*tz'ihb'*) or carved (*uxul?*) vessels, including plates (*lak*, Figure 4.1a), drinking cups (*uk'ib'*, Figure 4.1b), and rounded bowls (*jaay*, Figure 4.1c; Houston and Taube 1987; MacLeod 1990; MacLeod and Stross 1990; Stuart 1987). More than this, many Primary Standard Sequences turned out to describe their vessels as containers intended for particular foods and drinks, especially *kakaw* (cacao, *Theobroma cacao* or *Theobroma bicolor*; Stuart 1988). The tra-

Figures 4.1a–4.1c. Terms for kinds of vessels in Classic Maya writing: (a) **la-ka**, *lak*, "plate," on a codex-style vessel from the area of Calakmul (K1892); (b) **yu-k'i-b'i**, *yuk'ib'*, "his drinking instrument," on a codex-style vessel from the area of Calakmul (K6751); (c) **ja-yi**, *jaay*, "clay vessel," on a polychrome vessel from the area of El Zotz (K7147). (Note that the standard in Maya epigraphy is to render hieroglyphic transliterations in boldface, transcriptions in italics, and translations in ordinary type.) Drawings by Nicholas Carter.

dition of inscribing vessels with Primary Standard Sequences originated in northern Petén and southern Campeche no later than the third century CE and persisted until the Maya collapse of the ninth century. Within that tradition, local styles and technologies proliferated in the Late Classic period, from the area of Oxkintok in the Yucatán Peninsula to Copán in the south, although some important sites never produced many inscribed pots (Stuart 2006b:188–190).

Scenes of palace life, painted on many pots with dedicatory texts, provide visual evidence of how foodstuffs in their raw forms or as prepared dishes were given, displayed, and consumed in royal courts. Further representations of food and drink come from mural paintings, including the mythic narratives in the Late Preclassic murals of the Las Pinturas building at San Bartolo (Saturno, Taube, and Stuart 2005); vignettes of market life on the seventh-century platform walls of Str. Sub 1-4 in the Chiik Nahb complex at Calakmul (Carrasco Vargas and Cordeiro Baqueiro 2012;

Martin 2012); and ritual offerings depicted in the Late Postclassic Temple of the Diving God at Tulum (Miller 1982). Finally, the four surviving Postclassic codices contain images connected to food, including offering scenes and depictions of deities related to agriculture. This wide range of extant sources provides a glimpse of the local diversity of pre-Columbian Maya foodstuffs and related practices, but also collectively attests to more widespread trends in food conceptualization and use.

Eating, Drinking, and Their Objects in Classic Mayan Texts

Generic terms for "eating" and "drinking" appear in Classic Mayan as *we'* and *uk'*, respectively; their corresponding logograms depict a human head with the signs for "water" or "tamal" over the mouth (Figure 4.2a, b; Boot 2005b; Stuart 1995:39, Fig. 2.9a; Zender 1999:75–76). Although both terms can and do appear as inflected verbs, they occur more often in derived form—"his eating instrument" or "his drinking instrument"—in Primary Standard Sequences on the plates, bowls, and cups used for those purposes (e.g., Boot 2003; Boot 2005a:7–8, 12–15; Prager 2018; Stuart 1995:115; Stuart 2005a; Zender 2000; and see Houston and Taube 1987). Paired together (whether as a poetic couplet or a compound logogram analogous to the paired variants of **TZ'AK**, "to set in order," is unclear; see Stuart 2003), *uk'* and *we'* seem to refer to feasting or to consumption generally (Figure 4.2c; Houston, Stuart, and Taube 2006:111; Hull 2010:237; Stuart et al. 1999:II-36). Other verbs describe the consumption of specific kinds of food: meat (*k'ux*; see Tokovinine 2007), maize bread and similar foods (*mak'*, a Yucatec word attested in the Dresden Codex; Figure 4.2d), and soft foods or drinks (*och*; Figure 4.2e).

The two foodstuffs most commonly recorded in hieroglyphic texts are among the most critical culturally and socially: maize and cacao. The former, though rarely documented in its raw state of *ixiim* (maize grains; Figure 4.3a) or *nal* (maize on the cob; Figure 4.3b), was the basic ingredient in several foods that are frequently referenced: a maize gruel called *sa'* (Figure 4.3c) or *ul* (Figure 4.3d); another corn-based drink, *sakha'* (Figure 4.3e), served cold during special events; and the steamed cornbread tamal, or *waaj* (Figure 4.3f; Beliaev, Davletshin, and Tokovinine 2010:264–266; Grube 1990:324–325; Hellmuth 1987, Fig. 411; Hull 2010:246–248; Martin 2012:64–66, 72, Figs. 6, 12; Stone and Zender 2011:224–225; Taube 1989; Thomas 1882:156). This last could also be combined with *ha'*, "water," in a difrasismo for "bounty" or "sustenance" (Houston, Stuart, and

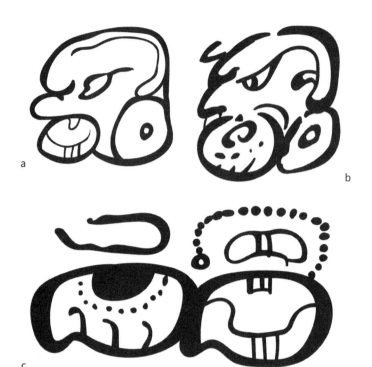

Figures 4.2a–4.2e. Terms for eating and drinking in Classic and Postclassic Mayan writing: (a) **WE'**, *we'*, "eat," from a polychrome vessel from the area of Xultun (K4572); (b) **UK'**, *uk'*, "drink," from a codex-style vessel from the area of Calakmul (K2067); (c) logogram for "feast," from the Dresden Codex, pg. 5; (d) **ma-k'a**, *mak'*, "eat [maize bread]," from the Dresden Codex, pg. 13; (e) **OCH-chi-ya**, *ochiiy*, "ate [soft foods]," from the Dresden Codex, pg. 10. Drawings by Nicholas Carter.

Figures 4.3a–4.3f. Terms for maize-based foods in Classic and Postclassic Maya writing: (a) **i-IXIIM**, *ixiim*, "maize kernels," from a polychrome vessel from the area of Altar de Sacrificios, now in the collection of the Princeton Art Museum (K791); (b) **NAL**, *nal*, "maize cob," "place," from Tikal Stela 31; (c) **SA'-la**, *sa'al*, "maize gruelish," from an Early Classic stuccoed vessel with a lid (K7529); (d) **u-lu**, *ul*, "maize gruel," from a painted vessel from the area of Xultun (K1547); (e) **SAK-HA'**, *sakha'*, "white water," "maize drink," from an Early Classic polychrome vessel (K4995); (f) **WAAJ-wa-ji**, *waaj*, "tamal," from the Dresden Codex, pg. 14. Drawings by Nicholas Carter.

Taube 2006:108–113; Hull 2003:442; Hull 2010:237). The Classic Mayan word *kakaw*, denoting the raw fruit and seed of the cacao tree and their derivatives, was borrowed from a Mesoamerican language spoken to the west of the Maya region, although scholars disagree on precisely which one (Dakin and Wichmann 2000; Kaufman and Justeson 2006; Macri 2005; Stuart 1988). A foreign origin for this lexeme may explain why *kakaw* is consistently spelled out with syllabic signs (Figure 4.4a; Matsumoto 2017: 111; Zender 1999:121–123), in contrast to other common foods that have logograms (e.g., maize; see Taube 1989; Zender 2014).

The hieroglyphic corpus records a number of protein-rich foods, too, of which the most accessible and regularly consumed would have been legumes: black beans (*b'u'l*; Figure 4.4b; see Houston, Stuart, and Robertson 1998:282) and lima beans (*ib'*; Figure 4.4c; Prager 2018; Tokovinine 2014). Wild and domestic meat animals included deer (*chih*; Figure 4.4d), turkeys (*kutz*; Figure 4.4e), iguanas (*huh*; Figure 4.4f), dogs (*tz'i'* or *ok*; Figure 4.4g; see Cunningham-Smith et al., this volume), and fish (*kay* or *chay*). Although most often recorded as fillings for tamales (Hull 2010: 236), meat and fish were surely also consumed as main dishes and in other forms in ancient times as they are today (Förstemann 1880:23; cf., e.g., Brasseur de Bourbourg 1869, Pls. VIII–XVIII, XXII; Joyce 1933, Pl. VI.12; Prager 2018). One form of preparation is even suggested by the name of the captive sculpted on the tread of Step I of Hieroglyphic Stairway 3 at Yaxchilán: *popol chay*, perhaps "fish [roasted in] a mat" (Houston, Robertson, and Stuart 2001, Table 9; see Graham 1982:166).

The greatest variety of preparations attested in the corpus pertains to drinks, although the precise ingredients of many are unknown. *Ul*, for instance, could be prepared "sour" (*pah* or *paj*), "bitter" (*ch'aj*), or "chocolaty" (*kakawal*; Beliaev, Davletshin, and Tokovinine 2010:263; Grube 1990:325; see also Strupp Green 2010). Cacao is variously described as "new" (*ach*), "ripe" (*k'an*), "sweet" (*tzah*), or flavored with a variety of additives, including "honey" (*kab'* or *chab'*), "lima bean" (*ib'*), "cherry" (*suutz*), and possibly "chile" (*ich*; Beliaev, Davletshin, and Tokovinine 2010:260–262; Stuart 2016; Tokovinine 2014:13). Such mixtures are best attested on Early Classic vessels; by the Late Classic period, almost all cacao is designated in Primary Standard Sequences with one or two of three adjectives or their variants: *ixiimte'el*, *tzih*, or *yutal* (Stuart 2006b:201). All three terms have straightforward, plausible translations, but chemical data may impose constraints on how they should be read in context, as discussed in more detail below (Loughmiller-Cardinal 2018). Other mixtures are still less understood, such as the term *b'ukuutz kakaw* that describes cacao on a

Figures 4.4a–4.4g. Terms for edible plants and animals in Classic and Postclassic Maya writing: (a) **ka-wa**, *kakaw*, "cacao," from a Late Classic polychrome vessel (K8947); (b) **b'u-la**, *b'u'l*, "beans," from a polychrome vessel from the area of Río Azul (K2914); (c) **IB'-IL**, *ib'il*, "of lima beans," from an unprovenanced codex-style bowl (see Prager 2018, Fig. 4); (d) **chi-hi-IL**, *chihil*, "of deer meat," from a polychrome plate from the area of El Zotz (K5460); (e) **ku-tzu**, *kutz*, "turkey," from the Dresden Codex, pg. 17; (f) **HUH-WAAJ**, *huh waaj*, "iguana tamal," from the Dresden Codex, pg. 33; (g) **TZ'I'**, *tz'i'*, "dog," from Tonina Monument 83. Drawings by Nicholas Carter.

squash skeuomorph vessel from Acanceh (Miller and Martin 2004, Pl. 74; see also Grube and Gaida 2006:140, Abb.14.1; Stuart 2006b:192–193).

Terms for comestibles recorded in Classic Maya inscriptions mainly denote drinks, with few hieroglyphic references to the substantial meat consumption suggested by archaeological, ethnohistorical, and ethnographic research (see Bronson 1966; Cunningham-Smith et al., this volume; Emery 2004; Lentz 1999; Masson and Peraza Lope 2008; Masson et al., this volume; Scherer, Wright, and Yoder 2007; White et al. 2001). References to animal foods mainly take the form of representational art. A number of painted ceramic vessels, as well as a unique stone monument from the Puuc site of Tabi, show men hunting animals, including deer, armadillos, and rodents (K1373; Mayer 1987, Pl. 165; Proskouriakoff 1950: 165). Other vessels depict supernatural entities, particularly dangerous *way* spirits, carrying trussed deer on their backs or blowing the conch shell horns that hunters evidently used to communicate or to drive their prey (K771, K808). Edible domesticated animals in Classic Maya art include dogs (portrayed, for instance, in Jaina-style figurines, like Yale Art Gallery Object No. 1973.88.4), turkeys (K1001, K2010), and rabbits (K511, K2026).

A final, important point is that most glyphic and iconographic references to things eaten and drunk occur on painted surfaces, like murals or bark paper codices, or on painted or modeled ceramic vessels. This pattern likely reflects conventional differences in genre and discourse among various media. Maya books document a range of religious rites, many of which entailed presenting specific foods and other offerings to different gods. Ceramics especially lent themselves to food references in their inscriptions, since they were often implicated in activities of consumption or preparation (see LeCount 2010; Reents-Budet 1998). Other portable objects would have presented less obvious surfaces on which to write about food, especially since their brief texts were usually dominated by self-referential content (Houston and Taube 1987; Mathews 1979). Even an apparent exception, a mention of chocolate on a diminutive sculpture of a crouching dog from Tonina (Monument 89), actually underscores this tendency by referencing the foodstuff only in an epithet for the dog's owner, *aj kakaw* ("cacao person"; Stuart 2014).

The surviving corpus of stone monuments, in contrast, contains few references to social interactions, economic activities, or rituals in which food played a significant part. Eating and drinking are rarely implicated in any of the events—bloodletting, war, captive presentation, ball-playing, dynastic succession, deity impersonation, or calendrical rites—recorded on most monuments. Exceptions do exist, of course, including Panel 3 from Piedras Negras (discussed below), which records the consumption of a fermented cacao beverage in the context of a court visit (Houston, Stuart, and Taube 2006:108; O'Neil 2012:154–156, 162). Altars K and U from Copán likewise record elite imbibing of another alcoholic drink, pulque, in the text on Altar K following a dedication ceremony (Beliaev, Davletshin, and Tokovinine 2010:266–267; Bíró 2010; Grube 2004:63; Grube and MacLeod 1989:2–3, Fig. 1; Tokovinine 2016:16). Representation of food and drink in the epigraphic corpus is thus significantly skewed in favor of those situations and media that pre-Columbian tradition prescribed as appropriate for recording.

Picturing and Writing Ancient Maya Food

Most foods named in the hieroglyphic corpus are depicted in Maya art as well, with maize and cacao again predominating. The latter is regularly depicted in unprepared form, most commonly as pods growing from cacao trees or held in the hands of humans or animals (K631; Grube and Gaida 2006:126, Abb. 12.12–12.13; Miller and Martin 2004, Pl. 40; Stone and Zender 2011:218–219; but see Miller and Martin 2004, Pl. 37). In contrast, maize usually appears as prepared food, especially tamales, although there are some images of the raw staple (Mayer 2009:80–81, Figs. 3–5, Fig. 7; Stone and Zender 2011:224–225; Taube 1985, Fig. 6). The Dresden and Madrid codices offer the clearest illustrations of tamales whose various fillings are indicated by animals drawn atop them in whole or part: turkey, fish, deer, and iguana, the last sometimes represented by spines on the tamale's surface (see Hull 2010:236). Although there is no clear archaeological evidence before the tenth century CE for the flat *comales*, or griddles, indicative of tortilla production, a Jaina-style figurine of a woman proffering thick, tortilla-like maize bread provides clear iconographic evidence that this staple was made and eaten at least as early as the Late Classic period as well (cf. Ardren, this volume; Miller and Martin 2004, Pl. 57; Taube 1989:33–34).

In some cases, images of raw or prepared foods are accompanied by glyphic texts that disambiguate or reinforce their identity. The irregular sphere held by the woman in scene NE-E1 of the Chiik Nahb murals at Calakmul, wrapped in what appear to be leaves, is marked as a ball of salt by a nearby caption identifying the woman as an *aj atz'aam* ("salt person"; García, cited in Martin 2012:69; Martin 2012:68, Fig. 19). Likewise, some of the roughly pyramidal objects protruding from the bowls held by several gods in the Dresden Codex may represent piles of cacao beans, given references to *kakaw* in the associated text (Förstemann 1880:10, 13). Moreover, some hieroglyphic signs are used as icons in nonlinguistic representations, a phenomenon most clearly illustrated by tamales. Although some appear as simple, lumpish circles, with or without color indicating additional spices or sauces (K1599, K6500; Saturno, Taube, and Stuart 2005, Fig. 5), others are rendered with the same sign used in the hieroglyphic script as the logogram for "tamale" (**WAAJ**), making their identification explicit (Figure 4.5). Through parallel use of the same graph in iconography and writing, Maya artisans simultaneously evoked and reinforced the connection between its rounded, drawn form and its referent, the warmed mass of corn dough that they and their peers would have eaten daily.

Glyphic labels were more frequent and perhaps more necessary with food whose visual representations were ambiguous or, as in the case of the salt bundle, obscured by an external covering. The two glyphs **chi-hi** on an olla shown on K732, for instance, indicate that the jar, and possibly also the cups held by two individuals facing it, contain pulque (*chih*). But some artisans used captions to underscore the identity of a food even when the straightforward imagery makes the label seem redundant. Chiik Nahb scene SE-S2, for one, doubly marks the identity of the food in question: the artist drew the internal features of the tamale logograph in the two circles sitting in front of the woman and glyphically identified her in an adjacent caption as the "tamale person" (*aj waaj*), with pre- and post-posed phonetic complements on the term for "tamale" (**wa-WAAJ-ji**) leaving no room for ambiguity (Martin 2012:65, Figs. 10, 12). Not all portrayals are so easily interpreted, however. The nature of some comestibles piled up in ceramic containers remains uncertain due to their abstruse visual form or undeciphered label, or because they lack glyphic explanation altogether (K2707, K4825, K8000; Brasseur de Bourbourg 1869, Pl. VII–X; Dresden Codex 30, in Förstemann 1880:59; García Barrios 2017:178–179; Martin 2012:69–70).

Some provisions, especially liquids, are not themselves illustrated but instead denoted indirectly by their containers (K504; Miller and Martin 2004, Pls. 4, 14). Others receive implicit reference in depictions of preparation activities: the presence of the ubiquitous maize, for instance, can be assumed in most images of women bent over a metate (K1272; Joyce 1933, Pls. VI.8–VI.9). Yet other foods would have been ground before eating, too, which could be signaled by context; indeed, one painted vessel with an individual at a grindstone next to a cacao tree may indicate prepa-

Figure 4.5. Seated Maize Deity holding the logogram **WAAJ**, *waaj*, "tamal," from the Dresden Codex, pg. 14. Drawing by Nicholas Carter.

ration of those beans for consumption (Miller and Martin 2004, Fig. 26). Unsurprisingly, these implicit visual references are often accompanied by hieroglyphic labels. Captions in the Chiik Nahb murals, for instance, specify that the men in scenes SE-S1 and SE-E1 are imbibing *ul*, "atole" (Martin 2012:62–64, Figs. 4, 6). Bundles were particularly useful vehicles for denoting granular foodstuffs, like legumes, cacao nibs, or salt, that would be too small to draw individually and tricky to illustrate in bulk (see K8963; Martin 2012:68–69; Stuart 2006a:137–141; Tokovinine and Beliaev 2013: 179). Some bundles are marked in such illustrations with glyphs naming or counting their contents, a practice that, if it had real-world analogs, would have been useful for accounting and transportation (see Miller and Martin 2004, Pl. 31; Stuart 2006a, Fig. 11; Tokovinine and Beliaev 2013, Fig. 7.5). Since the Primary Standard Sequence, the example par excellence of Classic Maya tagging practices, typically specifies vessels' intended contents, it is likely that these and other more humble containers were labeled as well (Grube 1990, 1991; MacLeod 1990; see Coe 1973; Houston and Taube 1987).

Maize, Cacao, and Pulque in Ancient Maya Writing

With such a wide range of food and drink attested in ancient Maya writing and art, it would be impractical to explore in detail the meanings and stories associated with each. Instead, three key comestibles are featured here: maize, cacao, and pulque. All three were probably in wide, even ubiquitous use through all periods of Maya cultural history and in all parts of the Maya world, although their consumption may have been socially limited in various ways. Each food anchored a cluster of mythic narratives, social values, and practices of production and consumption.

Maize

Since its domestication at least five thousand years ago (Colunga-García Marín and Zizumbo-Villarreal 2004; Piperno and Flannery 2001), maize has been widely cultivated and consumed throughout Mesoamerica. But where and how it appears in the Maya iconographic and epigraphic record presents a specific conception of this staple, one that emphasizes the performative modes and contexts of its use and thus reflects the normatively maize-based cuisine of Classic Maya society (see Goody 1982).

It is likely that in ancient times as today, only a small amount of maize was eaten plain, cooked and perhaps salted but otherwise unaltered. Most kernels were probably removed from the cob and processed with lime before being ground. Lime treatment, or nixtamalization, is a process whose origin and development remain archaeologically unclear, but whose ongoing use for at least three thousand years in Mesoamerica has been driven by two key benefits: reduction of the labor required to grind maize, by breaking down the kernel's durable external pericarp or shell; and enhanced nutrition, by releasing niacin and amino acids inherent in the maize and contributing additional calcium from the lime (Cheetham 2010:346; see Cravioto et al. 1945; Trejo-Gonzalez, Feria-Morales, and Wild-Altamirano 1982). The masa, or dough, produced by grinding the saturated kernels was used as the basis for beverages and gruels or was baked into solid foods like tamales. Flavor could be modified by adding fruit, vegetable, or protein fillings to tamales, or a range of spices and seasonings to liquid and solid dough. Yet the iconographic and epigraphic data are too limited in scope and quantity to tell us much about functional or notional differences between different styles of preparation. Nor do they offer insight into the cultural values that may have been assigned to different varieties of maize, as suggested by comparison with ethnographic studies (see Arias et al. 2000; Tuxill et al. 2010; Wellhausen, Roberts, and Hernández X. 1952).

What we can say is that maize held unparalleled cultural importance to ancient Mayas, standing for food and vegetable abundance even when its actual dietary importance varied (see A. Chase and D. Chase 2001:128–130 for evidence of a maize- and protein-rich "palace diet"). The Maize Deity is one of the oldest and most recognizable deities in Mesoamerican religion, with roots in Middle Formative Olmec culture (Taube 1996). Two versions of the Maize Deity, one shown with a distinctive "tonsure" and the other with his head transforming into an ear of maize, are represented in Classic art (Schellhas 1904:24–25; Taube 2009:41). The Classic Maya knew this figure as Juun Ixiim, "One Maize" (Stuart 2005b:182; Zender 2014), and a complicated set of myths surrounding him—somewhat variable over space and time, and pieced together mainly from iconography accompanied by a few hieroglyphic captions—present the life cycle of maize in terms of his death and resurrection. In its rough outlines, the story has Juun Ixiim die by decapitation and enter a watery underworld where he may be transported in a canoe by a pair of aged deities. There, he becomes a fruiting cacao tree (see below), a source of further wealth for the chthonic God L, until impregnating one of that deity's daughters with twin sons (Martin 2006; Stone and Zender 2011:219). Later, his sons—forerunners of the Hero Twins from the *Popol Vuh*, a K'iche' narrative recorded in the sixteenth century—and beautiful young women, who may be his wives or the wives or daughters of God L, adorn the Maize Deity with jewels before his triumphant emergence from the split carapace of the earth, represented as a cosmic turtle (Taube 1985; Taube 2009:41–42; see, e.g., K626, K1004, K1892). Maya rulers often impersonated the Maize Deity in various rites, and Alexandre Tokovinine (2013) argues that some accounts of dynastic origins were connected to local versions of that deity. Maize was, and in traditional Maya religions continues to be, considered the substance of humankind itself: unlike previous races formed from mud or wood, current humans are described in the *Popol Vuh* as made from maize dough, and it is through the consumption of maize that infants were and still are socialized into human society (Christenson 2006, 2010; cf. Scherer 2015:25–26; see Christenson 2003:lines 4882–4939).

Unlike cacao, maize in its raw state was not a sufficiently high-status item of tribute or exchange to be well represented in writing or image. The only surviving visual record of what was probably a busy, local commerce in unprocessed maize comes from the Chiik Nahb murals, which have been interpreted as a unique representation of market exchange in the Classic Maya visual corpus (Martin 2012). Yet finished maize products do appear as socially important tokens in courtly and ritual contexts. Painted scenes often represent tamales or similar dishes being raised up, either in the hand or in a ceramic receptacle, as offerings from a visitor or supplicant to another (usually male) individual, whose superior status is registered by his elevated position and more elaborate dress (K2923, K6418; Coe 1973, No. 30). In other contexts, plates of tamales sit in front of such a person, implying his reception or possession of them (K1775; Coe 1973, Nos. 13, 48).

But maize was not simply an earthly good. As the substance of ancestral bodies, it was, like human blood, also an acceptable sacrifice to the gods, a theme abundantly attested in Maya iconography (Dütting 1991; Stross 1992; Taube 1985). Three of the four known Maya codices contain images of tamales being offered to or by various deities (Brasseur de Bourbourg 1869, Pls. XXI–XXIII; Förstemann 1880:13–16, 54–57; Love 1994, Pls. 2, 16). That these tamales are sometimes accompanied by the glyphs for copal incense (*pom*) underscores the food's ritual function. Diego de Landa recorded Yucatec Maya people placing corn dough in the mouths of their deceased before they were interred, revealing that the cosmological significance of maize, like that of its patron deity, was not limited to life on earth (Scherer 2015:76; Tozzer 1941:130, 220). Carbonized maize cobs or kernels recovered from cache and cave deposits thought to be ritual in nature provide paleoethnobotanical evidence that raw maize, too, could be offered (e.g., Brady et al. 1997:95; Lentz 1991:272; Morehart 2011:114–116). More systematic study of the pre-Columbian imagery and limited archaeological data is needed if we are to tease out possible nuances in what forms of maize were presented, in what contexts, and for what reasons.

Pulque

At the time of Spanish contact, Yucatec Maya people consumed two main sorts of alcoholic drinks: pulque, made from the fermented sap of magueys (*Agave* spp.), and a kind of mead named *balche'* after the tree (*Lonchocarpus* spp.) whose bark was a key ingredient (see Vail and Dedrick, this volume). In most Mayan languages, *chih*, *kih*, and cognate words denote primarily the maguey plant and secondarily its products, including pulque and rope made from maguey fibers (Kaufman 2003:1161–1163). In Classic Mayan, *chih* was "pulque" and "maguey," and circumstantial evidence connected to deities of intoxication, discussed below, suggests that it may also have referred to meads. In traditional pulque production, before and after the Spanish Conquest, the "heart" or central leaves of a mature maguey plant are cut out and the resulting cavity left covered for up to a year. Then, the cavity walls are scraped twice a day and the sap collected as it accumulates (Escalante et al. 2016:3–5). In the Late Classic period, fermentation probably took place in globular ceramic jars with narrow necks, apparently with maguey leaves stuffed into their mouths.

In colonial times, Yucatec *balche'* recipes called for honey dissolved in *suhuy ha'*—"virgin water" collected from caves or cenotes into which no woman had entered—in addition to plant ingredients including the bark of the *balche'* tree itself (Thompson 1970:184). The Postclassic Madrid Codex illustrates rituals involving pots marked with so-called "Kaban curls," which may indicate *kab'* ("honey"; see Vail and Dedrick, this volume) or the strong odor of *balche'* (see Houston 2010), along with what may be bee antennae (Figure 4.6). Yet there is no clear evidence for *balche'* in the Classic Maya epigraphic or iconographic corpora: instead, in painted scenes on ceramic vessels, jars presumably containing alcoholic beverages appear filled with maguey leaves protruding from their mouths or marked with the glyphs **chi** or **chi-hi** for *chih*, or both. The best example is probably a polychrome vase in the Museum of Fine Arts Boston (K1092) depicting a party of inebriated elite youths (*ch'ok*), one of whom bears the fitting title of *aj chih* ("pulque person"; Figure 4.7).

Figure 4.6. Alcoholic drink in a jar marked with possible bee antennae and **KAB'** sign, from the Madrid Codex, pg. 50. Drawing by Nicholas Carter.

Figure 4.7. Drinker with a vessel containing maguey leaves and labeled **CHI**, *chih*, "pulque," along with a hieroglyphic caption identifying him as **AJ-chi-ji**, *aj chij*, "pulque person," from a polychrome vessel (K1092). Drawing by Nicholas Carter.

In other scenes of intoxication, ceramic or gourd enema clysters accompany or replace drinking vessels. The identity of psychoactive substances used in enemas by the ancient Maya has been the subject of some speculation—did they include tobacco, *Datura* spp., or other hallucinogens?—but a carved scene on an unprovenanced door jamb, probably from Campeche, shows a man carrying a jar labeled *chih* with a clyster resting on top (see Barrera Rubio and Taube 1987, Fig. 2; Spenard et al., this volume). Enemas, at least those taken in the same settings as drinks, may thus simply have been a way of enhancing the effects of pulque.

There are four known narrative texts describing pulque consumption, as opposed to illustrations with or without brief captions, in the Maya hieroglyphic corpus (Tokovinine 2016:16). Pulque drinking may have been especially socially salient at Copán, since three of those references come from Late Classic texts at that site. Two of these date to the reign of Copán's sixteenth and penultimate king, Yax Pahsaj Chan Yopaat, who ruled from 783 CE until 810 or a little later. The first, on an unnamed altar, only says that this king "drank pulque" (*yuk'ij chih*); the second, on Altar U (Grube 2004:63), situates the ruler's drinking in a ritual context, telling us that he "impersonated [the god] Akan in pulque drinking" (*u b'aah ahn akan ti uk' chih*). The third reference comes from Altar K (688 CE; see Grube and MacLeod 1989) and describes pulque drinking by the twelfth ruler K'ahk' U Ti' Witz' K'awiil: a building was ceremonially dedicated, "and then he drank white maize-gruel pulque" (*i uk' sak sa' chih*). The final hieroglyphic account of pulque drinking, on an inscribed stairway riser, comes not from Copán but from the site of La Corona, a vassal polity subject to Calakmul. The text states that a lord of La Corona "drank" (*uk'uun*) and "offered" or "gave pulque" (*yak'aw chih*), although the recipients, whether human or divine, are unstated (Martin 2008; Tokovinine 2016:16). Despite these references, and in contrast to the abundance of ceramic vessels designated for cacao- or maize-based beverages, only one known Classic Maya vessel, excavated from a royal tomb at Tikal, was explicitly labeled as its owner's "drinking instrument for pulque" (*yuk'ib' ta chih*) (Stuart 2005a:145). Unlike typical cacao vases, this vessel was carved from wood covered with painted stucco—only the stucco coating now survives—and could be closed with a lid, variances that may reflect culinary practices or environmental requirements specific to pulque (Houston 2018:67).

Unlike the Maize Deity, supernatural beings connected with pulque in Maya mythology are dangerous, even malevolent entities. The most explicit such association is with a being called Mok Chih, "Sickness Pulque" or perhaps "Bee Pulque," a variant or aspect of God A' (Akan, "Groan";

Figure 4.8. Mok Chih with bee wings and antennae protruding from under his hat, from a codex-style vessel from the area of Calakmul (K2286). Drawing by Nicholas Carter.

Grube 2004:66–70; Grube and Stuart 1987:10). Like other members of the Akan complex, he is, among other things, a deity of illness, his body marked with black paint on the face and "death" or "darkness" signs on the torso and limbs. Mok Chih is distinguished from these other characters by the knot (*mok* in Yucatec) worn over his mouth and nose, by the bees or other insects he carries in his hands or in a jar, and, in at least one case, by insect antennae on his head (Figure 4.8; Grube 2004:67–68). This apine imagery hints at the use of honey in producing alcoholic beverages, whether as an additive to pulque or as the primary fermented ingredient in a Classic analogue to *balche'*. A "Pulque Akan" (*chihil akan*) is named in a Late Classic inscription at Tortuguero, paired with a deity of cacao, as one of the patron gods of a local ruler (Gronemeyer and MacLeod 2010).

What is probably the same deity—*chihil k'uh* or "Pulque God"—is referenced in a caption (Drawing 90) painted on a stalagmite in the most remote part of the cave of Naj Tunich in the southern Maya Mountains, an important pilgrimage site during the seventh century CE (MacLeod and Stone 1995, Fig. 7-34; Stone 1995:121–125). Beyond the stalagmite, researchers encountered a chamber containing an altar and, a little farther on, the skeleton of a child sacrificial victim (Brady 1989:351, 362–363; MacLeod n.d.). Caves have a long association in Mesoamerica with child sacrifice and deities of rain; their connection here with Akan as a "pulque god" might be explained if some Late Classic alcoholic beverages, like *balche'* at the time of Spanish contact, had to be prepared with "virgin water" (see Spenard et al., this volume).

It is hard to separate ritual from recreational uses of pulque and related beverages in ancient Maya iconography. In the courtly contexts depicted on ceramic vessels and recounted on the monuments discussed above, such a distinction likely did not exist. In any event, Maya art suggests certain social rules about communal pulque consumption in representation and reality, one of which appears to have been that lords preferred to be depicted as providers rather than as consumers of this drink. As discussed by Tokovinine (2016), a number of Late Classic polychrome vessels depict lords of Motul de San José and Dos Pilas seated on platforms in palatial interiors, surrounded by courtiers and conspicuously displayed food and drink, including jars of pulque. Captions tell us that these scenes depict the kings' "image with pulque" (*u b'aah ti chih* or *u b'aah ta chih*), yet it is the rulers' subordinates, if anyone, who are depicted doing the actual drinking. In these contexts, superiors' provision of socially significant beverages likely encouraged social cohesion with their subjects, while simultaneously reinforcing preexisting status differences between them. Further social restrictions concerned tipplers' sex: raucous drinking parties like the one depicted on the MFA vessel were all-male affairs, important to forming social bonds among elite youth on the cusp of leadership (Houston 2009). Women are never shown drinking pulque or enjoying its effects, although they do sometimes offer it to men or, perhaps even more commonly, administer it in enemas.

Cacao

All wild species of cacao are native to northern South America, and it remains a subject of controversy whether cultivated cacao derives from populations domesticated separately in South America and Mesoamerica (e.g., Ogata, Gómez-Pompa, and Taube 2006) or was introduced to Mesoamerica as a South American domesticate (e.g., Motomayor et al. 2002). In any event, the earliest archaeological evidence for the consumption of cacao-based beverages in Middle America comes from the Ulúa Valley of Honduras (Henderson et al. 2007), where lightly fermented beverages made from the flesh of cacao pods may have been consumed. By the Classic period, Maya people were also preparing drinks from toasted cacao seeds, ground to a powder and mixed with water and various flavoring agents.

Within Mesoamerica, certain regions were better suited than others for cacao cultivation, especially parts of the Gulf Coast, the Soconusco region of the Pacific Coast, and a belt stretching along coastal Belize and inland along the Sarstoon River valley (Caso Barrera and Aliphat Fernández 2006a, 2006b). Control of those regions was important to the economies of Mesoamerican states in the Late Postclassic period, including the Aztec Triple Alliance, the Chontal kingdom of Acalan, and the Itza kingdom at Nojpetén (Bergmann 1969; Caso Barrera and Aliphat Fernández 2006a:32–35; Scholes and Roys 1968:29–30). Yet with sufficient care, cacao could also be grown in less favorable regions in sinkholes and other natural depressions (Gómez-Pompa, Salvador Flores, and Aliphat Fernández 1990), potentially supplementing the agricultural economies of kingdoms that nevertheless were not major producers (e.g., Garrison, Houston, and Alcover Firpi 2019).

Cacao was a highly prestigious food among the ancient Maya, as it was for other Mesoamerican peoples, and at least in Late Postclassic and colonial times, cacao beans served as a kind of currency (Bauer 2001:34–35; Fowler 2006:307–308; Millon 1955). Cacao forms the subject of one of the riddles in the "Language of Zuyua" in the colonial Yucatec *Book of Chilam Balam of Chumayel*, the understanding of which was among the qualifications for lordly status: the froth on a cup of chocolate, colored red with annatto paste, is likened to the crests of male cardinals (Barrera Vásquez and Rendón 1969:139). A similarly high value, as well as analogous associations with elite rank, is reflected in the prominent place cacao receives in scenes on painted ceramics depicting displays of wealth in courtly settings. Even more so, cacao's importance is evident from the high frequency with which it appears in Primary Standard Sequences on a variety of vessel types. Besides those dedicatory texts, a handful of ancient Maya textual and iconographic references to cacao occur in other media. The best known of these is surely Piedras Negras Panel 3, which provides rare monumental insight into the role of chocolate in dynastic political interactions by recording the consumption of a fermented cacao beverage (*kal kakaw*) during a reception of visitors in the local royal court (Houston, Stuart, and Taube 2006:108; O'Neil 2012:154–156, 162).

Within the corpus of Primary Standard Sequences, the most common term for a kind of ceramic vessel is *uk'ib'*, "drinking-instrument," from a root *uk'*, "drink." This term applies to vessel forms ranging from tall, cylindrical, barrel-shaped, or (in a few cases) rectangular prismatic vases to shorter, proportionally wider bowls and cups with straight, flared, or rounded sides (Kettunen and Helmke 2019:34). Most *uk'ib'* vessels of whatever form are described in their dedicatory texts as intended for cacao, and indeed some are painted with scenes of courtly life in which tall vases are used to raise a froth on a cacao beverage by pouring it back and forth between containers (Stuart 1988:156; e.g., K511). Yet containers depicted in such use lack texts or other decorations, and, as recent archaeometric research suggests (Loughmiller-Cardinal 2018), many of the most ornately decorated cylindrical vases may not actually have been used for liquid preparations of cacao.

Through gas and liquid chromatography/mass spectrometry, chemical residues of cacao, including the active ingredients theobromine and caffeine, have been identified in numerous ancient Maya pots. Among these are Middle Preclassic spouted vessels from Belize (Hurst et al. 2002); an Early Classic vessel from Río Azul with a narrow neck and a locking lid (Hall et al. 1990; Hurst et al. 1989; Stuart 1988); and eleven vessels of various forms from Early Classic royal mortuary contexts at Copán, including two small, cylindrical cups and two cylindrical pots with tripod bases, their containers slightly wider than they are tall (McNeil, Hurst, and Sharer 2006). Yet of seventy tall, cylindrical vases analyzed by Jennifer Loughmiller-Cardinal (2018), of which sixty-one bore dedicatory inscriptions, none contained the chemical signatures of cacao. Indeed, tall, cylindrical *uk'ib'* vessels tend not to show the evaporation rings or staining that would be expected if they had contained liquid cacao; instead, their interiors may exhibit vertical scrape or pockmarks, especially toward the bottoms of the walls. As Loughmiller-Cardinal (2018:4–5) suggests, these patterns of use-wear and the absence of cacao residues might be reconciled with textual descriptions of tall cylinders as "drinking instruments for cacao" if the vessels were used to store or serve dry cacao beans, with a wooden or bone implement used to scoop out quantities to be ground and mixed with liquids in other containers.

In that case, epigraphers face a choice between two possibilities about the term *uk'ib'* as applied to vessels whose dedicatory texts say they are for cacao. Do essentially all Primary Standard Sequences accurately describe the uses to which the pots were put or not? If the texts all tell the truth about their vessels, but some of those vessels did not contain cacao drinks, then the cultural category of *uk'ib'* must have included multiple kinds of vessels that facilitated drinking—that is, not only cups and bowls from which liquid was consumed but also other vessels, including ornately decorated cylinders, that played a different role in the formal presentation and service of cacao. Alternatively, *uk'ib'* in the strict sense might have referred only to drinking vessels. In that case, all Primary Standard Sequences referring to cacao do state that their vessels are for cacao beverages, but many of those statements—perhaps mainly the ones on tall, ornate vases—beautified and enhanced the value of pots without literally corresponding to their use.

If the first of these two possibilities is correct, it would have implications for interpreting the three modifiers most frequently applied to cacao in Primary Standard Sequences, which have proven difficult to understand in context. The first of these is *yutal*, for which various interpretations have been proposed. In some proposals, *yutal* derives from a root **ut* meaning "food" (Reents-Budet 1994:75, 161) or "seed" (Alfonso Lacadena, personal communication 2005, cited in Beliaev, Davletshin, and Tokovinine 2010:258), with the initial *y-* the prevocalic third-person ergative pronoun, so that *yutal kakaw* would be "cacao sustenance" or "the seeds of cacao." Yet linguistic evidence from Ch'orti' and one instance in the hieroglyphic corpus of *u yutal* among the titles of an elite youth (Stuart 2006b:188) indicate that the root is not *ut* but *yut*. Dmitri Beliaev and colleagues (2010:258–260) identify *yut* as a cognate of Ch'orti' *yutir*, "fruit," and conclude that *yutal kakaw* means "fruity cacao"—a beverage made either with cacao nibs flavored with other fruits or from the flesh of cacao pods. Complicating these proposals, a fragment of a royal throne recently discovered at the site of Ixtutz, where it had been removed from its original context and reset in antiquity (Mara Antonieta Reyes, personal communication to Nicholas Carter 2017), bears an inscription describing it as a *yutal tz'am* ("*yutal* throne"). Meanings connected to fruit and seeds seem unlikely here, and it is worth considering a suggestion by John Justeson (personal communication to Jennifer Loughmiller-Cardinal 2017, cited in Loughmiller-Cardinal 2018:6) that Classic Mayan *yutal* is a cognate of proto-Tzeltalan **yut*, "inside." Conceivably, *yutal kakaw* in Primary Standard Sequences could describe cacao as the "contents" of vessels, while a *yutal tz'am* might be something like an "interior throne" or the carved "face" (**ut*; see Beliaev, Davletshin, and Tokovinine 2010:259) of a bench.

A second common term in Primary Standard Sequences, *tzih*, modifies *kakaw* but also appears alone as the intended beverage for some vessels. As adjectives, *tzih* and the derived form *tzihil* mean "fresh," "pure," or "raw," and although a noun *tzi* does mean "nixtamalized maize" or "cooked maize" in K'iche', the most likely sense of *tzih* when it occurs by itself in dedicatory texts is as a term for unmixed cacao (Grube 1990:326; Stuart 2006b:195–197). The third, highly frequent modifier is *ixiimte'* (maize tree) or *ixiimte'el* (maize-tree-like, of a maize tree). A number of unrelated fruiting plant species, some of them poisonous, are known as "maize tree" in different modern Mayan languages (Stuart 2006b:198–199). Ancient Maya beverages combining cacao and maize are known from other terms, such as *sakha'* ("white water"), *kakawal ul* ("chocolaty gruel"), and perhaps *sa'al kakaw* ("gruelish cacao"; Beliaev, Davletshin, and Tokovinine 2010: 266). Yet as Simon Martin (2006) argues, *ixiimte'el kakaw* may refer not to cacao mixed with maize or other ingredients, but to myths surrounding cacao itself.

As Martin reconstructs the narrative, between his death and his triumph over the powers of the underworld, the Maize Deity grows into a magical tree, the *ixiimte'*, from which sprout cacao pods and, eventually, the head of the Maize Deity himself. K'awiil, a deity of lightning and agricultural abundance, is involved in some way with the Maize Deity's escape from captivity, and paintings on architectural capstones from sites in Campeche depict this deity holding sacks or baskets stuffed with cacao beans (Martin 2006:173). This episode is depicted on several painted vessels (K631 and K5615), while a few other works, including an incised, unprovenanced Early Classic vase (K6547) and the sarcophagus of K'ihnich Janab' Pakal at Palenque (Robertson 1983, Figs. 174–202), depict elite Maya men and women growing into cacao or other fruiting trees after death. Usually, but not always—the Palenque sarcophagus is a notable exception—beings undergoing that postmortem transformation have in common an inverted position, with the head and chest down and the feet rising behind (Taube 2003:461). Another unprovenanced, Early Classic vessel, a stone bowl in the Dumbarton Oaks museum collection, shows the Maize Deity or an impersonator sitting or lying on a matwork cushion, his body adorned with cacao pods and marked with "wood" or "tree" property qualifiers (Martin 2006, Fig. 8.1; see Stone and Zender 2011:13–15). Ancestors, the Maize Deity, and the so-called Pax Deity—an anthropomorphic form of the logogram **TE'**, "tree" (Taube 2005:27)—appear on ceramic cache vessels and on stone censers and censer lids at Copán in the Late Classic period (McNeil, Hurst, and Sharer 2006:237–249).

A survey of ceramic vessels documented by Barbara and Justin Kerr (1989, 1990, 1992, 1994, 1997, 2000) and by Traci Ardren and Michael Coe reveals variations according to style—corresponding to centers or regions of production—in how cacao is described in Primary Standard Sequences (Table 4.1a–f). Among fifty-one seventh- and eighth-century codex-style vessels from the Mirador Basin, *tzih* was referenced in three dedicatory texts and *tzih kakaw* in one; *yutal kakaw* was far more popular, with twenty-four references (47.06%), followed by *ixiimte'el kakaw* and variants, with twelve (23.52%). Similar proportions appear in a sample of twenty-eight vessels stylistically connected to the area of Naranjo and Holmul, from the late sixth into the eighth century: *yutal kakaw* appeared in twelve texts (42.86%) and *ixiimte'el kakaw* in eight (28.57%), with only one reference to *tzih*. In contrast, of seventeen vessels in the distinctive red-background style produced at El Zotz at the beginning of the Late Classic period (Houston 2008:8), eleven (64.71%) were for *tzihte'el kakaw* (fresh tree cacao), with *kakaw* mentioned by itself on only one vessel. More balanced ratios are attested on fifteen pots from the area of Río Azul and Xultun: four refer to *ixiimte'el kakaw*, three to *tzih*, three to *yutal kakaw*, and three to both *yutal* and *tzih* as distinct beverages. Turning to the north, the texts on Chochola-style and similar carved vessels emphasize *tzih*: five of thirteen such vessels (38.46%) are intended for *tzihil kakaw*, three (23.08%) for *tzih*, and two (15.38%) for *yutal tzihil*.

Whether such regional and temporal variation in dedicatory texts corresponds to divergent cacao recipes or simply represents different ways of talking about a common beverage remains to be established. Based on the evidence discussed above, there is little reason to think that *tzih* or *ixiimte'el kakaw* were preparations of cacao with flavoring agents, and even *yutal* may not be a reference to "fruit" at all. As Stuart (2006b:201) points out, a diversity of terms for cacao in the Early Classic period gives way to widespread emphases on *yutal*, *tzih*, and *ixiimte'el kakaw* in the Late Classic. It is thus quite possible that all three sorts of cacao most often referenced in Primary Standard Sequences are not necessarily prepared beverages, but simply "cacao" in a broad sense that included dry beans (perhaps stored or presented in decorated cylinders) and drinks made from them (drunk from shorter pots, bowls, and cups). At the same time, their distribution suggests that they indexed culturally salient conceptions of *kakaw*, particularly when considering the striking infrequency with which that generic term appears unmodified in these same corpora (see Tables 4.1a–f).

In eastern Petén at the end of the Early Classic period, a few artists were concerned with the origins of the cacao to be put in the pots they painted. One vessel's dedicatory text says that it is for *ixiimte' sa'al kakaw*, where *sa'al* might refer to maize gruel (*sa'*) or to the precinct within Naranjo after which the ruling dynasty was named (Stuart 2005a:29–30; Tokovinine

Table 4.1a–f. Results from a survey of vessel contents recorded in Primary Standard Sequence texts on vessels that have been attributed to different regions in the Maya Lowlands, organized by region

Contents	Count	% Total
a. Mirador Basin		
yutal [. . .] ha'	1	1.96
ixiimte'el	1	1.96
kakaw (?)	1	1.96
ixiim kakaw	4	7.84
ixiimte'el kakaw	7	13.73
tzih kakaw	1	1.96
yutal kakaw	24	47.06
yutal ixiimte'el kakaw	1	1.96
tzih	3	5.88
ul	7	13.73
kakawal ul	1	1.96
Total	51	100.0
b. Naranjo and Holmul style		
ixiimte'el kakaw	8	28.57
su:tz(?) kakaw	1	3.57
yutal kakaw (incl. single origin)	12	42.86
yutal ixiimte'el kakaw	3	10.71
tzih u yutal kakaw	1	3.57
ul	3	10.71
Total	28	99.99
c. El Zotz		
kakaw	1	5.88
kakaw and tzih	1	5.88
tzih/tzihil/tzihte'el kakaw	11	64.71
sak chihil we'/waaj	2	11.76
ul	2	11.76
Total	17	99.99
d. Río Azul and Xultun		
ixiimte'el kakaw	4	26.67
tzih kakaw	1	6.67
yutal kakaw	3	20.0
tzih	3	20.0
yutal, tzih	3	20.0
ul	1	6.67
Total	15	100.01

Table 4.1a–f. Continued

Contents	Count	% Total
e. Motul de San José region		
ixiimte'el kakaw	2	25.0
tzihil ixiimte'el kakaw	2	25.0
yutal kakaw	3	37.5
tzih	1	12.5
Total	8	100.0
f. Chochola and similar carved style		
ixiimte' kakaw	1	7.69
tzih/tzihil kakaw	5	38.46
tzih/tzit	3	23.08
yutal tzihil	2	15.38
ul	1	7.69
ch'aj ul	1	7.69
Total	13	99.99

and Fialko 2007). Two other vessels, adorned by one scribe for the important Naranjo ruler Aj Numsaaj Chan K'ihnich in the late sixth or early seventh century CE, were intended for *yutal ho'kab' kakaw*. Here, *ho'kab'*, "Five Lands," is the dynastic name pertaining to a kingdom whose Late and Terminal Classic capitals were at Ixtutz and Ixtonton, in the western Maya Mountains. In the sixteenth century, a key trade route passed near those sites, connecting Manche cacao growers south of the mountains with elite consumers at Nojpetén to the north (Caso Barrera and Aliphat Fernández 2006a, 2006b). Still another pot, this one from Río Azul, was intended for *wintik kakaw* and *koxoom mul kakaw*, where *wintik* and *koxoom mul* may also be place-names (Stuart 2006b:193–194). As Stuart suggests, these toponymic references, concentrated as they are in the Eastern Lowlands, may reflect the regional economic importance of cacao cultivation and trade.

Conclusion

The hieroglyphic and representational records contain a wealth of information about ancient Maya food. Scholars have identified numerous terms for solid foods and beverages, as well as for the kinds of vessels used in their storage, presentation, and consumption. Maize gruels and particularly cacao are best attested in the corpus of Primary Standard Sequences, but fermented beverages join those two as materially and ritually important. Epigraphic and iconographic evidence has permitted identification of deities associated with those foods and the reconstruction of some of the myths about those characters: Juun Ixiim, including in his form as the *ixiimte'*, and Mok Chih and other members of the Akan complex. Also evident are social limits on who should consume or refrain from certain comestibles—cacao was a food for nobility, pulque a drink for men—and conventions about their presentation and display.

Archaeological and epigraphic data also continue to encourage reconsideration and refinement of the meanings attributed to Classic Maya food and of interpretations of their referents. In particular, scholars have identified changes over time and variation over space in the terms used with the maize- and cacao-based drinks best attested in the ceramic corpus. Some of those expressions, especially in the Early Classic period, describe ingredients added to cacao beverages, or the geographic origins of cacao; by the Late Classic, the three modifiers in most common use—*yutal*, *tzih*, and *ixiimte'el*—vary regionally in their frequency but may all describe cacao itself rather than additives. Readings of *yutal* related to "fruit" and "seeds" are put in some doubt by the adjective's use to describe a throne, and the most widespread term for cacao vessels, *uk'ib'*, may be best interpreted as a general term for items involved in the preparation and service of beverages rather than a specific designation for drinking vessels. It is an open question whether these lexical changes reflect some shift in Maya *haute cuisine* from the Early to the Late Classic, perhaps a narrowing of former variation. If the suggestions advanced here about *ixiimte'el*, *tzih*, and *yutal* are correct, and if the inscribed polychrome cylinders of the Late Classic period tended to contain dry beans rather than prepared drinks, the problem may best be solved not by epigraphic means but through chemical analyses of small, uninscribed vessels. Meanwhile, connections between Mok Chih, honey, and caves raise the possibility that the Classic Maya of the Central and Southern Lowlands had a tradition of ritual mead consumption like that of the Yucatec Maya at the time of the Conquest, and that the category *chih* should be understood to include drinks fermented from honey as well as those made from maguey sap.

All these epigraphic successes, the identification of foods and ingredients in Maya texts and the elucidation of mythic narratives, make it clear how vital epigraphy is to the anthropology of Mesoamerican culinary practices. At the same time, advances in archaeometry check epigraphic interpretation while offering some new insights into Classic Maya taxonomies of foods and their containers. These two tendencies are not contradictory, but demonstrate—if further demonstration were needed—that epigraphic and archaeological interpretation should advance together in dialogue.

References

Arias, L., J. Chávez, V. Cob, L. Burgos, and J. Canul. 2000. "Agromorphological Characters and Farmer Perceptions: Data Collection and Analysis. Mexico." In *Conserving Agricultural Biodiversity in Situ: A Scientific Basis for Sustainable Agriculture*, ed. Devra I. Jarvis, B. R. Sthapit, and Linda Sears, 95–100. Rome: International Plant Genetic Resources Institute.

Barrera Rubio, Alfredo, and Karl A. Taube. 1987. "Los relieves de San Diego: Una nueva perspectiva." *Boletín de la Escuela de Ciencias Antropológicas de la Universidad de Yucatán* 14(83):3–18.

Barrera Vásquez, Alfredo, and Silvia Rendón, eds. 1969. *El libro de los libros de Chilam Balam*. 4th ed. Colección Popular 42. Mexico City: Fondo de Cultura Económica.

Bauer, Arnold J. 2001. *Goods, Power, and History: Latin America's Material Culture*. Cambridge: Cambridge University Press.

Beliaev, Dmitri, Albert Davletshin, and Alexandre Tokovinine. 2010. "Sweet Cacao and Sour Atole: Mixed Drinks on Classic Maya Ceramic Vases." In *Pre-Columbian Foodways: Interdisciplinary Approaches to Food, Culture, and Markets in Ancient Mesoamerica*, ed. John E. Staller and Michael D. Carrasco, 257–272. New York: Springer.

Bergmann, John F. 1969. "The Distribution of Cacao Cultivation in Pre-Columbian America." *Annals of the Association of American Geographers* 59(1):85–96.

Bíró, Péter. 2010. "A New Look at the Inscription of Copan Altar K." *The PARI Journal* 11(2):22–28.

Boot, Erik. 2003. "A New Classic Maya Vessel Type Collocation on a Uaxactun-style Plate." Accessed December 31, 2018. mayavase.com/bootplate.pdf.

———. 2005a. "A Preliminary Overview of Common and Uncommon Classic Maya Vessel Type Collocations in the Primary Standard Sequence." Rijswijk, the Netherlands. Accessed December 31, 2018. mayavase.com/BootVesselTypes.pdf.

———. 2005b. "A Vessel Fit for a Feast: Kerr No. 3091." Accessed December 31, 2018. mayavase.com/FitforaFeast.pdf.

Brady, James E. 1989. "An Investigation of Maya Ritual Cave Use with Special Reference to Naj Tunich, Petén, Guatemala." PhD diss., Department of Archaeology, University of California, Los Angeles.

Brady, James E., Gene A. Ware, Barbara Luke, Allan Cobb, John Fogarty, and Beverly Shade. 1997. "Preclassic Cave Utilization Near Cobanerita, San Benito, Petén." *Mexicon* 19(5):91–96.

Brasseur de Bourbourg, Charles É. 1869. *Manuscrit Troano: Études sur le système graphique et la langue des Mayas*. Paris: Imprimerie impériale.

Bronson, Bennet. 1966. "Roots and the Subsistence of the Ancient Maya." *Southwestern Journal of Anthropology* 22(3):251–279.

Carrasco Vargas, Ramón, and María Cordeiro Baqueiro. 2012. "The Murals of Chiik Nahb Structure Sub 1-4, Calakmul, Mexico." In *Maya Archaeology 2*, ed. Charles Golden, Stephen D. Houston, and Joel Skidmore, 8–59. San Francisco: Precolumbia Mesoweb Press.

Caso Barrera, Laura, and Mario Aliphat Fernández. 2006a. "Cacao, Vanilla and Annatto: Three Production and Exchange Systems in the Southern Maya Lowlands, XVI–XVII Centuries." *Journal of Latin American Geography* 5(2):29–52.

———. 2006b. "The Itza Maya Control over Cacao: Politics, Commerce, and War in the Sixteenth and Seventeenth Centuries." In *Chocolate in Mesoamerica: A Cultural History of Cacao*, ed. Cameron L. McNeil, 289–306. Gainesville: University Press of Florida.

Chase, Arlen F., and Diane Z. Chase. 2001. "The Royal Court of Caracol, Belize: Its Palaces and People." In *Royal Courts of the Ancient Maya*. Vol. 2, *Data and Case Studies*, ed. Takeshi Inomata and Stephen D. Houston, 102–137. Boulder: Westview Press.

Cheetham, David. 2010. "Corn, Colanders, and Cooking: Early Maize Processing in the Maya Lowlands and Its Implications." In *Pre-Columbian Foodways: Interdisciplinary Approaches to Food, Culture, and Markets in Ancient Mesoamerica*, ed. John E. Staller and Michael D. Carrasco, 345–368. New York: Springer.

Christenson, Allen J. 2003. *Popol Vuh: Literal Poetic Version, Translation and Transcription*. Vol. 2. New York: O-Books.

———. 2006. "You Are What You Speak: Maya as the Language of Maize." In *Maya Ethnicity: The Construction of Ethnic Identity from Preclassic to Modern Times*, ed. Frauke Sachse, 209–216. Markt Schwaben, Germany: Verlag Anton Saurwein.

———. 2010. "Maize Was Their Flesh: Ritual Feasting in the Maya Highlands." In *Pre-Columbian Foodways: Interdisciplinary Approaches to Food, Culture, and Markets in Ancient Mesoamerica*, ed. John E. Staller and Michael D. Carrasco, 577–600. New York: Springer.

Coe, Michael D. 1973. *The Maya Scribe and His World*. New York: Grolier Club.

Colunga-García Marín, Patricia, and Daniel Zizumbo-Villarreal. 2004. "Domestication of Plants in Maya Lowlands." *Economic Botany* 58(1):101–110.

Cravioto, R. O., R. K. Anderson, E. E. Lockhart, F. de P. Miranda, and R. S. Harris. 1945. "Nutritive Value of the Mexican Tortilla." *Science* 102(2639):91–93. doi: 10.1126/science.102.2639.91.

Dakin, Karen, and Søren Wichmann. 2000. "Cacao and Chocolate: A Uto-Aztecan Perspective." *Ancient Mesoamerica* 11(1):55–75.

Dütting, Dieter. 1991. "In Search of Kawil and Chaac: Blood and Maize in Maya Epigraphy." *Tribus* 40:83–135.

Emery, Kitty. 2003. "The Noble Beast: Status and Differential Access to Animals in the Maya World." *World Archaeology* 34(3):498–515. doi:10.1080/0043824021000026477.

———. 2004. "In Search of the 'Maya Diet': Is Regional Comparison Possible in the Maya Area?" *Archaeofauna* 13:37–56.

Escalante, Adelfo, David R. López Soto, Judith E. Velázquez Gutiérrez, Martha Giles-Gómez, Francisco Bolívar, and Agustín López-Munguía. 2016. "Pulque, a Traditional Mexican Alcoholic Fermented Beverage: Historical, Microbiological, and Technical Aspects." *Frontiers in Microbiology* 7:1026.

Förstemann, Ernst. 1880. *Codex Dresdensis: Die Mayahandschrift der Königlichen Öffentlichen Bibliothek zu Dresden*. Leipzig, Germany: Verlag der A. Naumann'schen Lichtdruckerei.

Fowler, William R. 2006. "Cacao Production, Tribute, and Wealth in Sixteenth-Century Izalcos, El Salvador." In *Chocolate in Mesoamerica: A Cultural History of Cacao*, ed. Cameron L. McNeil, 307–321. Gainesville: University Press of Florida.

García Barrios, Ana. 2017. "The Social Context of Food at Calakmul, Campeche, Mexico: Images Painted on the Pyramid of Chiik Nahb'." In *Constructing Power and Place in Mesoamerica: Pre-Hispanic Paintings from Three Regions*, ed. Merideth Paxton and Leticia Staines Cicero, 171–190. Albuquerque: University of New Mexico Press.

Garrison, Thomas G., Stephen D. Houston, and Omar Alcover Firpi. 2019. "Recentering the Rural: Lidar and Articulated Landscapes among the Maya." *Journal of Anthropological Archaeology* 53:133–146.

Gómez-Pompa, Arturo, José Salvador Flores, and Mario Aliphat Fernández. 1990. "The Sacred Cacao Groves of the Maya." *Latin American Antiquity* 1(3):247–257.

Goody, Jack. 1982. *Cooking, Cuisine, and Class: A Study in Comparative Sociology*. Cambridge: Cambridge University Press.

Graham, Ian. 1982. *Corpus of Maya Hieroglyphic Inscriptions: Volume 3, Part 3: Yaxchilán*. Cambridge, MA: Peabody Museum of Archaeology and Ethnology, Harvard University.

Gronemeyer, Sven, and Barbara MacLeod. 2010. "What Could Happen in 2012: A Re-Analysis of the 13-*Bak'tun* Prophecy on Tortuguero Monument 6." *Wayeb Notes* 34.

Grube, Nikolai. 1990. "The Primary Standard Sequence in Chocholá Style Ceramics." In *The Maya Vase Book: A Corpus of Rollout Photographs of Maya Vases*, ed. Barbara Kerr and Justin Kerr, 2:320–330. New York: Kerr Associates.

———. 1991. "An Investigation of the Primary Standard Sequence on Classic Maya Ceramics." In *Sixth Palenque Round Table, 1986*, ed. Virginia M. Fields, 8:223–232. Norman: University of Oklahoma Press.

———. 2004. "*Akan*—The God of Drinking, Disease and Death." In *Continuity and Change: Maya Religious Practices in Temporal Perspective*, ed. Daniel Graña-Behrens, Nikolai Grube, Christian M. Prager, Frauke Sachse, Stefanie Teufel, and Elisabeth Wagner, 59–76. Acta Mesoamericana, Vol. 14. Markt Schwaben, Germany: Verlag Anton Saurwein.

Grube, Nikolai, and Maria Gaida. 2006. *Die Maya: Schrift und Kunst*. Berlin and Cologne: SMB-DuMont.

Grube, Nikolai, and Barbara MacLeod. 1989. "A Primary Standard Sequence on Copán Altar K." *Copán Note* 55:1–9.

Grube, Nikolai, and David S. Stuart. 1987. *Observations on T110 as the Syllable ko*. Research Reports on Ancient Maya Writing 8–10. Washington, DC: Center for Maya Research.

Hall, Grant D., Stanley M. Tarka Jr., W. Jeffrey Hurst, David Stuart, and Richard E. W. Adams. 1990. "Cacao Residues in Ancient Maya Vessels from Rio Azul, Guatemala." *American Antiquity* 55(1):138–143.

Hellmuth, Nicholas M. 1987. *Monster und Menschen in der Maya-Kunst: Eine Ikonographie der alten Religionen Mexikos und Guatemalas*. Graz, Austria: Akademische Druck-u. Verlagsanstalt.

Henderson, John S., Rosemary A. Joyce, Gretchen R. Hall, W. Jeffrey Hurst, and Patrick E. McGovern. 2007. "Chemical and Archaeological Evidence for the Earliest Cacao Beverages." *Proceedings of the National Academy of Sciences* 104(48): 18937–18940.

Houston, Stephen D. 2008. "In the Shadow of a Giant." *Mesoweb*. Accessed February 24, 2020. www.mesoweb.com/zotz/articles/Shadow-of-a-Giant.pdf.

———. 2009. "A Splendid Predicament: Young Men in Classic Maya Society." *Cambridge Archaeological Journal* 19(2):149–178.

———. 2010. "Maya Musk." *Maya Decipherment*. Accessed December 31, 2018. decipherment.wordpress.com/2010/06/17/maya-musk.

———. 2018. *The Gifted Passage: Young Men in Classic Maya Art and Text*. New Haven: Yale University Press.

Houston, Stephen D., John Robertson, and David Stuart. 2001. *Quality and Quantity in Glyphic Nouns and Adjectives*. Research Reports on Ancient Maya Writing 47. Washington, DC: Center for Maya Research.

Houston, Stephen D., David Stuart, and John Robertson. 1998. "Disharmony in Maya Hieroglyphic Writing: Linguistic Change and Continuity in Classic Society." In *Anatomía de una civilización: Aproximaciones interdisciplinarias a la cultura maya*, ed. Andrés Ciudad Real, María Yolanda Fernández Marquínez, José Miguel García Campillo, Maria Josefa Iglesias Ponce de León, Alfonso Lacadena García Gallo, and Luis Tomás Sanz Castro, 275–296. Madrid: Sociedad Española de Estudios Mayas.

Houston, Stephen D., David Stuart, and Karl A. Taube. 2006. *The Memory of Bones: Body, Being, and Experience among the Classic Maya*. Austin: University of Texas Press.

Houston, Stephen D., and Karl A. Taube. 1987. "'Name Tagging' in Classic Maya Script." *Mexicon* 9(2):38–41.

Hull, Kerry M. 2003. "Verbal Art and Performance in Ch'orti' and Maya Hieroglyphic Writing." PhD diss., Department of Anthropology, University of Texas at Austin.

———. 2010. "An Epigraphic Analysis of Classic-Period Maya Foodstuffs." In *Pre-Columbian Foodways: Interdisciplinary Approaches to Food, Culture, and Markets in Ancient Mesoamerica*, ed. John E. Staller and Michael D. Carrasco, 235–256. New York: Springer.

Hurst, W. Jeffrey, Robert A. Martin, Stanley M. Tarka, and Grant D. Hall. 1989. "Authentication of Cocoa in Maya Vessels Using High-Performance Liquid Chromatographic Techniques." *Journal of Chromatography* 466:279–289.

Hurst, W. Jeffrey, Stanley M. Tarka, Terry G. Powis, Fred Valdez, and Thomas R. Hester. 2002. "Archaeology: Cacao Usage by the Earliest Maya Civilization." *Nature* 418(6895):289–290.

Joyce, Thomas A. 1933. "The Pottery Whistle-Figurines of Lubaantun." *Journal of the Royal Anthropological Institute of Great Britain and Ireland* 63:xv–xxv.

Kaufman, Terrence. 2003. *A Preliminary Mayan Etymological Dictionary*. FAMSI.org.

Kaufman, Terrence, and John Justeson. 2006. "The History of the Word for 'Cacao' and Related Terms in Ancient Meso-America." In *Chocolate in Mesoamerica: A Cultural History of Cacao*, ed. Cameron L. McNeil, 117–139. Gainesville: University Press of Florida.

Kerr, Barbara, and Justin Kerr, eds. 1989. *The Maya Vase Book: A Corpus of Rollout Photographs of Maya Vases*. Vol. 1. New York: Kerr Associates.

———. 1990. *The Maya Vase Book: A Corpus of Rollout Photographs of Maya Vases*. Vol. 2. New York: Kerr Associates.

———. 1992. *The Maya Vase Book: A Corpus of Rollout Photographs of Maya Vases*. Vol. 3. New York: Kerr Associates.

———. 1994. *The Maya Vase Book: A Corpus of Rollout Photographs of Maya Vases*. Vol. 4. New York: Kerr Associates.

———. 1997. *The Maya Vase Book: A Corpus of Rollout Photographs of Maya Vases*. Vol. 5. New York: Kerr Associates.

———. 2000. *The Maya Vase Book: A Corpus of Rollout Photographs of Maya Vases*. Vol. 6. New York: Kerr Associates.

Kettunen, Harri, and Christopher Helmke. 2019. *Introduction to Maya Hieroglyphs*. 7th ed. N.p.: Wayeb.

LeCount, Lisa J. 2010. "Ka'kaw Pots and Common Containers: Creating Histories and Collective Memories among the Classic Maya of Xunantunich, Belize." *Ancient Mesoamerica* 21(2):341–351. doi:10.1017/S095653611000026X.

Lentz, David L. 1991. "Maya Diets of the Rich and Poor: Paleoethnobotanical Evidence from Copan." *Latin American Antiquity* 2(3):269–287. doi:10.2307/972172.

———. 1999. "Plant Resources of the Ancient Maya: The Paleoethnobotanical Evidence." In *Reconstructing Ancient Maya Diet*, ed. Christine D. White, 3–18. Salt Lake City: University of Utah Press.

Loughmiller-Cardinal, Jennifer. 2018. "Distinguishing the Uses, Functions, and Purposes of Classic Maya 'Chocolate' Containers: Not All Cups Are for Drinking." *Ancient Mesoamerica* 30(1):1–18.

Love, Bruce. 1994. *The Paris Codex: Handbook for a Maya Priest*. Austin: University of Texas Press.

MacLeod, Barbara. 1990. "Deciphering the Primary Standard Sequence." PhD diss., Department of Anthropology, University of Texas at Austin.

———. n.d. "Celebrations in the Heart of the Mountain." *Bulletin of the Association for Mexican Cave Studies*. In press.

MacLeod, Barbara, and Andrea Stone. 1995. "The Hieroglyphic Inscriptions of Naj Tunich." In *Images from the Underworld: Naj Tunich and the Tradition of Maya Cave Painting*, by Andrea Stone, 155–184. Austin: University of Texas Press.

MacLeod, Barbara, and Brian Stross. 1990. "The Wing-Quincunx." *Journal of Mayan Linguistics* 7(1):14–27.

Macri, Martha J. 2005. "Nahua Loan Words from the Early Classic Period: Words for Cacao Preparation on a Río Azul Ceramic Vessel." *Ancient Mesoamerica* 16(2):321–326. doi:10.1017/S0956536105050200.

Martin, Simon. 2006. "Cacao in Ancient Maya Religion: First Fruit from the Maize Tree and Other Tales from the Underworld." In *Chocolate in Mesoamerica: A Cultural History of Cacao*, ed. Cameron McNeil, 154–183. Gainesville: University Press of Florida.

———. 2008. "Three Panels from La Corona?/Site Q K9126, K9127, K9128." Accessed December 31, 2018. mayavase.com/corona/La_Corona.html.

———. 2012. "Hieroglyphs from the Painted Pyramid: The Epigraphy of Chiik Nahb

Structure Sub 1-4, Calakmul, Mexico." In *Maya Archaeology 2*, ed. Charles Golden, Stephen Houston, and Joel Skidmore, 60–81. San Francisco: Precolumbia Mesoweb Press.

Masson, Marilyn A., and Carlos Peraza Lope. 2008. "Animal Use at the Postclassic Center of Mayapán." *Quaternary International* 191(1):170–183.

Mathews, Peter. 1979. "The Glyphs on the Ear Ornament from Tomb A-1/1." In *Excavations at Altun Ha, Belize, 1964–1970*, ed. David M. Pendergast, 79–80. Toronto, Ontario: Royal Ontario Museum.

Matsumoto, Mallory E. 2017. "From Sound to Symbol: Orthographic Semantization in Maya Hieroglyphic Writing." *Writing Systems Research* 9(2):99–122.

Mayer, Karl Herbert. 1987. *Maya Monuments: Sculptures of Unknown Provenance, Supplement 1*. Maya Monuments, Vol. 4. Berlin: Von Flemming.

———. 2009. "The Capstone 6 from Dzibilnocac, Campeche." *Mexicon* 31(4):77–83.

McNeil, Cameron L., W. Jeffrey Hurst, and Robert J. Sharer. 2006. "The Use and Representation of Cacao during the Classic Period at Copan, Honduras." In *Chocolate in Mesoamerica: A Cultural History of Cacao*, ed. Cameron L. McNeil, 224–252. Gainesville: University Press of Florida.

Miller, Arthur G. 1982. *On the Edge of the Sea: Mural Painting at Tancah-Tulum, Quintana Roo, Mexico*. Washington, DC: Dumbarton Oaks Research Library and Collection.

Miller, Mary Ellen, and Simon Martin. 2004. *Courtly Art of the Ancient Maya*. London: Thames and Hudson.

Millon, René F. 1955. "When Money Grew on Trees: A Study of Cacao in Ancient Mesoamerica." PhD diss., Faculty of Political Science, Columbia University.

Morehart, Christopher T. 2011. *Food, Fire and Fragrance: A Paleoethnobotanical Perspective on Classic Maya Cave Rituals*. BAR International Series 2186. Oxford: Archaeopress.

Motamayor, Juan C., A. M. Risterucci, P. A. Lopez, Carlos F. Ortiz, A. Moreno, and C. Lanaud. 2002. "Cacao Domestication I: The Origin of the Cacao Cultivated by the Mayas." *Heredity* 89(5):380–386.

Ogata, Nisao, Arturo Gómez-Pompa, and Karl A. Taube. 2006. "The Domestication and Distribution of *Theobroma cacao* L. in the Neotropics." In *Chocolate in Mesoamerica: A Cultural History of Cacao*, ed. Cameron L. McNeil, 69–89. Gainesville: University Press of Florida.

O'Neil, Megan E. 2012. *Engaging Ancient Maya Sculpture at Piedras Negras, Guatemala*. Norman: University of Oklahoma Press.

Piperno, D. R., and K. V. Flannery. 2001. "The Earliest Archaeological Maize (*Zea mays* L.) from Highland Mexico: New Accelerator Mass Spectrometry Dates and Their Implications." *Proceedings of the National Academy of Sciences* 98(4):2101–2103.

Prager, Christian M. 2018. "The Term 'Lima Bean Vessel' in the Classic Mayan Lexicon." *Research Note 11*. Bonn: Textdatenbank und Wörterbuch des Klassischen Maya. https://mayawoerterbuch.de/wp-content/uploads/2018/12/twkm_note_11.pdf.

Proskouriakoff, Tatiana. 1950. *A Study of Classic Maya Sculpture*. Washington, DC: Carnegie Institution.

Reents-Budet, Dorie. 1994. *Painting the Maya Universe: Royal Ceramics of the Classic Period*. Durham, NC: Duke University Press.

———. 1998. "Elite Maya Pottery and Artisans as Social Indicators." *Archaeological Papers of the American Anthropological Association* 8(1):71–89.
Robertson, Merle Greene. 1983. *The Sculpture of Palenque, Vol. I: The Temple of the Inscriptions*. Princeton: Princeton University Press.
Saturno, William, Karl A. Taube, and David Stuart. 2005. *The Murals of San Bartolo, El Petén, Guatemala, Part I: The North Wall*. Ancient America 7. Barnardsville, NC: Center for Ancient American Studies.
Schellhas, Paul. 1904. *Representation of Deities of the Maya Manuscripts*. Trans. Selma Wesselhoeft and A. M. Parker. 2nd ed. Papers of the Peabody Museum of American Archaeology and Ethnology, Vol. 4, No. 1. Cambridge, MA: Peabody Museum at Harvard University.
Scherer, Andrew K. 2015. *Mortuary Landscapes of the Classic Maya: Rituals of Body and Soul*. Austin: University of Texas Press.
Scherer, Andrew K., Lori E. Wright, and Cassady J. Yoder. 2007. "Bioarchaeological Evidence for Social and Temporal Differences in Diet at Piedras Negras, Guatemala." *Latin American Antiquity* 18(1):85–104. doi:10.2307/25063087.
Scholes, France V., and Ralph L. Roys. 1968. *The Maya-Chontal Indians of Acalan-Tixchel: A Contribution to the History and Ethnography of the Yucatan Peninsula*. Norman: University of Oklahoma Press.
Stone, Andrea J. 1995. *Images from the Underworld: Naj Tunich and the Tradition of Maya Cave Painting*. Austin: University of Texas Press.
Stone, Andrea, and Marc Zender. 2011. *Reading Maya Art: A Hieroglyphic Guide to Ancient Maya Painting and Sculpture*. New York: Thames and Hudson.
Stross, Brian. 1992. "Maize and Blood: Mesoamerican Symbolism on an Olmec Vase and a Maya Plate." *RES: Anthropology and Aesthetics* 22(Autumn):82–107.
Strupp Green, Judith. 2010. "Feasting with Foam: Ceremonial Drinks of Cacao, Maize, and Pataxte Cacao." In *Pre-Columbian Foodways: Interdisciplinary Approaches to Food, Culture, and Markets in Ancient Mesoamerica*, ed. John E. Staller and Michael D. Carrasco, 315–343. New York: Springer.
Stuart, David. 1987. *Ten Phonetic Syllables*. Research Reports on Ancient Maya Writing 14. Washington, DC: Center for Maya Research.
———. 1988. "The Río Azul Cacao Pot: Epigraphic Observations on the Function of a Maya Ceramic Vessel." *Antiquity* 62(234):153–157.
———. 1995. "A Study of Maya Inscriptions." PhD diss., Department of Anthropology, Vanderbilt University, Nashville, TN.
———. 2003. "On the Paired Variants of TZ'AK." *Mesoweb*. Accessed December 31, 2018. mesoweb.com/stuart/notes/tzak.pdf.
———. 2005a. "Glyphs on Pots: Decoding Classic Maya Ceramics." In *Sourcebook for the 29th Maya Meetings at Texas*, ed. David Stuart, 110–197. Austin: University of Texas at Austin.
———. 2005b. *The Inscriptions from Temple XIX at Palenque: A Commentary*. San Francisco: Pre-Columbian Art Research Institute.
———. 2006a. "Jade and Chocolate: Bundles of Wealth in Classic Maya Economics and Ritual." In *Sacred Bundles: Ritual Acts of Wrapping and Binding in Mesoamerica*, ed. Julia Guernsey and F. Kent Reilly III, 127–144. Barnardsville, NC: Boundary End Archaeology Research Center.
———. 2006b. "The Language of Chocolate: References to Cacao on Classic Maya

Drinking Vessels." In *Chocolate in Mesoamerica: A Cultural History of Cacao*, ed. Cameron McNeil, 184–201. Gainesville: University Press of Florida.
———. 2014. "The Chocolatier's Dog." *Maya Decipherment*. Accessed January 31, 2020. decipherment.wordpress.com/2014/03/26/the-chocolatiers-dog.
———. 2016. "Chili Vessels." *Maya Decipherment*. Accessed December 31, 2018. decipherment.wordpress.com/2016/03/24/chili-vessels.
Stuart, David S., Stephen D. Houston, and John S. Robertson. 1999. "Recovering the Past: Classic Maya Language and Classic Maya Gods." In *Notebook for the XXIIIrd Maya Hieroglyphic Forum at Texas*. Austin: Department of Art and Art History, the College of Fine Arts, and the Institute of Latin American Studies, University of Texas.
Taube, Karl. 1985. "The Classic Maya Maize God: A Reappraisal." In *Fifth Palenque Round Table, 1983*, ed. Virginia M. Fields, 7:171–181. San Francisco: Pre-Columbian Art Research Institute.
———. 1989. "The Maize Tamale in Classic Maya Diet, Epigraphy, and Art." *American Antiquity* 54(1):31–51.
———. 1996. "The Olmec Maize God: The Face of Corn in Formative Mesoamerica." *RES: Anthropology and Aesthetics* 29/30:39–81.
———. 2003. "Ancient and Contemporary Maya Conceptions about Field and Forest." In *The Lowland Maya Area: Three Millennia at the Human-Wildland Interface*, ed. Arturo Gómez-Pompa, Michael Allen, Scott Fedick, and Juan Jiménez-Osornio, 461–492. Binghamton, NY: Haworth Press.
———. 2005. "The Symbolism of Jade in Classic Maya Religion." *Ancient Mesoamerica* 16(1):23–50.
———. 2009. "The Maya Maize God and the Mythic Origins of Dance." In *The Maya and Their Sacred Narratives: Text and Context in Maya Mythologies*, ed. Geneviève Le Fort, Raphaël Gardiol, Sebastian Matteo, and Christophe Helmke, 41–52. Proceedings of the 12th European Maya Conference, Geneva, December 7–8, 2007. Markt Schwaben, Germany: Verlag Anton Saurwein.
Thomas, Cyrus. 1882. *A Study of the Manuscript Troano*. Vol. 5, *Contributions to North American Ethnology*. Washington, DC: Government Printing Office.
Thompson, J. Eric S. 1970. *Maya History and Religion*. Norman: University of Oklahoma Press.
Tokovinine, Alexandre. 2007. "Of Snake Kings and Cannibals: A Fresh Look at the Naranjo Hieroglyphic Stairway." *The PARI Journal* 7(4):15–22.
———. 2013. *Place and Identity in Classic Maya Narratives*. Studies in Pre-Columbian Art and Archaeology, No. 37. Washington, DC: Dumbarton Oaks Research Library and Collection.
———. 2014. "Beans and Glyphs: A Possible IB Logogram in the Classic Maya Script." *The PARI Journal* 14(4):10–16.
———. 2016. "'It Is His Image with Pulque': Drinks, Gifts, and Political Networking in Classic Maya Texts and Images." *Ancient Mesoamerica* 27(1):13–29.
Tokovinine, Alexandre, and Dmitri Beliaev. 2013. "People of the Road: Traders and Travelers in Ancient Maya Words and Images." In *Merchants, Markets, and Exchange in the Pre-Columbian World*, ed. Kenneth G. Hirth and Joanne Pillsbury, 169–200. Washington, DC: Dumbarton Oaks Research Library and Collection.

Tokovinine, Alexandre, and Vilma Fialko. 2007. "Stela 45 of Naranjo and the Early Classic Lords of Sa'aal." *The PARI Journal* 7(4):1–14.

Tozzer, Alfred M. 1941. *Landa's Relación de las cosas de Yucatán: A Translation*. Papers of the Peabody Museum of American Archaeology and Ethnology, Vol. 18. Cambridge, MA: Peabody Museum at Harvard University.

Trejo-Gonzalez, Augusto, Alejandro Feria-Morales, and Carlos Wild-Altamirano. 1982. "The Role of Lime in the Alkaline Treatment of Corn for Tortilla Preparation." In *Modification of Proteins: Food, Nutritional, and Pharmacological Aspects*, ed. Robert E. Feeney and John R. Whitaker, 245–263. Washington, DC: American Chemical Society.

Tuxill, John, Luis Arias Reyes, Luis Latournerie Moreno, Vidal Cob Uicab, and Devra I. Jarvis. 2010. "All Maize Is Not Equal: Maize Variety Choices and Mayan Foodways in Rural Yucatan, Mexico." In *Pre-Columbian Foodways: Interdisciplinary Approaches to Food, Culture, and Markets in Ancient Mesoamerica*, ed. John E. Staller and Michael D. Carrasco, 467–486. New York: Springer.

Wellhausen, E. J., L. M. Roberts, and E. Hernández X. 1952. *Races of Maize in Mexico: Their Origin, Characteristics and Distribution*. Cambridge, MA: Bussey Institution of Harvard University.

White, Christine D., David M. Pendergast, Fred J. Longstaffe, and Kimberley R. Law. 2001. "Social Complexity and Food Systems at Altun Ha, Belize: The Isotopic Evidence." *Latin American Antiquity* 12(4):371–393. doi:10.2307/972085.

Zender, Marc U. 1999. "Diacritical Marks and Underspelling in the Classic Maya Script: Implications for Decipherment." Master's thesis, Department of Archaeology, University of Calgary.

———. 2000. "A Study of Two Uaxactun-Style Tamale Serving Vessels." In *The Maya Vase Book: A Corpus of Rollout Photographs of Maya Vases*, ed. Barbara Kerr and Justin Kerr, 6:1038–1055. New York: Kerr Associates.

———. 2014. "On the Reading of Three Classic Maya Portrait Glyphs." *The PARI Journal* 15(2):1–14.

CHAPTER 5

Plant Foodstuffs of the Ancient Maya: Agents and Matter, Medium and Message

SHANTI MORELL-HART

From *Fighting with Food* (Young 1971) to *Feasts* (Dietler and Hayden 2001), anthropological literature has long demonstrated the active social role of food, as substance as much as symbol. Foodstuffs create obligation, bind people together, mark differences, ritualize practice, and incentivize social movement. In the ancient Maya area, alongside faunal and mineral ingredients, botanical foodstuffs occupied special positions. Beyond basic nutritional building blocks, plants were active agents in large-scale terraforming projects (Dunham et al. 2009), fickle ingredients in long-distance trade (Batún Alpuche 2009), and central figures in large-scale ceremonial feasts and ritual offerings (McNeil 2009). They were also key players in incantations found in *Ritual of the Bacabs: A Book of Maya Incantations* (Roys 1965 [1779]), a colonial document transcribed from oral traditions. Aside from these loftier stations, even day-to-day botanical activities served to reinforce or overturn social norms through the medium of food collection, preparation, consumption, and conceptualization. Social messages were ingested as much as they were transformed and maintained through ingestion.

In spite of the critical role of botanical ingredients, food studies in the Maya area have tended to focus on durable actors and elements, including faunal remains such as shark teeth and deer bones (see Brown and Freiwald, this volume; Cunningham-Smith et al., this volume), or nondurable actors that nonetheless leave durable co-actors behind, as in the case of ceramics used in salt production (McKillop and Sills 2017). The presumed perishability and thus invisibility of many plant foods has been challenged by a mounting body of evidence in the form of phytoliths, pollen, starch grains, seeds, wood, and even chemical residues (see Spenard et al., this volume). Here, I draw on this diverse set of botanical residues to consider the doings of plant agents in ancient Maya societies. I use published work by other scholars, as well as paleoethnobotanical data I've collected from multiple sites throughout the Maya Lowlands. Botanical residues reveal that food plants were manipulated for social ends as frequently as they actively manipulated the worlds around them. Drawing from the writings of Charles Saunders Peirce, Marshall McLuhan, and Mary Weismantel, among others, I also consider how foods operated simultaneously as icons, indices, and symbols, often independently of human intentions and sometimes in opposition to them.

Although colleagues and I have previously documented the role of economic plants in ancient Mesoamerican societies, and particularly in Mesoamerican foodways (Farahani et al. 2017; Morehart and Morell-Hart 2015; Morell-Hart 2005, 2011, 2015a, 2015b; Morell-Hart, Joyce, and Henderson 2014; Morell-Hart et al. 2019; Morell-Hart, Dine, et al. 2018; Morell-Hart, Watson, et al. 2018), this review is intended to recast plants as more active players in cuisine, landscape, and society. I foreground the utility of posthumanist approaches in this endeavor. The strength of a posthumanist approach in Maya archaeology is not simply to "add value" to things—such as ancient plant foods—but rather to grant them active roles; to blur the boundaries between strict human and nonhuman categories. Foods and plants represent "a materiality that materializes" (Coole and Frost 2010:9); they are actants "within an agentic assemblage that includes ... metabolism, cognition, and moral sensibility" (Bennett 2007:145). Such views of food are borne out in evidence from ancient Maya communities as much as from contemporary societies around the world. This framing is complementary to (and sometimes overlaps with) other frameworks such as historical ecology; relational approaches; political economy; and diverse theorizations of landscape, semiotics, and practice. Many of these approaches take for granted the notion that food is more than subsistence; that human-environmental connections are dynamic; and that "people don't eat species, they eat meals" (Sherratt 1991:1).

How Did Ancient Maya People Socialize Food Plants?

When it comes to ancient Maya foods, we cannot even take edibility for granted. "Food"—not simply a biological given—is part social construction, molded by individual tastes and preferences. What is potentially edible is not always regarded as food (Fischler 1980:940; Soler 1997 [1973]:55), and furthermore, what is considered "food" is not always

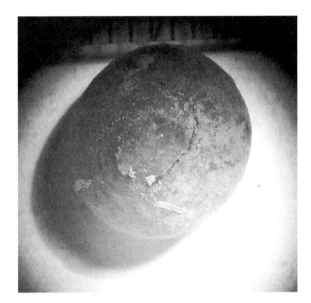

Figure 5.1.
Ramón (Brosimum alicastrum) fruit recovered from the site of Río Amarillo, Honduras. Photo by the author.

technically edible. People throughout the ancient Maya world would have had to negotiate the human "omnivore's paradox," a sort of double bind in which, when confronted with new foods, we are torn between feelings of neophobia (fear of unknown and potentially harmful foods) and neophilia (attraction to unknown and novel foods; Fischler 1980). In the contemporary Maya area, the nutritious and flavor-neutral *ramón* fruit (*Brosimum alicastrum*) is frequently cited as solely a famine food, if eaten at all, while the wicked-looking and stinging *chaya* plant (*Cnidoscolus* spp.) is consumed far and wide. Friar Diego de Landa claimed in 1566 that northern Maya people consumed *ramón* (*ox*) "on occasion," implying some degree of frequency, but to date I have recovered only a single charred fruit out of approximately four hundred samples from across the Maya region (Figure 5.1; Morell-Hart 2015b), while other researchers have had slightly better luck with wood charcoal (Dussol et al. 2017).

What makes some food plants fine to consume and others inedible? That is, if there are unquestioned food taken-for-granteds—the *doxic* marking of food that is "good to think" and "good to eat"—then how did these practices, ingredients, and recipes initially make their way into Maya society? The aesthetics of taste, as Farrington and Urry (1985:154) argue, could be responsible for the first practices of cultivation, a position that runs counter to arguments favoring simple "staple crop" caloric maximization and diet optimization (see Boone and Smith 1998:153). When applied to the Maya area, beyond obvious condiments such as pepperleaf (*Piper auritum*) and chile peppers (*Capsicum* spp.; Figure 5.2), this raises the possibility that the emergence of key staple crops such as maize, beans, and squash was tied more closely to their flavors than to their caloric content.

Furthermore, what made some food plants prized luxuries, while others languished as unremarkable or low valued? And under what conditions did quotidian foods become highly prized, in some cases becoming sumptuary or commodified? Food plants such as cacao (*Theobroma cacao*) were frequently incorporated into Classic Maya ritual practice and funerary contexts (Beliaev, Davletshin, and Tokovinine 2009; Carter and Matsumoto, this volume; Hall et al. 1990; McNeil 2006, 2009; Prufer and Hurst 2007), as well as widely traded inter- and intra-regionally (Crown and Hurst 2009; Harrison-Buck 2017). Political models have framed cacao as an elite-controlled ritual foodstuff or market commodity (e.g., McAnany 1995), with some limited use as currency (Stuart 2006), while other models frame the emergence of cacao in terms of dowries, bride wealth, and principles of descent and lineage formation (e.g., Harrison-Buck 2017). Such arguments have also been applied to a variety of wetland agricultural commodities (Fedick 2017; Guderjan et al. 2017) that generally receive less scholarly attention. In the case of agricultural surplus products such as maize, some scholars have argued that their value was stored in imperishable tokens and currencies such as jade, copper, and stone axes (Freidel and Reilly 2010:64). Whatever the contingencies, it is likely that

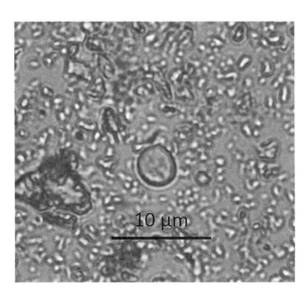

Figure 5.2. Chile pepper (*Capsicum annuum*) starch grain recovered from the sonicated residue of a mano, Piedras Negras, Guatemala. Photo by the author.

 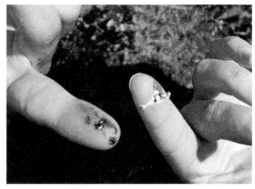

Figure 5.3. (L) Nopal cactus (*Opuntia* sp.) edible "pad" (stem) with cochineal insect webbing; (R) crushed cochineal insects and carmine color used in dyes. Photos by the author.

cacao and maize, like other botanical foodstuffs, came to be valued differently from community to community and household to household as they traveled along the numerous pathways described above.

Historically, trajectories of valued plant agents have taken convoluted routes. Although the earliest consumption practices related to cacao in the Formative period seemed to have primarily involved the fruit (Joyce and Henderson 2007), the seed of cacao came to be more greatly prized in later Classic period beverages across the Maya area. (Cacao has been a primary scholarly focus, but similar arguments could be made for maize, perhaps also first consumed in fermented beverages.) Hyperprized food plants such as cacao—operating as gifts, commodities, and trade goods—not only reflected social relations (Graeber 2001; Mauss 1954) but also actively shifted over time. Such shifts could be the movement of staple food to surplus product to regularly traded commodity, or rare commodity to frequently consumed to staple food. These movements were necessarily tied to broader relationships between home gardens and markets noted by Fedick (2017), Sheets (2000), and others.

Beyond their subsistence value, food plants were also critical components in the production of valuable trade products. As documented at Cozumel by Batún Alpuche (2009), various flowering plants (including food plants) were used to attract bees for apiculture, an activity also widely documented in the Maya area in contemporary times (Imre 2010; Rico-Gray, Chemás, and Mandujano 1991; Vail and Dedrick, this volume). This is also the case for the edible prickly pear cactus (*Opuntia* spp.) used in cochineal production (Figure 5.3; Baron 2018:104; Bricker and Miram 2002).

Whether common or luxury, staple or commodity for ancient communities, in the archaeological record some Maya plant foods appear as more frequent social actors, while others appear much less frequently. A cast of common characters have been recovered from Maya archaeological sites, including staples like maize (Figure 5.4) and fruits such as the *sapote* (*Manilkara* sp.). Then there are infrequent players, as in the case of presumed staple crops such as beans (*Phaseolus* spp.) and presumed luxury crops like cacao (see Fernández Souza, Zimmermann, and Jiménez Álvarez, this volume). There are also surprising absences, such as papaya (*Carica papaya*) and the highly prized vanilla (*Vanilla planifolia*). In some cases, these "absences" are directly related to archaeological visibility. A plant like the vanilla orchid leaves behind no diagnostic phytoliths or starch grains, and has seeds so tiny they would be extraordinarily difficult to recover using flotation or wet sieving. In such instances, valued food plants may be visible if they persist as chemical signatures (see Spenard et al., this volume) or as relict stands of plants that have persevered for centuries (Ross 2008). Such is likely the case with the thick vanilla vines currently growing in profusion around the central cenote of the archaeological site of T'isil (Fedick, Mathews, and Sorensen 2012). Although this type of relict evidence carries its own analytical pitfalls (see Miksicek et al. 1981; Ross 2008), sometimes it may be the only evidence available for the ancient cultivation and use of otherwise invisible plants. For extended discussions of botanical residue

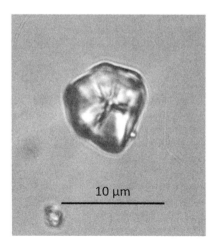
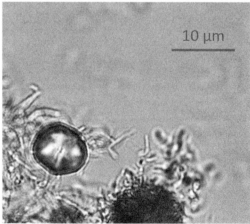

Figure 5.4. (L) Maize (*Zea mays*) starch grains recovered from the sonicated residue of human tooth calculus (Piedras Negras, Guatemala) and (R) the sonicated residue of an obsidian blade fragment (Río Amarillo, Honduras). Photos by the author.

preservation and archaeological visibility, see Miksicek (1987), Pearsall (2015), Piperno (2006), and VanDerwarker, Alvarado, and Webb (2015).

The variation in botanical visibility nonetheless belies the values some plants carried and the extent to which Maya people actively negotiated their social and natural environments to incorporate novel plants into their foodways. However much a given food plant was prized, we see a complicated dance between perishability, processing regimes, geographical habitat, relative shortages and harvest quantities, the value of food plants in local cuisines, necessity in ritual practices, modes of transport, distances to market, and prices of acquisition. The values of individual food plants thus represented heterogeneous socialization across diverse contexts and with diverse actors; they were not a roster of intrinsic values that were defined homogeneously across ancient Maya marketplaces.

How Did Food Plants Socialize Ancient Maya People?

To turn the coin: how did food plants socialize Maya people? Posthumanist approaches that foreground the agency of plants prove helpful in such understandings. If we follow the arguments of scholars like Michael Pollan (2001:xiii), food plants such as maize have used human societies for millennia, effectively domesticating human beings to facilitate propagation: "Through trial and error [domesticated] plant species have found that the best way to [reproduce themselves] is to induce animals—bees or people, it hardly matters—to spread their genes." Such perspectives are in the minority, and in archaeology, only a handful of scholars exploring alternate ontologies have considered plants as actants (e.g., Hastorf 2017:3–4; Van der Veen 2014). More commonly, scholars explore the agency of plants primarily through the myriad ways that people socialize other people using plants. This may take place in the context of politically charged feasting (e.g., Ardren, this volume; Brown and Freiwald, this volume; Dietler 1996; Goldstein and Hageman 2009; Lamoureux-St-Hilaire, this volume; LeCount 2001) or socially charged daily practice (Allison 2013 [1991]; Bourdieu 1984 [1979]; Lentz, Lane, and Thompson 2014). Some scholars in the Maya area have cast the agency of plants in a semi-active sort of way, either as a dynamic factor in daily or ritual life (Morehart and Butler 2010) or as the floral component of an active landscape (Ford and Nigh 2009, 2010). It takes only a small nudge to these arguments to see how—in the household, feast, or landscape—food plants dynamically impacted human societies and were active agents in their own right.

In the broader anthropological literature, we have a robust history of granting agency to nonhuman entities, networks, and assemblages (Appadurai 1988; Hodder 2011; Knappett and Malafouris 2008; Latour 2005; Miller 2005; Taylor 2008). Studies of subsistence are among the easiest and most obvious routes to challenge the exceptionality of human agency, given that eating is shared by all creatures, and all creatures need to eat to survive. Moreover, food is composed of substances that both transform human beings and are transformed by them, in the material sense as well as the symbolic. Foods, plants, and food plants have the power to effect heterodoxy and orthodoxy. People bend over backward to accommodate plants—not only to get them to germinate and survive but to thrive and produce a robust harvest.

What might be the utility of posthumanist approaches in foodways studies generally and Maya plant food studies in particular? First, a general argument can be made for broadening modes of understanding, introducing novel perspectives, and addressing alterity, especially when considering the human as "a non-fixed and mutable condition" (Ferrando 2013: 27). Second, we can consider the breakdown between food technology, matter, and the human self, as Donna Haraway (1991) has done in defining cyborgs and human-technological hybrids. In this case, we could consider the transformation and incorporation of substances such as maize *atole* through consumption (Bennett 2007). Third, following Coole and Frost (2010:7), among others, we can rewrite matter as a process of materialization, not something static, fixed, or passive (Ferrando 2013:27). Similar arguments have been made by Bennett (2007, 2009) in considering the vibrant and even "vagabond" nature of matter, as food "reveals materiality's instability, vagrancy, activeness" (2007:136) through impacts on a broader assemblage of actors and forces—along with transformation through ingestion. Fourth, these attentions to matter allow us to critically evaluate "sustainable" plant food practices in the Maya area, whether in the present or the past. To quote Ferrando (2013.32): "The way humans inhabit this planet, what they eat, how they behave, what relations they entertain, creates the network of who and what they are: it is not a disembodied network, but (also) a material one, whose agency exceeds the political, social, and biological" (similar to Coole and Frost 2010:4 and Bennett 2007, 2009).

These last two points are critical when we consider the relationships between plant foods and ancient Maya communities and our contemporary understandings of sustainability and resilience. In the context of the so-called Maya collapse (Aimers 2007; Wright and White 1996), posthumanist perspectives help us counter Jared Diamond–style narratives—stories that push us toward geographic determinism on the one hand yet a societal "choice" to fail or succeed on the other. Many studies have already countered these arguments, portraying ancient Maya people as neither fallible idiots nor greedy overconsumers in the face of widespread agricultural troubles. Rather, they are shown to be frequently creative and cautious stewards who negotiated forces sometimes outside their control (Fedick 1996; Ford and Nigh 2009; McAnany and Gallareta Negrón 2009; McNeil, Burney, and Pigott Burney 2010).

Maya food plants are well-represented in models of environmental shifts, emergence of food crises, and warfare related to dietary duress (Aimers and Hodell 2011; Lentz 2001; Zarger 2009), but they are generally cast as passive objects manipulated by Maya societies and subject to broader environmental forces. Posthumanist approaches provide complementary and sometimes parallel perspectives. Such approaches foreground crop plants like maize as active actors in broad human-environmental networks instead of isolated dependents on humans or failed agricultural crops resulting from poor human choices. Plant foods are unstable and active materials, entangled in broader foodways and wider environments. Crops are always becoming. Feasts are always becoming. Their materiality is not a product but a process, with a limited fixity that is constantly subjected to environmental and social winds, and simultaneously contributing to socio-environmental trajectories. The search for staple foodstuffs was the impetus for migration, in some cases, while the pursuit of sumptuary foods such as cacao and annatto led to trade and even bloodshed (Caso Barrera and Aliphat Fernández 2006; Kaplan et al. 2017:532). Luxury food plants such as vanilla thus participated in their own materialization, directing human intentions and activities in a number of ways.

Homelands and Botanical Itineraries

Classic Maya plant foods were interconnected with broader ecologies just as assemblages of plant foods can be placed in broader contexts of ritualized activities and quotidian practices. The notion of transported landscapes (Berman and Pearsall 2008; Siegel et al. 2015) represents an excellent example of one way that plants socialized people, who in turn sought to replicate plant relationships in new territories. At the core of this idea is the premise that people re-create homeland environments by moving familiar biota to new habitats, to "produce predictability, ensure comfort, and provide a preferred diet in their new surroundings" (Berman and Pearsall 2008:181). In this model, human colonizers transferred "portmanteau biota" (Crosby 1986) from ancestral homelands, along with cultural practices including "plant knowledge, food preparation techniques, and cuisine," and applied these practices to new settings (Berman and Pearsall 2008:182).

Although this phenomenon has been more extensively documented in island contexts such as the Caribbean and South Pacific (Rick et al. 2013), we also have ample evidence of transported landscapes in the Maya area. At the level of individual ingredients, we can simply track the itineraries of various foodstuffs into the Maya landscape. Maize was first domesticated in the Balsas region of central Mexico (Piperno et al. 2009), while domesticated beans and squash have multiple origin points, both in Mesoamerica and South America. Chocolate (*Theobroma cacao*) may have been brought from the Amazon basin to Mesoamerica prior to domestication, then domesticated in Mesoamerica (Clement et al. 2010). Of the palms, the domesticated peach palm (*Bactris* sp.) likely arrived from South America (Clement et al. 2010), while the *cocoyol* (*Acrocomia* spp.) probably came from Brazil (Lanes et al. 2014), and the *cohune* (*Attalea cohune*) seems to have been originally distributed along only the Pacific coast of Mexico and into Central America (Lentz 2000). Three frequently consumed *chaya* varietals, autochthonous as wild versions in many parts of southeastern Mesoamerica, represent domesticated versions that are not only varietals but clones of the same original plant. These *chaya* plants had to be transported directly across the Maya landscape as cuttings, as they only reproduce vegetatively rather than through seed plantings (McKey et al. 2010; Ross-Ibarra and Molina-Cruz 2002). Domesticated *chaya* plants generally have low archaeological visibility, but root material was tentatively identified in raised fields in Belize (Hather and Hammond 1994; Miksicek 1983).

Important root and tuber crops also emerged in other locations and spread to the Maya area. The roles of these crops have shifted in models of Maya foodways, from occasional ingredient (Turner and Miksicek 1984; Fernández Souza, Zimmermann, Jiménez Álvarez, this volume) to a potentially extensively cultivated staple (Sheets et al. 2012). Regardless, increasing evidence indicates their importance in quotidian and feast foods across ancient southeastern Mesoamerica (Bronson 1966; Hather and Hammond 1994; Lentz, Dunning, and Scarborough 2015; Morell-Hart 2011; Sheets et al. 2012; Simms, Berna, and Bey 2013; Trabanino García and Liendo Stuardo 2012; Turner and Miksicek 1984). So where did these starchy ingredients originate? Sweet potato (*Ipomoea batatas*) may have had two separate points of domestication: Mesoamerica and South

America, though these two gene pools subsequently became entangled at various points in human history (Roullier et al. 2013). Manioc (*Manihot esculenta*) appears to have been domesticated in the Amazon basin, the home of its closest wild relative, then moved north (Olsen and Schaal 2001).

Even in this abbreviated list, we see the movement of prized food plants on the landscape into new homes, then the duplication of successful efforts across the Maya region. All of these ingredients, at one time foreign to some part of the Maya area, eventually made their way into the heart (and soul) of the Maya world. Some may have begun as trade novelties and sumptuary items, but eventually many were planted—sometimes as full assemblages of nonautochthonous plants—by Maya people looking to reconstruct homelands both nearby and distant. This recasts food taxa as active agents in the formulations of landscape, effectively bending people to their needs. Humans in these cases served plants by providing free passage and tending to their needs before serving those same plants as food.

Management of Plants and Management for Plants

When novel plants made their way into the Maya area—or autochthonous plants came to be highly prized—people invested heavily in landscape modification and management to make plants comfortable in their homes. Lentz, Dunning, and Scarborough (2015) discuss the construction of plant niches at Tikal through intensive landscape investment, while Ford and Nigh (2009, 2010) have addressed the management of specific wild plant resources through agroforestry and other tending practices. In my own work, I have recovered evidence of nondomesticated species across the Maya area, at the sites of Río Amarillo (Honduras), T'isil (Mexico), and Piedras Negras (Guatemala). Such plant foods have included sorrel (*Oxalis* spp.), hoja santa (*Piper auritum*), and various palm (Arecaceae) fruits. Evidence of nondomesticated plant foods has also been documented by other scholars (Lentz et al. 1996) and corroborated by faunal remains of nondomesticated species (Emery 2002). The presence of nondomesticated species in cultural contexts indexes an engagement with the environment that is not predicated entirely on agriculture or even adventitious gathering during hunting and fuel collection. The frequent presence of noncultivated plants indicates that plants sometimes got people to make special trips to collect them.

Beyond moving and maintaining plant ingredients on the landscape, we have ample evidence of ancient Maya people constructing special facilities and tools to support food production, processing, storage, and serving. Plant food storage, as discussed by a roster of authors (Fedick 2017; Lamoureux-St-Hilaire, this volume; Miksicek et al. 1981; Puleston 1971; Sheets 1998, 2000), involved construction or modification of specialized facilities such as underground *chultunes* or aboveground cribs. Some preservation of plant foods required the acquisition of other materials, a few of which (e.g., salt and honey) were costly relative to more distant areas where the food preservation was taking place (Fedick 2017). Other preservation materials were relatively cheap, accessible, and widespread (e.g., wood for smoking), as discussed by Reina and Hill (1980).

Even the most basic kitchen setup would have involved an array of culinary equipment to help process plant foods (Farahani et al. 2017), including obsidian blades, hearths, metates, wooden implements, gourd containers, and ceramic vessels. Plant foods pushed people to mold ceramics for particular purposes—frothing chocolate, grating salsas, serving maize tamales in royal courts, and warming tuber soups (see Ardren, this volume; Simms et al. 2013). Plant foods also required people to be particular about obsidian blades, a type of kitchen tool that was ubiquitous across the Maya area and used by all social classes, though obsidian is found as a resource in only a few regions. Moreover, preparing plant foods using all this culinary equipment—from grinding maize on metates, to constructing a stone *piib* roasting pit, to carefully feeding fuel into a three-stone hearth—would have required the training of budding cooks and servers (O'Connor and Anderson 2016).

As Allison (2013 [1991]) has revealed, it's not always a question of socializing people to negotiate food properly, but rather of negotiating food properly to socialize people. Such acculturation through food has taken many forms (Allison 2013 [1991]; Hastorf 2017; Weismantel 1988; Young 1971:41). In the Maya area, learning how to get two snacks out of a single *cocoyol* palm fruit (Figure 5.5), how to nixtamalize maize properly, and how to eat the safe part of the *guapinol* bean pod (Figure 5.6) were all practices that passed on knowledge of plants through formal and informal training. But this training also socialized and acculturated learners in ways that went beyond simply attaching knowledge to plants. Such acculturation inculcated, maintained, or transformed identity through age-appropriate tasks, gender-specific activities, and status-related practices—all tailored to particular plants and botanical foodstuffs. These processes thus impli-

Figure 5.5. Two snacks in one from the *cocoyol* palm fruit (*Acrocomia mexicana*): (L) edible yellow mesocarp (tastes of butter) and (R) hard endosperm (tastes of coconut). Photos by the author.

Figure 5.6. The *guapinol* (*Hymenaea courbaril*) fruit (L) and seed (R). The edible portion is not the pericarp (pod) or the seeds (beans), but rather the edible powdery pulp. It tastes somewhat of yeast, lending it the English name "stinkingtoe." *Guapinol* trees currently grow near Copán, Honduras, and one seed has been recovered archaeologically by Guy Hepp at the Formative period site of La Consentida in coastal Oaxaca (Bérubé, Hepp, and Morell-Hart 2020). Photos by the author.

cated plant foods themselves as actants in the human performance and interpretation of identity.

How Did Maya Food Plants Operate as Media?

As many scholars have demonstrated, the selection of plant foods for ancient Maya people went beyond personal preference or biological necessity to encompass an array of social dimensions. So what sorts of things do we see "written" in the food medium instead of paint or stone? Food plants were loci that encoded multiple shifting messages, in a heterotopic sense (Foucault 1986). Maya plant foods were used in ritualized practices as well as in quotidian meals, with differences marked in temporality, context, and assemblage. For example, although compositionally almost identical, corn tortillas and corn tamales occupy very different positions in terms of form, manner of preparation, labor invested, and symbolic importance (Brumfiel 1991; García Barrios 2017; see also Carter and Matsumoto, this volume). Maya food plants bore different messages in sometimes identical matters, whether or not these matters were interpreted the same way over time or space, or from individual to individual.

David Sutton (2001:5) claims that "anthropological work has produced a broad consensus that food is about commensality—eating to make friends—and competition—eating to make enemies." As Young (1971) and Weismantel (1988) point out, food, and by implication the labor connected with it, holds potential as a means of social control and social mediation. Relations of domination and resistance can be expressed through food practices, just as food symbols can be used in ideological discourse.

In the Maya area, feasting is the most common route to explore commensality and ideology in the food medium. Many scholars start with the work of Michael Dietler (1996), who categorizes different feasts by the most prominent role that each plays: entrepreneurial feasts (empowerment), patron/role feasts (legitimation based on quantity), and diacritical feasts (legitimation based on style). As Linda Brown and Andrea Gerstle describe in their discussion of feasting at Joya de Cerén (2002), the creation of a feast has very recognizable material correlates. It takes special objects and spaces to prepare and present necessary feast items, not just specialized foodstuffs. In other ancient Maya communities, these aspects may have played into maintenance of relations, transformations of relations, and the general movement and shoring up of social capital (see Ardren, this volume; Brown and Freiwald, this volume; Lamoureux-St-Hilaire, this volume). At the household level, this could have been expressed in the form of preferential seating; earlier serving; more numerous courses; or serving food that was expensive, labor-intensive, or more concentrated (following Appadurai 1981). For the Maya area, Reents-Budet (2006:202) has even gone so far as to call banquets "the cornerstone and focal point of an elite economic system based on feasting with its concomitant gift giving that included both basic commodities and luxury goods."

Feasting took place in all sectors of ancient Maya society, but it varied in terms of opulence and scale. Regardless, the plant foods incorporated into the feast—from achiote to maize—would have been the medium through which relations were maintained or transformed, and social capital would have been amassed. It is no accident that foodstuffs are almost ubiquitous in scenes of courtly Maya life (Figure 5.7). Such scenes frequently depict maize tamales on platters, drinks served in cylindrical vessels, and additional unmarked foodstuffs. These provisions were placed adjacent to and underneath royal benches, perhaps as welcoming snacks for visiting dignitaries but likely also as conspicuous markers of abundance.

Food was also a dynamic medium in more spiritual matters. As Appadurai (1981:496) notes, food is sometimes thought to be "the fundamental link between men and gods." In the Maya area, plant food offerings were a common part of ritualized practice in pre-Columbian times (Brown and Gerstle 2002; McAnany 1995; Morehart and Butler 2010; Spenard et al., this volume) as much as in historic and contemporary times (Caso Barrera and Aliphat Fernández 2006). In the sacred *Book of Chilam Balam of Chumayel*, the sweet potato is identified specifically as an item among the four sets of objects belonging to the "Four Quarters of the World" (Roys 1967 [1933]:63), suggesting its importance in the cosmological as well as the quotidian realm. Included in Landa's list of flora ingredients are *Lonchocarpus* roots used in the preparation of *balche'* drinks for ceremonies (see also Vail and Dedrick, this volume). *Sakha'* is used as a spiritual drink "for a wide variety of ceremonies such as field clearing, sowing maize, maize growing, watermelon ceremonies, sowing beans, harvesting of honey, hunting, bad winds, and new house dedication" (Gabriel 2004:160, cited in Hull 2010:246). Work at Colha (Powis et al. 2002) and Río Azul (Hall et al. 1990) has confirmed the use of cacao in ritualized practice through residue analyses of several burial-context vessels. Various authors (Brown and Gerstle 2002; Brown and Freiwald, this volume; Hall et al. 1990; Morehart 2001, 2004; Powis et al. 2002) have identified a number of plant food taxa acting in ritual contexts outside of burials, including cacao, achiote, squash seeds, palms, and maize. However, although their presence indicates their special importance in Maya foodways, like sweet potatoes, all these plants were also commonly consumed. Moreover, food plants acted in ritualized practice in a number of ways (buried with the dead; burned in offerings; invoked in *Ritual of the Bacabs*, the sacred Maya text transcribed in the eighteenth century) but were not necessarily physically consumed by participants (see Morehart and Butler 2010 and the "fourth obligation"). In all of these cases, plant food was a medium through which the living communed with the supernatural.

Ingesting hallucinogenic plants would seem a more obvious medium through which to commune with the divine, but actual botanical evidence of such plants remains scant in the Maya area. Hallucinogenic plants such as the water lily, jimson weed, and the morning glory may have been used, but in spite of optimism expressed by some scholars (Dobkin de Rios 1974), the botanical evidence remains scant (though see also Spenard et al., this volume, on chemical signatures of *Datura*). To date, no macrobotanical or microbotanical elements with hallucinogenic properties have been recovered in the detritus of ritual contexts. However, tobacco (*Nicotiana* spp.), a plant with limited psychoactive properties, makes an occasional appearance at lowland Maya sites (Dedrick 2013) and nearby (Morell-Hart, Joyce, and Henderson 2014; Morell-Hart et al. 2019). Tobacco, though primarily inhaled through smoking, was also ingested as a tea (see below) and has been cited as a medium of magical protection when applied to tamale pots "to ensure that the food turns out well; if not, it is said that half of the tamales will come out well-cooked, while the other half remains raw" (Groark 2010:20).

We can also consider how social meanings were invoked differently through different senses, using a variety of substances and materials (Hastorf 2017; Hurcombe 2007; Ouzman 2001; Sutton 2013). Some scholars highlight the importance of the sight, smell, and taste of food, which can draw out the senses and generate remembering (Hamilakis 1999, Sutton 2013). Yannis Hamilakis has emphasized the importance of studies of food aesthetics, as "food consumption is primarily an act of incorporation which involves emotions, pleasures and feelings" (1999:39). Plant food aesthetics in the Maya area took on many dimensions. We could consider the seasonings and condiments used to flavor foods, and the specific pungency of some plant foods such as epazote (*Chenopodium ambrosoides*) or achiote (*Bixa orellana*), documented at sites such as Copán (Lentz 1991b), Joya de Cerén (Brown and Gerstle 2002), and in my own work at Piedras Negras. Olfactory sensations would have included the scents of

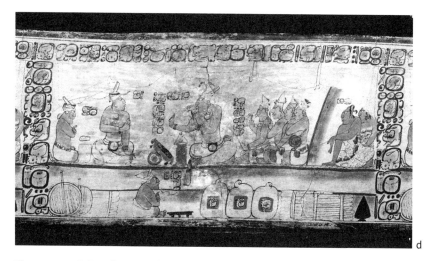

d

Figures 5.7a–d. Courtly scenes featuring plant foodstuffs, from rollout images of Classic period cylindrical vessels. Opposite, from top to bottom: Figure 5.7a, K1775: ruler receives offerings in the form of vases and bowls, tamales are underneath/next to thrones; Figure 5.7b, K8001: two panels with rulers on thrones, tamales are underneath/next to thrones; Figure 5.7c, K504: lord presents offering in vessel to deities, and maize tamales and *atole* are represented, with other foods depicted underneath/next to thrones. Above: Figure 5.7d, K2914: ruler with attendants, holding flowers, perhaps in marriage negotiation, and the tribute underneath/next to throne includes three bags of cacao beans. All images by Justin Kerr, used with permission.

food cooking, the smoke of the hearth fire, and the smell of freshly sliced guavas. Frequent sounds would have included cacao beans cracking as they toasted, maize being ground on the metate, and beans bubbling over the hearth. Such smells and sounds may have symbolized special occasions, produced slightly altered states, or simply indexed "home."

Across the board, it is evident that plant foodstuffs served as distinct media and sometimes the singular medium to convey a variety of messages—from person to person, household to household, community to deity. Plant food was a medium that connected Maya people directly to the divine, along with bloodletting, and it was the medium through which Maya people communicated with the dead via their offerings. Botanical foods and drinks were social lubricants that were shared, sometimes binding people together and sometimes asserting differences (see Ardren, this volume; Brown and Freiwald, this volume; Fernández Souza, Zimmermann, and Jiménez Álvarez, this volume; Hendon, this volume). Plant food was the means through which economic and social capital could be shored up and spent. These foods encoded the same messages of power, authority, and identity as those etched into stelae, but were directly served and consumed in feasts and other ritualized events. Quotidian foods also regularly conveyed social messages, in some cases more durably than infrequent ritualized practices, effecting social reproduction through diverse plant food media. The frequent reproduction of plant recipes conveyed social messages through multiple senses, before and after the plant sustenance was fully ingested.

Like the differences between messages transmitted in portable ceramic versus those in planted stone, critical distinctions existed between the plant medium and other types of media in portability, durability, replicability, and visibility. With botanical foodstuffs, in particular, perishability and edibility of edible matter are additional critical qualities under consideration, to understand the active role of plants as icons, indices, and symbols. Moreover, beyond simply the medium, plant foods frequently served as messengers, as more direct and iconic markers of sociality. I make this distinction in spite of Marshall McLuhan's caution that "the 'content' of any medium is always another medium" (2003 [1964]:19). That is, you can say some of the same things as when using other media, but sometimes the medium itself is the message. Just so with ancient Maya plant foods.

How Did Maya Food Plants Operate as Messages?

In the Maya area, food plants acted as messages in a number of assemblages. Building agricultural terraces, digging canals, fertilizing sediments, and raising fields (Fedick and Morrison 2004; Miksicek 1990) were practices with obvious end goals that served humans and plants alike. But these efforts also served as narratives of labor organization, whether to reinforce social affiliations, social obligations, or social hierarchies. Similarly, feasts delivered a payload of delicious foods, but as with large-scale terraforming, required social cooperation and social buy-in, or social coercion and force. At face value, feasts were measures of commensality and social saliency, and agricultural terraces were useful features to produce food plants, but each also represented labor investment, value encoded and symbolized through practice. Food plants were the primary movers in each of these cases, as both the motivators for, and the medium of, sociality. So, although large-scale agricultural endeavors and large-scale feasting events had end goals—terraces for food crops and feasts of food crops—ultimately it was participation in collective labor that delivered the messages to Maya people.

The Maya feast sometimes served as the medium, as described earlier, but also acted as the message itself, both in terms of the entire plant food assemblage and the individual food plants served. Particular botanical commodities and difficult-to acquire luxury foods communicated messages of social distinction (Bourdieu 1984 [1979]; Sutton 2013). Messages encoded in trade plants such as cacao or annatto would have been available to some folks and not others, given the uneven distribution of these plants (similar to arguments made by Henderson and Joyce [2006]). Dorie Reents-Budet (2006) describes the drinking of cacao-based beverages represented in Maya ceramic scenes as key parts of social and political life, especially in the context of the feast, which differentiated social class and special occasion. Particular plant ingredients found in a community may have been available to some households and not others, as David Lentz (1991b) and Julia Hendon (this volume) describe (see also Fernández Souza, Zimmermann, Jiménez Álvarez, this volume, and similar arguments about fauna by Masson et al., this volume). Such studies demonstrate the different scales of social difference conveyed through the plant messages ingested or simply observed at a remove. As Christine Hastorf (2017:7) affirms, "Food—the material and the idea—is an ethnic marker, a group identifier, and a medium for exclusion and inclusion."

How were different meanings expressed differently by Maya people through various plant foods? Writings on ceramic vessels sometimes prescribe food contents (such as atole) as well as spell out practices ("implement for drinking"; Helmke et al. 2017). "Intended contents" marked on vessels (Helmke et al. 2017:17) might be contrasted with unintended consequences, such as the ideological reinforcement of maintaining particular vessels for atole or reserving frothed chocolate consumption for royalty. Hull (2010) addresses representations of tortillas and tamales, and how they are marked differentially on ceramics based on content. He argues that the pairing of "water" and "tamale" is a stand-in for "bountiful times" in augury (Hull 2010:237). Stephen Houston and Karl Taube (2001) have also made ample arguments about the role of maize as represented epigraphically and iconographically. Taube (1996) further addresses the many ways that plant food symbols were mobilized in ideological discourse, as in the use of maize and general agricultural fertility iconography to solidify trade networks and consolidate power.

Even tobacco, not usually considered a food plant, has been documented to have been chewed, drunk, and eaten; added to water or cane liquor; and consumed as medicinal tea (Groark 2010:14). The use of tobacco snuff, held as a quid in the cheek or on the tongue, has been described as "eating" (Groark 2010:9). As Kevin Groark (2010:11) documents, tobacco (*Nicotiana tabacum*) is sometimes represented as "elder brother," a botanical helper, due to the effects of his nicotine on fatigue, pain, hunger, memory, mood, and attention. In some cases, tobacco is argued to be personified as the Classic Maya "Old God L" (Carlson 2011). During the Late Classic period, tobacco bottles were traded widely throughout the Maya area, although "perhaps the contents, not the bottles, were the desired trade items" (Houston, Stuart, and Taube 2006:116). Tobacco seeds, though miniscule and very difficult to discover, have been recovered from several sites (Dedrick 2013; Morell-Hart, Joyce, and Henderson 2014).

Moreover, as Houston and Taube (2000:271) note, "Throughout Mesoamerica, the dead are 'fed' with fragrance, whether it be in the form of incense, flowers, or the aroma of cooked food. . . ." Thus, "rather than eating actual food, the spirits consume the breath or aroma, whether of food, flowers, incense, or blood" (Taube 2004:73). Freidel and Reilly take this a step further, claiming that in the broader cosmology of Mesoamerica, "everyone was made of the same material: maize, the flesh of god." By extension, then, "the quotidian work of ordinary people: planting, cultivating, harvesting, storing, cooking, eating, weaving, modeling, and carving, were all expressions of the same creation" (Freidel and Reilly 2010:636). This is echoed in Hastorf's (2017:6) statement that ". . . meals are not just cultural events, they are also agents; they are techniques of the body and exist through meaningful practices that get carried along through bodily repetition and memory." Ritual and quotidian foodstuffs alike invoked memory; conveyed meaning; and instantiated, maintained, and transformed identities in relation to spiritual matters.

The passing on of recipes and the reproduction of meals may also have reconnected consumers to their lineage while incorporating heritage into their bodies (Hastorf 2017:235). The study of isotopic signatures has made it abundantly clear that we embody what we eat. The inscription of plant foods into the human skeleton has been well documented in the Maya area through isotopic work (Gerry 1997; Reed 1999; Scherer, Wright, and Yoder 2007; Somerville, Fauvelle, and Froehle 2013; Whittington and Reed 1997). The bioarchaeologist's act of reading isotopes of plant foods such as maize, beans, agave, and cacti shifts these plants from food media to dietary messengers. Nitrogen and carbon isotopic signatures become an index of social inequality, of shifts in Maya dietary regimes over time, of resiliency of Maya populations to environmental and nutritional stressors, and of dietary heterogeneity in elite subsets of Maya communities. These readings of isotopic signatures transform the Maya consumers themselves into media—into the canvases upon which food plants have scrawled their signatures.

How Were Ancient Maya Food Plants Matters Beyond Subsistence?

In a survey of communities across the Maya Lowlands, we find that people have very different perspectives on plant foods in terms of their flavors and even basic edibility. What is considered only a "famine food" or "cattle food" in some locations (e.g., the undisturbed *ramón* fruits in Naranjal, Mexico) becomes a contemporary resource for optimizing nutrition and marketing new foodstuffs in another (e.g., packaged *ramón* cookies in Copán, Honduras). Just as most of us would be hard-pressed to reduce the entirety of our diet to nutrition-optimized protein shakes, so people in the past opted for particular foods beyond the need to simply maximize calories or reduce food risk (in the sense of Bettinger 1991).

In rewriting matter as a process of materialization, and given the "vagabond" nature of matter (Bennett 2007), we are pointed toward semiosis—both the role of food matter in meaning-making and the role of meaning-making in construing "food." What we consume is not just calories and flavors. We ingest signs, which is where the work of Charles Saunders Peirce proves helpful. As Peirce defined it, "a sign is anything, of whatsoever mode of being, which mediates between an object and an interpretant; since it is both determined by the object relatively to the interpretant, and determines the interpretant in reference to the object, in such wise as to cause the interpretant to be determined by the object through the mediation of this 'sign'" (Peirce and Houser 1998:410). This relationship encapsulates the spirit of the posthumanistic approach to the assemblage, yet foregrounds meaning in human worlds. Peirce's detailed explorations of different signs are useful for defining and positioning icons, indices, and symbols (Peirce and Houser 1998; Peirce and Wiener 1958) in broader assemblages and networks of matter and materialization.

Examples from elsewhere demonstrate the utility of this approach. Andrea Adolph (2009:163), in her portrait of foodways during World War I, elucidates coping mechanisms employed by desperate British cooks who found themselves short on supplies. In one example, she describes the "culinary trickery" of substituting fish with Jerusalem artichokes and anchovy paste. Such culinary swapping, here called "making do," emerges as a dynamic interplay between culinary expectations and subversive everyday tactics. Foods were made to be iconically similar to missing ingredients, indices of kitchen craftsmanship, and symbolic of times when sumptuous meals were more the order (a sort of "remembrance of repasts"). Similarly, Mary Weismantel (1988) has described the ways that food symbols can be used to resist or assimilate dominant political modes that marginalize certain identities and privilege others. As she notes, the use of rice in place of barley on an Andean plate can be a sign of socioeconomic affluence, a meal's "starch," household struggles between mothers and children, globalization of available products, dominant Hispanic ideologies, resistance to and assimilation of these ideologies, ethnic positioning, and flavor preferences — any of which is either contested or taken for granted in a given meal space.

Plant foods in the ancient Maya area occupied all of these roles, operating as signs and substances both. We see many courtly scenes depicted in ceramics and murals where dishes are placed near the throne or bench of an important Maya personage (Reents-Budet 2006; see Figures 5.7a–d). Many of these dishes contain tamales, and some liquid chocolate; while others contain unknown foods and beverages hidden in jars, platters, and bowls (Beliaev, Davletshin, and Tokovinine 2009; Helmke et al. 2017; Stuart 2006). Were these iconic representations of courtly performance (McNeil, Hurst, and Sharer 2006)? Indices of wealth and abundance? We see no scenes depicting large food stores, contrary to the phenomenon of conspicuous food store displays frequently documented in Mississippian sites (Blitz 1993) and Inkan sites (D'Altroy 1985). Outside of the Maya area, conspicuous stores indexed wealth, symbolized moral rectitude (similarly to Kahn 1986), or indicated divine favor. Even rapidly abandoned Maya sites with ample evidence of small-scale food storage do not show evidence of conspicuous food stores (Inomata and Stiver 1998; Lamoureux-St-Hilaire, this volume; Sheets 2000). It may be that nearby maize and manioc fields (Sheets et al. 2012), though not represented in Maya courtly art, instead served as conspicuous enough signs of "food in the bank."

In other semiotic matters, we see the naming of Maya people with plant foods, as exemplified in the stunning murals painted on the exterior of a Calakmul pyramid (Carrasco Vargas, Vázquez López, and Martin 2009). Glyphic descriptions and representations of figures labeled "maize-gruel person," "maize-bread person," and "maize-grain person" demonstrate identities at least temporarily wrapped up in foodstuffs. These Calakmul

Figure 5.8. Rollout image of Classic period cylindrical vessel (K1092), depicting an event with a pulque-marked vessel and a drunk man marked as "the pulque one" supported by two other figures. Image by Justin Kerr, used with permission.

figures may have been attached specialists, temporary purveyors of feast foods, marketplace vendors, or generalized representatives of common roles—that is, icons, indices, or symbols of plant food practices. Maize and cacao are also incorporated into Classic period titles (Hull 2010:250)—for example, "he of new corn" for a ruler from Xcalumkin or "he of cacao" in the title for a scribe at Itzimte. A drunkard in one famous scene from a Classic period ceramic vessel was even identified as "the pulque one," simply translated as "drunkard" (Figure 5.8; Hull 2010:250, referencing Houston, Stuart, and Taube 2006:194). This clearly inebriated figure was made iconically similar to a drunk person, indexed drunkenness, and was marked with "the pulque one" symbol. Getting at the very core of humanity, in the *Popol Vuh*—the sacred origin text transcribed in the seventeenth century—the current race of human beings is represented as crafted of maize by the gods. This narrative transforms human beings into icons of maize plants, indexes the close relationship between maize and human life, and symbolizes core cosmological elements related to agricultural practices.

Along with the Maya use of plant foods in spiritually and emotionally charged ritual signification, quotidian practices carried their own weight. It is in the ordinary and unremarkable that social messages, taken for granted, are passed along without comment and reproduced without challenge. That is, foods are often "unmarked," a naturalized part of the everyday (similarly to Bourdieu 1984 [1979]). As Weismantel (1988:7) claims, "It is because they are ordinarily immersed in everyday practice in a material way that foods, abstracted as symbols from this material process, can condense in themselves a wealth of ideological meanings." As previously noted, tortillas and tamales—both made with maize dough—occupied very different roles at different points in time, in terms of form, manner of preparation, labor invested, and symbolic importance (see Carter and Matsumoto, this volume). Daily messages were encoded in storage and cooking and were read in the needs of crops for water, weeding, and fertilizer. Such food practices went without saying because they came without saying, to paraphrase Pierre Bourdieu. Residues of plants recovered from Río Amarillo, Piedras Negras, and T'isil consistently represent a spectrum of wild and gathered plants, indexing regular and common visits to wilder zones or fallow areas (Morell-Hart 2005, 2015b; Morell-Hart and Dine et al. 2018, Morell-Hart and Watson et al. 2018). These practices in turn may inculcate notions of landscape as William Hanks has described them in Yucatec Maya communities (1990; 2017), where language used to describe zones of agricultural practice shifts in relation to notions of place and positionality (deixis). The matter of plant residues indexes the social matters of daily life and does not simply represent the stuff of inert ingredients.

In times of strife, food plants may also have contributed to restoring some degree of normality to displaced Maya families, if cooks were able to re-create treasured and familiar dishes (following similar arguments by Elizabeth Dunn [2018]). Depending on the timing and mobility of Maya families relocating on the landscape, there may have been transportation of home landscapes and ingredients—cuttings of *chaya*, papaya seeds to plant—as well as the transport of recipes and ideas about the symbolic uses of plants and their critical roles as ritual participants. Foods in the Maya area, as worldwide (Sutton 2013), would have encoded cherished memories, symbolized as individual ingredients, specific recipe mixtures, or prominent features of the landscape.

Final Thoughts

From transported landscapes to wars, plants played a dynamic role in the lives of ancient Maya people, a role that goes far beyond basic food ingredients to get at semiosis and sociality. Food plants acted as basic matters of subsistence, as ritual actors, as petitioners to the gods, as players in royal performances. Food plants spurred people to all sorts of action: making, gifting, and trading specific vessels; traveling long distances and spending capital; engaging in trade wars and actual wars (Caso Barrera and Aliphat Fernández 2006; Kaplan et al. 2017).

When we take as given the deep entanglement of plants and people, we position ourselves to understand relationships that are not predicated on the centrality of human lives, actions, and preoccupations. To acknowledge the limits of our persistent perception of things as discrete entities — and understand the scaffolding built on them — is not to deny distributed agency or the potency of an assemblage. A Peircean approach proves helpful in this endeavor, as his work emphasizes the impact of broader contexts on individual practices (Peirce and Houser 1998). Peirce's triadic formulation also provides space for transformation over time by expanding the basic Saussurean dyad of signifier-signified (i.e., form of the concept-conceptualized) and incorporating space for interpretation. This formulation has implications for the ways that plant foods come to be symbolically important, and the ways they acquire positive meanings related to identity, community, and spirituality. The reshifting of plants in broader assemblages can manifest either a larger or smaller constrained repertoire of possibilities — can offer more or less optionality over time.

As Jane Bennett has put it, "to acknowledge nonhuman materialities as participants in a political ecology is not to claim that everything is always a participant, or that all participants are alike. Persons, worms, leaves, bacteria, metals, and hurricanes have different types and degrees of power, as different persons have different types and degrees of power" (2009: 108–109). To acknowledge the persistent power of food plants is not to deny the uniquely human experience or the particular effects of human agency. In the same way, to take the human as the analytical focal point is not to deny the persistent power of things. We can still go beyond thinking of food plants as inert symbols, matter, and media to give them their due as dynamic actors, mediators, and messengers. We can understand our human role as diminished in the grand scheme of things. But we can still acknowledge how human actions loom larger in the imaginations of human actors than the actions of plants (growing quietly in a field or resting cooked on a plate). Human relations of domination and resistance were expressed through plant food practices, just as plant food symbols were mobilized by humans in ideological discourse. Studying the deliberate manipulation of such relationships and symbols has fueled much of the critical anthropological endeavor.

Plant foods in the Maya area shifted power relations, operating as both medium and message. A posthumanist yet anthropological perspective in the Maya area can recognize the active position of plants in broad networks without undermining the role of human actors in social inequality. Plant foods were semiotically charged as indices, icons, and symbols.

Plants in the ancient Maya area operated as food media, as the basic matter of subsistence, and as messengers of social relations and sacred meanings. They occupied active roles, as indices of relationships between trade partners, as re-created simulacra of homelands, and as emblems of divine favor. In this way, plant foods were vibrant matters. Without plant foods, alliances could not be cemented, labor could not be amassed, the dead could not be celebrated, the gods could not be fed. In short, posthumanist perspectives allow us to go far beyond the basic matter of Maya subsistence to get at the heart of sociality—through its stomach.

References

Adolph, Andrea. 2009. *Food and Femininity in Twentieth-Century British Women's Fiction*. Farnham and Burlington, VT: Ashgate.

Aimers, James J. 2007. "What Maya Collapse? Terminal Classic Variation in the Maya Lowlands." *Journal of Archaeological Research* 15(4):329–377.

Aimers, James J., and David Hodell. 2011. "Societal Collapse: Drought and the Maya." *Nature* 479(7371):44–45.

Allison, Anne. 2013 [1991]. "Japanese Mothers and *Obentōs*: The Lunch-Box as Ideological State Apparatus." In *Food and Culture: A Reader*, ed. Carole Counihan and Penny Van Esterik, 154–172. New York: Routledge.

Appadurai, Arjun. 1981. "Gastro-Politics in Hindu South Asia." *American Ethnologist* 8(3):494–511.

———, ed. 1988. *The Social Life of Things: Commodities in Cultural Perspective*. Cambridge: Cambridge University Press.

Baron, Joanne P. 2018. "Ancient Monetization: The Case of Classic Maya Textiles." *Journal of Anthropological Archaeology* 49:100–113.

Batún Alpuche, Adolfo Iván. 2009. "Agrarian Production and Intensification at a Postclassic Maya Community, Buena Vista, Cozumel, Mexico." PhD diss., Anthropology, University of Florida.

Beliaev, Dmitri, Albert Davletshin, and Alexandre Tokovinine. 2009. "Sweet Cacao and Sour Atole: Mixed Drinks on Classic Maya Ceramic Vases." In *Pre-Columbian Foodways: Interdisciplinary Approaches to Food, Culture, and Markets in Ancient Mesoamerica*, ed. John E. Staller and Michael D. Carrasco, 257–272. New York: Springer.

Bennett, Jane. 2007. "Edible Matter." *New Left Review* 45 (May–June):133–145.

———. 2009. *Vibrant Matter: A Political Ecology of Things*. Durham, NC: Duke University Press.

Berman, Mary Jane, and Deborah M. Pearsall. 2008. "At the Crossroads: Starch Grain and Phytolith Analyses in Lucayan Prehistory." *Latin American Antiquity* 19(2):181–203.

Bérubé, Éloi, Guy David Hepp, and Shanti Morell-Hart. 2020. "Paleoethnobotanical Evidence of Early Formative Period Diet in Coastal Oaxaca, Mexico." *Journal of Archaeological Science: Reports* 29 (February 2020).

Bettinger, Robert L. 1991. "Hunter-Gatherers as Optimal Foragers." In *Hunter-Gatherers: Archaeological and Evolutionary Theory*, 83–112. New York: Plenum Press.

Blitz, John H. 1993. "Big Pots for Big Shots: Feasting and Storage in a Mississippian Community." *American Antiquity* 58(1):80–96.

Boone, James L., and Eric A. Smith. 1998. "Is It Evolution Yet? A Critique of Evolutionary Archaeology." *Current Anthropology* 39(S1):141–174.

Bourdieu, Pierre. 1984 [1979]. *Distinction: A Social Critique of the Judgement of Taste*. Cambridge, MA: Harvard University Press.

Bricker, Victoria R., and Helga-Maria Miram. 2002. *An Encounter of Two Worlds: The Book of Chilam Balam of Kaua*. New Orleans, LA: Tulane University Middle American Research Institute.

Bronson, Bennet. 1966. "Roots and the Subsistence of the Ancient Maya." *Southwestern Journal of Anthropology* 22(3):251–279.

Brown, Linda A., and Andrea I. Gerstle. 2002. "Structure 10: Feasting and Village Festivals." In *Before the Volcano Erupted: The Ancient Cerén Village in Central America*, ed. Payson Sheets, 97–103. Austin, TX: University of Texas Press.

Brumfiel, Elizabeth M. 1991. "Weaving and Cooking: Women's Production in Aztec Mexico." In *Engendering Archaeology: Women and Prehistory*, ed. Joan M. Gero and Margaret W. Conkey, 224–251. Oxford: Blackwell.

Carlson, John B. 2011. "Lord of the Maya Creations on His Jaguar Throne: The Eternal Return of Elder Brother God L to Preside over the 21 December 2012 Transformation." *Proceedings of the International Astronomical Union* 7(S278):203–213.

Carrasco Vargas, Ramón, Verónica Vázquez López, and Simon Martin. 2009. "Daily Life of the Ancient Maya Recorded on Murals at Calakmul, Mexico." *Proceedings of the National Academy of Sciences* 106(46):19245–19249.

Caso Barrera, Laura, and Mario Aliphat Fernández. 2006. "Cacao, Vanilla and Annatto: Three Production and Exchange Systems in the Southern Maya Lowlands, XVI–XVII Centuries." *Journal of Latin American Geography* 5(2):29–52.

Clement, Charles R., Michelly de Cristo-Araújo, Geo Coppens D'Eeckenbrugge, Alessandro Alves Pereira, and Doriane Picanço-Rodrigues. 2010. "Origin and Domestication of Native Amazonian Crops." *Diversity* 2(1):72–106.

Coole, Diana, and Samantha Frost. 2010. "Introducing the New Materialisms." In *New Materialisms: Ontology, Agency, and Politics*, ed. Diana Coole and Samantha Frost, 1–43. Durham, NC: Duke University Press.

Crosby, Alfred W. 1986. "Biotic Change in Nineteenth-Century New Zealand." *Environmental Review* 10(3):189–198.

Crown, Patricia L., and W. Jeffrey Hurst. 2009. "Evidence of Cacao Use in the Prehispanic American Southwest." *Proceedings of the National Academy of Sciences* 106(7):2110–2113.

D'Altroy, Terence. 1985. "Staple Finance, Wealth Finance, and Storage in the Inka Political Economy." *Current Anthropology* 26(2):187–206.

Dedrick, Maia. 2013. "The Distributed Household: Plant and Mollusk Remains from K'axob, Belize." Master's thesis, Department of Anthropology, University of North Carolina at Chapel Hill.

Diamond, Jared. 2006. *Collapse: How Societies Choose to Fail or Succeed*. New York: Penguin Group USA.

Dietler, Michael. 1996. "Feasts and Commensal Politics in the Political Economy:

Food, Power and Status in Prehistoric Europe." In *Food and the Status Quest: An Interdisciplinary Perspective*, ed. Polly Wiessner and Wulf Schiefenhövel, 87–125. Oxford: Berghahn Books.

Dietler, Michael, and Brian Hayden, eds. 2001. *Feasts: Archaeological and Ethnographic Perspectives on Food, Politics, and Power*. Washington, DC: Smithsonian Institution Press.

Dobkin de Rios, Marlene. 1974. "The Influence of Psychotropic Flora and Fauna on Maya Religion." *Current Anthropology* 15(2):147–164.

Dunham, Peter S., Marc A. Abramiuk, Linda Scott Cummings, Chad Yost, and Todd J. Pesek. 2009. "Ancient Maya Cultivation in the Southern Maya Mountains of Belize: Complex and Sustainable Strategies Uncovered." *Antiquity* 83(319):1–3.

Dunn, Elizabeth Cullen. 2018. "Nothing." In *No Path Home: Humanitarian Camps and the Grief of Displacement*, 91–112. Ithaca, NY: Cornell University Press.

Dussol, Lydie, Michelle Elliott, Dominique Michelet, and Philippe Nondédéo. 2017. "Ancient Maya Sylviculture of Breadnut (*Brosimum alicastrum* Sw.) and Sapodilla (*Manilkara zapota* [L.] P. Royen) at Naachtun (Guatemala): A Reconstruction Based on Charcoal Analysis." *Quaternary International* 457:29–42.

Emery, Kitty F. 2002. "The Noble Beast: Status and Differential Access to Animals in the Maya World." *World Archaeology* 34:498–515.

Farahani, Alan, Katherine L. Chiou, Rob Q. Cuthrell, Anna Harkey, Shanti Morell-Hart, Christine A. Hastorf, and Payson D. Sheets. 2017. "Exploring Culinary Practices through GIS Modeling at Joya de Cerén, El Salvador." In *Social Perspectives on Ancient Lives from Paleoethnobotanical Data*, ed. Matthew P. Sayre and Maria C. Bruno, 101–120. New York: Springer.

Farrington, Ian S., and James Urry. 1985. "Food and the Early History of Cultivation." *Journal of Ethnobiology* 5(2):143–157.

Fedick, Scott L. 1996. "Introduction: New Perspectives on Ancient Maya Agriculture and Resource Use." In *The Managed Mosaic: Ancient Maya Agriculture and Resource Use*, ed. Scott L. Fedick. Salt Lake City: University of Utah Press.

———. 2017. "Plant-Food Commodities of the Maya Lowlands." In *The Value of Things: Prehistoric to Contemporary Commodities in the Maya Region*, ed. Jennifer P. Mathews and Thomas H. Guderjan, 163–173. Tucson: University of Arizona Press.

Fedick, Scott L., Jennifer P. Mathews, and Kathryn Sorensen. 2012. "Cenotes as Conceptual Boundary Markers at the Ancient Maya Site of T'isil, Quintana Roo, México." *Mexicon* 34(5):118–123.

Fedick, Scott L., and Bethany A. Morrison. 2004. "Ancient Use and Manipulation of Landscape in the Yalahau Region of the Northern Maya Lowlands." *Agriculture and Human Values* 21(2):207–219.

Ferrando, Francesca. 2013. "Posthumanism, Transhumanism, Antihumanism, Metahumanism, and New Materialisms." *Existenz* 8(2):26–32.

Fischler, Claude. 1980. "Food Habits, Social Change and the Nature/Culture Dilemma." *Social Science Information* 19(6):937–953.

Ford, Anabel, and Ronald Nigh. 2009. "Origins of the Maya Forest Garden: Maya Resource Management." *Journal of Ethnobiology* 29(2):213–236.

———. 2010. "The Milpa Cycle and the Making of the Maya Forest Garden." *Research Reports in Belizean Archaeology* 7:83–190.

Foucault, Michel. 1986. "Of Other Spaces." *Diacritics* 16(1):22–27.
Freidel, David, and F. Kent Reilly III. 2010. "The Flesh of God: Cosmology, Food, and the Origins of Political Power in Ancient Southeastern Mesoamerica." In *Pre-Columbian Foodways: Interdisciplinary Approaches to Food, Culture, and Markets in Ancient Mesoamerica*, ed. John E. Staller and Michael D. Carrasco, 635–680. New York: Springer.
Gabriel, Marianne. 2004. "Elements, Action Sequences and Structure: A Typology of Agrarian Ceremonies." *Acta Mesoamericana* 14:157–164.
García Barrios, Ana. 2017. "The Social Context of Food at Calakmul, Campeche, Mexico." In *Constructing Power and Place in Mesoamerica: Pre-Hispanic Paintings from Three Regions*, ed. Merideth Paxton and Leticia Staines Cicero, 171–190. Albuquerque: University of New Mexico Press.
Gerry, John P. 1997. "Bone Isotope Ratios and Their Bearing on Elite Privilege among the Classic Maya." *Geoarchaeology* 12(1):41–69.
Goldstein, David J., and John B. Hageman. 2009. "Power Plants: Paleobotanical Evidence of Rural Feasting in Late Classic Belize." In *Pre-Columbian Foodways: Interdisciplinary Approaches to Food, Culture, and Markets in Ancient Mesoamerica*, ed. John E. Staller and Michael D. Carrasco, 421–440. New York: Springer.
Graeber, David. 2001. *Toward an Anthropological Theory of Value: The False Coin of Our Own Dreams*. New York: Palgrave.
Groark, Kevin P. 2010. "The Angel in the Gourd: Ritual, Therapeutic, and Protective Uses of Tobacco (*Nicotiana tabacum*) among the Tzeltal and Tzotzil Maya of Chiapas, Mexico." *Journal of Ethnobiology* 30(1):5–30.
Guderjan, Thomas H., Sheryl Luzzadder-Beach, Timothy Beach, Steven R. Bozarth, and Samantha Krause. 2017. "Production of Ancient Wetland Agricultural Commodities." In *The Value of Things: Prehistoric to Contemporary Commodities in the Maya Region*, ed. Jennifer P. Mathews and Thomas H. Guderjan, 30–48. Tucson: University of Arizona Press.
Hall, Grant D., Stanley M. Tarka Jr., W. Jeffrey Hurst, David Stuart, and Richard E. W. Adams. 1990. "Cacao Residues in Ancient Maya Vessels from Río Azul, Guatemala." *American Antiquity* 55(1):138–143.
Hamilakis, Yannis. 1999. "Food Technologies/Technologies of the Body: The Social Context of Wine and Oil Production and Consumption in Bronze Age Crete." *World Archaeology* 31(1):38–54.
———. 2008. "Time, Performance, and the Production of a Mnemonic Record: From Feasting to an Archaeology of Eating and Drinking." In *DAIS: The Aegean Feast*, ed. Louise A. Hitchcock, Robert Laffineur, and Janice L. Crowley, 3–19. Liège, Belgium: Université de Liège.
Hanks, William F. 1990. *Referential Practice: Language and Lived Space among the Maya*. Chicago: University of Chicago Press.
———. 2017. "The Plurality of Temporal Reckoning among the Maya." *Journal de la Société des américanistes* (Tiempos Mayas–Maya Times). https://doi.org/10.4000/jsa.15294.
Haraway, Donna J. 1991. *Simians, Cyborgs, and Women: The Reinvention of Nature*. New York: Routledge.
———. 2006 [1990]. "A Cyborg Manifesto: Science, Technology, and Socialist-

Feminism in the Late 20th Century." In *The International Handbook of Virtual Learning Environments*, ed. J. Weiss, J. Nolan, J. Hunsinger, and P. Trifonas, 117–158. Dordrecht, Netherlands: Springer.

Harrison-Buck, Eleanor. 2017. "The Coin of Her Realm: Cacao as Gendered Goods among the Prehispanic and Colonial Maya." In *The Value of Things: Prehistoric to Contemporary Commodities in the Maya Region*, ed. Jennifer P. Mathews and Thomas H. Guderjan, 104–123. Tucson: University of Arizona Press.

Hastorf, Christine A. 2017. *The Social Archaeology of Food: Thinking about Eating from Prehistory to the Present*. New York: Cambridge University Press.

Hather, Jon G., and Norman Hammond. 1994. "Ancient Maya Subsistence Diversity: Root and Tuber Remains from Cuello, Belize." *Antiquity* 68(259):330–335.

Helmke, Christophe G. B., Yuriy Polyukhovych, Dorie J. Reents-Budet, and Ronald L. Bishop. 2017. "A Bowl Fit for a King: A Ceramic Vessel of the Naranjo Court Bearing the Komkom Emblem Glyph." *The PARI Journal* 18(1):9–24.

Henderson, John S., and Rosemary A. Joyce. 2006. "Brewing Distinction: The Development of Cacao Beverages in Formative Mesoamerica." In *Chocolate in Mesoamerica: A Cultural History of Cacao*, ed. Cameron L. McNeil, 140–153. Gainesville: University Press of Florida.

Hodder, Ian. 2011. "Human-Thing Entanglement: Towards an Integrated Archaeological Perspective." *Journal of the Royal Anthropological Institute* 17(1):154–177.

Houston, Stephen D., David Stuart, and Karl A. Taube. 2006. *The Memory of Bones: Body, Being, and Experience among the Classic Maya*. Austin: University of Texas Press.

Houston, Stephen D., and Karl Taube. 2000. "An Archaeology of the Senses: Perception and Cultural Expression in Ancient Mesoamerica." *Cambridge Archaeological Journal* 10(02):261–294.

Hull, Kerry M. 2010. "An Epigraphic Analysis of Classic-Period Maya Foodstuffs." In *Pre-Columbian Foodways: Interdisciplinary Approaches to Food, Culture, and Markets in Ancient Mesoamerica*, ed. John E. Staller and Michael D. Carrasco, 235–256. New York: Springer.

Hurcombe, Linda. 2007. "A Sense of Materials and Sensory Perception in Concepts of Materiality." *World Archaeology* 39(4):532–545.

Imre, Dylan M. 2010. "Ancient Maya Beekeeping (ca. 1000–1520 CE)." *University of Michigan Undergraduate Research Journal* 7:42–50.

Inomata, Takeshi, and Laura R. Stiver. 1998. "Floor Assemblages from Burned Structures at Aguateca, Guatemala: A Study of Classic Maya Households." *Journal of Field Archaeology* 25(4):431–452.

Joyce, Rosemary A., and John S. Henderson. 2007. "From Feasting to Cuisine: Implications of Archaeological Research in an Early Honduran Village." *American Anthropologist*, n.s., 109(4):642–653.

Kahn, Miriam. 1986. *Always Hungry, Never Greedy: Food and the Expression of Gender in a Melanesian Society*. Cambridge: Cambridge University Press.

Kaplan, Jonathan, Federico Paredes Umaña, W. Jeffrey Hurst, D. Sun, Bruce Stanley, Luis Barba Pingarrón, and Mauricio Obregón Cardona. 2017. "Cacao Residues in Vessels from Chocolá, an Early Maya Polity in the Southern Guatemalan Piedmont, Determined by Semi-quantitative Testing and High-Performance Liquid Chromatography." *Journal of Archaeological Science: Reports* 13:526–534.

Knappett, Carl, and Lambros Malafouris, eds. 2008. *Material Agency: Towards a Non-Anthropocentric Approach*. Boston: Springer.

Landa, Diego de. 1978 [1566]. *Yucatan Before and After the Conquest*. New York: Dover.

Lanes, Éder C.M., Sérgio Y Motoike, Kacilda N. Kuki, Carlos Nick, and Renata D. Freitas. 2014. "Molecular Characterization and Population Structure of the Macaw Palm, *Acrocomia aculeata* (Arecaceae), *Ex Situ* Germplasm Collection Using Microsatellites Markers." *Journal of Heredity* 106(1):102–112.

Latour, Bruno. 2005. *Reassembling the Social: An Introduction to Actor-Network-Theory*. New York: Oxford University Press.

LeCount, Lisa J. 2001. "Like Water for Chocolate: Feasting and Political Ritual among the Late Classic Maya at Xunantunich, Belize." *American Anthropologist* 103(4):935–953.

Lentz, David L. 1991a. *Acrocomia mexicana*: La palma de los antiguos mesoamericanos. *Yaxkin* 12(1):78–101.

———. 1991b. "Maya Diets of the Rich and Poor: Paleoethnobotanical Evidence from Copan." *Latin American Antiquity* 2(3):269–287.

———. 2000, ed. *Imperfect Balance: Landscape Transformations in the Precolumbian Americas*. Historical Ecology Series. New York: Columbia University Press.

———. 2001. "Diets under Duress: Paleoethnobotanical Evidence from the Late Classic Maya Site of Aguateca." Paper presented at the 66th Annual Meetings of the Society for American Archaeology, New Orleans, LA.

Lentz, David L., Marilyn P. Beaudry-Corbett, Maria Luisa R. de Aguilar, and Lawrence Kaplan. 1996. "Foodstuffs, Forests, Fields, and Shelter: A Paleoethnobotanical Analysis of Vessel Contents from the Ceren Site, El Salvador." *Latin American Antiquity* 7(3):247–262.

Lentz, David L., Nicholas P. Dunning, and Vernon L. Scarborough. 2015. "Defining the Constructed Niche of Tikal: A Summary View." In *Tikal: Paleoecology of an Ancient Maya City*, ed. David L. Lentz, Nicholas P. Dunning, and Vernon L. Scarborough, 280–295. Cambridge: Cambridge University Press.

Lentz, David L., Brian Lane, and Kim Thompson. 2014. "Food, Farming, and Forest Management at Aguateca." In *Life and Politics at the Royal Court of Aguateca: Artifacts, Analytical Data, and Synthesis*, ed. Takeshi Inomata and Daniela Triadan, 201–215. Salt Lake City: University of Utah Press.

Mauss, Marcel. 1954. *The Gift: Forms and Functions of Exchange in Archaic Societies*. Glencoe, IL: Free Press.

McAnany, Patricia Ann. 1995. *Living with the Ancestors: Kinship and Kingship in Ancient Maya Society*. Austin: University of Texas Press.

McAnany, Patricia Ann, and Tomás Gallareta Negrón. 2009. "Bellicose Rulers and Climatological Peril? Retrofitting Twenty-First-Century Woes on Eighth-Century Maya Society." In *Questioning Collapse: Human Resilience, Ecological Vulnerability, and the Aftermath of Empire*, ed. Patricia Ann McAnany and Norman Yoffee, 142–175. Cambridge: Cambridge University Press.

McAnany, Patricia A., Ben S. Thomas, Steven Morandi, Polly A. Peterson, and Eleanor Harrison. 2002. "Praise the Ajaw and Pass the Kakaw: Xibun Maya and the Political Economy of Cacao." In *Ancient Maya Political Economies*, ed. Marilyn A. Masson and David A. Freidel, 123–139. Walnut Creek, CA: Altamira Press.

McKey, Doyle, Marianne Elias, Benoît Pujol, and Anne Duputié. 2010. "The Evolutionary Ecology of Clonally Propagated Domesticated Plants." *New Phytologist* 186(2):318–332.

McKillop, Heather, and E. Cory Sills. 2017. "The Paynes Creek Salt Works, Belize: A Model for Ancient Maya Salt Production." In *The Value of Things: Prehistoric to Contemporary Commodities in the Maya Region*, ed. Jennifer P. Mathews and Thomas H. Guderjan, 67–86. Tucson: University of Arizona Press.

McLuhan, Marshall. 2003 [1964]. *Understanding Media: The Extensions of Man (Critical Edition)*. Edited by W. Terrence Gordon. Corte Madera, CA: Gingko Press.

McNeil, Cameron L. 2006. "Traditional Cacao Use in Modern Mesoamerica." In *Chocolate in Mesoamerica: A Cultural History of Cacao*, ed. Cameron L. McNeil, 341–366. Gainesville: University Press of Florida.

———. 2009. "Death and Chocolate: The Significance of Cacao Offerings in Ancient Maya Tombs and Caches at Copan, Honduras." In *Pre-Columbian Foodways: Interdisciplinary Approaches to Food, Culture, and Markets in Ancient Mesoamerica*, ed. John E. Staller and Michael D. Carrasco, 293–314. New York: Springer.

McNeil, Cameron L., David A. Burney, and Lida Pigott Burney. 2010. "Evidence Disputing Deforestation as the Cause for the Collapse of the Ancient Maya Polity of Copan, Honduras." *Proceedings of the National Academy of Sciences* 107(3):1017–1022.

McNeil, Cameron L., W. Jeffrey Hurst, and Robert J. Sharer. 2006. "The Use and Representation of Cacao during the Classic Period at Copan, Honduras." In *Chocolate in Mesoamerica: A Cultural History of Cacao*, 224–252. Gainesville: University Press of Florida.

Miksicek, Charles H. 1983. "Macrofloral Remains of the Pulltrouser Area: Settlements and Fields." In *Pulltrouser Swamp: Ancient Maya Habitat, Agriculture, and Settlement in Northern Belize*, ed. B. L. Turner II and Peter D. Harrison, 94–104. Austin: University of Texas Press.

———. 1987. "Formation Processes of the Archaeobotanical Record." *Advances in Archaeological Method and Theory* 10:211–247.

———. 1990. "Early Wetland Agriculture in the Maya Lowlands: Clues from Preserved Plant Remains." In *Ancient Maya Wetland Agriculture: Excavations on Albion Island, Northern Belize*, ed. Mary Pohl, 295–312. Boulder, CO: Westview Press.

Miksicek, Charles H., Kathryn J. Elsesser, Ingrid A. Wuebber, Karen Olsen Bruhns, and Norman Hammond. 1981. "Rethinking Ramón—a Comment on Reina and Hill's Lowland Maya Subsistence." *American Antiquity* 46(4):916–919.

Miller, Daniel. 2005. "Materiality: An Introduction." In *Materiality*, ed. Daniel Miller, 1–50. Durham, NC: Duke University Press.

Morehart, Christopher T. 2001. "Plants of the Underworld: Ritual Plant Use in Ancient Maya Cave Ceremonies." Paper presented at the American Anthropological Association Annual Meetings, Washington, DC.

———. 2004. "Paleoethnobotany in the Maya Lowlands: The Belize River Valley." Paper presented at the The 69th Annual Meetings of the Society for American Archaeology, Montreal, Canada.

Morehart, Christopher T., and Noah Butler. 2010. "Ritual Exchange and the Fourth Obligation: Ancient Maya Food Offering and the Flexible Materiality of Ritual." *Journal of the Royal Anthropological Institute* 16(3):588–608.

Morehart, Christopher T., and Shanti Morell-Hart. 2015. "Beyond the Ecofact:

Toward a Social Paleoethnobotany in Mesoamerica." *Journal of Archaeological Method and Theory* 22(2):483–511.

Morell-Hart, Shanti. 2005. *Analysis of Macrobotanical Remains from Structure 13M-2 at the Site of T'isil*. University of California, Berkeley Paleoethnobotany Lab Report No. 61. Submitted to University of California, Berkeley, Berkeley, CA.

———. 2011. "Paradigms and Syntagms of Ethnobotanical Practice in Pre-Hispanic Northwestern Honduras." PhD diss., Anthropology, University of California, Berkeley.

———. 2015a. "Paleoethnobotanical Analysis, Post-Processing." In *Method and Theory in Paleoethnobotany*, ed. John M. Marston, Jade d'Alpoim Guedes, and Christina Warinner, 371–390. Boulder: University Press of Colorado.

———. 2015b. *Proyecto Arqueológico Río Amarillo Copán (PARAC): Macrobotanical Scan of 2011 Excavation Samples*. Submitted to McMaster Paleoethnobotany Research Facility (MPERF), Hamilton, ON.

Morell-Hart, Shanti, Harper Dine, Sarah Watson, and Shane Teesdale. 2018. "Análisis Paleoetnobotánicos de Macabilero y Piedras Negras (2016–2018)." In *Proyecto Paisaje Piedras Negras—Yaxchilán: Informe de la Tercera Temporada de Investigación*, ed. Monica Urquizú and Omar A. Alcover. Guatemala City: Dirección General del Patrimonio Cultural y Natural del Instituto de Antropología e Historia (IDAEH).

Morell-Hart, Shanti, Rosemary A. Joyce, and John S. Henderson. 2014. "Multi-Proxy Analysis of Plant Use at Formative Period Los Naranjos, Honduras." *Latin American Antiquity* 25(1):65–81.

Morell-Hart, Shanti, Rosemary A. Joyce, John S. Henderson, and Rachel Cane. 2019. "Ethnoecology in Pre-Hispanic Central America: Foodways and Human-Plant Interfaces." *Ancient Mesoamerica* 30(3):535–553.

Morell-Hart, Shanti, Sarah Watson, Harper Dine, and Meghan MacLeod. 2018. "Análisis Paleoetnobotánicos de Budsilhá, El Infiernito, El Porvenir y Sak Tz'i'-Lacanjá Tzeltal (2018)." In *Proyecto Arqueológico Busiljá-Chocoljá: Informe de la Novena Temporada de Investigación*, ed. Andrew K. Scherer and Charles W. Golden. Mexico City: Instituto Nacional de Antropología e Historia (INAH).

O'Connor, Amber M., and Eugene N. Anderson. 2016. *K'oben: 3,000 Years of the Maya Hearth*. Lanham, MD: Rowman and Littlefield.

Olsen, Kenneth M., and Barbara A. Schaal. 2001. "Microsatellite Variation in Cassava (*Manihot esculenta*, Euphorbiaceae) and Its Wild Relatives: Further Evidence for a Southern Amazonian Origin of Domestication." *American Journal of Botany* 88(1).131–142.

Ouzman, Sven. 2001. "Seeing Is Deceiving: Rock Art and the Non-Visual." *World Archaeology* 33(2):237–256.

Pearsall, Deborah M. 2015. *Paleoethnobotany: A Handbook of Procedures*. 3rd ed. Walnut Creek, CA: Left Coast Press.

Peirce, Charles S., and Nathan Houser. 1998. *The Essential Peirce: Selected Philosophical Writings*. Vol. 2 (1893–1913). Bloomington: Indiana University Press.

Peirce, Charles S., and Philip P. Wiener. 1958. *Values in a Universe of Chance: Selected Writings of Charles S. Peirce (1839–1914)*. Stanford, CA: Stanford University Press.

Piperno, Dolores R. 2006. *Phytoliths: A Comprehensive Guide for Archaeologists and Paleoecologists*. Lanham, MD: Altamira Press.

Piperno, Dolores R., Anthony J. Ranere, Irene Holst, Jose Iriarte, and Ruth Dickau. 2009. "Starch Grain and Phytolith Evidence for Early Ninth Millennium BP Maize from the Central Balsas River Valley, Mexico." *Proceedings of the National Academy of Sciences of the United States of America* 106(13):5019–5024.

Pollan, Michael. 2001. *The Botany of Desire: A Plant's-Eye View of the World*. New York: Random House.

Powis, Terry G., Fred Valdez Jr., Thomas R. Hester, W. Jeffrey Hurst, and Stanley M. Tarka Jr. 2002. "Spouted Vessels and Cacao Use among the Preclassic Maya." *Latin American Antiquity* 13(1):85–106.

Prufer, Keith M., and W. Jeffrey Hurst 2007. "Chocolate in the Underworld Space of Death: Cacao Seeds from an Early Classic Mortuary Cave." *Ethnohistory* 54(2): 273–301.

Puleston, Dennis E. 1971. "An Experimental Approach to the Function of Classic Maya Chultuns." *American Antiquity* 36(3):322–335.

Reed, David M. 1999. "Cuisine from Hun-Nal-Ye." In *Reconstructing Ancient Maya Diet*, ed. Christine D. White, 183–196. Salt Lake City: University of Utah Press.

Reents-Budet, Dorie. 2006. "The Social Context of Kakaw Drinking among the Ancient Maya." In *Chocolate in Mesoamerica: A Cultural History of Cacao*, ed. Cameron L. McNeil, 202–223. Gainesville: University Press of Florida.

Reina, Ruben E., and Robert M. Hill. 1980. "Lowland Maya Subsistence: Notes from Ethnohistory and Ethnography." *American Antiquity* 45(1):74–79.

Reno, Joshua. 2013. "Waste." In *The Oxford Handbook of the Archaeology of the Contemporary World*, ed. Paul Graves-Brown, Rodney Harrison, and Angela Piccini, 261–272. Oxford: Oxford University Press.

Rick, Torben C., Patrick V. Kirch, Jon M. Erlandson, and Scott M. Fitzpatrick. 2013. "Archeology, Deep History, and the Human Transformation of Island Ecosystems." *Anthropocene* 4:33–45.

Rico-Gray, V., A. Chemás, and S. Mandujano. 1991. "Uses of Tropical Deciduous Forest Species by the Yucatecan Maya." *Agroforestry Systems* 14(2):149–161.

Ross, Nanci Jane. 2008. "The Impact of Ancient Maya Forest Gardens on Modern Tree Species Composition in NW Belize." PhD diss., University of Connecticut.

Ross-Ibarra, Jeffrey, and Alvaro Molina-Cruz. 2002. "The Ethnobotany of Chaya (*Cnidoscolus aconitifolius* ssp. *aconitifolius* Breckon): A Nutritious Maya Vegetable." *Economic Botany* 56(4):350–365.

Roullier, Caroline, Anne Duputié, Paul Wennekes, Laure Benoit, Víctor Manuel Fernández Bringas, Genoveva Rossel, David Tay, Doyle McKey, and Vincent Lebot. 2013. "Disentangling the Origins of Cultivated Sweet Potato (*Ipomoea batatas* [L.] Lam)." *PLOS ONE* 8(5):e62707.

Roys, Ralph L., trans. and ed. 1965 [1779]. *Ritual of the Bacabs: A Book of Maya Incantations*. Norman: University of Oklahoma Press.

———, trans. 1967 [1933]. *The Book of Chilam Balam of Chumayel*. Norman: University of Oklahoma Press.

Scherer, Andrew K., Lori E. Wright, and Cassady J. Yoder. 2007. "Bioarchaeological Evidence for Social and Temporal Differences in Diet at Piedras Negras, Guatemala." *Latin American Antiquity* 18(1):85–104.

Sheets, Payson D. 1998. "Place and Time in Activity Area Analysis: A Study of Elevated Contexts Used for Artifact Curation at the Ceren Site, El Salvador." *Revista Española de Antropología Americana* 28:63–98.

———. 2000. "Provisioning the Ceren Household: The Vertical Economy, Village Economy, and Household Economy in the Southeastern Maya Periphery." *Ancient Mesoamerica* 11(2):217–230.

Sheets, Payson D., David L. Lentz, Dolores R. Piperno, John Jones, Christine C. Dixon, George Maloof, and Angela Hood. 2012. "Ancient Manioc Agriculture South of the Cerén Village, El Salvador." *Latin American Antiquity* 23(3):259–281.

Sherratt, Andrew. 1991. "Palaeoethnobotany: From Crops to Cuisine." In *Paleoecologia e Arqueologia II: Trabalhos dedicados a A. R. Pinto da Silva*, ed. F. Queiroga and A. P. Dinis, 221–236. Portugal: Centro de Estudos Arqueológicos Famalicenses.

Siegel, Peter E., John G. Jones, Deborah M. Pearsall, Nicholas P. Dunning, Pat Farrell, Neil A. Duncan, Jason H. Curtis, and Sushant K. Singh. 2015. "Paleoenvironmental Evidence for First Human Colonization of the Eastern Caribbean." *Quaternary Science Reviews* 129(2015):275–295.

Simms, Stephanie R., Francesco Berna, and George J. Bey III. 2013. "A Prehispanic Maya Pit Oven? Microanalysis of Fired Clay Balls from the Puuc Region, Yucatán, Mexico." *Journal of Archaeological Science* 40(2):1144–1157.

Soler, Jean. 1997 [1973]. "The Semiotics of Food in the Bible." In *Food and Culture: A Reader*, ed. Carole Counihan and Penny Van Esterik, 55–66. Routledge, New York.

Somerville, Andrew D., Mikael Fauvelle, and Andrew W. Froehle. 2013. "Applying New Approaches to Modeling Diet and Status: Isotopic Evidence for Commoner Resiliency and Elite Variability in the Classic Maya Lowlands." *Journal of Archaeological Science* 40(3):1539–1553.

Stuart, David. 2006. "The Language of Chocolate: References to Cacao on Classic Maya Drinking Vessels." In *Chocolate in Mesoamerica: A Cultural History of Cacao*, ed. Cameron L. McNeil, 184–201. Gainesville: University Press of Florida.

Sutton, David E. 2001. *Remembrance of Repasts: An Anthropology of Food and Memory*. Oxford: Berg.

———. 2013. "Cooking Skills, the Senses, and Memory: The Fate of Practical Knowledge." In *Food and Culture: A Reader*, ed. Carole Counihan and Penny Van Esterik, 299–319. New York: Routledge.

Taube, Karl A. 1996. "The Olmec Maize God: The Face of Corn in Formative Mesoamerica." *RES: Anthropology and Aesthetics* 29/30:39–81.

———. 2004. "Flower Mountain: Concepts of Life, Beauty, and Paradise among the Classic Maya." *RES: Anthropology and Aesthetics* 45:69–98.

Taylor, Timothy F. 2008. "Materiality." In *Handbook of Archaeological Theories*, ed. R. Alexander Bentley, Herbert D. G. Maschner, and Christopher Chippindale, 297–320. Lanham, MD: Altamira Press.

Trabanino García, Felipe, and Rodrigo Liendo Stuardo. 2012. "Arqueología de las plantas en Chinikiha." Paper presented at the Primera Conferencia Intercontinental (First International Conference) of the Society for American Archaeology, Panama.

Turner, B. L., and Charles H. Miksicek. 1984. "Economic Plant Species Associated with Prehistoric Agriculture in the Maya Lowlands." *Economic Botany* 38(2):179–193.

Van der Veen, Marijke. 2014. "The Materiality of Plants: Plant-People Entanglements." *World Archaeology* 46(5):799–812.

VanDerwarker, Amber M., Jennifer V. Alvarado, and Paul Webb. 2015. "Analysis and Interpretation of Intrasite Variability in Paleoethnobotanical Remains: A Consideration and Application of Methods at the Ravensford Site, North Carolina." In *Method and Theory in Paleoethnobotany*, ed. John M. Marston, Jade d'Alpoim Guedes, and Christina Warinner, 205–234. Boulder: University Press of Colorado.

Weismantel, Mary J. 1988. *Food, Gender, and Poverty in the Ecuadorian Andes*. Philadelphia: University of Pennsylvania Press.

Whittington, Stephen L., and David M. Reed. 1997. "Commoner Diet at Copan: Insights from Stable Isotopes and Porotic Hyperostosis." In *Bones of the Maya: Studies of Ancient Skeletons*, ed. Stephen L. Whittington and David M. Reed, 157–170. Tuscaloosa: University of Alabama Press.

Wright, Lori E., and Christine D. White. 1996. "Human Biology in the Classic Maya Collapse: Evidence from Paleopathology and Paleodiet." *Journal of World Prehistory* 10(2):147–198.

Young, Michael W. 1971. *Fighting with Food: Leadership, Values and Social Control in a Massim Society*. Cambridge: Cambridge University Press.

Zarger, Rebecca K. 2009. "Mosaics of Maya Livelihoods: Readjusting to Global and Local Food Crises." *NAPA Bulletin* 32(1):130–151.

CHAPTER 6

Food, Friend, or Offering: Exploring the Role of Maya Dogs in the Zooarchaeological Record

PETRA CUNNINGHAM-SMITH, ASHLEY E. SHARPE,
ARIANNE BOILEAU, ERIN KENNEDY THORNTON,
AND KITTY F. EMERY

Introduction

Remains of the domestic dog (*Canis lupus familiaris*) can be found at virtually every site in pre-Columbian Mesoamerica, from the burial mounds of ancient nobles, to the ritual caches of ceremonial temples, to the kitchen middens of low-status households. Their images appear in ancient codices, on elaborately decorated ceramic pottery and murals, and in the chronicles of the Spanish conquerors. Previous research suggests that Mesoamerican dogs served not only as food but also as sentinels, companions, ritual sacrificial offerings, and the source of commodities like skins, medicines, and raw material for crafting. In this chapter, we explore the role of dogs as food, arguing that despite their ubiquity in archaeological deposits, these animals were never simple fare and, if they were food at all, it was only as a "sometime food" eaten with the full cognizance of the symbolic meaning of the dog beyond its nutritional value.

Dogs were almost certainly the domesticated companions of the first inhabitants of the Maya area, having accompanied the first human settlers across the Americas during the late Pleistocene (Leathlobhair et al. 2018). The earliest Mesoamerican remains of domestic dogs are found in the Tehuacán Valley and date to about 3000 BCE (Flannery 1967). The earliest dog remains found in the areas inhabited by the ancient Maya date to the Middle Preclassic period (ca. 1200–300 BCE), such as at Cuello (Wing and Scudder 1991), Ceibal (Sharpe 2016), Cerros (Carr 1986), Colha (Shaw 1991), and other places. Faunal analyses at these early sites revealed a high proportion of dog remains, often in midden contexts, leading researchers to suggest that dogs, an easily accessible protein and fat source, were an important food commodity during the rise of early Maya society (Clutton-

Brock and Hammond 1994:825; White et al. 2001:91). Wing (1978:39) argued that early Mesoamerican dependence on dogs for food was comparable to that of European dependence on domestic animals beginning in the Neolithic. Dogs are not isolated to early periods but are also found at Classic and Postclassic sites (Götz and Stanton 2013; Hamblin 1984; Masson and Peraza Lope 2008; Teeter 2004). An early chronological review of the distribution of dog remains across the Maya world substantiated the high frequency of dog bones in early deposits (Emery 2004b). It also revealed similarly high numbers of dogs in Postclassic and Colonial/Historical deposits, but a lower abundance during the Classic period.

Several seminal works contributed to the growing corpus on dogs as food. A careful study of the distribution and treatment of dog remains at Cuello (Clutton-Brock and Hammond 1994; Wing and Scudder 1991) found that dogs had a mortality pattern of about one year of age, suggesting slaughter when the animals had reached an "optimal" size for meat return. Isotopic studies revealed that dog diets included substantial proportions of C4 plants, likely maize (at Cuello 30%–40% during the Preclassic [Tykot, van der Merwe, and Hammond 1996; van der Merwe et al. 2002], at Colha increasing from early to later periods of the Preclassic [White et al. 2001, 2004], and at Lagartero during the Classic period [White et al. 2004]). This pattern was interpreted as humans sharing food with their closest animal companions (dogs are often used as proxies for human diet) or as the result of changing dog husbandry practices.

However, other researchers have suggested that the more important role for dogs in Maya society involved ritual and ceremony (Emery et al. 2013; Shaw 1995; Stanchly and Awe 2015). The dog's role as a ritual actor is actually much better documented than its use as food. The Spanish bishop Diego de Landa described the use of puppies and young dogs as sacrificial offerings and remarked that dogs and humans were often used for sacrifices (Tozzer 1941:143–145). Maya iconographers (Vail and Hernández 2007) also note that dogs and humans play similar and sometimes interchangeable roles as sacrificial victims in certain depicted ceremonies, suggesting the high value of dogs as offerings. In Mexico, Bernardino de Sahagún described the sacrifice of dogs with cotton cords about their necks, which were interred with their owners to accompany them to the underworld (Anderson and Dibble 1952). Their role symbolizing death, reincarnation, and regeneration is echoed in the *Popol Vuh*, a historic Maya creation narrative with ancient roots. In this narrative, the Hero Twins, Hunahpu and Xbalanque, sacrifice a dog and then bring it back to life, prompting the Lords of Death to clamor for their own sacrifice and resurrection (Tedlock 1996:134).

Diego de Landa also described the consumption of dog meat and hearts during certain rites (Tozzer 1941:155), a description that aligns with proposals that dogs were an important special occasion food. Shaw (1995) cited the association of dog remains with elite communal buildings and ceremonial ceramics, together with the deposition of high numbers of dog remains in single-layer deposits, as evidence that dogs were a preferred food for public ritual and political feasts. She argued that dogs may have been preferred to other ritual animals for this role because they could be managed and stored. Dogs are found in some deposits and interpreted as the remains of feasting (see Rosenswig 2007:21; Shaw 1999). They were the lead actors in the probable feast deposit at Lagartero excavated by Ekholm (1990) and analyzed by Koželsky (2005), who found nearly half of the deposit consisted of dog. White and colleagues' (2004) and White's (2004) isotopic analysis of the Lagartero dogs showed that they had eaten an almost exclusively vegetarian diet, primarily maize, suggesting that the animals had been husbanded and fattened for the feast. As a special menu item, dogs may have been used during feasting to maintain relations among equals or to emphasize political and social differences, as discussed by Fernández Souza, Zimmermann, and Jiménez Álvarez (this volume).

Dogs are also found in a range of special contexts, including caves, caches, and burials, suggesting that their ritual roles were not isolated to that of being food (Pohl 1983). As a few examples, many dogs were found in burials at the island community of Cozumel, off the Yucatán coast (Hamblin 1984:117); at Mayapán, dog skulls were found in ritual cenotes (Pollock and Ray 1957); at Cancuén, puppies dominated the fauna from a politically controlled central *aguada*, or water retention pond (Thornton and Demarest 2019); and complete dog skeletons were recovered in the tombs of elite nobles at Kaminaljuyu (Emery et al. 2013:412; Kidder, Jennings, and Shook 1946). Based on strontium and oxygen isotope data, two dogs recovered from Middle Preclassic monumental structures at the ceremonial core of Ceibal were found to have been imported to the site from the distant volcanic highlands, suggesting "foreign" dogs were sometimes sought for rituals (Sharpe et al. 2018). Another dog identified by Moholy-Nagy (2008) at Tikal and listed in the appendix she prepared with Coe was found to have isotopic values indicating that it had eaten marine animals (White et al. 2004:155–156). Although this initially was interpreted as the result of dogs having been fed table scraps by seafood-eating rulers, this may instead constitute another example of an imported dog, since there is no evidence that seafood was commonly consumed at inland Tikal.

Modern ethnographic accounts of dog consumption in other parts of the world, as well as archaeological remains of dog consumption beyond Mesoamerica, suggest that even in societies where large numbers of dogs are bred specifically for consumption (for example, South Korea and China), they are still not a frequent source of protein (Kim 2008; Li, Sun, and Yu 2017; Podberscek 2009). Part of this is due to the difficulty of breeding substantial numbers of dogs to meet daily dietary needs. In South Korea, for example, where millions of dogs are bred every year for food, they are mainly eaten for special occasions, particularly at certain times of the year, and breeding is timed to facilitate this availability (Podberscek 2009). Furthermore, there is a compartmentalization of the use of dogs in these societies, in that certain breeds are recognized as "food" dogs and never companions, whereas other breeds, particularly small "toy" breeds, are viewed as pets.

Historically, dogs in preindustrial Korea and China were consumed on occasion, including certain seasonal festivals, but there is no evidence that they were raised in large numbers as they are today (Kim 2008); in fact, most dogs were scavengers living on the periphery of human communities, so their consumption was likely opportunistic. In the archaeological record of Europe and the Middle East, evidence for direct dog consumption (e.g., cutting and dismemberment of dog skeletons) is inconsistent over time and space. Evidence of occasional dog consumption and purposeful butchering has been found from sites in Late Bronze Age Greece (Lipovitch 2006), Iron Age Crete (Snyder and Klippel 2003), Roman period Slovakia (Chrószcz et al. 2015), Bronze Age to Iron Age Palestine (Maeir, Hitchcock, and Horwitz 2013), and elsewhere. Yet faunal analysts working in these areas specify that evidence of dogs as food is usually rare compared to the abundance of evidence of other domestic or hunted animals. Dogs appear to have been ubiquitous across the landscape but not abundant.

What, then, is really known about the role of dogs as food in the ancient Maya area? Here, we present a detailed evaluation of a large compilation of data on dog remains from archaeological sites across the Maya area, using published and unpublished data from the authors as well as a comprehensive review of the literature. Based on this analysis, we argue that the role of dogs as food among the ancient Maya should be interpreted with caution. While dogs were sometimes eaten, evidence suggests that, as indicated by archaeological and ethnographic evidence of dog consumption elsewhere in the world, they were never a basic commodity or an everyday food. The role of dogs in the Maya world was varied and complex. Detailed zooarchaeological analysis is essential to understanding what their role would have been, with attention to context of recovery, distribution of skeletal remains, and markings left on the bones and teeth.

Study Methods

This chapter presents a comparative analysis of dog remains from across the Maya world and from the Preclassic through Historic periods. Our selected study assemblages include those that are published or publicly accessible through the internet, as well as unpublished data that are the intellectual property of the authors and have been approved for use by the original analyst or data curation facility (in situations where the analyst is not known or is no longer available to provide permission). Although we have attempted to be as thorough as possible, this does not represent the full extent of zooarchaeological analyses in the Maya region, since many are not publicly available or are in progress, while still others did not provide sufficient detail to allow us to assess dog data. Sites from the study area were excluded if there were no published data of sufficient resolution to allow us to include it in our quantifications, and as a result, some known sites are not included here. For a complete list of sources and sites, please see Emery et al. (2018).

In our chronological review, we provide information only on dated assemblages that fit into broad chronological period categories, including Preclassic (ca. 2000 BCE–200 CE), Classic (ca. 200–1000 CE), Postclassic (ca. 1000–1500 CE), and Colonial/Historic periods (ca. 1500–1800 CE). Our chronological period categories are intentionally broad in order to cover the range of archaeological interpretations from different sites. Internal site period spans are reported as provided in the publications, and as a result, some period categories may overlap between sites. For example, some temporal overlap may exist among site assemblages classified by the excavators as Contact or Colonial because the "Colonial period" begins temporally earlier in the area of first Spanish impacts than in the frontier zones where the Maya were in extended "contact" with the Spanish but not under Colonial dominion until the later half of the seventeenth century. We grouped here "Contact" and "Colonial" periods under the inclusive category of Colonial/Historic.

For our overall assessment of dog distributions, we compared dog specimen counts to overall mammal counts to avoid the bias inherent in comparing different taxonomic classes. Our review includes data on where dog bones were recovered contextually, the types of remains (body portions, side, age), and the treatment of those remains (burning, butchering, artifact manufacture) to highlight the possible meanings behind the human-dog interaction exemplified by the zooarchaeological remains.

To compare the contexts within which dog remains are found, we chose to classify contexts as "political," which includes those areas that functioned as governing structures or public places; "ritual," which includes burials, caches, and special function deposits; and "quotidian," which are all other spaces, whether at the household or elite level. In most cases, remains were assigned to a context based on how it was defined in the publication, or on information provided by the archaeologist in assemblages identified by the authors. To examine possible differential use of animal parts, we present body portions as a combined total of elements within that portion. We also calculated a ratio of the number of elements within each portion relative to the expected number found in a complete dog body (see Table 6.1 for elements included in each body portion and expected numbers of bones). We also present element body side as the proportion of right or left elements from all side-able elements (not including axial elements or those that could not be sided) for all dogs from a given period. We recorded juvenile/immature animals using the information provided by analysts and considering "unfused" as equivalent of juvenile/immature.

In our analysis, we distinguish between human-made modification marks resulting from artifact manufacture and marks resulting from butchery or skinning. We included anything defined by the analyst as "butchery mark" (or similar) as evidence of cutting, skinning, or disarticulation for consumption. Cut or other modification marks clearly identified as having an association with a finished nondietary product, such as cutting to make a bone tube, polishing, or carving/incising, are identified as artifactual modifications. Drilled stray dog teeth are considered finished artifacts, but we do not count unmodified teeth as such. Finally, we recorded the presence of burned elements. A more detailed description of the methods used in this study can be found in Emery et al. (2018).

Results

General Overview

In this study, we examined the zooarchaeological analyses of 151 faunal assemblages in the Maya area (Table 6.1; also see Emery et al. 2018). These include sites with and without dog remains to determine how often dogs occur in Maya assemblages. Of these, dogs were recovered from 82 percent of the sites. These include 14,461 individual dog remains (Number of Identified Specimens, or NISP), from an original 273,401 mammal elements. Although dogs are ubiquitous across the landscape, they are not found at all sites in the Maya area. Altogether, dogs make up just over 7 percent of mammal elements reported, indicating that although they were the only domestic Mesoamerican mammal, they were not a principal resource, but rather only one of the many mammals the Maya used.

Figure 6.1 shows the proportions of dogs recovered in the four different periods analyzed in this study. Prior studies have emphasized the higher proportions of dogs in early periods (Carr 1986; Clutton-Brock and Hammond 1994; Shaw 1999; Wing and Scudder 1991) or, relatively speaking, the lower proportions in Classic periods (Emery 2004b). Our comprehensive study bears out that conclusion. Our review shows that Classic period assemblages do indeed tend to have lower overall proportions of dog specimens than do assemblages from other chronological phases. However, that proportion ranges among site assemblages from no or very few dogs at all (even in fairly robust mammalian assemblages, e.g., Calakmul, La Joyanca, and Xultun) to above 20 percent at sites like Ek Balam, Mayapán, and Dzibilchaltun. As suggested in earlier studies, Preclassic and Postclassic assemblages are somewhat more dog-rich, but these still have, on average, less than 10 percent of dog remains in the assemblages. However, the variability among sites is high, and some include between 20 percent and 60 percent of dog remains (e.g., Preclassic Ceibal [32%] and Tikal [60%], Postclassic Mayapán [29%] and Champotón [47%]). As in the Classic period, most Colonial/Historic sites also have lower proportions (<10%) of dogs, but here again there are exceptions. For example, the analyses of remains from the site of Ek Balam in northern Yucatán report 70 percent of dogs, a proportion that is highly significant because the assemblage includes 705 dog specimens (deFrance and Hanson 2008).

Together these outliers indicate a considerable variation in proportion of dog remains to mammal remains in all time periods. Even if dogs may have been more common, proportionally, at more sites during the Preclassic and Postclassic periods than in the other periods, they were still not equally abundant at every site during those periods, with some sites apparently having far more dog remains than others. Thus, if dogs were a source of food, they were clearly not a primary nutritional resource, and their popularity was highly variable among sites during all time periods. In the following sections, we explore the evidence for whether dogs may have been used for food or for other purposes.

Context of Recovery

We identified a considerable degree of proportional variability in the contexts of recovery of dog remains both within and among chronological

Table 6.1. Summary of data used in the analysis of dog remains distribution and characteristics. Averages are of values across all assemblages to represent variability. Raw data available in Emery et al. (2018).

Data Categories	Preclassic (72% of total assemblages contain dog remains)			Classic (79% of total assemblages contain dog remains)		
	Dog NISP (#assemblages)	Max (Min=0)	Average	Dog NISP (#assemblages)	Max (Min=0)	Average
Period Dog Distribution						
NISP dogs	3,840 (58)	1,065	80.00	4,475 (77)	1,003	63.03
NISP dog as % of mammals		59.76	9.31		26.54	4.45
Context of Dog Remains*	2,900 (24)			4,034 (46)		
% quotidian		100.00	39.78		100.00	14.94
% political		100.00	43.69		100.00	39.25
% ritual		100.00	16.54		100.00	45.72
% NISP Juvenile** of Aged Dog Remains	811 (10)	90.03	20.25	1,560 (33)	50.00	12.78
% NISP Left of Sided Dog Remains	572 (13)	100.00	46.79	1,280 (37)	100.00	45.96
Treatment of Dog Remains***	2,582 (14)			2,840 (40)		
% burned		100.00	8.32		50.00	4.28
% butchered		2.94	0.44		11.11	0.49
% artifactually modified		1.59	0.33		100.00	14.41
Dog Body Portion NISP****	2,868 (23)			4,078 (47)		
front limb (2 each humerus, radius, ulna)	213	82	7.43	349	71	8.56
hind limb (2 each femur, patella, tibia, fibula)	123	35	4.29	186	38	4.56
feet (30 carpal/tarsal, 20 metapodial, 56 phalanx)	497	216	17.33	459	159	11.26
crania (18 cranial portion, 2 mandible)	408	153	14.23	475	175	11.65
isolated teeth (42)	839	258	29.25	2,032	1,003	49.83
axial (33 vertebra, 26 rib, 2 scapula, 2 pelvis)	787	387	27.44	573	151	14.05

Data Categories	Postclassic (74% of total assemblages contain dog remains)			Colonial (70% of total assemblages contain dog remains)			
	Dog NISP (#assemblages)	Max (Min=0)	Average	Dog NISP (#assemblages)	Max (Min=0)	Average	
Period Dog Distribution							
NISP dogs	2,644 (31)			749 (9)			
NISP dog as % of mammals		1,103	94.43		705	83.22	
Context of Dog Remains*	4,318 (13)	100.00	10.50	749 (8)	70.15	8.69	
% quotidian		100.00	16.51		100.00	40.63	
% political		100.00	31.21		100.00	46.48	
% ritual		100.00	52.28		100.00	12.89	
% NISP Juvenile** of Aged Dog Remains	1,828 (10)	100.00	20.53	36 (5)	100.00	22.07	
% NISP Left of Sided Dog Remains	660 (7)	66.67	42.66	38 (5)	75.00	38.79	
Treatment of Dog Remains***	1,359 (7)			42 (5)			
% burned		5.00	0.81		0.00	0.00	
% butchered		33.33	5.34		25.00	5.00	
% artifactually modified		100.00	15.57		0.00	0.00	
Dog Body Portion NISP****	4,470 (13)			43 (6)			
front limb (2 each humerus, radius, ulna)	283	211	6.33	6	2	13.95	
hind limb (2 each femur, patella, tibia, fibula)	393	322	8.79	3	2	6.98	
feet (30 carpal/tarsal, 20 metapodial, 56 phalanx)	225	100	5.03	12	12	27.91	
crania (18 cranial portion, 2 mandible)	653	498	14.61	8	5	18.60	
isolated teeth (42)	1,613	1,103	36.09	12	10	27.91	
axial (33 vertebra, 26 rib, 2 scapula, 2 pelvis)	1,303	964	29.15	2	2	4.65	

Table 6.1. Continued

	Undated/Mixed (23% of total assemblages contain dog remains)			Total (82% of total assemblages contain dog remains)		
Data Categories	Dog NISP (#assemblages)	Max (Min=0)	Average	Dog NISP (#assemblages)	Max (Min=0)	Average
Period Dog Distribution						
NISP dogs	391 (40)	125	10.57	14,461 (151)	2,341	106.33
NISP dog as % of mammals		23.33	3.25		100.00	7.11
Context of Dog Remains*	231 (13)			12,232 (83)		
% quotidian		75.00	8.73		100.00	23.42
% political		100.00	57.89		100.00	35.33
% ritual		100.00	33.38		100.00	41.21
% NISP Juvenile** of Aged Dog Remains	269 (14)	77.23	17.64	4,504 (52)	100.00	18.85
% NISP Left of Sided Dog Remains	101 (12)	69.23	35.03	2,651 (55)	100.00	48.39
Treatment of Dog Remains***	368 (17)			7,191 (63)		
% burned		5.13	0.30		50.00	3.21
% butchered		16.67	1.45		25.00	0.70
% artifactually modified		100.00	8.02		100.00	12.57
Dog Body Portion NISP****	268 (16)			11,727 (84)		
front limb (2 each humerus, radius, ulna)	37	12	13.81	888	211	7.57
hind limb (2 each femur, patella, tibia, fibula)	11	4	4.10	716	322	6.11
feet (30 carpal/tarsal, 20 metapodial, 56 phalanx)	58	20	21.64	1,251	237	10.67
crania (18 cranial portion, 2 mandible)	33	14	12.31	1,577	498	13.45
isolated teeth (42)	61	26	22.76	4,557	1,103	38.86
axial (33 vertebra, 26 rib, 2 scapula, 2 pelvis)	68	56	25.37	6,134	1,103	76.65

*Context designations are based on author/analyst definitions. Where possible, designations were premised on the specific contexts of dog remains recovery, but where that information was not available, more general contextual designations were used. For example, cave assemblages were considered "ritual" unless the author/analyst provided alternative interpretations.

**Age designations are based on classifications provided by the authors/analysts based on long bone fusion and tooth eruption. While some dog elements fuse during sub-adulthood, these are rarer, and thus the focus of "juvenile" is on dogs under one year of age and generally even younger.

***All treatment data are based on analyst/author definition of modifications. Burning categories include browning, charring, and calcining. Butchery categories include skinning, disarticulation, and meat/bone butchery. Artifact categories include finished and unfinished artifacts and debitage.

****Unlike other data categories, averages for body portion analysis are of total period NISP instead of per assemblage percentage. Cranial portions include 1 each occipital and basisphenoid/sphenoid, 2 each temporal, parietal, zygomatic, auditory bulla, frontal, maxilla, nasal, palatine. Vertebrae include 7 cervical, 13 thoracic, 7 lumbar, 1 sacrum, 5 caudal. Dog caudal vertebral counts are known to vary between breeds, but 5 is a standard average.

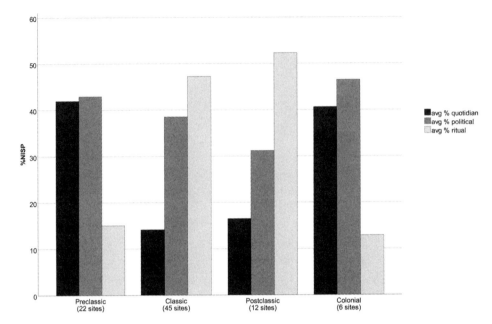

Figure 6.1. Proportion of dog remains found in Preclassic (ca. 2000 BCE–200 CE), Classic (ca. 200–1000 CE), Postclassic (ca. 1000–1500 CE), and Colonial/Historic (ca. 1500–1800 CE) assemblages at Maya sites

periods (Table 6.1). While the proportion of dogs recovered in political contexts is most similar among the periods and is usually fairly high (between 31% and 58% of mammals), and quotidian contexts have the lowest number of remains in all periods (between 9% and 41%), the proportion of dogs found in ritual deposits is also highly variable (between 13% and 52%). Interestingly, the Preclassic and Colonial/Historic periods are most similar in terms of where dogs are found contextually, whereas the Classic and Postclassic periods share a different proportional distribution among contexts. During the Preclassic and Colonial/Historic periods, dogs found in ritual contexts are least common (below 17%), whereas dogs found in politically significant contexts exceed 40 percent and are more common in quotidian contexts than in other periods. During the Classic and Postclassic periods, this pattern is reversed, with ritual context assemblages including 45 percent or more dog remains. This is related, in part, to the use of dog teeth and other artifacts in ritual contexts. Dog ornaments, such as teeth, are particularly common in Classic period burials, such as the site of Caracol (Teeter 2004:189). Teeth are also found in high quantities in other Classic and Postclassic ritual contexts, such as Actun Polbilche (1,103 teeth; Pendergast 1974) and Cahal Pech (1,003 teeth; Burke et al. 2017).

Animal Age at Time of Death

A total of fifty-two assemblages were used to determine whether dogs were adult or juvenile/immature at the time of death. Of 4,504 elements assessed for age, 859 (19%) were found to be juveniles (Table 6.1). Across time periods, similar distributions can be found for Preclassic, Postclassic, and Colonial/Historic periods. Only the Classic period results show a lower percentage of juvenile/immature animals. The average number of juvenile animals across time periods remains relatively constant; however, a few sites have proportions of juvenile elements greater than 30 percent. While animals raised to maturity and slaughtered at a similar age might indicate husbandry for meat consumption, a high percentage of juvenile animals may suggest alternative uses. The use of puppies in Maya ritual ceremonies was documented by Diego de Landa (Tozzer 1941), and puppies have been found in ritual contexts and human burials at a number of Maya sites (Hamblin 1984; Thornton and Demarest 2019; Valdez 1995). However, it is important to point out that the lack of juvenile animals at most sites may not indicate more dogs being raised for meat consumption but may simply point to poor preservation and recovery of the small cartilaginous bones typical of young puppies outside of special deposits (often excavated with finer screens and closer attention to animal remains) and deposits that might be expected to provide better preservation (such as crypts or *aguadas*).

Skeletal Portion Distribution and Sides

The results of the skeletal portion analysis (Figure 6.2) reveal a similar pattern emerging for most time periods. For the most part, dog skeletal elements are found in similar proportions to what would be expected if all skeleton parts were used and deposited in the same manner, without any preferential separation of certain parts. The only exceptions are the axial and forelimb elements for the Colonial/Historic period assemblages, which are respectively underrepresented and overrepresented, and the paw elements for the Preclassic, Classic, and Postclassic period sites, which are underrepresented. Axial and paw elements tend to be less frequently encountered than the other body parts, perhaps due to a combination of preservation issues (the central body and organs of animals are likely to

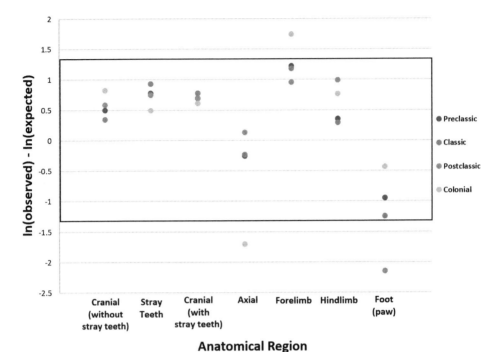

Figure 6.2. Skeletal body portions of dogs across time periods. Natural log difference between observed and expected proportions of elements was calculated following Reitz and Wing (2008:223–224). Standard deviation (region within black box) is 1.32. For axial portions, Preclassic and Postclassic have nearly the same value (-0.29).

be the most attractive to predators and decomposers), identifiability (fragmentary ribs and vertebrae of dog-sized mammals are difficult to distinguish between species), and recovery methods (small carpals, tarsals, and phalanges are likely to be lost, even when screening with a ¼" mesh).

We expected that stray teeth might be overrepresented at Maya sites due to their preferred use as ornamental objects, but this was not the case. Despite evidence from studies of other species for the ritual use of animal crania (Brown and Emery 2008; Masson 1999), we also did not find evidence of overrepresentation of cranial elements such as might be expected from ritual caching of heads. Rather, teeth, and cranial elements in particular, were found about as frequently as would be expected during all phases (some unusual teeth caches notwithstanding, such as at Actun Polbilche). It is possible that larger teeth used for ornaments, such as canines and carnassials, appear in higher abundance at sites, whereas smaller teeth such as incisors are less frequently recovered due to their size, but this will need to be explored in more detail in the future. We also speculated whether there would be evidence of combined cranial and paw associations reflective of the use of dog skins in ways similar to the use of skins of jaguars and other cats. However, the overall low number of paw elements indicates that either dog skins were not made or that paws were not left attached to skins. More broadly, the fact that most cranial and limb elements appear in roughly equal proportions indicates that, at the community level at least, complete animals were used and there were no preferences for certain portions (this does not preclude the possibility that dog portions may have been differentially distributed among residences within a site, since our study did not examine the data at that level).

Regarding element sides, there is no clear evidence that either left- or right-side elements were recovered in higher than expected quantities (see Table 6.1). Again, though, it is important to consider that the broad data may mask details found at a more specific level. In no period were left-sided elements recovered more frequently than right-sided elements (see Table 6.1), although the proportions were close to 50 percent. The Colonial/Historic period had the lowest proportion of left-sided elements (39%), but side data from only five sites (thirty-eight elements) were included from this period, whereas the others have hundreds of sided elements, suggesting that, like a coin toss, when more data are included, the proportion of right to left elements approaches 50:50. This pattern also coincides with the results of the skeletal distribution analysis, indicating that, at least at the site level, dogs were not frequently separated, with the parts used for different functions. A meaningful bias toward either left- or right-sided elements remains possible in specific contexts at some sites, perhaps a result of a method of butchering or even a symbolic meaning for a ritual, but the results of our analysis cannot speak to within-site patterning.

Treatment—Burning, Butchery, and Artifactual Modification

Overall, less than one-fifth of dog remains reported from sites with data regarding burning, butchery, or other artifactual processing show any sign of these modifications. Evidence for burning is exceedingly rare at most sites (Figure 6.3a), usually amounting to only a few specimens per site per period, or less than 5 percent of the dog remains recovered. Preclassic sites with more than a few specimens tend to have less burning reported than Classic period sites (at low frequencies, such as that of Aguacatal, with only one burned bone identified by Emery and Thornton [Table 1], such

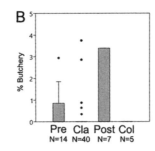
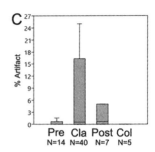

Figure 6.3. Proportion of burned, butchered, and modified dog specimens across time periods. Extreme outliers are not shown here for visualization purposes.

comparative evaluations are not useful). Postclassic sites also have low levels of burning (<1% of bones on average). There is no reported evidence of burned dog remains at the Colonial/Historic era sites in this study, but this period has very few assemblages with reported treatments, so this observation may not reflect broad patterns. Besides Aguacatal, Preclassic sites had less than 10 percent of dog remains burned. In the Classic period assemblages from Dos Pilas (26.7% burned), all but one of the burned dog specimens are teeth, often perforated, and most are from a single structure occupied very late in the sequence of occupation at the site (Emery 2010). At the neighboring site of Aguateca (17.1% burned), the burned dog remains are more skeletally diverse but either are part of a termination ritual at the main palace or were secondarily burned during the destruction of the houses by invaders in the final days of Aguateca's occupation (Emery 2014). Hamblin (1984:114) reported thirteen burned bones at the Postclassic site of Cozumel, but as most of these were found in ceremonial contexts, she suggested that they were the result of ritual sacrifice rather than quotidian consumption.

Even less evidence exists for butchering than for burning among the dog remains reported in this study. Distinguishing butchering marks from those that are the result of artifactual manufacture is often difficult and debatable in archaeology (Olsen and Shipman 1988). Nevertheless, using all data of marks reported as butchery (or simply "cut" without further qualifications), we find remarkably little butchery evidence on Maya dogs overall (Figure 6.3b). The Postclassic period has the most evidence of butchery, although this is from two assemblages at the site of Lamanai (33% and 3% of dogs in both assemblages). The high proportion of butchered dog remains in one of the two assemblages may be due, in part, to the analyst's (Boileau's) previous expertise in identifying taphonomic characteristics on fauna. Lamanai also has the only evidence of a Colonial/Historic era butchered dog bone.

Evidence of artifactual modifications, including drilling, polishing, and incising, is far more common than evidence of either burning or butchering (Figure 6.3c). Stray drilled dog teeth, often canines, are particularly common at many sites. Interestingly, it seems that most modified dog specimens come from Classic period assemblages. Caracol, for example, has one of the highest proportions (and raw NISP quantities) of modified dog remains, many of which were isolated tooth ornaments found in the burial of a woman (Teeter 2004:188–189). Before and after the Classic period, dog artifacts are fairly rare, although drilled dog teeth and polished long bone pieces are found on occasion (e.g., dog teeth pendants and bone artifacts at Middle Preclassic households at Ceibal [Sharpe 2016] and a collection of over one thousand dog teeth at Postclassic Actun Polbilche [Pendergast 1974]). No artifactually modified dog teeth or bones from Colonial or Historic era occupations were found in the reports used in this study, supporting a suggestion that the use of dogs as a material resource had gone out of favor in the generations following European contact. However, it could also be argued that due to the overall lack of Colonial and Historic era sites assessed for zooarchaeological remains in the Maya region, the absence of modified dog specimens may be a product of sampling bias.

Discussion and Conclusion

Dogs have long been cited as a source of sustenance in the Maya region, but as this study shows, dogs more likely had a diverse set of uses across time and space, far beyond a place on the quotidian menu. In this analysis, we tested the common assumption that dogs were an important and commonplace source of food in the ancient Maya world. A series of predictions guided our test: We expected that if dogs were commonly consumed by the Maya populace, then they would appear at most archaeological sites. They should also be expected, as a common food item, to appear in most quotidian contexts, in fairly high quantities compared to other mammals, and generally in higher proportions than are found in ritual contexts. As well, we would expect evidence of butchery activities on the bones, such as cutting and hack marks, and evidence of burning indicating cooking and roasting activities. The proportions resulting from these lines of evidence should be expected to resemble those found for other common food species such as deer or peccary.

We also explored several other forms of evidence that could indicate food use or perhaps other specialized uses. One of these is evidence for a preponderance of juvenile dogs, those young enough to have either been considered particularly tender eating or, just as possibly, particularly symbolic as ritual agents. Another of these is evidence for selective body part distribution. Although dogs are intermediate sized, differential use and discard of different body parts might indicate preferential consumption of meatier parts, a common measure for food animals. Body part distributions might also indicate other uses of dogs, not all associated with food. We do not have any direct information about which parts of the dog body would have been considered most "edible" (culturally speaking) to the ancient Maya, but we do know that dog teeth were used as adornments and that animal skins and heads were frequently given special treatment and often included skulls and foot bones. It is also interesting to consider that ulnae of other species (cats and perhaps also others at Aguateca; see Emery 2014) were used as scepters and possible totems, and dog bones other than teeth have been found modified into artifacts (Sharpe 2016).

Another skeletal distribution difference that has been cited in many contexts, and not just for animals, is that of left and right aspects. The meaning of body sides is well documented among the modern Maya, and the left side in particular has been suggested as representative of important natural and ritual components (Brown 2004:43; Emery 2004a:109; Palka 2002). Pohl (1983:89) found higher proportions of left elements in birds and deer in ritual contexts, suggesting that if dogs were being used in special functions, it is possible that not only the portion of the dog body but also the side of the animal would be important. Finally, we might expect to find fewer specimens in ritual contexts or as artifacts, although those uses do not preclude food consumption. Following our analysis of 151 assemblages from the Preclassic through Colonial/Historic periods, we found that only some of these expectations were supported, and only at some sites in some time periods.

Dogs make up less than 10 percent of the mammal fauna for most of the assemblages that were analyzed, a value we found to be consistent for all time periods. We also found that proportions of dogs varied widely among assemblages and sites of the same time period, revealing that dog presence and practices of use at contemporaneous sites were not standard across the Maya world. Thus, if dogs were a food resource, they were not a common food item; rather, they were one resource among many, and one that was not consistently present or used in the same way at every site.

Dogs were rare in quotidian contexts, although these contexts are admittedly rare across sites in general because of a prior lack of excavation focus on these areas. However, in assemblages from sites where excavators did review households outside the site centers, such as Classic period Motul de San José (only 2% in quotidian contexts vs. 96% in deposits from political/ceremonial locations), dogs are no more common in quotidian contexts than they are in other contexts. In contrast, dogs are very common in ritual contexts, often in the form of artifacts such as perforated teeth, but also often as nonartifactual material. This indicates that if dogs were a food item, it was not within the confines of all domestic homes, certainly not the nonelite homes, and it was not solely a food without associated other uses as artifacts and ritual participants. This contrasts with such animals as agouti, armadillo, and other medium-sized animals that are typically found ubiquitously in households of the rich and poor alike and are not often found as artifacts or in ritual deposits.

Evidence of burning and butchery was also lacking at the vast majority of sites. Butchery marks are rare in all animal remains in the Maya world—the ancient Maya butchers were skilled, and their knives were sharp. However, cut and hack marks were rare in all time periods even in comparison to those found on deer or other food animals. Burning is much more common on ancient animal bones, but burned dog remains in this study were very rare and were primarily found in ritual deposits, not in deposits that might be assumed to be associated with cooking, such as household middens. If dogs were used as food, they were not commonly roasted or cooked in such a way that the evidence was taphonomically visible. This does not preclude cooking, since, as several authors have noted (Götz 2014; Hamblin 1984), dogs could have been cooked in the *píib* or as soups and stews, or in any number of other indirect heating situations.

Among the categories of information that might only provide evidence for or against food use in the details of their findings are age, body part distribution, and "ritual" use. Our examination of reported dog ages at death showed that these were variable among assemblages, but overall the majority (over 80%) of bones were fused and teeth were erupted, indicating that the dogs were at least subadults, and were not juveniles (puppies), in similar proportions across time and space. We do not know at what age dogs might have "tasted best" for the ancient Maya, but in countries that still consume dogs, they are reportedly brought to market when they are around a year old (Bökönyi 1969; Podberscek 2009). At that point in age, many of the larger bones are fused, and adult dentition is in place (Sutton, Byrd, and Brooks 2018). This does not mean that the Maya did not prefer suckling dog, but it does indicate that the market value of a dog is higher when it reaches, but does not much surpass, mature size. Our finding that some site assemblages contained much larger proportions of young dogs in ritual deposits (such as at Cerros, Cancuén, and Lagartero) suggests that young dogs may have been more valued as ritual agents than as food, as proposed by Thornton and Demarest (2019:12).

Dog skeletal portions are found within the statistically expected proportions for the most part, with the exception of a lower-than-expected proportion of paw bones for most periods. This discrepancy does not support the prediction that certain meatier body parts such as haunches were selectively procured for food; rather, it appears that the entire dog was used. Whole body use in other zooarchaeological analyses has been cited as evidence of ritual deposition (Losey et al. 2011) and of feasting (Whitcher Kansa and Campbell 2004). Since our analysis examines remains at the site level, this might just indicate that the whole body was used, perhaps in many different areas and by many different people, across a site. More detailed analysis would be needed to clarify the actual distributions. However, it is intriguing that several deposits specifically described as related to feasting are represented by fairly complete bodies (e.g., Lagartero [Koželsky 2005] and Chinikihá [Montero López 2011]). We also found no bias for left- or right-sided elements at sites and, therefore, no indication of a particular side preference. This neither supports nor discredits the hypothesis of dogs as food, but it does indicate that whatever use the dog had, at the site level, its use did not emphasize one side of the dog's body over another.

Although our focus has been on the use of dogs as food, our results suggest a much broader role for the Maya dog. We are not the first to suggest this, and Stanchly and Awe (2015), for example, have highlighted many of the important considerations we raise here. Although dogs may have been consumed and could easily have been raised and fattened in one's household, their use by the Maya took on many meanings and roles, as did maize, a basic food that was a staple of the Maya diet (see Hendon, this volume). Special foods are intrinsic to all cultures and in many ways define cultural tastes. But a dog's role in ceremony and ritual cannot be assumed to have been limited to even "special food" uses. Some additional evidence can be found in the chronological assessment of trends in dog remain distributions and characteristics.

In terms of context, many dogs were found in areas of sites associated with a political function, doubtless in part a result of the preponderance of our assemblages that were from political contexts, a fact caused by the bias toward excavations in the political site cores of Maya communities.

Nonetheless, their consistent presence in these areas is important to note, particularly considering suggestions that dogs may have been important actors at feasting events that may have been community oriented or politically linked (see Koželsky 2005; Rosenswig 2007). Dogs were uncommon in most quotidian contexts but were more common in quotidian contexts during Preclassic and Colonial/Historic times (with certain exceptions, for example, in the small quotidian sample discussed by Emery et al. [2013] in Preclassic Kaminaljuyu). They were more common in ritual contexts during the Classic and Postclassic periods, particularly as dog teeth (including unmodified teeth) in burials and caches and as other artifacts such as bone tubes. Together, these observations suggest that, whether food-related or not, by the Classic and Postclassic periods, dogs seem to have become a ritually significant resource, especially used for political activities. Indeed, instances such as the numerous dog teeth recovered in Classic, but not Preclassic or Colonial/Historic, special deposits, and unusual cases such as the Postclassic ceremonial sacrifices of entire dogs in the Mayapán cenote (Pollock and Ray 1957) and a probable similar situation at Cancuén (Thornton and Demarest 2019), suggest a notable association between dogs and symbolically significant activities during the Classic and Postclassic periods. Ritual activities involving dogs seem to decrease during the Colonial/Historic period, perhaps due to religious changes resulting from the introduction of European Christian practices, and dogs are once again found in high proportions only in quotidian and political contexts during this period.

The lack of direct evidence of dog bones as a common food source in the Maya region could be explained in several ways, based on ethnographic and archaeological evidence of dog consumption in other societies. In general, even in countries today where dog consumption is a cultural norm and dogs are even bred for this purpose, dogs are not consumed on a regular basis because dog breeding is not as easy or profitable as rearing other animals (Kim 2008; Podberscek 2009). It is possible that, just as in societies today, the Maya had different breeds of dogs that were culturally compartmentalized into acceptable "food" and "friend" categories, although this would warrant further research and likely genetic or osteometric verification.

It is interesting to speculate, then, what cultural bounds marked the transition where dogs passed from "nonfood" to "food." Were dogs mainly used as food for special events or at certain times of the year? Were they eaten by only certain parts of the population (as Podberscek [2009] observes, eating dog meat in South Korea is more commonly a male pastime)? Were all dogs viewed as a potential walking larder or only certain dogs? Were dogs perhaps viewed as companions and, more distantly, a potential source of food while alive, but once slaughtered and prepared for a meal, they crossed the fateful border from friend to food? Many families in Western societies may be familiar with the concept of the latter, in that there is a clear culturally derived mental division between a live pet piglet or chick and an amorphous shrink-wrapped package of bacon or chicken breast at the store.

In sum, this study found that the use of dogs throughout the Maya region varied significantly across time and space. There is no evidence to strongly support the hypothesis that they were a common food item. More than likely, dogs were used to serve a variety of functions. Our compilation of dog data is the first step in a larger effort to tease apart the finer details of how dogs were used in the past. We have made this data available on Open Context (Emery et al. 2018) and hope that, as more research is performed, more data will become available and could be added to the growing compilation to help explain the diverse use of dogs over time and space. We also hope that finer-grained analyses at the household and activity-area level can be used to discern many of the patterns that were not visible in this study as a result of the nature of this analysis.

Acknowledgments

The authors wish to thank Kristen Koželsky, Elizabeth Graham, and Elizabeth Wing for their generous permission to use their unpublished data. We also thank the excavators and analysts whose work creates the foundation for this study, and the institutions of Belize (Belize Institute of Archaeology), Guatemala (Instituto de Antropología e Historia de Guatemala), Honduras (Instituto Hondureño de Antropología e Historia), and Mexico (Instituto Nacional de Antropología e Historia de México) who graciously permitted excavation and analyses of these materials. This chapter has been greatly enhanced by the comments of two anonymous reviewers, Carolyn Freiwald, and Traci Ardren, without whose invitation and patience we would not have had the opportunity to participate in this volume.

References

Anderson, Arthur J. O., and Charles E. Dibble. 1952. *Translation of Fray Bernardino de Sahagún Florentine Codex Book 3, Number 14, Part IV*. Santa Fe, NM: School of American Research.

Bökönyi, Sándor. 1969. "Archaeological Problems and Methods of Recognizing Animal Domestication." In *The Domestication and Exploitation of Plants and Animals*, ed. Peter J. Ucko and G. W. Dimbleby, 219–229. Chicago: Aldine.

Brown, Linda A. 2004. "Dangerous Places and Wild Spaces: Creating Meaning with Materials and Space at Contemporary Maya Shrines on El Duende Mountain." *Journal of Archaeological Method and Theory* 11(1):31–58.

Brown, Linda A., and Kitty F. Emery. 2008. "Negotiations with the Animate Forest: Hunting Shrines in the Guatemalan Highlands." *Journal of Archaeological Method and Theory* 15(4):300–337.

Burke, Chrissina C., Gavin B. Wisner, Katie K. Tappan, Dylan M. Wilson, and Norbert Stanchly. 2017. "Analysis of Faunal Remains from the Upper Belize River Valley Sites of Baking Pot, Cahal Pech, Lower Dover, and Xunantunich." In *The Belize Valley Archaeological Reconnaissance Project: A Report of the 2016 Field Season*, ed. Claire E. Ebert, Chrissina C. Burke, Jaime J. Awe, and Julie A. Hoggarth, 22:407–438. Waco, TX: Institute of Archaeology, Baylor University.

Carr, H. Sorayya. 1986. "Faunal Utilization in a Late Preclassic Maya Community at Cerros, Belize." PhD diss., Tulane University.

Chrószcz, Aleksander, Maciej Janeczek, Zora Bielichová, T. Gralak, and V. Onar. 2015. "Cynophagia in the Púchov (Celtic) Culture Settlement at Liptovská Mara, Northern Slovakia." *International Journal of Osteoarchaeology* 25(4):528–538.

Clutton-Brock, Juliet, and Norman Hammond. 1994. "Hot Dogs: Comestible Canids in Preclassic Maya Culture at Cuello, Belize." *Journal of Archaeological Science* 21(6):819–826.

deFrance, Susan D., and Craig A. Hanson. 2008. "Labor, Population Movement, and Food in Sixteenth-Century Ek Balam, Yucatán." *Latin American Antiquity* 19(3):299–316.

Ekholm, Susana M. 1990. "Una ceremonia de fin-de-ciclo: El gran basurero ceremonial de Lagartero, Chiapas." In *La Época Clásica: Nuevos hallazgos, nuevas ideas*, ed. Amalia Cardos de Méndez, 455–467. Mexico City: Museo Nacional de Arqueología, Instituto Nacional de Antropología e Historia.

Emery, Kitty F. 2004a. "Animals from the Maya Underworld: Reconstructing Elite Maya Ritual at the Cueva de los Quetzales, Guatemala." In *Behaviour Behind Bones: The Zooarchaeology of Ritual, Religion, Status and Identity*, ed. Sharyn Jones O'Day, Wim Van Neer, and Anton Ervynck, 101–113. Oxford: Oxbow Books.

———. 2004b. "In Search of the 'Maya Diet': Is Regional Comparison Possible in the Maya Tropics?" *Archaeofauna* 13:37–55.

———. 2009. "Perspectives on Ancient Maya Bone Crafting from a Classic Period Bone-Artifact Manufacturing Assemblage." *Journal of Anthropological Archaeology* 28(4):458–470.

———. 2010. *"Dietary, Environmental, and Societal Implications of Ancient Maya Animal Use in the Petexbatun: A Zooarchaeological Perspective on Collapse."* Vanderbilt Institute of Mesoamerican Archaeology 5. Nashville: Vanderbilt University Press.

———. 2014. "Aguateca Animal Remains." In *Life and Politics at the Royal Court of Aguateca: Artifacts, Analytical Data, and Synthesis*, ed. Takeshi Inomata and Daniela Triadan, 158–200. Salt Lake City: University of Utah Press.

Emery, Kitty F., and Kazuo Aoyama. 2007. "Bone, Shell, and Lithic Evidence for Crafting in Elite Maya Households at Aguateca, Guatemala." *Ancient Mesoamerica* 18(1):69–89.

Emery, Kitty F., Petra Cunningham-Smith, Ashley E. Sharpe, Erin K. Thornton, and Arianne Boileau. 2018. "Database of Archaeological Information on Maya Dogs

(*Canis lupus familiaris*) from Preclassic through Colonial Periods." Open Context. DOI: doi.org/10.6078/M7J964F6. Accessed October 11, 2018. http://opencontext.org/projects/d4e82e22-d96f-4d01-a15a-fc5ec7958435.

Emery, Kitty F., Erin K. Thornton, Nicole Cannarozzi, Stephen D. Houston, and Héctor Escobedo. 2013. "Archaeological Animals of the Southern Maya Highlands: Zooarchaeology of Kaminaljuyu." In *The Archaeology of Mesoamerican Animals*, ed. Christopher M. Götz and Kitty F. Emery, 381–416. Archaeobiology 1. Atlanta: Lockwood Press.

Flannery, Kent V. 1967. "Vertebrate Fauna and Hunting Patterns." In *The Prehistory of the Tehuacan Valley*. Vol. 1, *Environment and Subsistence*, ed. Douglas S. Byers, 132–177. Austin: University of Texas Press.

Götz, Christopher M. 2014. "¿Solamente contextos culturales?—Evaluación del papel de la tafonomía en la zooarqueología maya de las tierras bajas mayas del norte de la Península de Yucatán." *Etnobiología* 12(2):20–38.

Götz, Christopher M., and Travis W. Stanton. 2013. "The Use of Animals by the Pre-Hispanic Maya of the Northern Lowlands." In *The Archaeology of Mesoamerican Animals*, ed. Christopher M. Götz and Kitty F. Emery, 191–232. Archaeobiology 1. Atlanta: Lockwood Press.

Hamblin, Nancy L. 1984. *Animal Use by the Cozumel Maya*. Tucson: University of Arizona Press.

Kidder, Alfred V., Jesse D. Jennings, and Edwin H. Shook. 1946. *Excavations at Kaminaljuyu, Guatemala*. Carnegie Institution of Washington Publication 576. Washington, DC: Carnegie Institution.

Kim, Rakhyun E. 2008. "Dog Meat in Korea: A Socio-Legal Challenge." *Animal Law* 14(2):201–236.

Koželsky, Kristin L. 2005. "Identifying Social Drama in the Maya Region: Fauna from the Lagartero Basurero, Chiapas, Mexico." Master's thesis, Florida State University.

Leathlobhair, Máire Ní, Angela R. Perri, Evan K. Irving-Pease, Kelsey E. Witt, Anna Linderholm, James Haile, Ophelie Lebrasseur, Carly Ameen, Jeffrey Blick, Adam R. Boyko, et al. 2018. "The Evolutionary History of Dogs in the Americas." *Science* 361(6397):81–85.

Li, Peter J., Jiang Sun, and Dezhi Yu. 2017. "Dog 'Meat' Consumption in China: A Survey of the Controversial Eating Habit in Two Cities." *Society and Animals* 25(6):513–532.

Lipovitch, David R. 2006. "Modeling a Mycenaean Menu: Can Aegean Populations Be Defined in Near Eastern Contexts Based on Their Diet?" *Scripta Mediterranea* 27–28:147–159.

Losey, Robert J., Vladimir I. Bazaliiskii, Sandra Garvie-Lok, Mietje Germonpré, Jennifer A. Leonard, Andrew L. Allen, et al. 2011. "Canids as Persons: Early Neolithic Dog and Wolf Burials, Cis-Baikal, Siberia." *Journal of Anthropological Archaeology* 30(2):174–189.

Maeir, Aren M., Louise A. Hitchcock, and Liora Kolska Horwitz. 2013. "On the Constitution and Transformation of Philistine Identity." *Oxford Journal of Archaeology* 32(1):1–38.

Masson, Marilyn A. 1999. "Animal Resource Manipulation in Ritual and Domestic Contexts at Postclassic Maya Communities." *World Archaeology* 31(1):93–120.

Masson, Marilyn A., and Carlos Peraza Lope. 2008. "Animal Use at the Postclassic Maya Center of Mayapán." *Quaternary International* 191(1):170–183.

Moholy-Nagy, Hattula. 2008. *The Artifacts of Tikal—Ornamental and Ceremonial Artifacts and Unworked Material*. Tikal Museum Monographs, Tikal Report 27A. Philadelphia: University of Pennsylvania Museum of Archaeology and Anthropology.

Montero López, Coral. 2011. "From Ritual to Refuse: Faunal Exploitation by the Elite of Chinikihá, Chiapas, during the Late Classic Period." PhD diss., La Trobe University, Bundoora, Victoria, Australia.

Olsen, Sandra L., and Pat Shipman. 1988. "Surface Modification on Bone: Trampling versus Butchery." *Journal of Archaeological Science* 15(5):535–553.

Palka, Joel W. 2002. "Left/Right Symbolism and the Body in Ancient Maya Iconography and Culture." *Latin American Antiquity* 13(4):419–443.

Pendergast, David M. 1974. *Excavations at Actún Polbilche, Belize*. Archaeology Monograph 1. Toronto: Royal Ontario Museum.

Podberscek, Anthony L. 2009. "Good to Pet and Eat: The Keeping and Consuming of Dogs and Cats in South Korea." *Journal of Social Issues* 65(3):615–632.

Pohl, Mary D. 1983. "Maya Ritual Faunas: Vertebrate Remains from Burials, Caches, and Cenotes in the Maya Lowlands." In *Civilization in the Ancient Americas: Essays in Honor of Gordon R. Willey*, ed. Richard M. Leventhal and Alan L. Kolata, 55–103. Albuquerque: University of New Mexico Press.

Pollock, H. E. D., and Clayton E. Ray. 1957. "Notes on Vertebrate Animal Remains from Mayapan." *Carnegie Institution of Washington Current Reports* 41:633–656.

Reitz, Elizabeth J., and Elizabeth S. Wing. 2008. *Zooarchaeology*. 2nd ed. Cambridge Manuals in Archaeology. Cambridge: Cambridge University Press.

Rosenswig, Robert M. 2007. "Beyond Identifying Elites: Feasting as a Means to Understand Early Middle Formative Society on the Pacific Coast of Mexico." *Journal of Anthropological Archaeology* 26(1):1–27.

Sharpe, Ashley E. 2016. "A Zooarchaeological Perspective on the Formation of Maya States." PhD diss., University of Florida.

Sharpe, Ashley E., Kitty F. Emery, Takeshi Inomata, Daniela Triadan, George D. Kamenov, and John Krigbaum. 2018. "Earliest Isotopic Evidence in the Maya Region for Animal Management and Long-Distance Trade at the Site of Ceibal, Guatemala." *Proceedings of the National Academy of Sciences* 115(14):3605–3610.

Shaw, Leslie C. 1991. "The Articulation of Social Inequality and Faunal Resource Use in the Preclassic Community of Colha, Northern Belize." PhD diss., University of Massachusetts.

———. 1995. "The Importance of Dog in Ritual Feasting in the Maya Preclassic." Paper presented at the 60th Annual Meeting of the Society for American Archaeology, Minneapolis, MN.

———. 1999. "Social and Ecological Aspects of Preclassic Maya Meat Consumption at Colha, Belize." In *Reconstructing Ancient Maya Diet*, ed. Christine D. White. 83–102. Salt Lake City: University of Utah Press.

Snyder, Lynn M., and Walter E. Klippel. 2003. "From Lerna to Kastro: Further Thoughts on Dogs as Food in Ancient Greece; Perceptions, Prejudices and Reinvestigations." *British School at Athens Studies* 9:221–231.

Stanchly, Norbert, and Jaime J. Awe. 2015. "Ancient Maya Use of Dog (*Canis lupus familiaris*): Evidence from the Upper Belize River Valley." *Research Reports in Belizean Archaeology* 12:227–237.

Sutton, Lerah K., Jason H. Byrd, and Jason W. Brooks. 2018. "Age Determination in Dogs and Cats." In *Veterinary Forensic Pathology*, ed. Jason W. Brooks, 2:151–163. New York: Springer.

Tedlock, Dennis. 1996. *Popol Vuh: The Mayan Book of the Dawn of Life*. Rev. ed. New York: Touchstone.

Teeter, Wendy G. 2004. "Animal Utilization in a Growing City: Vertebrate Exploitation at Caracol, Belize." In *Maya Zooarchaeology: New Directions in Method and Theory*, ed. Kitty F. Emery, 177–191. Monograph 51. Los Angeles: Cotsen Institute of Archaeology at UCLA.

Thornton, Erin Kennedy, and Arthur A. Demarest. 2019. "At Water's Edge: Ritual Maya Animal Use in Aquatic Contexts at Cancuén, Guatemala." *Ancient Mesoamerica* 30(3):473–491.

Tozzer, Alfred M. 1941. *Landa's Relación de las Cosas de Yucatan: A Translation*. Papers of the Peabody Museum of American Archaeology and Ethnology, Vol. 18. Cambridge, MA: Peabody Museum at Harvard University.

Tykot, Robert H., Nikolaas J. van der Merwe, and Norman Hammond. 1996. "Stable Isotope Analysis of Bone Collagen, Bone Apatite, and Tooth Enamel in the Reconstruction of Human Diet: A Case Study from Cuello, Belize." In *Archaeological Chemistry*, ed. Mary Virginia Orna, 355–365. ACS Symposium Series 625. Washington, DC: American Chemical Society.

Vail, Gabrielle, and Christine Hernández. 2007. "Human Sacrifice in Late Postclassic Maya Iconography and Texts." In *New Perspectives on Human Sacrifice and Ritual Body Treatments in Ancient Maya Society*, ed. Vera Tiesler and Andrea Cucina, 120–164. Interdisciplinary Contributions to Archaeology. New York: Springer.

Valdez, Fred. 1995. "Religion and Iconography of the Preclassic Maya at Rio Azul, Peten, Guatemala." In *Religión y sociedad en el área maya*, ed. Carmen Varela Torrecilla, Juan Luis Bonor Villarejo, and María Yolanda Fernández Marquínez, 211–218. Mesa Redonda 4. Madrid: Sociedad Española de Estudios Mayas.

van der Merwe, Nikolaas J., Robert H. Tykot, Norman Hammond, and Kim Oakberg. 2002. "Diet and Animal Husbandry of the Preclassic Maya at Cuello, Belize: Isotopic and Zooarchaeological Evidence." In *Biogeochemical Approaches to Paleodietary Analysis*, ed. Stanley H. Ambrose and M. Anne Katzenberg, 23–38. Advances in Archaeological and Museum Science 5. Boston: Springer.

Whitcher Kansa, Sarah, and Stuart Campbell. 2004. "Feasting with the Dead?—A Ritual Bone Deposit at Domuztepe, South Eastern Turkey (c. 5550 cal BC)." In *Behavior Behind Bones: The Zooarchaeology of Ritual, Religion, Status and Identity*, ed. Sharyn Jones O'Day, Wim van Neer, and Anton Ervynck, 2–13. Oxford: Oxbow Books.

White, Christine D. 2004. "Stable Isotopes and the Human-Animal Interface in Maya Biosocial and Environmental Systems." *Archaeofauna* 13:183–198.

White, Christine D., Mary E. D. Pohl, Henry P. Schwarcz, and Fred J. Longstaffe. 2001. "Isotopic Evidence for Maya Patterns of Deer and Dog Use at Preclassic Colha." *Journal of Archaeological Science* 28(1):89–107.

———. 2004. "Feast, Field, and Forest: Deer and Dog Diets at Lagartero, Tikal, and

Copan." In *Maya Zooarchaeology: New Directions in Method and Theory*, ed. Kitty F. Emery, 141–158. Los Angeles: Cotsen Institute of Archaeology at UCLA.

Wing, Elizabeth S. 1978. "Use of Dogs for Food: An Adaptation to the Coastal Environment." In *Prehistoric Coastal Adaptations: The Economy and Ecology of Maritime Middle America*, ed. Barbara L. Stark and Barbara Voorhies, 29–41. New York: Academic Press.

Wing, Elizabeth S., and Sylvia J. Scudder. 1991. "The Exploitation of Animals." In *Cuello: An Early Maya Community in Belize*, ed. Norman Hammond, 84–97. Cambridge: Cambridge University Press.

CHAPTER 7

Celebrating Sihó: The Role of Food and Foodways in the Construction of Social Identities

LILIA FERNÁNDEZ SOUZA, MARIO ZIMMERMANN, AND SOCORRO DEL PILAR JIMÉNEZ ÁLVAREZ

For human beings, food is much more than a way to resolve subsistence needs. Producing, preparing, cooking, and serving dishes play fundamental roles in how people see themselves and relate to one another. The study of food offers a deep perspective on many aspects of society because choices about what people eat and how they prepare and consume foodstuffs depend on numerous factors, including class, ethnicity, gender roles, technology, religion, and cultural values (Allen and Sachs 2012:25; Armelagos 2003:106; Ayora-Díaz 2012; Dietler 1996; Dirks and Hunter 2013:5; Inness 2001:5–6; Moore 2013:79). As mentioned by Ardren in the introduction to this volume, food provides a social glue because most of its associated processes involve some sort of social interaction (Armelagos 2003:105; Hastorf 2012:218; 2017). Meals may help create or reinforce group and family ties. Sharing food is an endearing way to strengthen affections, build memories, and close deals, but it can simultaneously be used to mark differences and establish social, political, or economic ranking (Appadurai 1981; Dietler 1996; Hastorf 2012, 2017; Hendon, this volume). In both senses, food is a powerful agent, closely involved with the construction of social identities at different levels.

In this chapter, we explore the role of food and foodways in the construction and negotiation of social identities at Sihó, Yucatán, a northern lowland Maya settlement that reached its peak during the Late Classic (600–900 CE) and Terminal Classic periods (850–1000 CE). Using data from household contexts, we were able to obtain insight into the food consumption patterns of Sihó's inhabitants. Based on the comparison of culinary equipment, spot-test chemical analyses, zooarchaeological evidence, and starch grains from seven residential compounds representative of different status groups, we discuss how food may have contributed to creating community identities as well as emphasizing social and political differences between the inhabitants of the site.

Food and Politics: The Flavor of Power

Food is a critical element in the construction of community identity (Appadurai 1981; Dietler 1996; Hastorf 2012, 2017; Morell-Hart, this volume). Based on his studies in South Asia, Appadurai (1981:496) stresses that food may serve two opposed semiotic functions: on one hand, it constructs social relations founded in equality, solidarity, or intimacy. On the other, food may also sustain relations characterized by rank and segmentation (see also Hendon, this volume).

According to Hastorf (2017:231, 532), some products, which she recognizes as "signature foods," activate community identities. In the case of the Maya, this would be maize. Maize was a primordial staple food for the whole of Mesoamerica, although every culture had its particularities about selected species and forms of preparation. This cultigen became a significant staple around the Middle Preclassic period (Clark, Pye, and Gosser 2007:31). From that time, symbolic elements like green stone celts linked to the Maize Deity appear regularly in the archaeological record, paving the way for the symbolism of divine rulership and the expression of Maya rulers as an embodiment of the Maize Deity (Clark, Pye, and Gosser 2007; Freidel and Reilly 2010). As suggested by Ardren (this volume), maize cultivation played an important role in the foundation of Maya structural power, and it was a leading protagonist in religious and political narratives of the Maya area. On the other hand, maize was, and still is, a very versatile food that has been prepared in a wide variety of meals and drinks and can be combined with many different animal or vegetable ingredients. As mentioned by Hendon (this volume), maize is a good example of a staple food with several meanings and roles. The ancestral importance of maize is evidenced in different Mayan languages, in which the word *waaj* was ubiquitous (Zender 2008). Frequently translated today as "tortilla," *waaj*, scholars agree, should be read as "tamale" in the Classic period (Taube 1989; Zender 2008).

Feasts are recognized by several authors as important occasions to create community ties through meals that differ, slightly or in a significant way, from quotidian food (Appadurai 1981; Brown and Freiwald, this volume; Dietler 1996; Hastorf 2012, 2017; Lamoureux-St-Hilaire, this volume; LeCount 2001). As expressed by Dietler (1996:89), feasts are ritualized social events that symbolically express social relations. Some feasts involve and reinforce relations between equals, such as the potluck, in which every participant brings a different dish to share (Hastorf 2017: 271). Others are used as strategies and mechanisms that contribute to creating or emphasizing social and political inequalities, highlighting exclusion or rivalry, as seen in the concept of "gastropolitics." Appadurai (1981: 495) defines gastropolitics as "conflict or competition over specific cultural or economic resources as it emerges in social transactions around food." Dietler (1996:98; see also Lamoureux-St-Hilaire, this volume; LeCount 2001; Morell-Hart, this volume) has proposed the term "diacritical feast"—mentioned by Hastorf (2017:202) as "competitive feast"—to refer to events with distinguished cuisines and styles of consumption that exhibit and naturalize rank and status differences, which may be expressed through exclusive or expensive foods and service vessels. These differences may be deployed to distinguish between "high" and "low" cuisines, or as a means to emphasize the wealth and political power of one group over another. As mentioned by Hendon (this volume), luxury foods or a "high cuisine" are not necessarily (or at least not only) determined by particular ingredients but may be the result of refined ways of processing or of the selection of particularly fine cuts of meat.

Besides their leading role in defining and reinforcing the relationships between humans, foodways and feasts are central ingredients in the worship of ancestors and deities (Freidel and Reilly 2010; Hastorf 2012). In the case of the Maya, the Maize Deity and other supernatural beings who provided an abundance of rain, crops, and sustenance were invoked in community ceremonies, as mentioned in pre-Columbian and colonial documents like the Dresden and Madrid codices and Bishop Landa's *Relación de las cosas de Yucatán* (Landa 2001; Vail and Looper 2014:124; Velásquez García 2017:43). Hastorf (2017:271) discusses the case of Joya de Cerén, an unusually well-preserved site as a result of a volcano eruption that covered it with ashes; at Cerén, evidence shows a communal way to cultivate and store food in households that contained both domestic and ritual spaces. There, food played a central role in the relationship between household members, who were linked to the Rain Deity and could have shared an ontology of fertility. Feasting and practicing communal rituals could have strengthened self-identity in the communities and reinforced ties between families (Hastorf 2017:271).

In succeeding years, Yucatec historic sources demonstrate the importance of feasts as social and political arenas that united rulers and commoners in banquets that offered special dishes that were uncommon in quotidian life, especially for nonelite members of the community. For example, the New Year Ceremonies, recorded in the Dresden Codex (Velásquez García 2017) and later described by Bishop Landa (2001), were festivities dedicated to deities in which delicate and elaborate meals were served. The house of the ruler was a central place for the ceremony, reinforcing his political power and social influence.

Food Differences among the Maya

The ancient Maya diet has been approached from a variety of disciplines that include zooarchaeology, paleoethnobotany, chemistry, epigraphy, and history (Barba Pingarrón 2007; Farriss 2012; Götz 2005, 2011, 2014; Hendon, this volume; Landa 2001; Lentz 1999; Matos 2014; Morell-Hart, this volume; Morell-Hart, Joyce, and Henderson 2014; Stuart 2006; Vail and Dedrick, this volume; Vail and Looper 2014), with the result that we have a general overview of vegetal and animal sources that were commonly consumed. As previously mentioned, maize constituted the main staple, but in Yucatán, many other plants offered seeds, fruits, leaves, and roots for a wide variety of meals, such as beans, pumpkins, yams, sweet potatoes, bush spinach, avocados, sapotes, *prunus* (cherries or *capulines*), and others. Animals like deer, turkey, curassow, wild pig, iguana, and fish were some of the most frequent sources of meat. Unsurprisingly, regional differences existed, derived from environmental diversity between coastal or inland areas, as well as from variations in humidity or soil quality, and some regions had fish and seafood, salt or good cocoa, while others did not.

Besides regional variations, differences between Maya elites and commoners have been recognized in both pre-Columbian and post-Conquest times. In Yucatán, the term *almehen* referred to nobility that survived through the Colonial period (Restall 1997:88). From Yucatecan colonial documents, Farriss (2012; see also Patch 2014:446–447; Restall 1997) emphasizes the fact that colonial Maya society was far from homogeneous, as the Spaniards may have assumed. Important differences can be seen with respect to the size and complexity of house gardens, or *solares*; colonial Maya elites had a greater quantity and larger *solares* with a variety of fruit trees, as well as orchards and croplands with beehives located outside settlements, and sometimes even private access to cenotes, or sinkholes, that reached the water table. The commoners, or *macehuales*, used to have turkeys or chickens, and sometimes one or two pigs, but cows and horses were exclusively for the elite. According to Farriss (2012:241–242), the pantry of colonial Maya nobility included lard, honey, cacao, pumpkin seeds, and spices, which were used to enrich the local diet of corn and beans. Game and fish were part of upper-class meals, but not so much of the meals of commoners, who ate meat much less frequently, because their consumption was limited to special events such as communal feasts (Roys 1972:44; see also Farriss 2012). Elites received most of their foodstuffs from commoners. Friar Diego de Landa (2001:46–47) notes that both farming and hunting were done communally, and the lords received their part in meat, fish, and salt. The lords' lands were also worked by commoners.

It is important to realize, though, that there was not a simple binary social division: for example, based on the Ixil testaments (1765–1769 CE), a series of Yucatecan wills dictated during the Colonial period, Restall (1997: 96, 97) proposed a social hierarchy consisting of at least eight levels: lower commoners, lower-middle commoners, upper-middle commoners, upper commoners, lower *almehenob*, middle *almehenob*, upper *almehenob*, and *indios hidalgos*. Given this, it seems likely that there would have been dramatic differences between the upper *almehenob* and the lower commoners, including, probably, myriad variances of wealth and, possibly, diet, based not only on the social status of an individual but also on the town or community to which he or she belonged.

In the case of pre-Columbian times, discussions regarding the segmentation of ancient Maya society have moved away from a traditional dichotomic perspective that only envisioned "elites" and "commoners" toward a picture that recognizes the multistratified character of the region's past populations (Chase and Chase 1992; Lohse and Valdez 2004; Marcus 2004; White 1999). Differences may be seen within a site but also between different sites, according to their political and economic power. We review three of the ways these differences have been identified in the Maya area that are relevant to our discussion of Sihó.

In an analysis of faunal remains from households that represent different socioeconomic levels at a series of lowland sites, Christopher Götz (2010) observed that the volume of bones and MNI is greatest at the highest-ranked site, Chichén Itzá, and lower at smaller sites such as Sihó. Within these communities, the most elaborate architectural groups generally surpassed humbler residences in the same categories. Differences in meat consumption may also be found between the central and peripheral areas of a settlement, as evidenced by zooarchaeological remains from Mayapán (Masson et al., this volume). Finally, higher-status consumers did not only fare better in terms of sheer quantities but also managed to acquire a broader array of species. Götz (2010) concludes that the proportion of meat in the diet, as well as the possibility to access limited goods, signaled group identity.

Another line of evidence is carbon and nitrogen isotopic studies of human bone, which have obtained results that fit with the above-mentioned patterns. For example, Metcalfe et al. (2009) and White et al. (2001) demonstrated that the elites in sites such as Chau Hiix, Lamanai, Altun Ha, and Pacbitun, in Belize, were consuming more maize than individuals from lower social strata. Similarly, Chase and colleagues (2001) state that members of Caracol's highest social segment consumed a "palace diet," which was rich in maize and meat when compared to the diet of the lower strata at the same site. On the other side, while Wright (2003) did not find any differences in terms of maize consumption, the ancient inhabitants of Tikal also differed when it came to meat consumption, with elites ingesting higher quantities. In Piedras Negras, Scherer et al. (2007) observed a kind of homogeneous isotopic pattern during the peak of the site, while finding differences during subsequent politically stressed times, which showed diet inequality between social strata.

Special attention has long been paid to cocoa as a plant food and status marker among the ancient Maya. Its control by elites was proven through the decipherment of the Primary Standard Sequences (PSS), which informed scholars about the variety of ways the ancient Maya enjoyed flavored cocoa and corn beverages, served in beautiful carved or painted vessels (Beliaev, Davletshin, and Tokovinine 2009; Kettunen and Helmke 2010; Stuart 2006). According to Stuart (2006:192), cocoa was the most frequently mentioned beverage in the PSS, and epigraphers have found numerous ways it was consumed: Stuart (2006:193) finds *tzih kakaw* (pure cacao), *ach' kakaw* (new cacao), and *yutal k'an kakaw* (ripe cacao); Beliaev, Davletshin, and Tokovinine (2009) mention *yutal kakaw* (fruity cacao, maybe cacao with fruits or a beverage prepared with cocoa fruit flesh instead of the seeds), *kaab'il* or *chab'il kakaw* (cacao with honey), and *tzah kakaw* (sweet cacao); and Kettunen and Helmke (2010:45) describe *chak kakaw* (red cacao) and *om? kakaw* (frothy cacao). Interestingly, Vela (2012) reported a pottery dish fragment with chemical evidence of cocoa, which suggests that cocoa could have been served in food instead of drink, maybe as a sauce or proto-*mole*.

In addition to the exquisite beverages described in the PSS, the elegant wares used at high-status feasts, such as delicate dishes, bowls, and vases, were signs of wealth exclusiveness and exclusion, because only elites had access to them. The elaborate meals and drinks mentioned in pre-Columbian texts and in ethnohistoric sources required specialized kitchen equipment that included a wide variety of pottery, gourd, or basketry receptacles; flint and obsidian blades; grinding instruments; and diverse cooking facilities and serving implements (Ardren 2015; Ardren, this volume; García Barrios and Carrasco Vargas 2008; Fernández Souza 2016; Fernández Souza, Toscano Hernández, and Zimmermann 2014; Morell-Hart, this volume; Simms et al. 2013; Toscano Hernández et al. 2011). Some of these objects are archaeologically identifiable and provide critical evidence to approach an understanding of cuisine preparation processes, the spaces in which these tasks were performed, and the possible agents who participated in them.

Culinary Scenarios: Residences at Sihó, Yucatán

Sihó is located in the Mexican state of Yucatán, on the northwestern plains of the Yucatán Peninsula, about 30 km inland from the coast (Figure 7.1). It has an area of about 10 km². During the mapping project directed by Rafael Cobos between 2001 and 2003, more than one hundred structures were registered, at least thirteen of which have vaulted architecture. With the exception of two of them, all of the vaulted structures are located at the center of the site. Around the central area, numerous compounds suggest the use of perishable superstructures. Excavations led by archaeologists from the Autonomous University of Yucatán were first carried out from 2001 to 2003, when five structures in two high-status architectural groups were studied. In 2013, a new project started, working on much less voluminous nonelite residential units.

The site was first settled during the Middle Preclassic period, and there is evidence of occupation through the Terminal Classic period. After 1050 CE, the settlement seems to have been visited only occasionally (Cobos and Lacadena García-Gallo 2019; Cobos et al. 2002; Jiménez Álvarez 2007; Jiménez Álvarez et al. in press). Some of its most important architecture was built and the settlement's demographic peak occurred during the Late and Terminal Classic periods.

The Central Group of Sihó (Figure 7.2) is a complex architectural compound, in which Structure 5D1, a pyramid-like temple, served as one of the city's hallmarks. South of the Central Group, the Main Plaza contains large stone monoliths known as stelae, monuments that exhibited portraits and written information about the rulers (Lacadena García-Gallo 2011; Schele and Freidel 1990). Unfortunately, most carved stelae at Sihó are quite damaged, and some of the monuments are plain, with no visible

Figure 7.1. Map of the Yucatán Peninsula with location of Sihó. Illustration by María J. Novelo-Pérez.

carving, suggesting they were painted; as a consequence, we do not have information about the name of the ruling family. Str. 5D2 is a range or palace-type vaulted building located on the west side of an open area or patio delimited by 5D1 in the east, range Str. 5D7 in the north, and Str. 5D17 in the south, a basal platform that possibly supported a perishable construction. Excavation of Str. 5D2 and Str. 5D7, in 2003, clearly defined a residential area due to the presence of large, legless grinding stones (locally known as metates), domestic pottery, and faunal remains (Cobos et al. 2004; Fernández Souza 2010; Götz 2005; Jiménez Álvarez 2007; Tun Ayora 2004). The legless metates present an especially valuable in situ artifact category, as their weight and volume make them too heavy to be transported.

Group 5D16, situated about two hundred meters north of the Central Group, is also an elite residential compound. It consists of an elevated platform with a frontal stairway, whose main structure is a palace-type building, designated Str. 5D16. This structure is located north of an open area or patio that is also flanked by two ancillary structures, Str. 5D20 in the east and Str. 5D19 in the west. A subterranean water storage unit, or *chultun*, is situated west of Str. 5D19. Unlike the Central Group, this

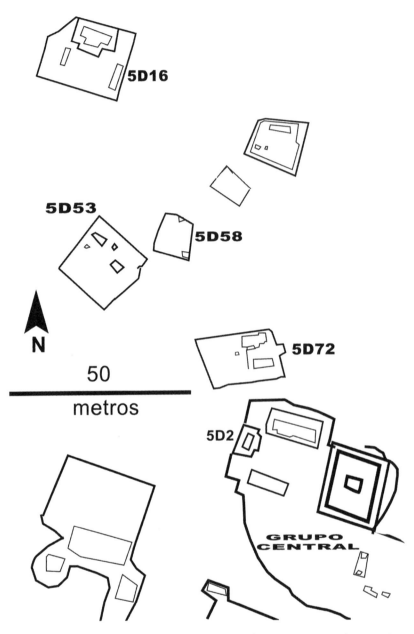

Figure 7.2. Groups and structures at the Center of Sihó. Illustration by María J. Novelo-Pérez, based on the map of Cobos and Inurreta (2002).

Figure 7.3. Structure 5D16. Photograph by Lilia Fernández Souza.

compound was exclusively residential, with no religious, administrative, or political structures or monuments in evidence (Cobos et al 2002, 2004; Fernández Souza 2010; Peniche May 2004, 2011).

Group 5D72, located northwest of the Central Group, is more modest and has no vaulted or masonry architecture (Figure 7.3). Nonetheless, the basal platform of its main building, Str. 5D72, mimics the plan of elite Strs. 5D2 and 5D16, although it is much smaller and simpler. The basal platform of Str. 5D72 has relatively well-cut stones, but its superstructure was perishable. It defined the northern side of a patio for which the southern side was marked by Str. 5D73, another semi-perishable building (Figure 7.4). All together, these structures occupy about half of a bigger open platform; in its center there was a small and poorly preserved square stone feature. Cobos and Inurreta (2002) proposed that this feature was possibly an altar. At the southern end of the platform, next to Str. 5D73, is a small, circular human-made depression. Its shallowness suggests that it was not a water storage feature. Adjacent soils showed modest levels of phosphate enrichment and relatively high concentrations of both carbonate and protein residues (Matos 2014), and its location next to one of the six grinding stones of the group suggests that it was associated with food preparation or storage.

In spite of the nonmonumental character of Group 5D72, excavation of Test Pit 1, located at the center of Str. 5D72, revealed a construction offering of three greenstone earplugs. Based on architectural characteristics and access to valuable goods like the greenstone, we suggest that Group 5D72 could have been occupied by a sort of "middle socioeconomic status" household, similar to what Restall (1997) identified as lower or middle *almehenob*.

Group 5D53 (Figure 7.5) consists of seven simple basal platforms over a square platform, delimitated by large rough-cut stones. None of the structures were similar to, nor as elaborate as, those from Group 5D72. All of the construction was limited to platforms built of a single course of stone with perishable walls and roofs. Nonetheless, the group was a complex space, because the structures were organized in such a way as to form discrete spaces, probably patios or relatively private areas. Five legless metates were distributed across the open space, one of which was found inside a small oval structure with elevated levels of chemical residues (Fernández Souza et al. 2014). Group 5D58 is also a residential compound organized on a platform delimited by large rough-cut stone. It is even simpler than 5D53, with only three small alignments constructed from irregular stones that should have supported perishable structures. Organization of the domestic space is also simpler, because the three structures look toward a single big, central patio.

Figure 7.4. Hypothetical reconstruction of Group 5D72 at Sihó. Illustration by Lilia Fernández Souza.

Figure 7.5. Hypothetical reconstruction of Group 5D53 at Sihó. Illustration by Lilia Fernández Souza.

Finally, Strs. 4D5, 4D9, and 4D10a are the most modest constructions of our sample. 4D5 and 4D10a were low foundations resting directly on the ground surface, with no platform and no well-cut stones in their construction, and 4D9 is a leveling of the bedrock with some irregular stone alignments. Associated pottery appears to support the domestic character of these three structures.

Material Evidence of Culinary Practices

The excavation and analysis of these domestic compounds provided data about the kitchen practices performed at Sihó, as evidenced by culinary equipment, chemical residues left by foods and food preparation, and traces of vegetal and animal products. With respect to culinary equipment, we focus on three classes of implements: grinding stones, pottery, and obsidian blades.

Grinding Stones

During the 2001 and 2003 field season, 285 metates were reported across the entire site, ranging from dispersed fragments to complete in situ artifacts (Pat Cruz 2006:60). Compared to metates, only 32 manos were found, either fragmented or complete, during excavations (Pat Cruz 2006:105). According to Pat Cruz (2006:90), 283 of the 285 grinding stones—90 percent of which were in use during the Late Classic period—demonstrated a certain homogeneity in size, with a range between 40 × 32 cm in width and 121 × 74 cm in length. Among his concluding remarks, Pat Cruz (2006: 124) states that "there is no marked difference in relation to the form and size of metates between vaulted and non-vaulted buildings." But, even though Pat Cruz did not find a difference in the form and size of metates between elite and commoner structures, there were important numerical variations, with the number of grinding stones associated with architectural complexity. According to the map by Cobos and Inurreta (2002), as well as Pat Cruz's study (2006), and newer data from the 2001–2003 and 2013–2017 excavations, a higher number of grinding stones were found associated with higher-status buildings. About 20 metates were found at the Central Group, at Strs. 5D1, 5D2, 5D7, and 5D17. In contrast, small structures with low basal platforms or with no basal platforms at all, such as 4D10, 4D10a, 5D47, 5D50, 5D51, 5D52, and 5D59, had no grinding stones. In the middle, there was variation: for example, Str. 5D16, a non-central palace, possibly pertaining to secondary elite, had 8 metates. Some compounds, such as 5D53 and 5D58, which are relatively similar to each other, have simple basal platforms for perishable superstructures, which house an average of 5 to 6 metates. Str. 4D5 had 1 metate. There were a few fragments of small tripod grinding stones, one of which was found in low-status Str. 4D9. Fragments of imported basalt metates were found in Str. 5D2 (a hand, two fragments, and a leg) and 5D16 (a leg and a fragment), while these were absent in nonelite structures excavated in 2013, 2015, and 2017.

Most grinding stones at Sihó are large, basin-like legless metates, easily identified and recorded from the surface (Pat Cruz 2006). This is useful to the archaeologist but problematic in certain aspects—it opens up a number of possibilities to explain their number, because the large metates may have been used by more than one generation, implying that not all of them were necessarily in use at the same time. Considering this, we compared the number of grinding stones from the structures that were excavated in seasons 2001–2004 and 2013–2017 (Table 7.1). All the structures were excavated horizontally, following the same excavation strategies, while looking for activity area surfaces, and it is possible to propose that grinding stones were at least partially contemporaneous during the Late and Terminal Classic periods.

Table 7.1. Number of grinding stones by household group at Sihó, Yucatán, Mexico, registered in the 2001–2004 and 2013–2017 field seasons

Household Group	Number of Grinding Stones
5D2/5D7	20
5D16	8
5D72	6
5D53	5
5D58	5
4D5	1
4D10	0

The high number of metates in the Central Group may be the result of activities performed in the residential, administrative, and religious compound of the royal elite. Something similar was reported by Toscano Hernández et al. (2011; Fernández Souza et al. 2014) in the kitchen, or k'oben, area of the palace at Kabah. In the kitchen of the Kabah palace, a long basal platform located next to the palace, there were more than thirty metates in association with animal bone, high quantities of ceramics suggesting storage, ash, and chemical and archaeobotanical residues that support the hypothesis of a complex area for culinary activities.

On the other hand, secondary elite, or upper commoners such as the inhabitants of Group 5D16, may have had fewer grinding stones because they inhabited less complex households and did not have to prepare royal banquets. More difficult to explain is the absence of grinding stones in the lowest-status structures. On the other hand, it is important to consider other possible explanations, such as the number and longevity of the members in the households or the number of nuclear families in each compound.

Pottery

There are also differences between these various domestic structures in terms of their ceramic samples. In the case of elite Strs. 5D16 and 5D2, during the Late Classic Jolin I Complex, there was abundant and mostly monochrome domestic pottery with a wide repertoire of forms, including jars, basins, and tripod plates (Jiménez Álvarez 2007:192). The inhabitants of these structures also had access to imported pottery, and during the Terminal Classic period, they used a diagnostic and delicate elite ware named Ticul Thin Slate (Jiménez Álvarez 2007:200).

In the case of nonelite structures, Jiménez Álvarez and colleagues (in press) identified marked differences between 5D72, 5D53, and 5D58. Str. 5D72 shares the pattern of 5D2 and 5D16, with the presence of fine paste wares such as Silho and Chablekal, as well as imported fine pottery wares like La Chontalpa, Huimanguillo, and Jalpa, although in lesser quantities than at the elite compounds. In contrast, none of these are found in 5D53 or 5D58. Consequently, Jiménez Álvarez et al. (in press) suggest that 5D72 inhabitants had access to prestige goods, unlike the inhabitants of the 5D53 and 5D58 households.

Obsidian Blades

Morell-Hart (this volume; Morell-Hart, Joyce, and Henderson 2014) has mentioned obsidian blades as part of the culinary equipment for processing plant foods. At Sihó, there were clear differences in access to these artifacts. Elite contexts had the highest number of blades: around 310 in Group 5D16 and 188 in the patio of Strs. 5D2 and 5D7 at the Central Group. The quantity of obsidian blades diminished in a directly proportional rate to architectural complexity: Group 5D72 had 38, Group 5D53 had 15, Group 5D58 had 7, Str. 4D5 had 2, and Str. 4D10 did not have any obsidian blades. It is important to say, though, that no residue analyses have yet been performed on these obsidian blades, so it is not possible to say with certainty what they were cutting (Table 7.2).

Animal and Vegetal Diet

Evidence of food products comes from three sources: faunal remains, starch grains, and chemical residues recovered from pottery fragments and grinding stones. Götz (2005) analyzed faunal remains from three elite contexts at Sihó: Strs. 5D2 and 5D16, both of them horizontally excavated, and a test pit related to Strs. 5D13/5D14. In a midden area dated to the Late Classic and Terminal Classic periods based on ceramic evidence (Jiménez Álvarez 2004, 2007), and located next to the northern side of Str. 5D2's basal platform, Götz recovered 100 bone fragments. Ninety-three fragments corresponded to the Late Classic period and showed the presence of a variety of possibly edible fauna, including a large avian, probably great curassow (*Crax rubra*) or ocellated turkey (*Melleagris ocellate*); mammals such as *temazate*, or red brocket (*Mazama americana*), and White-tailed deer

Table 7.2. Number of obsidian blades by household group at Sihó, Yucatán, Mexico, registered in the 2001–2004 and 2013–2017 field seasons

Household Group	Number of Obsidian Blades
5D2/5D7	188
5D16	310
5D72	38
5D53	15
5D58	7
4D5	2
4D10	0

(*Odocoileus virginianus*); reptiles such as turtle (Testudinae cf. *Terrapene*), black iguana (*Ctenosaura similis*), rattlesnake (*Crotalus durissus*), and boa (*Boa constrictor*); and finally catfish (*Arius felis*) and manta ray (Myliobatoidei) (Götz 2005:2). Due to the absence of processing markers, Götz (2010: 167) proposed that the catfish and manta ray represent tool or ornament remains rather than food items. Another midden context was found in the monumental center of Sihó, in Test Pit 5, excavated between Strs. 5D13 and 5D14 (Pozuelo 2002), and ceramic evidence dating to the Late and Terminal Classic (Jiménez Álvarez 2007). Götz (2005:4) found 155 Late Classic bone fragments, consisting of ocellated turkey (*Meleagris ocellata*), dog (*Canis familiaris*), wild pig (Tayassuidae cf. *Tayassu tajacu*), deer (*Odocoileus virginianus* and Cervidae n.d.), and nondetermined mammal.

Götz (2005:3) reported 39 bone remains from Str. 5D16. It is important to stress that they were recovered from small middens on both sides of the building's stairway, suggesting that they were remains that accumulated due to sweeping instead of an important accumulation as in the much larger in situ midden at Str.5D2. This difference complicates comparison between the two elite residences. Only 15 percent of the faunal remains in Str. 5D16 belong to dog (*Canis familiaris*), deer (*Cervidae n.d.*), and a nondetermined mammal, while the rest of the bone fragments were rodents (*Rodentia n.d.* and *Orthogeomys hispidus*), black iguana (*Ctenosaura similis*), and boa (*Boa constrictor*). Preparation and consumption marks are present on those smaller animals. Again, a single catfish vertebra was found exhibiting clear signs of use-wear (Götz 2010:167–168). Archaeological interventions in nonelite structures did not provide faunal remains, despite the use of identical excavation methods.

With respect to vegetal components of the diet, starch grains have been recovered in pottery fragments, grinding stones, and soil samples from Strs. 5D2, 5D16, 5D72, 5D53, and 5D58 (Balam Lara, Chaparro, and Fernández Souza 2018; Herrera Parra 2018; Matos 2014; Novelo-Pérez et al. 2019). The five contexts all produced evidence for the presence of maize, beans, and sweet potato (*Ipomoea batatas*). Strs. 5D2 and 5D16, as well as 5D72, also had yam (*Dioscorea* spp.) and two types of beans, *Phaseolus vulgaris* and *Phaseolus lunatus* or *ib*, a very delicate and still quite appreciated bean in Yucatán. Our results do not show a significant difference with respect to the plant species consumed by the different households. Interestingly, Matos (2014) recovered a cocoa starch grain from one of the grinding stones at Group 5D72, which may support the hypothesis that the inhabitants of this household had access to luxury items, such as greenstone, imported pottery, and cocoa, although they were not part of the settlement's elite.

Chemical Residues in Pottery Fragments

Spot-test chemical analysis was carried out on a total of fifty-three sherds recovered from four of the excavated structures: 5D2, 5D16, 5D72, and 5D53. Materials from the first three structures correspond to Late Classic jars, basins, bowls, and tripod plate vessels. Chemical spot tests are semi-quantitative tests that detect residues in porous materials such as plaster floors or pottery. To access chemical residues captured within their porous matrix, bits of sherds were broken off and ground into a fine powder. In these procedures, we followed the protocol established by Luis Barba Pingarrón (2007; Barba Pingarrón, Ortiz Butrón, and Pecci 2014; Middleton et al. 2010), from the Anthropological Research Institute of the National Autonomous University of Mexico (UNAM). Analyses were completed for phosphates, carbonates, protein residues, fatty acids, and carbohydrate content. Phosphates are indicative of organic residues. Carbonates suggest the presence of lime, which may be the result of food processes like maize nixtamalization. Protein residues indicate residues of meat, blood, or other foods rich in proteins. Fatty acids result from substances like oil, animal fat, or resins. And carbohydrates are useful to identify the presence of vegetables. We compared our results with those offered by Balam Lara, Chaparro, and Fernández Souza (2018), who analyzed sherds from Str. 5D53 and from the Circular Feature at Group 5D72, and by Novelo-Pérez et al. (2019), who analyzed 143 sherds from elite contexts. All the studies followed the same spot-test procedures.

Of the fifty-three sherds analyzed by our team, twenty-four originated in elite contexts, from Strs. 5D2, 5D16, and test pits excavated during the 2001–2003 field seasons (Cobos et al. 2002; Fernández Souza 2010; Jiménez Álvarez 2007); twenty-one sherds came from Str. 5D72; and eight came from Str. 5D53 (Table 7.3).

Comparison of carbonates, carbohydrates, and fatty acids between the elite structures and two of the more modest residential structures (Group 5D72 and 5D53) did not offer significant differences, and values on the three sherd groups are relatively low. This may mean that the consumption of vegetables was similar in the different households and that, in general, the use of fat was low. Nonetheless, we did find differences in phosphates: on a scale from 0 to 6, the average from elite sherds was 3.79, while from 5D72 it was 4.57, and from 5D53 it was 4.25 (Chart 7.1). The difference between jars in both groups was more significant: 3.58 in the case of elite jars and 4.75 in the case of 5D72. This may suggest a more intensive use of containers in nonelite contexts, maybe due to nonelites having fewer jars available than the elites. Differences in protein residues were even more evident (Chart 7.2). Sherds from elite contexts had an average of 8.58, while 5D72 sherds averaged 7.43, and 5D53 averaged 7.56 (in the scale of protein residue analyses, their presence is identified above level 8). In both cases, the highest average was found in jars (8.71 in 5D2 and 5D16 structures, and 7.5 in 5D72; all the 5D53 sherds were from jars). One explanation is that some jars were used to prepare stews or meat broths. Those jars with protein residues and carbohydrates may indicate a combination of meat and vegetables. Jar number 10, from structure 5D2, is particularly interesting, because it has a relatively high protein residue level (9.5), the presence of fatty acids (2), and a little bit of carbohydrates (1), possibly suggesting a rich stew. In total, twenty-three pieces (95.83%) of the elite-context sherds presented protein residues, compared to four (19.04%) from Structure 5D72 and two (25%) from Structure 5D53.

Novelo-Pérez et al. (2019) obtained similar results by analyzing 143 pottery fragments from Sihó's elite contexts: jars, bowls, and basins showed the presence of protein residues. The lowest average was found on tripod dishes, possibly because they contained dry food and not drinks that may have permeated more deeply into the material. On the other hand, Balam Lara, Chaparro, and Fernández Souza (2018) performed spot-test analyses on 18 sherds from 5D72 and 14 sherds from 5D53 (Table 7.2). Sherds from 5D72 came from the Circular Feature area that presented high chemical residue values. The protein residues for these 18 sherds averaged 7.72, meaning low or absent. But 8 sherds had some evidence of protein resi-

Table 7.3. Spot-test chemical results for ceramics from household groups 5D2, 5D16, 5D72, and 5D53 at Sihó, Yucatán, Mexico

Structure	Form	Carbonates	Phosphates	Protein Residues	Carbo-hydrates	pH	Fatty Acids
5D2	Jar	3	3	9	1	9.35	2
5D2	Jar	2	3	9	1	9.46	1
5D2	Jar	2	4	9.5	0	9.38	1
5D2	Jar	2.5	3	8	1	9.3	1
5D16	Jar	3	4	8	0	9.33	0
B78	Jar	2.5	4	8.5	1	9.25	1
B85	Jar	3	3	8.5	1	9.14	1
CG	Jar	3	4	9	1	9.03	1
B78	Jar	3	4	9	0	9.17	1
5D2	Jar	3	3	9.5	1	9.42	2
5D2	Jar	3	5	8.5	1	9.37	1
5D2	Jar	2	3	8	1	9.39	1
	Average	2.67	3.58	8.71	0.75	9.29	1.08
B68	Basin	2	4	9	1	9.25	1
CG	Basin	2.5	3	9.5	1	9.23	1
CG	Basin	2	3	8	1	9.21	1
CG	Basin	2.5	5	7.5	1	9.3	2
5D2	Basin	2	3	8	1	9.4	1
5D16	Basin	2	4	8	1	9.33	1
	Average	2.17	3.67	8.33	1	9.28	1.16
5D2	Tripod dish	2	6	8.5	1	9.33	0
5D2	Tripod dish	3	3	9	1	9.22	1
B54	Tripod dish	2	3	8.5	1	9.15	2
	Average	2.33	4	8.67	1	9.23	1
5D2	Bowl	3	5	8	1	9.55	1
5D2	Bowl	3	5	8.5	1	9.37	1
CG	Bowl	3	4	9	1	9.46	1
	Average	3	4.67	8.5	1	9.46	1
5D72	Jar	3	5	9	1	9.1	1
5D72	Jar	2	5	7	1	9.13	0
5D72	Jar	3	5	7.5	1	8.97	2
5D72	Jar	2	6	7	1	9	1
5D72	Jar	3	4	9	1	8.91	2
5D72	Jar	3	3	7	1	9	1
5D72	Jar	3	4	8	0.5	9.01	2
5D72	Jar	2.5	4	7	0	9.06	1

Table 7.3. Continued

Structure	Form	Carbonates	Phosphates	Protein Residues	Carbo-hydrates	pH	Fatty Acids
5D72	Jar	2	5	7	1	8.91	1
5D72	Jar	2	5	7.5	1	9.06	1
5D72	Jar	2	5	7	1	9.05	0
5D72	Jar	3	6	7	1	8.97	1.5
	Average	2.54	4.75	7.5	0.875	9.01	1.12
5D72	Dish	3	4	7	0	9.08	0
5D72	Dish	2	5	7.5	1	8.99	0
5D72	Dish	3	5	7.5	1	9.24	1
5D72	Dish	2.5	5	7	1	9.18	0
5D72	Dish	2	5	7.5	1.5	8.93	1
5D72	Dish	3	4	7	1	8.96	1
5D72	Dish	2	5	7.5	1	9.06	1
5D72	Dish	2	2	7	1	8.93	1
5D72	Dish	2	4	8	1	8.98	1
	Average	2.39	4.33	7.33	0.94444	9.03	0.66
5D53	Jar	2	5	7.5	2	9.03	2
5D53	Jar	3	4	8	2	9.2	0
5D53	Jar	2	4	7.5	2	9.13	0
5D53	Jar	2	5	7	3	9.12	2
5D53	Jar	1	2	7	2	8.78	0
5D53	Jar	2	6	7.5	1.5	9.09	2
5D53	Jar	2	4	8.5	2	8.87	1
5D53	Jar	1	4	7.5	1.5	9.03	1
	Average	1.875	4.25	7.56	2	9.03	1

Note: Data are averaged by structure/status group and vessel type.

due (44%), which is a little higher presence than that in our own study of Str. 5D72, which seems to make sense in that we think the Circular Feature was in a specific area dedicated to preparation or storage of food. In the case of Str. 5D53, Balam Lara, Chaparro, and Fernández Souza (2018) found an average of 7.71 for protein residues, present in only 5 sherds (35% of the total). In the Balam Lara, Chaparro, and Fernández Souza (2018) results, as in ours and in those found by Novelo-Pérez et al. (2019), jars were, in general, the ceramic forms most enriched with protein residues (Table 7.4).

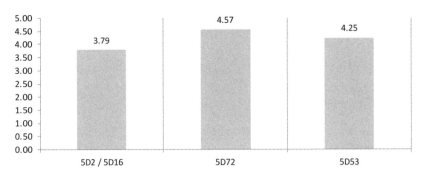

Chart 7.1. Phosphate levels from elite groups (5D2, 5D16) and nonelite groups (5D72 and 5D53) at Sihó, Yucatán, Mexico

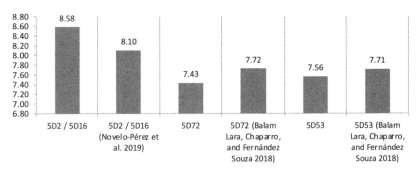

Chart 7.2. Protein residue levels from all household groups. Comparison with Balam Lara, Chaparro, and Fernández Souza (2018), and Novelo-Pérez et al. (2019).

Spot-test results suggest that the elite consumed more protein than did the nonelite inhabitants, including the middle socioeconomic status people who lived in Group 5D72 (Charts 7.3 and 7.4). Spot-test results do not give specific chemical markers, so we cannot say if protein residues came from animals or plants. Combining these results with Götz's animal remains analyses, however, it is possible to suggest that the elite of Sihó had access to a diet that was richer in protein than the nonelite households, and that part of this protein came from animal sources.

Foodways, Identities, and Social Interactions at Sihó

Archaeological patterns suggest that during the Late and Terminal Classic periods, Sihó was a multistratified settlement, as suggested by several au-

Table 7.4. Spot-test chemical results from Structures 5D72 and 5D53 at Sihó, Yucatán, Mexico (modified from Balam Lara, Chaparro, and Fernández Souza 2018)

Structure	Form	Fatty Acids	Carbonates	Protein Residues
5D72	Bowl	3	1	7.5
5D72	Jar	3	3	7
5D72	Jar/Basin	1	3	7
5D72	Bowl	0	0	7
5D72	Jar	1	1	8.5
5D72	Bowl/Jar	1	0	8
5D72	Dish	2	4	7.5
5D72	Jar	3	2	10
5D72	Jar	0	1	9
5D72	Dish	2	1	7.5
5D72	Dish	0	2	8
5D72	Jar	1	3	8
5D72	ND	1	1	7
5D72	Bowl/Jar	1	0	7
5D72	Bowl/Jar	1	1	7
5D72	ND	0	1	7
5D72	Jar	1	1	8
5D72	Jar	3	2	8
	Average	1.33	1.5	7.72
5D53	Basin	2	2	8.5
5D53	Jar	2	2	7.5
5D53	Jar	0	3	8
5D53	ND	0	2	7.5
5D53	Jar	2	2	7
5D53	Jar	0	0	7
5D53	Jar	0	1	7
5D53	Jar	2	2	7.5
5D53	Jar	1	2	8.5
5D53	Bowl/Jar	0	1	9
5D53	Bowl/Jar	1	1	7.5
5D53	ND	1	2	8
5D53	ND	2	0	7.5
5D53	Jar	2	2	7.5
	Average	1.07	1.57	7.71

Note: Data are averaged only by structure.

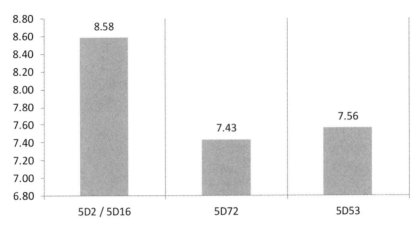

Chart 7.3. Protein residue levels from two elite (5D2 and 5D16) and two nonelite (5D72 and 5D53) groups at Sihó, Yucatán, Mexico

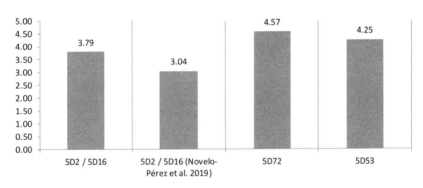

Chart 7.4. Phosphate levels from two elite (5D2 and 5D16) and two nonelite (5D72 and 5D53) groups at Sihó, Yucatán, Mexico. Comparison with Novelo-Pérez et al. (2019).

thors working at other Maya sites (Chase and Chase 1992; Lohse and Valdez 2004; Marcus 2004; White 1999), and as proposed by Restall (1997: 88) for colonial Yucatec Maya. From the royal court structures in the Central Group to the small huts inferred from simple stone alignments, we see a myriad of heterogeneous households with differentiated access to foodstuffs and goods such as imported pottery, obsidian blades, or greenstone.

What role did food and culinary practices play in the construction of social identities at Sihó? Were they significant in the way families or community members saw themselves and other actors? To answer this, we compare our data from Sihó to what is known from other Maya sites of this time period. We identify some culinary patterns that Sihó shared with other Maya sites. Maize, as the "signature food," and beans were ubiquitous in poor and rich house lots, and there is also evidence of consumption of yam and sweet potatoes as in numerous other Maya settlements (Matos 2014; Morell-Hart, this volume; Morell Hart, Joyce, and Henderson 2014). Animal species found at the site's palace structures were also commonly consumed by other Maya elite, including deer, wild pig, iguana, and possibly turkey, in addition to other small animals like rodents and turtles (Götz 2005, 2011). But apparently at Sihó, meat was a socially restricted food. In general terms, it is possible to say that Sihó's royal elite ate more meat than "middle socioeconomic status" people from 5D72 and possibly also more than the secondary elite group from Str. 5D16, for animal bones were more numerous in the Central Group than in Group 5D16, and chemical analyses confirmed that the elite were eating more protein than the rest of the households we studied. In this sense, the consumption of meat identified the elite of Sihó as a separate group within the settlement, and it probably connected the royal central group with other Maya rulers who shared similar practices. However, food consumption patterns do vary among elites from different sites, as there is little evidence for fish and seafood at Sihó when compared to bigger inland sites such as Chichén Itzá or Dzibilchaltun (Götz 2005, 2011, 2014). At the same time, differential access to meat within the settlement marked social distinctions from middle and lower classes, emphasizing asymmetrical relations, including social exclusion.

Besides food products, status differences were also expressed through culinary and service equipment: grinding stones, obsidian blades, and pottery containers were abundant in elite contexts and almost absent in the simplest house lots. It was not just a question of quantity: in the case of pottery, the Central Group had not only more but better-quality and imported containers, emphasizing their exclusiveness and power. As previously mentioned, "high cuisine" implies not only select ingredients but also refined ways of preparation and service. Delicate and well-prepared fare was probably an important component at an elegant table. Culinary practices may have played important roles in social competition and identity negotiation; as previously mentioned, "middle socioeconomic status" inhabitants of Group 5D72 mimicked some architectural features of palace structures 5D2 and 5D16 and had some access to elite pottery, as well as to greenstone objects and foodstuffs like cocoa. They did not have vaulted buildings, and, in many other aspects, they were more similar to lower-status households than to the royal or secondary elites they apparently tried to emulate. But in some ways, they were able to share some of the flavors, style, and sophistication that characterized high-status culinary practices at the site.

In Yucatán, historic sources demonstrate the importance of feasts and ceremonial meals dedicated to the deities in pre-Columbian times and to Catholic saints during the Colonial period. These were religious festivities, but they also reinforced political relations between lords and commoners. Landa (2001:72) described New Year ceremonies and explained that the lords, the priest, and the people offered food and beverages to the *bacabs* and other "demons." As part of the ritual, they traveled around the four corners of the town and, later, went to the *principal*'s house, where they danced and shared meals such as bread filled with venison heart or egg yolk, quail pastries, and other delicacies. According to Velásquez García (2016, 2017), Landa's narration is quite like New Year ceremonies as documented in the Dresden Codex. In the latter document, venison, fish, iguana, turkey, and a variety of tamales were depicted being served in dishes. Farriss (2012:420) affirms that for colonial Yucatec Maya, banquets strengthened social cohesion and reinforced rank and status categories between lords and commoners. On the other hand, such feasts allowed nonelite members of the community to eat and enjoy meals and beverages that were not accessible to them in quotidian life (Farriss 2012:420).

In the case of Sihó, the numerical discrepancy of grinding stones presents an interesting question. The Central Group had at least twenty metates, while 5D16 had only eight, and the other groups had six or fewer. This situation is similar to that of the royal kitchen at Kabah, where Toscano Hernández et al. (2011) reported more than thirty grinding stones related to the palace. This may imply that, in both sites, rulers offered banquets for numerous people. At Sihó, the main religious and administrative buildings are in the Central Group, suggesting that the royal elite could have concentrated on communal ritual events, forging bonds and reinforcing community identity with nonelites while also exhibiting generosity, culinary style, and wealth that was out of reach for most commoners. The middens with faunal remains, much more voluminous than those in Str. 5D16, could have been the result not only of a dietary difference between elites and commoners but of ritual practices that, as late pre-Columbian and early colonial documents state, served as vehicles of communication between humans and gods, and between lords and common people.

At Sihó, evidence suggests that food played a consistent role within a clearly stratified social structure: on the one hand, differential access to material goods such as elaborate architecture, stone monuments, greenstone, imported pottery, and obsidian objects helps us identify social groups who lived in a marked state of inequality, also reflected in their foodways. In this sense, in daily life, the elite seem to have eaten more nutritious and varied food and to have enjoyed it in numerous delicate and specialized pottery containers as a privilege and as a strategy to naturalize rank, reinforce status differences, and stress a sense of exclusion. But, on the other hand, banquets could have played a diacritic role in negotiation and construction of a communal identity that strengthened ties between elites and commoners, while at the same time reinforcing the position of the rulers in the ritual practices of the settlement. Many questions remain to be explored, but a promising path is now open to approach the multiple ways in which food and culinary practices contributed to define, reinforce, or challenge social and political identities of the ancient Maya.

References

Allen, Patricia, and Carolyn Sachs. 2012. "Women and Food Chains: The Gendered Politics of Food." In *Taking Food Public*, ed. Psyche Williams-Forson and Carole Couniham, 23–40. New York: Routledge.
Appadurai, Arjun. 1981. "Gastro-Politics in Hindu South Asia." *American Ethnologist* 8(3):494–511.
———. 1988. "How to Make a National Cuisine: Cookbooks in Contemporary India." *Comparative Studies in Society and History* 30(1):3–24.
Ardren, Traci. 2015. *Social Identities in the Classic Maya Northern Lowlands: Gender, Age, Memory, and Place*. Austin: University of Texas Press.
Armelagos, George. 2003. "Cultura y contacto: El choque de dos cocinas mundiales." In *Conquistas y comida: Consecuencias del encuentro de dos mundos*, ed. Janet Long, 105–129. Mexico City: UNAM.
Ayora-Díaz, Steffan Igor. 2012. *Foodscapes, Foodfields, and Identities in Yucatán*. Amsterdam: CEDLA Latin American Studies.
Balam Lara, Rosario G., Abigail Chaparro, and Lilia Fernández Souza. 2018. "Los recipientes cerámicos y la cultura gastronómica en Sihó, Yucatán." In *Los investigadores de la cultura maya: Gastronomía en la cultura Maya: usos cotidianos*, ed. Ma. del Rosario Domínguez, Miriam J. Gallegos, Ricardo A. Torres, and Miriam León, 109–123. Campeche City: Universidad Autónoma de Campeche.
Barba Pingarrón, Luis A. 2007. "Chemical Residues in Lime-Plastered Archaeological Floors." *Geoarchaeology: An International Journal* 22(4):439–452.
Barba Pingarrón, Luis, Agustín Ortiz Butrón, and Alessandra Pecci. 2014. "Los residuos químicos: Indicadores arqueológicos para entender la producción, preparación, consumo y almacenamiento de alimentos en Mesoamérica." *Anales de Antropología* 48(1):201–240.
Barrera Vásquez, Alfredo, dir. 1995. *Diccionario Maya Cordemex*. Mexico City: Editorial Porrúa.
Beliaev, Dmitri, Albert Davletshin, and Alexandre Tokovinine. 2009. "Sweet Cacao and Sour Atole: Mixed Drinks on Classic Maya Ceramic Vases." In *Pre-Columbian*

Foodways: Interdisciplinary Approaches to Food, Culture, and Markets in Ancient Mesoamerica, ed. John E. Staller and Miguel D. Carrasco, 257–272. New York: Springer.

Chase, Arlen F., and Diane Z. Chase. 1992. "Mesoamerican Elites: Assumptions, Definitions, and Models." In *Mesoamerican Elites: An Archaeological Assessment*, ed. D. Chase and A. Chase, 3–17. Norman: University of Oklahoma Press.

Chase, Arlen F., Diane Z. Chase, and Christine White. 2001. "El paisaje urbano maya: La integración de los espacios construidos y la estructura social de Caracol, Belice." In *Reconstruyendo la ciudad maya: El urbanismo en las sociedades antiguas*, ed. Andrés Ruiz Ciudad, María Josefa Iglesias Ponce de León, and María del Carmen Martínez Martínez, 95–122. Madrid: Sociedad Española de Estudios Mayas.

Clark, John, Mary E. Pye, and Dennis C. Gosser. 2007. "Thermolithics and Corn Dependency in Mesoamerica." In *Archaeology, Art, and Ethnogenesis in Mesoamerican Prehistory: Papers in Honor of Gareth W. Lowe*, ed. Lynneth Lowe and Mary E. Pye, 23–61. Provo, Utah: New World Archaeological Foundation, Brigham Young University.

Cobos, Rafael, Lilia Fernández Souza, Nancy Peniche May, Gabriel Tun Ayora, Daniel Pat Cruz, Vera Tiesler, Alfonso Lacadena García-Gallo, Socorro Jiménez Álvarez, and Christopher Götz. 2004. *Proyecto arqueológico: El surgimiento de la civilización en el occidente de Yucatán: Los orígenes de la complejidad social en Sihó*. Informe de actividades de la Temporada de Campo 2003 presentado al Consejo de Arqueología del INAH. Mérida, Mex.: Universidad Autónoma de Yucatán.

Cobos, Rafael, Lilia Fernández Souza, Vera Tiesler, Pilar Zabala, Armando Inurreta, Nancy Peniche May, Ma. Luisa Vázquez, and Diana Pozuelo Lorenzo. 2002. *Proyecto Arqueológico: El surgimiento de la civilización en el occidente de Yucatán: Los orígenes de la complejidad social en Sihó*. Informe de actividades de la Temporada de Campo 2001 presentado al Consejo de Arqueología del INAH. Mérida, Mex.: Universidad Autónoma de Yucatán.

Cobos, Rafael, and Armando Inurreta. 2002. "Informe del recorrido de superficie y mapeo realizado entre abril y julio de 2001, Proyecto Arqueológico Sihó." In *Proyecto arqueológico: El surgimiento de la civilización en el occidente de Yucatán: Los orígenes de la complejidad social en Sihó*, ed. R. Cobos, L. Fernández Souza, V. Tiesler, P. Zabala, A. Inurreta, N. Peniche May, M. L. Vázquez de Ágredos, and D. Pozuelo Lorenzo, 6–47. Informe de actividades de la Temporada de Campo 2001 presentado al Consejo de Arqueología del INAH. Mérida, Mex.: Universidad Autónoma de Yucatán.

Cobos, Rafael, and Alfonso Lacadena García-Gallo. 2019. "Un conjunto arquitectónico asociado con la elite de Sihó, Yucatán." *Revista Española de Antropología Americana* 49 (special number):139–155.

Dietler, Michael. 1996. "Feasts and Commensal Politics in the Political Economy: Food, Power, and Status in Prehistoric Europe." In *Food and the Status Quest: An Interdisciplinary Perspective*, ed. P. Wiessner and W. Schiefenhövel, 87–125. Oxford: Berghahn.

Dirks, Robert, and Gina Hunter. 2013. "The Anthropology of Food." In *Routledge International Handbook of Food Studies*, ed. Ken Albala, 3–13. New York: Routledge.

Farriss, Nancy M. 2012. *La sociedad maya bajo el dominio colonial*. Trans. María Palomar. Mexico City: CONACULTA.

Fernández Souza, Lilia. 2010. "Grupos domésticos y espacios habitacionales en las Tierras Bajas mayas durante el período Clásico." PhD diss., Universität Hamburg.
———. 2016. "Grinding and Cooking: An Approach to Mayan Culinary Technology." In *Cooking Technology: Transformations in Culinary Practice in Mexico and Latin America*, ed. Steffan Igor Ayora-Díaz, 15–28. London: Bloomsbury Academic.
Fernández Souza, Lilia, Socorro del Pilar Jiménez Álvarez, María Jesús Novelo-Pérez, Daniel Alberto Herklotz Balam, Héctor Abraham Hernández Álvarez, Alejandra Espinosa, Carlos Manuel Matos Llanes, and Joaquín Venegas de la Torre, eds. 2014. *Proyecto: La vida cotidiana en Sihó, Yucatán: Diversidad social y económica en grupos domésticos no elitarios de una comunidad del período Clásico*. Informe de actividades de la Temporada de Campo 2013 presentado al Consejo de Arqueología del INAH. Mérida, Mex.: Universidad Autónoma de Yucatán.
Fernández Souza, Lilia, Lourdes Toscano Hernández, and Mario Zimmermann. 2014. "De maíz y de cacao: Aproximaciones a la cocina de las élites mayas en tiempos prehispánicos." In *Estética y poder en la ciencia y la tecnología*, ed. Steffan Igor Ayora-Díaz and Gabriela Vargas Cetina, 107–130. Mérida, Mex.: Universidad Autónoma de Yucatán.
Freidel, David, and F. Kent Reilly. 2010. "The Flesh of God: Cosmology, Food, and the Origins of Political Power in Ancient Southeastern Mesoamerica." In *Pre-Columbian Foodways: Interdisciplinary Approaches to Food, Culture, and Markets in Ancient Mesoamerica*, ed. John E. Staller and Michael D. Carrasco, 635–680. New York: Springer.
García Barrios, Ana, and Ramón Carrasco Vargas. 2008. "Una aproximación a los estilos pictóricos de la Pirámide de Las Pinturas de la Acrópolis Chiik Nahb' de Calakmul." In *XXI Simposio de Investigaciones Arqueológicas en Guatemala, 2007*, ed. J. P. Laporte, B. Arroyo, and H. Mejía, 848–867. Guatemala City: Museo Nacional de Arqueología y Etnología.
Garine, Igor de. 1999. "Antropología de la alimentación: Entre naturaleza y cultura." In *Alimentación y cultura: Actas del Congreso Internacional 1998*, 1:13–34. Huesca, Spain: Museo Nacional de Antropología.
Götz, Christopher M. 2005. "El consumo de vertebrados en tres grupos habitacionales de Sihó, Yucatán." In *XVIII Simposio de Investigaciones Arqueológicas en Guatemala*, ed. J. P. Laporte, B. Arroyo, and H. Mejía, 781–797. Guatemala City: Museo Nacional de Arqueología y Etnología.
———. 2010. "Una mirada zooarqueológica a los modos alimenticios de los mayas de las tierras bajas del norte." In *Identidades y cultura material en la región maya*, ed. Héctor A. Hernández Álvarez and Marcos Pool Cab, 89–109. Mérida, Mex.: Universidad Autónoma de Yucatán.
———. 2011. "Diferencias socioeconómicas en el uso de animales vertebrados en las tierras bajas mayas del norte." In *Vida cotidiana de los antiguos mayas del norte de la Península de Yucatán*, ed. Rafael Cobos and Lilia Fernández Souza, 45–65. Mérida, Mex.: Ediciones de la Universidad Autónoma de Yucatán.
———. 2014. "La alimentación de los mayas prehispánicos vista desde la zooarqueología." *Anales de Antropología* 48(1):167–199.
Hastorf, Christine A. 2012. "Steamed or Boiled: Identity and Value in Food Preparation." *eTopoi: Journal for Ancient Studies*. Special Volume 2:213–242.

———. 2017. *The Social Archaeology of Food: Thinking about Eating from Prehistory to the Present*. New York: Cambridge University Press.

Herrera Parra, Esteban Moisés. 2018. "Actividades y espacios domésticos no elitarios en Sihó, Yucatán, durante el Clásico Tardío-Terminal: Una aproximación multivariable para su identificación." B.A. thesis, Universidad Autónoma de Yucatán, Mérida.

Inness, Sherrie A., ed. 2001. "Introduction: Eating Ethnic." In *Pilaf, Pozole, and Pad Thai: American Women and Ethnic Food*, ed. Sherrie A. Inness, 1–16. Amherst: University of Massachusetts Press.

Jiménez Álvarez, Socorro del Pilar. 2007. "Sihó: Una unidad política del occidente de Yucatán." Master's thesis, Facultad de Ciencias Antropológicas, Universidad Autónoma de Yucatán, Mérida.

Jiménez Álvarez, Socorro del Pilar, María J. Novelo-Pérez, and Daniel A. Herklotz Balam. 2014. "Informe preliminar de la cerámica hallada en la estructura 5D72." In *La vida cotidiana en Sihó, Yucatán: Diversidad social y económica en grupos domésticos no elitarios de una comunidad del período Clásico*, ed. Lilia Fernández Souza, Socorro del P. Jiménez Álvarez, Héctor A. Hernández Álvarez, María J. Novelo-Pérez, Daniel A. Herklotz Balam, Carlos M. Matos Llanes, María A. Espinosa, L. Joaquín Venegas de la Torre, 72–91. Informe de actividades de la Temporada de Campo 2013 presentado al Consejo de Arqueología del INAH. Mérida, Mex.: Universidad Autónoma de Yucatán.

Jiménez Álvarez, Socorro del Pilar, María J. Novelo-Pérez, Moisés Herrera Parra, Rosario Balam Lara, and Abigail Chaparro Pech. 2016. "Informe preliminar de la cerámica en las estructuras 5D54, 5D58, 5D57 y 5D72." In *La vida cotidiana en Sihó, Yucatán: Diversidad social y económica en grupos domésticos no elitarias de una comunidad del período Clásico*, ed. Lilia Fernández Souza, Socorro del P. Jiménez Álvarez, Héctor Hernández Álvarez, María Jesús Novelo-Pérez, Carlos M. Matos Llanes, Rosario G. Balam Lara, Rosario A. Chaparro Pech, E. Moisés Herrera Parra, Llorens Pujol Piza, María Alejandra Espinosa, and L. Joaquín Venegas de la Torre, 55–78. Informe de la Temporada 2015, dirigido al Consejo de Arqueología. Mérida, Mex.: Universidad Autónoma de Yucatán.

Kettunen, Harri, and Christophe Helmke. 2010. "Introducción a los Jeroglíficos Mayas." mesoweb.com/es/recursos/intro/JM2010.pdf.

Lacadena García-Gallo, Alfonso. 2011. "Historia y ritual dinásticos en Machaquilá (Petén, Guatemala)." *Revista Española de Antropología Americana* 41(1):205–240.

Landa, Diego de. 2001. *Relación de las cosas de Yucatán*. Mexico City: Editorial Porrúa.

LeCount, Lisa J. 2001. "Like Water for Chocolate: Feasting and Political Ritual among the Late Classic Maya at Xunantunich, Belize." *American Anthropologist* 103(4):935–953.

Lentz, David L. 1999. "Plant Resources of the Ancient Maya: The Paleoethnobotanical Evidence." In *Reconstructing Ancient Maya Diet*, ed. Christine White, 3–18. Salt Lake City: University of Utah Press.

Lohse, Jon C., and Fred Valdez Jr. 2004. "Examining Ancient Maya Commoners Anew." In *Ancient Maya Commoners*, ed. Jon C. Lohse and Fred Valdez Jr., 1–22. Austin: University of Texas Press.

Marcus, Joyce. 2004. "Maya Commoners: The Stereotype and the Reality." In *Ancient*

Maya Commoners, ed. Jon C. Lohse and Fred Valdez Jr., 255–284. Austin: University of Texas Press.

Matos, Carlos M. 2014. "Alimentación vegetal y áreas de actividad en la unidad habitacional 5D72 de Sihó, Yucatán: Etnoarqueología, análisis químico de suelos y paleoetnobotánica como herramienta de aproximación." B.A. thesis, Facultad de Ciencias Antropológicas, Universidad Autónoma de Yucatán, Mérida.

Metcalfe, Jessica Z., Christine D. White, Fred J. Longstaffe, Gabriel Wrobel, Della Collins Cook, and K. Anne Pyburn. 2009. "Isotopic Evidence for Diet at Chau Hiix, Belize: Testing Regional Models of Hierarchy and Heterarchy." *Latin American Antiquity* 20(1):15–36.

Middleton, William D., Luis Barba Pingarrón, Alessandra Pecci, James H. Burton, Agustín Ortiz Butrón, Laura Salvini, and Roberto Rodríguez Suárez. 2010. "The Study of Archaeological Floors: Methodological Proposal for the Analysis of Anthropogenic Residues by Spot Tests, ICP-OES, and GC-MS." *Journal of Archaeology Method and Theory* 17(3):183–208.

Moore, Katherine. 2013. "The Archaeology of Food." In *Routledge International Handbook of Food Studies*, ed. Ken Abdala, 74–86. New York: Routledge.

Morell-Hart, Shanti, Rosemary A. Joyce, and John S. Henderson. 2014. "Multi-Proxy Analysis of Plant Use at Formative Period Los Naranjos, Honduras." *Latin American Antiquity* 25(1):65–81.

Novelo-Pérez, María J., E. Moisés Herrera Parra, Lilia Fernández Souza, Iliana Ancona Aragón, and Socorro Jiménez Álvarez. 2019. "Pre-Columbian Culinary Landscapes: Reconstructing Elite Gastronomy at Sihó, Yucatán." *STAR: Science & Technology of Archaeological Research*, 1–13. DOI: 10.1080/20548923.2019.1674508.

Pat Cruz, Daniel. 2006. "Análisis de las piedras de molienda de Sihó, Yucatán." B.A. thesis, Universidad Autónoma de Yucatán, Mérida.

Peniche May, Nancy. 2004. "Aspectos de la organización económica de grupos domésticos de élite: Las industrias de talla de sílex de Sihó, Yucatán." B.A. thesis, Facultad de Ciencias Antropológicas, Universidad Autónoma de Yucatán, Mérida.

———. 2011. "Las industrias de pedernal de Yucatán y Campeche: Una perspectiva regional." In *Vida cotidiana de los antiguos mayas del norte de la Península de Yucatán*, ed. Rafael Cobos and Lilia Fernández Souza, 183–205. Mérida, Mex.: Ediciones de la Universidad Autónoma de Yucatán.

Patch, Robert W. 2014. "Sociedad, economía y estructura agraria, 1649–1812." In *Historia General de Yucatán*, ed. Sergio Quezada, Jorge Castillo Canché, and Inés Ortiz Yam, 2:431–496. Mérida, Méx.: Ediciones de la Universidad Autónoma de Yucatán.

Pozuelo Lorenzo, Diana. 2002. "Informe de los pozos de prueba de la Temporada 2001 excavados en Sihó." In *Proyecto arqueológico: El surgimiento de la civilización en el occidente de Yucatán: Los orígenes de la complejidad social en Sihó*, ed. R. Cobos, L. Fernández Souza, V. Tiesler, P. Zabala, A. Inurreta, N. Peniche May, M. L. Vázquez de Agredos, and D. Pozuelo Lorenzo, 69–91. Informe de actividades de la Temporada de Campo 2003 presentado al Consejo de Arqueología del INAH. Mérida, Mex.: Universidad Autónoma de Yucatán.

Restall, Matthew. 1997. *The Maya World: Yucatec Culture and Society, 1550–1850*. Stanford, CA: Stanford University Press.

Roys, Ralph L. 1972. *The Indian Background of Colonial Yucatan*. Norman: University of Oklahoma Press.

Schele, Linda, and David Freidel. 1990. *A Forest of Kings: The Untold Story of the Ancient Maya*. New York: Morrow.

Scherer, Andrew K., Lori E. Wright, and Cassady J. Voder. 2007. "Bioarchaeological Evidence for Social and Temporal Differences in Diet at Piedras Negras, Guatemala." *Latin American Antiquity* 18(1):85–104.

Simms, Stephanie R., Francesco Berna, and George J. Bey III. 2013. "A Prehispanic Maya Pit Oven? Microanalysis of Fired Clay Balls from the Puuc Region, Yucatán, México." *Journal of Archaeological Science* 40(2):1144–1157.

Stuart, David. 2006. "The Language of Chocolate: References to Cacao on Classic Maya Drinking Vessels." In *Chocolate in Mesoamerica: A Cultural History of Cacao*, ed. Cameron L. McNeil, 184–201. Gainesville: University Press of Florida.

Taube, Karl. 1989. "The Maize Tamale in Classic Maya Diet, Epigraphy, and Art." *American Antiquity* 54(1):31–51.

Toscano Hernández, Lourdes, Rocío Jiménez Díaz, Gustavo A. Novelo Rincón, David Ortegón Zapata, Aarón Duarte Medina, Karla Castro Chong, Nelda Marengo Camacho, Oyuki García Salas, and Julián Cruz Cortés, eds. 2011. *Proyecto investigación y restauración arquitectónica en Kabah, Yucatán: Informe de la Temporada 2010*. Informe de actividades presentado al Instituto Nacional de Antropología e Historia, Yucatán, Mérida.

Tun Ayora, Gabriel. 2004. "La organización de viviendas mayas prehispánicas: Análisis de estructuras domésticas asociadas a unidades habitacionales de élite en Sihó, Yucatán." B.A. thesis, Facultad de Ciencias Antropológicas, Universidad Autónoma de Yucatán, Mérida.

Vail, Gabrielle, and Matthew Looper. 2014. "World Renewal Rituals among the Postclassic Yucatec Maya and Contemporary Ch'orti Maya." *Estudios de Cultura Maya* 45:121–140.

Vela, Enrique. 2012. *El cacao y el chocolate*. *Arqueología Mexicana*, edición especial 45.

Velásquez García, Erik. 2016. *Códice de Dresde*. Parte 1. Edición facsimilar. *Arqueología Mexicana*, edición especial 67. arqueologiamexicana.mx.

———. 2017. *Códice de Dresde*. Parte 2. Edición facsimilar. *Arqueología Mexicana*, edición especial 72. arqueologiamexicana.mx.

White, Christine D. 1999. "Introduction." In *Reconstructing Ancient Maya Diet*, ed. Christine D. White, ix–xxvii. Salt Lake City: University of Utah Press.

White, Christine D., David M. Pendergast, Fred J. Longstaffe, and Kimberley R. Law. 2001. "Social Complexity and Food Systems at Altun Ha, Belize: The Isotopic Evidence." *Latin American Antiquity* 12(4):371–393.

Wright, Lori E. 2003. "La muerte y estatus económico: Investigando el simbolismo mortuorio y el acceso a los recursos alimenticios entre los mayas." In *Antropología de la eternidad: La muerte en la cultura maya*, ed. Andrés Ciudad Ruiz, Mario H. Ruz Sosa, and Ma. Josefa Iglesias Ponce de León, 175–193. Madrid: Sociedad Española de Estudios Mayas.

Zender, Marc. 2008. "A Study of Two Uaxactun-Style Tamale-Serving Vessels." In *The Maya Vase Book* 6, ed. Justin Kerr and Barbara Kerr, 1038–1055. New York: Kerr Associates.

CHAPTER 8

Cuisine and Feasting in the Copán and Lower Ulúa Valleys in Honduras

JULIA A. HENDON

This chapter considers cuisine and feasting in Late to Terminal Classic period societies living in what is now Honduras (Figure 8.1). During this time period, approximately the seventh to eleventh centuries CE, people living in the Copán valley in the mountains of western Honduras and in the Lower Ulúa valley, a broad, low-lying flood plain in the central part of the country, prepared, served, and ate meals made from local and imported ingredients. These meals most often brought together members of the same household and took place in the intimate confines of domestic space. However, food also played an important role in bringing together larger groups of people, including relatives, neighbors, acquaintances, and strangers. By turning the everyday acts of eating into elaborate and structured social occasions, meals became feasts.

Feasts played a central role in the celebration of achievements or milestones significant to the hosts. Such milestones may be part of the life cycle of the individual and family—birth, coming of age, marriage, death—or they may be connected to a calendar of events of religious or political importance. Commensality, the act of eating together, has "immense socializing power" (Simmel 1997:135) because it connects a natural behavior, something required for survival, directly to social relations and interactions. It celebrates the need for people to work together, to form social bonds, and to interact regularly. The daily meal at home or while working exemplifies commensality at an intimate social scale. Feasts serve to amplify commensality by including larger numbers of people, many of whom are not bound together by day-to-day interactions. Feasts express cultural notions of style, norms of behavior, and aesthetics through the provision, display, and consumption of large quantities of food and drink, including dishes and beverages made from special ingredients. Cuisine be-

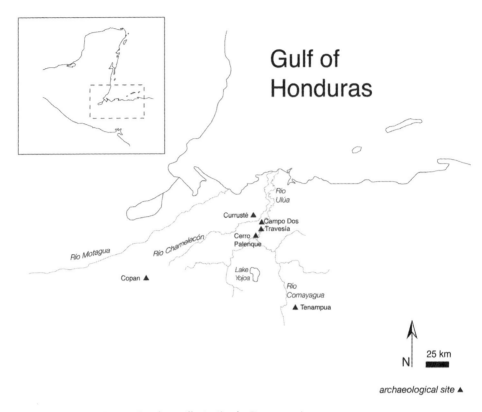

Figure 8.1. Western Honduras. Illustration by Rosemary Joyce.

comes part of this expression; in fact, ideas about food and feasting form an inextricable synergy that promotes social connections but also social differences and distinctions (Bourdieu 1984).

The meals at the heart of these exercises in commensality, competition, and cooperation must, therefore, fit into people's ideas about cuisine—a set of ideas and practices that center on food (Hastorf 2017). Cuisines may set people apart, but they also bring people together. Cuisine is something that characterizes because it is based on the where, how, what, and who of foodways (Hastorf 2017). The "where," according to Sidney Mintz (1996), is a geographically definable place. The "how" consists of the commonly used techniques of cooking and the actions associated with them, including ways of processing and manipulating, combining, and flavoring (Giard 1998; Rozin 1982). The "what" is composed of the ingredients used in cooking, including what Elisabeth Rozin (1982:197) refers to helpfully as the "flavoring practices." These ingredients may be local or imported.

What matters is how they are incorporated into the cuisine of the place. The ingredients themselves, many of which come from that geographically definable place, are the "what." The "who" encompasses who prepares and who consumes, who evaluates and who passes on the traditions.

Differences in content, preparation, presentation, and other aspects of making and serving food also allow cuisine to be used as a way of marking distinctions between members of different social classes, rural and urban dwellers, educated and uneducated, and so on (Albala 2014; Bourdieu 1984; Goody 1982). Marijke Van der Veen (2003:413) notes that prestige or "luxury foods [are] defined not as specific items of food but as foods offering a refinement of a basic food that is widely desired (not yet widely attained) *and* a means of distinction." Refinement may refer to differences in preparation or in how ingredients are juxtaposed with one another. It might be, for example, the conversion of a foodstuff into an alcoholic drink, as was done with cacao, maize, honey, and agave in Mesoamerica (Coe 1994; Cutler and Cárdenas 1947; Henderson and Joyce 2006; Tokovinine 2016; Vail and Dedrick, this volume; Vela 2014). It might be a particular cut of meat, such as the turkey parts or deer haunches that were considered most appropriate for Maya elite consumption (Coe 1994; Pohl 1994).

Comparing the Copán and Lower Ulúa valleys demonstrates the flexibility of cuisine, especially when considered as part of the specific social context of feasting (see also Hendon 2003, 2010). Whereas Copán residents used feasting as a way to reinforce social stratification, people living in the Lower Ulúa region used it as a way of keeping social distinctions from coalescing into an encompassing sociopolitical hierarchy (Hendon, Joyce, and Lopiparo 2014). The cuisines put on display through these feasts incorporated local and imported ingredients, domesticated and wild resources (Lentz 2000), and even items the taste of which may not agree with modern sensibilities. Eating was not limited to people. Deities, ancestors, and other supernatural beings were fed through offerings of raw ingredients, prepared dishes, and transformations of edible materials through, for example, burning (Stross 2010).

Settlement and Society in the Copán and Lower Ulúa Valleys

Location and interaction are the key factors in studying cuisine. Local identities throughout ancient Honduras are tied to natural and human-built landscapes that are part of a web of social relationships within and between settlements (Hendon 2010; Joyce, Hendon, and Lopiparo 2009;

Lopiparo 2007; Sheptak 2013). These landscapes include resources and technologies that contribute to cuisines that characterize and differentiate, that are inclusive and exclusive. Two regions, the Copán River valley in western Honduras and the Lower Ulúa River valley in north-central Honduras, have been the focus of extensive archaeological research. Tracing the beginnings of occupation in these regions is complicated, on the one hand, by the reuse of important locations and, on the other, by the changes to the landscape caused by natural processes such as sedimentation and changes in the courses of rivers (see Pope 1985; Turner et al. 1983; Wingard 2016). It is clear, however, that both valleys have long histories of being lived in, with settled agricultural life established by 1600 BCE in the Lower Ulúa valley (Joyce and Henderson 2001) and by 1400 BCE in the Copán valley (Hall and Viel 2004; Viel and Hall 1997). By the time of the period under discussion in this chapter, both valleys were at or near their peak population level for the region prior to Spanish colonization (Fash and Long 1983; Freter 1988; Joyce 2017; Webster 1999).

Residents of both valleys were organized into social houses (Hendon 2010). Social houses represent a flexible form of social organization found in many Mesoamerican societies (Gillespie 2000; Hendon 2007, 2010; Joyce 2000, 2007). A common investment in an estate lies at the heart of a social house. This investment is enacted and reinforced through practice, including both ritualized and day-to-day events and activities. A social house's estate includes rights, such as the right to carry out certain rituals or make or use of certain kinds of regalia. It provides a basis for claims to resources such as land, water, or labor. Material wealth is also central to a social house's estate. The structures that a social house builds, renovates, and maintains are the most enduring physical representation of the estate. The practice of burying the dead close to home helps create histories for these residences that afford space for both the living and the dead members of the social house. It is expected that the members of a social house may differ in their access to resources and to their status within the group. This ability to accommodate diversity represents one way that a social house strengthens itself and helps explain why burial practices and the buildings themselves within a large residential group vary (Hendon 2010; Lopiparo 2007).

The Copán River drainage in western Honduras covers an area of approximately four hundred square kilometers, about half of which is mountainous (Wingard 2016). Over time, the river has cut a series of small alluvial valleys into the land. The Copán pocket (that small alluvial valley where the archaeological site is located) was the most heavily settled, reaching

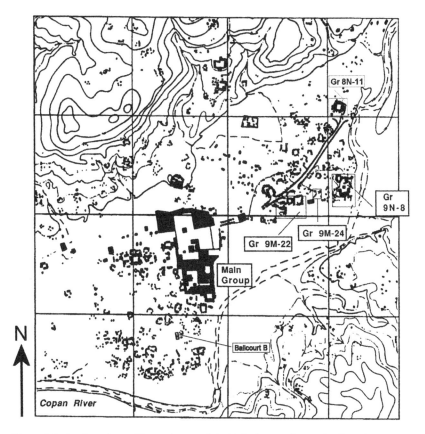

Figure 8.2. Copán valley settlement around the Main Group. Illustration by Julia Hendon, redrawn from Fash and Long 1983:Map 26A.

peak population in the Late Classic period, from about 600 to 900 CE (Figure 8.2). This pocket has the largest area of high-quality alluvial soils (Wingard 2016). During the Late to Terminal Classic period, the people living there were organized into a kingdom that included those living along the river and in the surrounding foothills. The physical and political center of this kingdom, known to archaeologists as the Main Group, is a complex of royal residences and monumental constructions dedicated to ritual, the ball game, and commemoration of royal histories written using the Maya hieroglyphic writing system (Fash 2001). These elements have convinced archaeologists that Copán was "fully Maya in its architecture, great art, hieroglyphic and calendric inscriptions" (Willey et al. 1994:1) by the time period under review in this chapter. All of these elements are also markers of a particular social and political system characterized by a succession of kings and associated nobility that seems to have developed starting in the fifth century CE when notable sociopolitical changes occurred, perhaps the result of foreign contact or incursion from the Lowland Maya Petén region or central Mexico (Sharer 2004; Stuart 2004).

At least three neighborhoods of large residential compounds cluster around the Main Group. Moving away from this core zone into the foothills, settlement becomes more dispersed and, for the most part, the houses become smaller, although some large compounds do occur in this more rural setting (see Fash 2001; Fash and Long 1983; Freter 1988; Hendon 2010; Leventhal 1979; and Willey and Leventhal 1979 for details of the settlement pattern in the valley). The basic residential unit is the patio group consisting of buildings arranged around a central open space or patio. When a household needed to expand, it might add on to an existing building. Wealthier social houses built additional patio groups that were connected to the original or founding group but usually maintained their own sense of privacy by being built around their own enclosed space (Hendon 1991). Most of the large compounds made up of many patio groups are found in the area around the Main Group. The social houses who lived in these impressive residences have some of the longest residential histories in the valley and are notable for the wealth represented in the architecture and kinds of objects they used in their daily life. Included among these objects are Ulúa polychrome pottery and clay figurines imported from the Lower Ulúa valley and adjacent regions such as the Lake Yojoa area and the Comayagua valley (Bill 1997; Gerstle 1987; Hendon 2010; Hendon, Joyce, and Lopiparo 2014; Joyce 2017; Viel 1993).

Study of the burials found in and around these patio groups provides evidence of the ways that social houses encompass complex systems of differentiation. The way people were buried varies both within and across patio groups. In other words, not all members of the social house living in a large stone-built compound within an easy walk of the Main Group were buried in the same way or with the same kinds of burial offerings, suggesting a continuous rather than segmented distribution of wealth and status. One finds a range of burials in patio groups, leading David Reed and Scott Zeleznik (2016:193) to conclude that the Copán burial program is marked by "degree of access, not exclusivity of access" (see also Diamanti 1991).

Nor does the health of the people who lived near the Main Group necessarily reflect a better standard of living in terms of the most basic aspects of nutrition and protection from disease. Paleopathology and paleodemography studies of the Copán skeletal sample reveal that people had similar levels of dietary deficits that affected growth, overall health status, morbidity, and mortality. Nutritional diseases or conditions such as anemia, dental diseases, and uneven growth patterns in childhood were widespread, occurring in people of various ages and both genders, and those who lived in rural or urban settings. People who were buried in tombs, with many valuable offerings, in locations that put them near the center of power may have been politically more important but were not any healthier than their contemporaries buried in the foothills in simple graves and accompanied by few or no offerings (Storey 1997, 1999, 2005; Whittington 1999; Whittington and Reed 1997). Thus, although the valley was centralized politically under the control of a ruling dynasty from at least the early 400s CE, a situation that undoubtedly created opportunities for some families to enrich themselves and gain political clout through their association with the royal family, this system was not so rigidly defined as to eliminate the need to express and enhance social distinction through culturally recognized means.

The Lower Ulúa River valley presents an interesting geographical and cultural contrast to the Copán kingdom (Figure 8.3). A "broad, long alluvial valley formed by three major, and numerous minor, rivers" (Joyce 1991:11) that empty into the Gulf of Honduras, the flood plain was densely settled during the seventh–eleventh centuries. This valley is a dynamic environment, as the rivers change course and periodically flood. Many of these areas were occupied for a long period of time, with people first living directly on the floodplain and then, around 200 CE, shifting to putting their houses and associated living spaces on *lomas*, where they also buried their dead. *Lomas* are foundation mounds that raise living spaces above ground level and are added to over time. Other groups of people settled in the areas less likely to flood, such as the foothills that form the edges of the valley. Stone is the favored building material for houses in the foothill settlements. Their builders still constructed foundation platforms to raise houses above ground level, replicating the idea of the *lomas* even when they were not needed to prevent the houses from being flooded (Hendon, Joyce, and Lopiparo 2014; Joyce 1991; Lopiparo 2003). Larger sites in both the valley bottom and the foothills represent places of larger aggregations of people. In other words, these places exhibit internal evidence of social differentiation within a shared framework of material culture and cultural values (Joyce and Hendon 2000). These towns and villages formed a network of societies whose connections reached into Belize, Guatemala, Nicaragua, Costa Rica, and El Salvador (Joyce 2017). During the Colonial period, indigenous people were multilingual, and there is every reason to suspect this was also the case for the period before the Spanish Conquest

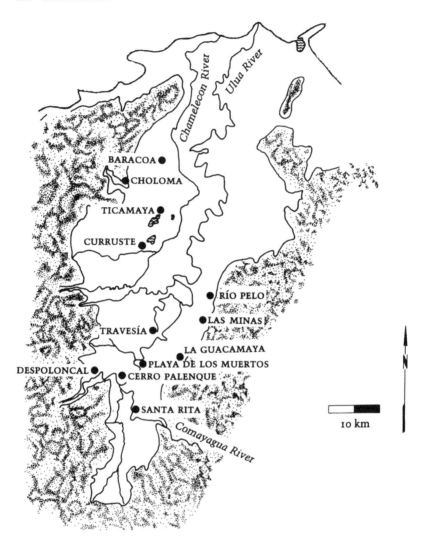

Figure 8.3. Settlement in the Lower Ulúa valley. Illustration by Than Saffel.

(Sheptak 2013). Languages such as Lenca and Tol have survived into more recent times (Ardón Mejía 1986; Chapman 1985, 1986).

The villages and towns occupied during this time period share a common material culture and visual imagery. Ulúa polychrome pottery, fine-paste pottery, clay figurines and other three-dimensional clay objects, and Ulúa marble vases represent items used in feasting, rituals, offerings, and gift exchange within the valley. The polychrome pottery, figurines, and vases were also desired by societies living farther away, including that of the Copán valley. Pottery and figurine production was decentralized and associated with important social and ritual events that encouraged social connections between different settlements. Unlike in the Copán valley, Lower Ulúa valley residents did not coalesce into a single political entity. While residents displayed material markers of affluence, they did not organize themselves into centralized settlement systems. The organizational principle is better characterized as heterarchy rather than hierarchy (Henderson and Joyce 2004; Hendon, Joyce, and Lopiparo 2014; Joyce 2017; Joyce and Hendon 2000; Lopiparo 2007). A set of more and less bounded settlements are tied together by multiple coordinate economic, social, and political networks based on shared practices.

> Heterarchy may be defined as the relation of elements to one another when they are unranked or when they possess the potential for being ranked in a number of different ways. For example, power can be counterpoised rather than ranked. Thus, three cities might be the same size but draw their importance from different realms: one hosts a military base, one is a manufacturing center, and the third is home to a great university. (Crumley 1995:3)

Heterarchies are social systems characterized by many different forms of social distinction that serve to differentiate individuals or groups or settlements from one another without creating a monolithic system (Crumley 1987, 1995; Crumley and Marquardt 1987). They are orderly but not necessarily hierarchical.

At the foothill town of Cerro Palenque, for example, one patio group is notably larger and built close to the ballcourt and associated monumental ritual structures (Hendon 2010; Joyce 1991). The smaller site of Campo Dos (CR-132) on the floodplain also possessed a ballcourt, even though it lacked monumental architecture like that found at Cerro Palenque. Residents of the village of Campo Dos and the town of Cerro Palenque wore jewelry made from imported jade and shell and used Ulúa marble vases, "the most precious and rarest luxury produced in the lower Ulúa valley" (Hendon, Joyce, and Lopiparo 2014:67; see Luke 2002, 2012). Both settlements were pottery-producing locations. Kilns and molds used to produce three-dimensional objects such as figurine whistles as well as fine-paste serving bowls were found in the largest residential group at Cerro Palenque, the one closest to the ballcourt (Hendon 2010). The Campo Dos workshop area is also near the ballcourt, which is itself surrounded by *lomas* (Lopiparo 2003, 2004).

Foodways in the Copán and Lower Ulúa Valleys

Understanding what people ate in the Copán and Lower Ulúa valleys relies on multiple lines of evidence. All of this research sheds light but has its limitations. The data are patchy for many reasons—sample availability and composition, preservation, researcher interests, and methods used being the most significant. In reviewing studies using plant or animal remains, stable isotopes, or residues, one finds that the different methods and materials sometimes produce complementary results and sometimes contradictory ones. Sometimes one method identifies a component of the diet invisible to other methods. Other times, comparing results creates a more nuanced understanding that may not align with ideas about how, for example, diet and social status relate to one another. In this section, I present an overview of diet in the two regions drawn from as many kinds of analyses as possible. My discussion uses a broader brush than any of the individual studies I draw on, and the reader should consult them for details of sampling, analytical techniques, and so on.

Mary Pohl (1994) studied faunal remains from houses near the Copán Main Group, in the more urban core. People living in this area ate more venison but fewer turtles than people living in other Maya regions. She also identified tapir, peccary, opossum, and coati. Dogs have been found but mostly buried more or less intact (Gerstle and Webster 1990; Pohl 1994). Other animals identified through faunal remains included pygmy owls and resplendent quetzals as well as several kinds of large Felidae and the large rodent *Cuniculus paca* (Ballinger and Stomper 2000; Pohl 1994; Reed 1998; Tremain 2016). Many remains of fresh and marine shellfish have been found (Beaubien 2004; Hendon 2010).

Bringing together species identifications from several sites in the Lower Ulúa valley, John Henderson and Rosemary Joyce (2004) demonstrate the importance of a wide range of animals to the local cuisine. Deer, dogs, opossums, peccaries, and fish have been found, along with traces of medium-sized mammals that cannot be more specifically identified. Tapirs, turkeys, and turtles appear in samples dating to the end of the period covered in this chapter. The turkeys were not native and may have come from the Yucatán Peninsula. Comparing these inventories with those from the Formative period site of Puerto Escondido reveals a decline in deer and other large mammals in favor of medium to small ones during the Late to Terminal Classic period.

The presence of many different plant species has been verified in the Lower Ulúa valley through the study of macroremains and microremains, including phytoliths and starch grains, and analysis of the chemical composition of residues on artifacts. Shanti Morell-Hart (2011) studied samples from four ancient settlements in the valley and was able to identify a wide range of plants. Maize and squash, such as *Cucurbita andreana*, *C. moschata*, and *C. maxima*, fit expectations about important contributors to the cuisine of the area. However, common beans (*Phaseolus vulgaris*) are surprisingly rare. Root crops, including *lirén* tubers (*Calathea* sp.), manioc (*Manihot*), achira (*Canna* sp.), and arrowroot (*Maranta*), contribute to the diet as do grains such as amaranth (*Amaranthus* sp.) and goosefoot (*Chenopodium* sp.). Many examples of the *Lamiaceae* (mint) family are noted. These may have provided flavoring elements. Papaya (*Carica papaya*), custard apples (*Annona* sp.), nances (*Brysonima crassifolia*), and hackberries (*Celtis* sp.) demonstrate that fruit was part of the cuisine. Traces of *Mammillaria* cacti may represent another component of people's meals. Among the traces of many types of palm trees is *Acrocomia*, which produces edible fruits and can be used to make a fermented drink.

Plant remains from the Copán valley reported by David Lentz (1991) provide evidence of maize and common bean consumption. Copán residents ate squash such as *Cucurbita moschata* and also used it in offerings. Important members of the gourd family include chayote (*Sechium edule*). Remains of palms (*Acrocomia* sp.), especially the coyol palm, suggest that people were making food or drink from these plants. Lentz identified traces of fruits, including avocado; *ciruela*, or hog plum (*Spondias* sp.); nance; and possibly sapote (*Pouteria* sp.), suggesting that the trees bearing these fruits were husbanded and cultivated in the valley. The residents of the region also made use of such wild species as wild grape (*Vitis* sp.), hackberry, and frijolillo (*Cassia* sp.). They did not eat root crops, however.

It is hardly surprising that the remains of plants and animals indicate other kinds of uses (Henderson and Joyce 2004; Lentz 1991; Morell-Hart 2011). Palms and grasses are used to make containers, mats, bedding, roofs, building materials, and so on. Bottle gourds (*Langenuria* sp.) turned up in Copán and Lower Ulúa samples. These inedible gourds can be turned into containers. Many of the plants that Morell-Hart identified are known to have had medicinal uses, making the distinction between food and medicine fuzzy and arbitrary. Animal bones as well as shells were shaped into tools or made into decorative regalia (Hendon 2010), while animals, or their parts, were important ritual offerings (Ballinger and Stomper 2000; Henderson and Joyce 2004). The pygmy owls and resplendent quetzal remains at Copán noted by Pohl (1994) and Tremain (2016) may have supplied feathers for ceremonial regalia. In the Lower Ulúa valley, copal

(*Protium*), a resin burned to create fragrant smoke, and tobacco (*Nicotiana*) have been found, suggesting that these central elements of Mesoamerican ritual practice were important parts of the ceremonial life of the valley's residents (Morell-Hart 2011).

By studying the pollen grains found in the floors of earlier religious buildings buried inside the massive Acropolis of the Main Group, Cameron McNeil (2012) sheds light on the use of plants in offerings. She notes the prevalence of four kinds of plants: maize, cattails (*Typha latifolia* L.), coyol palm, and *Bourreia*, a genus containing several species of flowering plant with fragrant white flowers. Maize and coyol are both edible, and *Bourreia huanita* flowers were added to cacao drinks, perhaps to enhance the aroma of the beverage. McNeil also calls attention to the fact that these plants have yellow or white flowers, in the case of coyol and *Bourreia*.

The material culture of food preparation, cooking, and eating offers more insight into cuisine. In a study of Copán ceramic vessels used for food preparation and cooking from the urban residences around the Main Group, I identified the following kinds of vessels (Hendon 1987, 2003). Comales, flat griddles useful for baking tortillas or other flat breads as well as toasting seeds or grains, made up about 5 percent of the ceramic rims I studied (Hendon 1987, Table 5.11). An earlier compilation of Copán ceramics by John Longyear (1952:25) also reported finding this useful type of cooking vessel. *Calderos*, large bowls, also served as food preparation and cooking vessels. Three-pronged braziers have a conical base supporting a shallow plate to which are attached three prongs. The base has cut-out areas, while the interior of the plate is often heavily burned. Several examples were found in association with food-preparation areas in Copán residences, leading me to propose that they were portable heating devices that could keep food warm (Hendon 1987:335–339). The Copán inventory also included plates and bowls in various sizes, some relatively plain, others decorated in various ways. Small and large drinking cups in the shape of a simple cylinder were also used. These, too, could be carefully decorated. Much of the fancy tableware was locally made but other pieces, particularly cylinders, were imported from the Comayagua and Lake Yojoa regions to the east (Joyce 2017:252–255). And finally, jars of various sizes were heavily used for storage and to store water or other liquids.

The Lower Ulúa valley residents had their own tradition of cooking and storage vessels based on local clays. Rosemary Joyce (2017:42–44) identifies a common suite of vessel forms for the valley. Jars of various sizes for storage and transport were crucial components of food preparation, just as they were in the Copán valley. Cooking pots include wide shallow bowls, deeper basins, and shallow plates, which Joyce notes probably served as griddles. They are thus similar to the Copán comales but may have been used for different kinds of cooking. Food was served and eaten in smaller bowls, plates, and cylinders. Again, the suite of forms is similar to what is found at Copán. Damaged starch grains found by Morell-Hart in ceramic sherds from Lower Ulúa valley sites further support the use of these vessels for cooking or serving food. Traces of palm phytoliths may "correspond with strips of palms used as ties binding and wrapping foods (tamales for example)" (Morell-Hart 2011:151).

Another important set of implements in both valleys is the combination of a grinding stone (metate) and a grinder (mano). Most often associated with processing maize, manos and metates can be used for many kinds of crushing, pounding, or grinding. Other ground-stone implements include bowls, mortars, and pestles (Hendon 1987; Joyce 1991). And finally, the artifact inventories of both regions are rich in tools made from obsidian or chert. Obsidian tools from the Lower Ulúa valley showed evidence of having been used to process parts of palm trees, various grasses, fibers or fruit from the Bromeliaceae family, and phytoliths from members of the Marantaceae family, such as arrowroot. Tools were used to process wood, maize, squash, and root crops (Morell-Hart 2011). Use-wear analysis of obsidian blades from Copán residences by John Mallory (1984) found evidence of sawing, slicing, and scraping—all of which can be taken as indirect evidence of processing a wide range of materials, including edibles.

The overall impression gained from the evidence for Copán and Lower Ulúa valley foodways is that of a core group of staples within a larger framework of variety. Maize and squash formed part of the diet in both regions. But people living in the two valleys also used many types of fruits, grains, seeds, herbs, and leafy plants in their meals. Nor were their cuisines based on identical suites of edibles. Lower Ulúa valley people ate *lirén* tubers, manioc, *achira*, and arrowroot as well as amaranth and goosefoot, foods that lend themselves to a variety of preparations and combine well with seasonings such as herbs. They ate beans less often, however, than residents of the Copán valley. Fruits were valued for their flavor but not always the same species. While both ate nances, Ulúa valley residents also preferred papaya, custard apples, and hackberries, whereas Copanecos ate hog plums and sapotes. Chile peppers, one of the hallmarks of Mexican cuisines, do not seem to have been part of the cooking traditions in either valley, a preference that continues to express itself in contemporary Honduran cuisine. Morell-Hart (2011:222) notes that there are several ways to identify chile peppers. In other words, it is not a particularly fugitive plant, and its absence seems to indicate lack of use rather than merely preservation issues.

Cacao (*Theobroma*) was an important part of indigenous economies in north-central Honduras, including the Lower Ulúa valley, before Spanish colonization and for some time afterward (Henderson 1977; Newson 1986; Roys 1957; Scholes and Roys 1948; Sheptak 2013). Documentary sources written after the Spanish established control of the region make it clear that the indigenous idea of a proper settlement included cacao groves and agricultural fields as well as buildings (Sheptak 2013). It is not surprising, therefore, that cacao was grown and used by some of the earliest known residents of the Lower Ulúa valley. Residue analyses of ceramics as old as 1150 BCE from the site of Puerto Escondido attest to the use of cacao (*Theobroma*) in fermented drinks (Henderson and Joyce 2006; Henderson et al. 2007; Joyce and Henderson 2007).

Colonial-period documents that include information about Maya society before the Spanish Conquest in the Yucatán Peninsula and Belize indicate that the desire to import cacao from north-central Honduras contributed to the establishment of long-distance trade relations between the two areas (Landa 1978; Roys 1957; Scholes and Roys 1948; Sheptak 2013). For the people in the Lower Ulúa region who grew the cacao and used it in their own meals, it signaled a homegrown sense of belonging that was not Maya but connected them to many different and more distant regions.

Residue analysis of ceramic vessels from Copán that date to the time period under discussion in this chapter attests to the use of cacao there as well (McNeil, Hurst, and Sharer 2006). It seems likely that Copanecos, especially those from wealthy social houses living near the Main Group, got their cacao through trade with towns in the Lower Ulúa valley and adjacent cacao-growing areas—also the source of the Ulúa polychrome eating and drinking vessels. Important as an ingredient in drinks and sauces in both areas, cacao nevertheless would have had a different set of associations—as a core element of local identity in the Lower Ulúa valley but as an exotic import in the Copán valley. Despite its origins in a culturally and linguistically distinct area, cacao may have been one way that the people in Copán developed a Maya identity and may have contributed to cuisine being a way of separating more prominent families from others. Many lines of evidence, such as residue analyses of vessels, decorative motifs, hieroglyphic texts, and later documentary sources, link cacao, for example, to Maya notions of value and high status. Yet the unusually well preserved village of Cerén in El Salvador provides clear evidence of cacao's presence in a nonelite setting (Lentz et al. 1996).

Cacao, root crops, seeds and grains, squash and beans, fruits, herbs, and even the lack of chile peppers begin to shape a sense of differences and similarities that contribute to cuisine. As noted earlier, paleoethnobotanical studies suggest that the Copán valley diet relied heavily on maize and lacked the variety seen in the diet of the Lower Ulúa valley, thanks to root crops such as manioc or grains such as amaranth. Stable isotope analysis of human skeletal remains from Copán support the conclusion that maize and beans were eaten all the time by people at all levels of society, although with some differences between men and women (Gerry 1997; Gerry and Chesson 2000; Gerry and Krueger 1997; Reed 1998, 1999; Reed and Zeleznik 2016; Whittington and Reed 1997).

Commensality in Context: Cuisine and Feasting

Cuisine starts with food but expands to include the how and why of preparation, serving, and consumption (Hastorf 2017). Commensality, as discussed at the beginning of this chapter, is also important to our understanding of cuisine's importance in the construction of identity and social relations. Excavations in both valleys show that feasting was something that happened in association with domestic places, providing the stage on which social identities were performed and negotiated (Hendon 2003, 2010; Hendon, Joyce, and Lopiparo 2014; Lopiparo 2003, 2007). The labor and skill required to produce food and drink of the quality needed for these events fell heavily on women, whose abilities to brew and cook were on display (Hendon 2010). Feasts go beyond mere eating because they are performances that require planning, cooperation, and skill. As the discussion at the beginning of the chapter emphasized, cuisines based on one or more staple foods are not necessarily identical. Preparation methods, flavoring principles, and ways of serving are all part of a cuisine. Cuisine must have depended in part on refinements rather than on a completely different set of raw ingredients. Sauces, fillings, and flavoring elements such as herbs, suggested by the plant and animal remains reviewed in this chapter, suggest ways that basic foodstuffs such as maize or root crops would be transformed into dishes that reflected local identities, created distinction, and fostered commensal relations.

As one might expect, the Copán royal family involved itself in hosting feasts, both in their living quarters on the south side of the Main Group and in the monumental space associated with massive religious and funerary structures (Andrews and Bill 2005; Aoyama 1995; Joyce 1986; Longyear 1952). The distribution of serving vessels, especially local and imported polychromes, and implements used for food preparation indicates that social houses living in larger and smaller patio groups located near the Main Group, in the generally wealthier and higher-status area, participated in status-enhancing feasts (Hendon 2003, 2010). Smaller and more rural patio groups clearly lacked the wealth or people to host elaborate feasts. Residents of these small sites may also have been involved in larger-scale feasting events through their social connections to the more substantial residential groups in the foothills or with residents of the inner zone. The presence of small amounts of fancy ceramics and censers at these rural sites (Gonlin 1993; see also Gonlin 1994, 2012) suggests that rural households also relied on the commensality encouraged by feasting to develop social relations and mark important life-cycle events. The many burials associated with residential places of all sizes provide one example of such an event. The death of children, something that happened often (Storey 1997), would have been an especially important moment to reinforce the emotional and psychological ties between members of the same family and the larger social house (Hendon, Joyce, and Lopiparo 2014).

Feasts hosted by noble social houses or royalty were occasions to demonstrate the ways that ingredients could be combined into special versions of everyday foods. Cacao, as evidenced by the analyses of McNeil, Hurst, and Sharer (2006), and venison (Pohl 1994) were items that higher-ranking and wealthier houses could offer to their peers and to lower-status rural dwellers. Serving beverages was not a simple task, however. Drinks made with cacao, maize, or other ingredients, for example, were not just about taste or alcohol content but also presentation. Served in tall, finely made and decorated drinking vessels, the liquid would be whipped or poured from a height to produce a frothy, foaming head on the surface of the liquid that seems to have been the quintessence of elegance and was highly valued (Hendon 2010; Stross 2011). Pohl's study revealed more deer bones in the trash deposits of households living near the Main Group. This finding, coupled with the stable isotope results that suggest that meat was not widely eaten at Copán (Gerry 1997; Gerry and Krueger 1997; Reed 1999), underscore the ways that feast dishes made with venison or other meats would have been a valued aspect of the meals served at these events.

Feasting in the Lower Ulúa valley was associated with life-cycle events and the ball game. Ballcourts used for communal events and rituals are found at several sites, some larger, such as Cerro Palenque, and some smaller, such as Campo Dos (Hendon 2010; Hendon, Joyce, and Lopiaro 2014). This proliferation of ballcourts represents one way that Lower Ulúa societies differed from the Copán valley where one ballcourt was built in the Main Group, with a second one added later in an adjacent residential area (Fash and Lane 1983; Joyce, Hendon, and Lopiparo 2009). Feasting in the Lower Ulúa valley, whether connected to a ball game or not, included dishes made from maize, manioc, and other ingredients that allowed for creativity in combining flavorings and in presentation. Tamales, suggested by the traces of palm strips in vessels analyzed by Morell-Hart (2011), would be one such festive dish that was more labor-intensive than the usual preparations of common ingredients. Copal and tobacco, used in rituals, would also have been part of these events (Morell-Hart 2011).

Lower Ulúa valley communities marked the end of feasts and associated ritual events in a deliberate manner. They broke many of the implements and ritual objects used during the event, burying them in or around *lomas*, or foundation mounds. One such event at Cerro Palenque was associated with the renewal of the western building. Censers and vessels for serving and eating were smashed on a pavement. This deposit was then buried by layers of broken objects, including figurines as well as more vessels. A single human femur was placed on top of this material. The bone and its supporting deposit were then covered by the staircase created as part of a renovation of the building foundation mound (Hendon 2010). Excavations by Jeanne Lopiparo at the site of Currusté (CR-32) provide another example. Currusté, like Campo Dos, is a valley settlement, but larger than its neighbor. It, too, was involved in crafting things out of clay, including impressively large three-dimensional figures, and may have had a ballcourt (now destroyed). Lopiparo found a dense and large deposit in one area of the site that included fine-paste serving vessels clearly broken in situ. Six large censers had been broken in a circle. One of these has been reconstructed and depicts a standing woman. Below the ring of censers lay several bundles of human long bones, covered by the remains of the feasting and ritual events (Hendon, Joyce, and Lopiparo 2014; Lopiparo 2008, 2009).

The similarity in feasting events between the larger and smaller sites in the Lower Ulúa valley argues in favor of heterarchy rather than hierarchy. The production of pottery vessels and figurines was also widely distributed between valley sites, suggesting a system of gift giving that reinforced social ties through the exchange of similar items (Hendon, Joyce, and Lopiparo 2014; Joyce 2017; Lopiparo 2003, 2004, 2007; Lopiparo and Hendon 2009; Lopiparo, Joyce, and Hendon 2005). Whereas Copán feasts reinforced the social hierarchy of powerful social houses living near the Main Group and certainly the power of the ruling family, Lower Ulúa valley feasts allowed for interaction within and across settlements of varying sizes. The food and drink served at these feasts allowed individuals and groups to demonstrate their ability to prepare dishes that agreed with the culturally developed ideas about how to prepare, serve, and consume food and drink—in other words, showing their understanding of the local cuisine in all its subtlety. The traces of plant and animal remains suggest that both areas had much to work with in terms of the core ingredients of dishes, such as meats, grains, starches, and vegetables, as well as flavoring principles and condiments. Feasting and cuisine emerge as flexible ways to build relationships that are sometimes hierarchical, sometimes heterarchical.

References

Albala, Ken. 2014. "Toward a Historical Dialectic of Culinary Styles." *Historical Research* 87(238):581–590.
Andrews, E. Wyllys, and Cassandra R. Bill. 2005. "A Late Classic Royal Residence at Copan." In *Copan: The History of an Ancient Maya Kingdom*, ed. E. Wyllys Andrews and William L. Fash, 239–314. Santa Fe: School of American Research Press.
Aoyama, Kazuo. 1995. "Microwear Analysis in the Southeast Maya Lowlands: Two Case Studies at Copán, Honduras." *Latin American Antiquity* 6(2):129–144.
Ardón Mejía, Mario. 1986. "Los indígenas jicaques de Honduras." *Tradiciones de Guatemala* 25:71–85.
Ballinger, Diane A., and Jeffrey Stomper. 2000. "The Jaguars of Altar Q, Copán, Honduras: Faunal Analysis, Archaeology, and Ecology." *Journal of Ethnobiology* 20(2): 223–236.
Beaubien, Harriet F. 2004. "Excavation and Recovery of a Funerary Offering of Marine Materials from Copán." In *Maya Zooarchaeology: New Directions in Method and Theory*, ed. Kitty F. Emery, 45–54. Los Angeles: Cotsen Institute of Archaeology at UCLA.
Bill, Cassandra R. 1997. "Patterns of Variation and Change in Dynastic Period Ceramics and Ceramic Production at Copán, Honduras." PhD diss., Dept. of Anthropology, Tulane University.
Bourdieu, Pierre. 1984. *Distinction: A Social Critique of the Judgement of Taste*. Trans. Richard Nice. Cambridge, MA: Harvard University Press.
Chapman, Anne. 1985. *Los hijos del copal y la candela*. Vol. 1, *Ritos agrarios y tradición oral de los lencas de Honduras*. Mexico City: Universidad Nacional Autónoma de México.
———. 1986. *Los hijos del copal y la candela*. Vol. 2, *Tradición católica de los lencas de Honduras*. Mexico City: Universidad Nacional Autónoma de México.
Coe, Sophie D. 1994. *America's First Cuisines*. Austin: University of Texas Press.
Crumley, Carole L. 1987. "A Dialectical Critique of Hierarchy." In *Power Relations and State Formation*, ed. Thomas C. Patterson and Christine Ward Gailey, 155–169. Washington, DC: American Anthropological Association.

———. 1995. "Heterarchy and the Analysis of Complex Societies." In *Heterarchy and the Analysis of Complex Societies*, ed. Robert M. Ehrenreich, Carole L. Crumley, and Janet E. Levy, 1–5. Archaeological Papers of the American Anthropological Association no. 6. Arlington, VA: American Anthropological Association.

Crumley, Carole L., and William H. Marquardt, eds. 1987. *Regional Dynamics: Burgundian Landscapes in Historical Perspective*. San Diego, CA: Academic Press.

Cutler, Hugh C., and Martín Cárdenas. 1947. "Chicha, a Native South American Beer." *Botanical Museum Leaflets* 13(3):33–60.

Diamanti, Melissa. 1991. "Domestic Organization at Copán: Reconstruction of Elite Maya Households through Ethnographic Models." PhD diss., Pennsylvania State University.

Fash, William L. 2001. *Scribes, Warriors and Kings: The City of Copán and the Ancient Maya*. London: Thames and Hudson.

Fash, William L., and Sheree Lane. 1983. "El juego de pelota B." In *Introducción a la arqueología de Copán, Honduras*, ed. Claude F. Baudez, 2:501–562. Tegucigalpa, Honduras: Proyecto Arqueológico Copán, Secretaría de Estado en el Despacho de Cultura y Turismo.

Fash, William F., and Kurt Z. Long. 1983. "Mapa arqueológico del valle de Copán." In *Introducción a la arqueología de Copán, Honduras*, ed. Claude F. Baudez, 3:5–48. Tegucigalpa, Honduras: Proyecto Arqueológico Copán, Secretaría de Estado en el Despacho de Cultura y Turismo.

Freter, AnnCorinne. 1988. "The Classic Maya Collapse at Copán, Honduras: A Regional Settlement Perspective." PhD diss., Pennsylvania State University.

Gerry, John P. 1997. "Bone Isotope Ratios and Their Bearing on Elite Privilege among the Classic Maya." *Geoarchaeology* 12(1):41–69.

Gerry, John P., and Meredith S. Chesson. 2000. "Classic Maya Diet and Gender Relationships." In *Gender and Material Culture in Archaeological Perspective*, ed. Moira Donald and Linda Hurcombe, 250–264. New York: St Martin's Press.

Gerry, John P., and Harold W. Krueger. 1997. "Regional Diversity in Classic Maya Diets." In *Bones of the Maya: Studies of Ancient Skeletons*, ed. Stephen L. Whittington and David M. Reed, 196–207. Washington, DC: Smithsonian Institution Press.

Gerstle, Andrea I. 1987. "Ethnic Diversity and Interaction at Copán, Honduras." In *Interaction on the Southeast Mesoamerican Frontier: Prehistoric and Historic Honduras and El Salvador*, ed. Eugenia J. Robinson, 2:328–356. BAR International Series 327. Oxford: British Archaeological Reports.

Gerstle, Andrea I., and David Webster. 1990. "Excavaciones en 9N-8, Conjunto del Patio D." In *Proyecto Arqueológico Copán Segunda Fase: Excavaciones en el área urbana de Copán*, ed. William T. Sanders, 3:25–378. Tegucigalpa, Honduras: Secretaría de Estado en el Despacho de Cultura y Turismo, Instituto Hondureño de Antropología e Historia.

Giard, Luce. 1998. "Doing-Cooking." In *The Practice of Everyday Life*. Vol. 2, *Living and Cooking*, 149–247. Trans. Timothy J. Tomasik. Minneapolis: University of Minnesota Press.

Gillespie, Susan D. 2000. "Rethinking Ancient Maya Social Organization: Replacing 'Lineage' with 'House.'" *American Anthropologist* 102(3):467–484.

Gonlin, Nancy. 1993. "Rural Household Archaeology at Copán, Honduras." PhD diss., Pennsylvania State University.

———. 1994. "Rural Household Diversity in Late Classic Copán, Honduras." In *Archaeological Views from the Countryside: Village Communities in Early Complex Societies*, ed. Glenn M. Schwartz and Steven E. Falconer, 177–197. Washington, DC: Smithsonian Institution Press.

———. 2012. "Production and Consumption in the Countryside: A Case Study from the Late Classic Maya Rural Commoner Households at Copán, Honduras." In *Ancient Households of the Americas: Conceptualizing What Households Do*, ed. John G. Douglas and Nancy Gonlin, 79–116. Boulder: University Press of Colorado.

Goody, Jack. 1982. *Cooking, Cuisine and Class: A Study in Comparative Sociology*. Cambridge: Cambridge University Press.

Hall, Jay, and René Viel. 2004. "The Early Classic Copan Landscape: A View from the Preclassic." In *Understanding Early Classic Copan*, ed. Ellen E. Bell, Marcello A. Canuto, and Robert J. Sharer, 17–28. Philadelphia: University of Pennsylvania Museum of Archaeology and Anthropology.

Hastorf, Christine A. 2017. *The Social Archaeology of Food: Thinking about Eating from Prehistory to the Present*. New York: Cambridge University Press.

Henderson, John S. 1977. "The Valle de Naco: Ethnohistory and Archaeology in Northwestern Honduras." *Ethnohistory* 24(4):363–376.

———. 1988. "Investigaciones arqueológicas en el Valle de Sula." *Yaxkin* 11(1):5–30.

Henderson, John S., and Rosemary A. Joyce. 2004. "Human Use of Animals in Prehispanic Honduras: A Preliminary Report from the Lower Ulúa Valley." In *Maya Zooarchaeology: New Directions in Method and Theory*, ed. Kitty F. Emery, 223–236. Los Angeles: Cotsen Institute of Archaeology at UCLA.

———. 2006. "Brewing Distinction: The Development of Cacao Beverages in Formative Mesoamerica." In *Chocolate in Mesoamerica: A Cultural History of Cacao*, ed. Cameron L. McNeil, 140–153. Gainesville: University Press of Florida.

Henderson, John, S., Rosemary A. Joyce, Gretchen R. Hall, W. Jeffrey Hurst, and Patrick E. McGovern. 2007. "Chemical and Archaeological Evidence for the Earliest Cacao Beverages." *Proceedings of the National Academy of Sciences* 104(48):18937–18940.

Hendon, Julia A. 1987. "The Uses of Maya Structures: A Study of Architecture and Artifact Distribution at Sepulturas, Copán, Honduras." PhD diss., Harvard University. cupola.gettysburg.edu/anthfac/32.

———. 1991. "Status and Power in Classic Maya Society: An Archeological Study." *American Anthropologist* 93(4):894–918.

———. 2003. "Feasting at Home: Community and House Solidarity among the Maya of Southeastern Mesoamerica." In *The Archaeology and Politics of Food and Feasting in Early States and Empires*, ed. Tamara L. Bray, 203–233. New York: Kluwer Academic/Plenum.

———. 2007. "Memory, Materiality, and Practice: House Societies in Southeastern Mesoamerica." In *The Durable House: House Society Models in Archaeology*, ed. Robin A. Beck, 292–316. Occasional Paper 35. Carbondale: Center for Archaeological Investigations, Southern Illinois University.

———. 2010. *Houses in a Landscape: Memory and Everyday Life in Mesoamerica*. Durham, NC: Duke University Press.

Hendon, Julia A., Rosemary A. Joyce, and Jeanne Lopiparo. 2014. *Material Rela-*

tions: The Marriage Figurines of Prehispanic Honduras. Boulder: University Press of Colorado.

Hendon, Julia A., Rosemary A. Joyce, and Russell Sheptak. 2009. "Heterarchy as Complexity: Archaeology in Yoro, Honduras." Revised version of a paper presented at the 58th Annual Meeting of the Society for American Archaeology, St. Louis, MO, in 1993. cupola.gettysburg.edu/anthfac/15.

Joyce, Rosemary A. 1986. "Terminal Classic Interaction on the Southeastern Maya Periphery." *American Antiquity* 51(2):313–329.

———. 1991. *Cerro Palenque: Power and Identity on the Maya Periphery*. Austin: University of Texas Press.

———. 2000. "Heirlooms and Houses: Materiality and Social Memory." In *Beyond Kinship: Social and Material Reproduction in House Societies*, ed. Rosemary A. Joyce and Susan D. Gillespie, 189–212. Philadelphia: University of Pennsylvania Press.

———. 2007. "Building Houses: The Materialization of Lasting Identity in Formative Mesoamerica." In *The Durable House: House Society Models in Archaeology*, ed. Robin A. Beck, 53–72. Occasional Paper 35. Carbondale: Center for Archaeological Investigations, Southern Illinois University.

———. 2017. *Painted Pottery of Honduras: Object Lives and Itineraries*. Leiden, Netherlands: Brill.

Joyce, Rosemary A., and John S. Henderson. 2001. "Beginnings of Village Life in Eastern Mesoamerica." *Latin American Antiquity* 12(1):5–24.

———. 2007. "From Feasting to Cuisine: Implications of Archaeological Research in an Early Honduran Village." *American Anthropologist* 109(4):642–653.

Joyce, Rosemary A., and Julia A. Hendon. 2000. "Heterarchy, History, and Material Reality: 'Communities' in Late Classic Honduras." In *The Archaeology of Communities: A New World Perspective*, ed. Marcello-Andrea Canuto and Jason Yaeger, 143–159. London: Routledge.

Joyce, Rosemary A., Julia A. Hendon, and Jeanne Lopiparo. 2009. "Being in Place: Intersections of Identity and Experience on the Honduran Landscape." In *The Archaeology of Meaningful Places*, ed. Brenda J. Bowser and María Nieves Zedeño, 53–72. Salt Lake City: University of Utah Press.

Landa, Diego de. 1978. *Landa's Relación de las cosas de Yucatán*. Ed. and trans. Alfred M. Tozzer. Papers of the Peabody Museum of American Archaeology and Ethnology, Vol. 18. Millwood, NY: Kraus Reprint.

Lentz, David L. 1991. "Maya Diets of the Rich and Poor: Paleoethnobotanical Evidence from Copán." *Latin American Antiquity* 2(3):269–287.

———. 2000. "Anthropocentric Food Webs in the Precolumbian Americas." In *Imperfect Balance: Landscape Transformations in the Pre-Columbian Americas*, ed. David L. Lentz, 89–120. New York: Columbia University Press.

Lentz, David L., Marilyn P. Beaudry-Corbett, Maria Luisa Reyna de Aguilar, and Lawrence W. Kaplan. 1996. "Foodstuffs, Forests, Fields, and Shelter: A Paleoethnobotanical Analysis of Vessel Contents from the Ceren Site, El Salvador." *Latin American Antiquity* 7(3):247–262.

Leventhal, Richard M. 1979. "Settlement Patterns at Copán, Honduras." PhD diss., Harvard University.

Longyear, John M., III. 1952. *Copán Ceramics: A Study of Southeastern Maya Pottery*. Publication 597. Washington, DC: Carnegie Institution of Washington.

Lopiparo, Jeanne. 2003. "Household Ceramic Production and the Crafting of Society in the Terminal Classic Ulúa Valley, Honduras." PhD diss., University of California, Berkeley.

———. 2004. "La evidencia arqueológica de la producción doméstica de la cerámica en el valle del río Ulúa." In *Memoria VII Seminario de Antropología de Honduras "Dr. George Hasemann,"* ed. Kevin Rubén Ávalos, 151–160. Tegucigalpa, Honduras: Instituto Hondureño de Antropología e Historia.

———. 2007. "House Societies and Heterarchy in the Terminal Classic Ulúa Valley, Honduras." In *The Durable House: House Society Models in Archaeology*, ed. Robin A. Beck, 73–96. Occasional Paper 35. Carbondale: Center for Archaeological Investigations, Southern Illinois University.

———. 2008. *Proyecto Arqueológico Currusté: Informe sobre la Primera Temporada*. Technical report on file with the Instituto Hondureño de Antropología e Historia, Tegucigalpa, Honduras.

———. 2009. *Proyecto Arqueológico Currusté: Informe sobre la Segunda Temporada*. Technical report on file with the Instituto Hondureño de Antropología e Historia, Tegucigalpa, Honduras.

Lopiparo, Jeanne, and Julia A. Hendon. 2009. "Honduran Figurines and Whistles in Social Context: Production, Use, and Meaning in the Ulúa Valley." In *Mesoamerican Figurines: Small-Scale Indices of Large-Scale Social Phenomena*, ed. Christina T. Halperin, Katherine A. Faust, Rhonda Taube, and Aurore Giguet, 51–74. Gainesville: University Press of Florida.

Lopiparo, Jeanne, Rosemary A. Joyce, and Julia A. Hendon. 2005. "Terminal Classic Pottery Production in the Ulúa Valley, Honduras." In *Geographies of Power: Understanding the Nature of Terminal Classic Pottery in the Maya Lowlands*, ed. Sandra L. López Varela and Antonia E. Foias, 107–119. BAR International Series 1447. Oxford: Archaeopress.

Luke, Christina. 2002. "Ulúa-Style Marble Vases." PhD diss., Cornell University.

———. 2012. "Materiality and Sacred Landscapes: Ulúa Style Marble Vases in Honduras." In *Beyond Belief: The Archaeology of Ritual and Religion*, ed. Yorke Rowan, 114–129. Archaeological Papers of the American Anthropological Association no. 21. Arlington, VA: American Anthropological Association.

Mallory, John K. 1984. "Late Classic Maya Economic Specialization: Evidence from the Copán Obsidian Assemblage." PhD diss., Pennsylvania State University.

McNeil, Cameron L. 2012. "Recovering the Color of Ancient Maya Floral Offerings at Copán, Honduras." *RES: Anthropology and Aesthetics* 61/62:300–314.

McNeil, Cameron L., W. Jeffrey Hurst, and Robert J. Sharer. 2006. "The Use and Representation of Cacao during the Classic Period at Copán, Honduras." In *Chocolate in Mesoamerica: A Cultural History of Cacao*, ed. Cameron L. McNeil, 224–252. Gainesville: University Press of Florida.

Mintz, Sidney W. 1996. *Tasting Food, Tasting Freedom: Excursions into Eating, Culture, and the Past*. Boston: Beacon Press.

Morell-Hart, Shanti. 2011. "Paradigms and Syntagms of Ethnobotanical Practice in Pre-Hispanic Northwestern Honduras." PhD diss., University of California, Berkeley.

Newson, Linda. 1986. *The Cost of Conquest: Indian Decline in Honduras under Spanish Rule*. Dellplain Latin American Studies no. 20. Boulder: Westview Press.

Pohl, Mary D. 1994. "Late Classic Maya Fauna from Settlement in the Copán Valley, Honduras: Assertion of Social Status through Animal Consumption." In *Ceramics and Artifacts from Excavations in the Copán Residential Zone*, ed. Gordon R. Willey, Richard M. Leventhal, Arthur A. Demarest, and William L. Fash, 459–476. Papers of the Peabody Museum of Archaeology and Ethnology, Vol. 80. Cambridge, MA: Peabody Museum at Harvard University.

Pope, Kevin O. 1985. "Paleoecology of the Ulúa Valley, Honduras: An Archaeological Perspective." PhD diss., Stanford University.

Reed, David M. 1998. "Ancient Maya Diet at Copán, Honduras." PhD diss., Pennsylvania State University.

———. 1999. "Cuisine from Hun-Nal-Ye." In *Reconstructing Ancient Maya Diet*, ed. Christine D. White, 183–196. Salt Lake City: University of Utah Press.

Reed, David M., and W. Scott Zeleznik. 2016. "The Maya in the Middle: An Analysis of Sub-Royal Archaeology at Copán, Honduras." In *Human Adaptation in Ancient Mesoamerica: Empirical Approaches to Mesoamerican Archaeology*, ed. Nancy Gonlin and Kirk D. French, 175–208. Boulder: University Press of Colorado.

Roys, Ralph L. 1943. *The Indian Background of Colonial Yucatan*. Carnegie Institution of Washington Publication 548. Washington, DC: Carnegie Institution of Washington.

———. 1957. *The Political Geography of the Yucatan Maya*. Carnegie Institution of Washington Publication 613. Washington, DC: Carnegie Institution of Washington.

Rozin, Elisabeth. 1982. "The Structure of Cuisine." In *The Psychobiology of Human Food Selection*, ed. Lewis M. Barker, 189–203. Westport, CT: AVI.

Scholes, Francis V., and Ralph L. Roys. 1948. *The Maya Chontal Indians of Acalan-Tixchel*. Carnegie Institution of Washington Publication 560. Washington, DC: Carnegie Institution of Washington.

Sharer, Robert J. 2004. "External Interaction at Early Classic Copán. In *Understanding Early Classic Copán*, ed. Ellen E. Bell, Marcello A. Canuto, and Robert J. Sharer, 299–317. Philadelphia: University of Pennsylvania Museum of Archaeology and Anthropology.

Sheptak, Russell N. 2013. *Colonial Masca in Motion: Tactics of Persistence of a Honduran Indigenous Community*. Leiden, Netherlands: Leiden University Repository. openaccess.leidenuniv.nl/handle/1887/20999.

Simmel, Georg. 1997. "The Sociology of the Meal." Trans. Mark Ritter and David Frisby. In *Simmel on Culture: Selected Writings*, ed. David Frisby and Mike Featherstone, 130–135. London: Sage.

Storey, Rebecca. 1997. "Individual Frailty, Children of Privilege, and Stress in Late Classic Copán." In *Bones of the Maya: Studies of Ancient Skeletons*, ed. Stephen L. Whittington and David M. Reed, 116–126. Washington, DC: Smithsonian Institution Press.

———. 1999. "Late Classic Nutrition and Skeletal Indicators at Copán, Honduras. In *Reconstructing Ancient Maya Diet*, ed. Christine D. White, 169–179. Salt Lake City: University of Utah Press.

———. 2005. "Health and Lifestyle (before and after Death) among the Copán Elite." In *Copán: The History of an Ancient Maya Kingdom*, ed. E. Wyllys Andrews and William L. Fash, 315–343. Santa Fe: School of American Research.

Stross, Brian. 2010. "This World and Beyond: Food Practices and the Social Order in

Mayan Religion." In *Pre-Columbian Foodways: Interdisciplinary Approaches to Food, Culture, and Markets in Ancient Mesoamerica*, ed. John E. Staller and Michael D. Carrasco, 553–576. New York: Springer.

———. 2011. "Food, Foam and Fermentation in Mesoamerica: Bubbles and the Sacred State of Inebriation." *Food, Culture and Society* 14(4):477–501.

Stuart, David. 2004. "The Beginnings of the Copán Dynasty: A Review of the Hieroglyphic and Historical Evidence." In *Understanding Early Classic Copán*, ed. Ellen E. Bell, Marcello A. Canuto, and Robert J. Sharer, 215–247. Philadelphia: University of Pennsylvania Museum of Archaeology and Anthropology.

Tokovinine, Alexandre. 2016. "It Is His Image with Pulque: Drinks, Gifts, and Political Networking in Classic Maya Texts and Images." *Ancient Mesoamerica* 27(1):13–29.

Tremain, Cara Grace. 2016. "Birds of a Feather: Exploring the Acquisition of Resplendent Quetzal (*Pharomachrus mocinno*) Tail Coverts in Pre-Columbian Mesoamerica." *Human Ecology* 44(4):399–408.

Turner, B. L., II, William Johnson, Gail Mahood, Frederick W. Wiseman, B. L. Turner, and Jackie Poole. 1983. "Habitat y agricultura en la región de Copán." In *Introducción a la arqueología de Copán, Honduras*, ed. Claude F. Baudez, 1:37–142. Tegucigalpa, Honduras: Secretaría de Estado en el Despacho de Cultura y Turismo.

Van der Veen, Marijke. 2003. "When Is Food a Luxury?" *World Archaeology* 34(3): 405–427.

Vela, Enrique. 2014. "Los usos del maguey." *Arqueología Mexicana* 57:56–65.

Viel, René. 1993. *Evolución de la cerámica de Copán, Honduras*. Tegucigalpa, Honduras: Instituto Hondureño de Antropología e Historia.

Viel, René, and Jay Hall. 1997. "El período formativo de Copán en el contexto de Honduras." *Yaxkin* 16:40–48.

Webster, David. 1999. "The Archaeology of Copán, Honduras." *Journal of Archaeological Research* 7(1):1–53.

Whittington, Stephen L. 1999. "Caries and Antemortem Tooth Loss at Copán: Implications for Commoner Diet." In *Reconstructing Ancient Maya Diet*, ed. Christine D. White, 151–167. Salt Lake City: University of Utah Press.

Whittington, Stephen L., and David M. Reed. 1997. "Commoner Diet at Copán: Insights from Stable Isotopes and Porotic Hyperostosis." In *Bones of the Maya: Studies of Ancient Skeletons*, ed. Stephen L. Whittington and David M. Reed, 157–170. Washington, DC: Smithsonian Institution Press.

Willey, Gordon R., and Richard M. Leventhal. 1979. "Prehistoric Settlement at Copán." In *Maya Archaeology and Ethnohistory*, ed. Norman Hammond and Gordon R. Willey, 75–102. Austin: University of Texas Press.

Willey, Gordon R., Richard M. Leventhal, Arthur A. Demarest, and William L. Fash. 1994. *Ceramics and Artifacts from Excavations in the Copán Residential Zone*. Papers of the Peabody Museum of Archaeology and Ethnology, Vol. 80. Cambridge, MA: Peabody Museum at Harvard University.

Wingard, John D. 2016. "Complementarity and Synergy: Stones, Bones, Soil, and Toil in the Copán Valley, Honduras." In *Human Adaptations in Ancient Mesoamerica: Empirical Approaches to Mesoamerican Archaeology*, ed. Nancy Gonlin and Kirk D. French, 73–93. Boulder: University Press of Colorado.

CHAPTER 9

Talking Feasts: Classic Maya Commensal Politics at La Corona

MAXIME LAMOUREUX-ST-HILAIRE

Few would dispute that sharing meals, or commensality, is of universal importance among human societies (Brown 1991:139; Douglas and Isherwood 1996:61). Many aspects of commensality have been explored by anthropological archaeologists, especially from the standpoint of feasting practices—that is, extraordinary and ritualized communal food consumption—which provide ideal occasions for (re)defining social relations through performance and material exchanges (Dietler 1996; Dietler and Hayden 2001; Van der Veen 2003). Among complex societies, the potential of feasts to simultaneously exclude and include political agents has been used to highlight how they are critical "for the enactment of sovereignty" (A. T. Smith 2015:69). Among the ancient Maya, feasting has been recognized as a political strategy used by royal courts to form alliances and reify status through material exchanges and conspicuous display (Ardren, this volume; Brown and Freiwald, this volume; Dahlin et al. 2010; Foias 2002, 2013; Halperin and Foias 2010, 2012; LeCount 2001, 2010; LeCount and Yaeger 2010; McAnany 2010; Reents-Budet 2000; Tokovinine 2016).

In this chapter, I move beyond material exchanges and hierarchy to address the communicational functions of feasting practices at Classic Maya royal courts. I present archaeological evidence from the late Late Classic (ca. 800 CE) regal palace of La Corona, Guatemala, to study the organization of politically charged feasts by the government of this polity. I argue that a central function of Classic Maya regal palaces was the orchestration of political gatherings centered around two entangled activities: communal food consumption and interpersonal communication. These recurring commensal events—featuring delicious food and drinks, reciprocal communication, and material exchanges—provided an institutional strategy corresponding to what Dietler (1996:98–99) defines as diacritical feasting.

Below, I first provide background information about the political institution of La Corona, Guatemala, after which I adopt a *chaîne opératoire*–like narrative to follow how foodstuffs, artifacts, and people flowed through carefully designed architectural settings and interacted in order to realize their political potential. This leads me to discuss palace kitchens and storage facilities, royal administration, and the distinct communicational settings designed by Classic Maya architects. I then analyze the relationship between royal-sponsored feasts and institutional communication to explore the sociopolitical value of food and the risks inherent to hosting feasts. Finally, I close this chapter with a commentary on certain methodological aspects of food archaeology.

The Regal Palace of La Corona in the Ninth Century

During the second half of the eighth century, the government of La Corona—a midsize polity located in northwest Petén, Guatemala (Figure 9.1)—was transformed by shifting geopolitical dynamics (Lamoureux-St-Hilaire 2018b). As the Kaanul hegemony receded from the Southern Lowlands, the La Corona rulers apparently weathered the political demise of their former overlords, filling in the regional political vacuum and acquiring more autonomy (Canuto, Barrientos Q., and Bustamante 2017). The fate of the post–Kaanul La Corona regime is reflected in the material record of its regal palace: an acropolis located west of the site's Main Plaza (Figure 9.1), measuring ca. 80 m × 55 m and 7–11 m in height, which supported a central platform surrounded by four architectural groups (the Northeast, Southeast, Southwest, and Northwest Groups; Canuto et al. 2017; Lamoureux-St-Hilaire 2018b). The palace's post-750 CE renovations and the dense middens associated with its subsequent occupations indicate that the government of La Corona remained dynamic and in sync with changing economic and political networks until the site's abandonment, ca. 900 CE (Lamoureux-St-Hilaire 2018b; Lamoureux-St-Hilaire et al. 2020).

Around 750 CE, royal architects decommissioned the two southern groups of the palace that were associated with the Kaanul hegemony, and then significantly renovated the Northeast and Northwest Groups (Canuto, Barrientos Q., and Bustamante 2017; Lamoureux-St-Hilaire 2018b:235–238; Lamoureux-St-Hilaire et al. 2020). This architectural program, spanning the Halcón B (ca. 750 CE) and Tucán (ca. 790–850 CE) construction phases, significantly altered the palace's spatial syntax. By

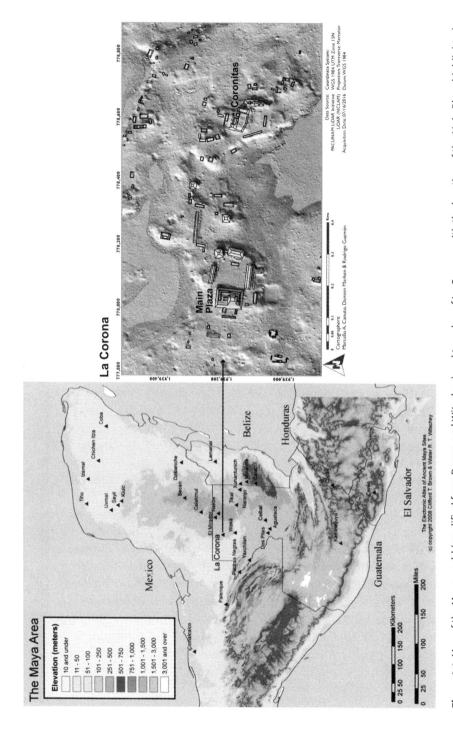

Figure 9.1. Map of the Maya world (modified from Brown and Witschey) and top plan of La Corona, with the location of the Main Plaza highlighted. Courtesy of the Proyecto Regional Arqueológico La Corona.

the ninth century, the two northern groups had become well-integrated, complementary complexes serving the residential, communicational, economic, administrative, and ceremonial functions of the royal court (Figure 9.2; Lamoureux-St-Hilaire 2018b).

This chapter builds on extensive architectural, artifactual, and geoarchaeological data (Lamoureux-St-Hilaire 2018a, 2018b; Lamoureux-St-Hilaire et al. 2019) produced by the author during five years of work in the Northeast and Northwest Groups of the La Corona regal palace under the umbrella of the Proyecto Regional Arqueológico La Corona, codirected by Marcello A. Canuto and Tomás Barrientos. Excavations and multi-proxy analyses revealed that the Northeast and Northwest Groups were designed, in part, to facilitate the accumulation, storage, and transformation of goods and food (Lamoureux-St-Hilaire 2018b; Lamoureux-St-Hilaire et al. 2019). The Northwest Group, with its storehouses, kitchens, craft areas, administrative section, and middens, was primarily dedicated to the ancillary activities supporting the daily subsistence of the court and its political feasts (see below; Lamoureux-St-Hilaire et al. 2019). Meanwhile, the Northeast Group, richly decorated with politically charged art, served as both the royal residential compound and the center stage for the La Corona regime (see below; Lamoureux-St-Hilaire 2018b). The articulating point between these two groups, a passageway structure monitored by royal administrators, channeled the flow of people and resources. All three sections of the regal palace played a key role in La Corona's commensal politics and are further discussed below.

The Beginning and End of Commensal Politics

A *chaîne opératoire* approach to goods and foodstuffs can adequately model the activities that occurred within the distinct areas of Classic Maya regal palaces (Lamoureux-St-Hilaire 2018b:71–77). Staples were acquired by royals, stored, transformed, served, consumed, or distributed, and the by-products of their transformation and consumption were finally discarded. Current scholarship suggests that staples were acquired by Classic Maya royals through tithing mechanisms (i.e., taxes and tribute; Foias 2002, 2013; McAnany 2010; McAnany et al. 2002). Consequently, this acquisition process should have taken place in courtly settings—a topic abundantly documented by iconographers and epigraphers (Jackson 2013, 2015; Miller and Brittenham 2013; Miller and Martin 2004). I believe this acquisition happened during courtly diacritical feasts that brought

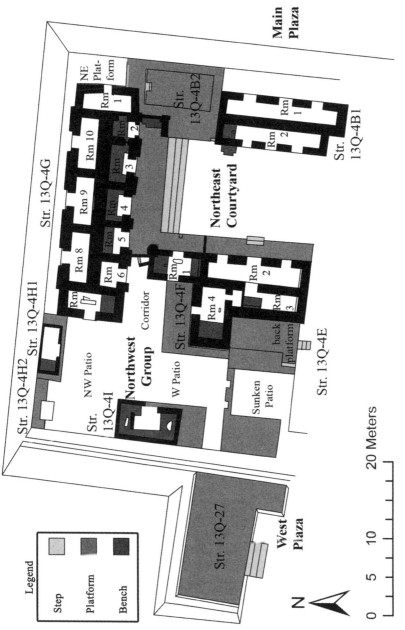

Figure 9.2. The north section of the La Corona regal palace. Map by the author.

together royals, some of their "international" allies, and their vassals (i.e., the leaders of local communities of production). These commensal events provided an incentive for vassals to gather and deliver their dues. Thus, through this exchange of tithe for feast, these gatherings substantiated the regime by materializing the reciprocal relationship between royals, allies, and vassals (Lamoureux-St-Hilaire 2018b:55–62).

In addition, this relationship was reified through the distribution of regalia—textiles, jewelry, ceramic containers, and other portable objects—to vassals (see below; Foias 2002, 2013; LeCount and Yaeger 2010; McAnany 2010, 2013; McAnany et al. 2002). A practical implication of both the acquisition and distribution steps of the *chaîne opératoire* is a need for storage facilities (Lamoureux-St-Hilaire 2018b:74; Morell-Hart, this volume). Indeed, the royals required adequate space for storing staples and regalia, and such storehouses should be found in association with reception areas. And while common sense and general archaeological theory dictate this, storage functions "are seldom mentioned by those interpreting palace room function" (McAnany 2010:178; for rare exceptions, see Smyth 2016; Vidal-Lorenzo, Vázquez-de-Ágredos-Pascual, and Muñoz-Cosme 2016).

A detailed discussion of Classic Maya courtly storage goes beyond the scope of this chapter, but I would like to highlight that distinct types of storehouses may be identified by somewhat elusive architectural features. In particular, taxes and tribute were likely stored near reception areas inside masonry rooms with restricted doorways and significant "empty space" fit for wooden architecture, such as shelving (Figure 9.3; Lamoureux-St-Hilaire 2018b:506–512; Vidal-Lorenzo, Vázquez-de-Ágredos-Pascual, and Muñoz-Cosme 2016). Meanwhile, foodstuffs were likely stored near kitchens in well-ventilated, semiperishable structures with internal subdivisions fit for supporting shelves, tables, and other storage devices (Lamoureux-St-Hilaire 2018b:204, 214–215).

It is impossible to gain an emic understanding of the reciprocal dynamics that balanced the exchanges of taxes and tribute for feasts and regalia. Most models of feudalism (Bloch 1961; Giddens 1973; Marx 1967; Seignobos 1902) suggest that all lords entertained a decidedly asymmetrical reciprocity with their vassals. Yet these models should be used carefully—and for Classic Maya regimes to last for centuries, the reciprocal arrangements and expectations defining these exchanges must have been in a certain state of balance. Just as offering taxes and tribute was a costly endeavor, preparing and hosting feasts was complex and labor-intensive. In addition, inclusion in diacritical royal-sponsored events yielded unique

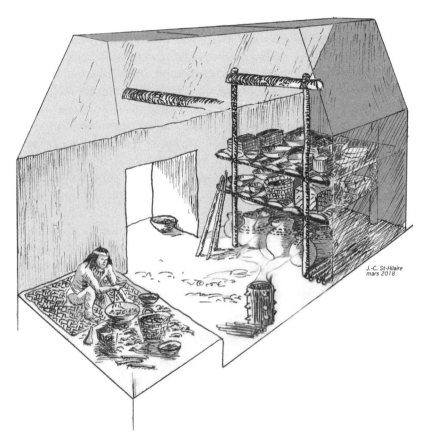

Figure 9.3. Artistic reconstruction of the interior of Room 7 of Str. 13Q-4G, looking northwest. Illustration by Jean-Claude St-Hilaire.

ideological and political value (Ardren, this volume; Brown and Freiwald, this volume). In other words, the intangible value of inclusion in royal feasts—and the tangible exchanges and consumption this entailed—may have been perceived by vassals as adequate to counterbalance the tithes and homage required of them (Lamoureux-St-Hilaire 2018b:59–62).

Beyond material trade, mutual information exchanges were a centerpiece of Classic Maya royal feasts (Lamoureux-St-Hilaire 2018b:47). Having gathered vassals and allies at court, royals could provide them with instructions or information. Conversely, royals certainly expected political partners to offer relevant information—exchanges that contributed to the immaterial value of feasts. Beyond exchanges of specific information, these governmental gatherings were likely used to coordinate events such as military expeditions, building efforts, or public ceremonies (see Restall 2001:345–346, on the stately matters discussed at colonial Yucatec courts). Some guests undoubtedly played more prominent roles in verbal exchanges, having access to privileged information. Thus, locations for courtly feasts required distinct communicational settings for accommodating groups of different sizes. A proxemics approach to this question suggests that adequate spaces for commensal politics occurred in areas of similar dimensions to Titicaca public plazas, or "relatively small spaces suitable for communication at close range" (Moore 1996:796). Beyond facilitating verbal communication, such settings allowed participants to appropriately examine one another's behavior and subtle material information encoded in regalia (Kolata 1993; Moore 1996:790–796).

Occasional gatherings in royal courtyards—the principal architectural groups of palaces—assembled the political community, which composed the crux of Classic Maya regimes (following Canuto and Lamoureux-St-Hilaire 2017). These regime-enacting events not only materialized a network through physical exchanges, they also entangled participants through reciprocal communication (Lamoureux-St-Hilaire 2018b:69–71). Although feasting was the focal point of these events, lubricating both kinds of exchange, they certainly featured some ritualized performance—as evidenced by the many performers and musicians in Classic Maya courtly scenes (Houston, Stuart, and Taube 2006; Miller and Martin 2004). Yet, unlike large public theatrical rituals, for which artistic performance was pivotal (Inomata 2006), diacritical royal-sponsored feasts did not emphasize unidirectional communication. I now turn to the ca. 800 CE regal palace of La Corona to contextualize these thoughts on courtly feasts and their role in fomenting exchanges of goods and information.

Commensal Politics in the Ninth-Century La Corona Regal Palace

Preparation

The Northwest Group of the La Corona regal palace was responsible for providing items and subsistence to its main occupants who resided and officiated in the Northeast Group. An extensive multiproxy data set—composed of architectural, macro- and microartifactual, paleobotanical, and geochemical data—indicates that this ancillary group fulfilled the role of storing foodstuffs, preparing meals, crafting different types of items, and managing the discard of refuse resulting from item and food transformation and consumption (Lamoureux-St-Hilaire 2018b; Lamoureux-St-Hilaire et al. 2019).

While the political apparatus responsible for acquiring staples was anchored in the Northeast Courtyard, the Northwest Group is where commensal politics were rooted. Its two kitchen areas, multiple storage facilities, and several middens reflect the lively ancillary activities that occurred there during the ninth century CE. Str. 13Q-4I, which featured a hearth, was used for both food preparation and for storing botanical foodstuffs, as indicated by geochemical and macrobotanical remains (Lamoureux-St-Hilaire 2018a; 2018b:434–435; Lamoureux-St-Hilaire et al. 2019). Similarly, Str. 13Q-4H2, a storehouse for meat-based products (as indicated by microartifactual and geochemical data), was coupled with an exterior kitchen area identified geoarchaeologically (Lamoureux-St-Hilaire 2018a; 2018b:375–376, 404, 433; Lamoureux-St-Hilaire et al. 2019). Str. 13Q-4H1 served a mix of domestic and ancillary functions (Lamoureux-St-Hilaire 2018b:433). Finally, Room 7 of Str. 13Q-4G was likely used for both food preparation and storage of serving vessels, with well over twenty reconstructible vessels (predominantly Nanzal Red bowls and dishes) found in storage in its northern half (Figure 9.3; Lamoureux-St-Hilaire 2018b:293–294, 433–434). The interconnected buildings and areas of the Northwest Group defined an ancillary group not unlike palace kitchens identified at Xunantunich (LeCount 2010) and Copán (Sanders 1989).

In addition, excavations in two middens associated with the Tucán occupation of the Northwest Group confirm these functions with a multifaceted data set composed of large amounts of butchered animal bones, carbonized remains of edible plants, and geochemical data reflecting the deposition of massive amounts of organic material (see below; Lamoureux-St-Hilaire 2018b:303–368, 379–403). Also found in the middens were significant proportions of vessels belonging to the three functional groups identified by Hendon (2002:216; this volume) as integral to ancient Maya feasting practices: (1) food preparation; (2) ritual food serving and eating; and (3) long-term or large-scale storage. These included many storage and cooking vessels: large Cambio Unslipped, Encanto Striated, and Tinaja Red jars (30–50 cm in diameter); large Chaquiste Impressed, Cambio Unslipped, Zubin Red, and Tinaja Red basins (36–45 cm in diameter); and large red- and black-slipped bowls of the Tinaja Red, Infierno Black, and Nanzal Red types (up to 60 cm in diameter; Lamoureux-St-Hilaire 2018b:303–332). To reiterate, these data strongly indicate that the Northwest Group was used to prepare large quantities of food.

Figure 9.4. Artistic reconstruction of the north half of the Northeast Courtyard, looking north. Illustration by Jean-Claude St-Hilaire. The front stage of Str. 13Q-4G features prominently, with the doorways to its rooms 3 and 4 in the center. Since only fragments of its stucco frieze were found, this depiction is inaccurate and was inspired by the Holmul frieze discovered by Francisco Estrada-Belli (with his permission).

Control

The Northwest Group's easternmost section, dubbed the Corridor, was composed of a mix of residential, administrative, and storage-oriented architecture, and was home to the principal royal administrators who managed the flow of people and things at court (Lamoureux-St-Hilaire 2018b:287–291, 431–433). Everyone and everything transiting between the Northeast and Northwest Groups passed through Room 1 of Str. 13Q-4F, a passageway building featuring two facing doorways and benches (Lamoureux-St-Hilaire 2018b:112–114, 290). The throne-like south bench, with its slanted backrest, was designed for seating court officials. Meanwhile, its platform-like north bench was lower and probably served to hold goods or food for inspection. I have hypothesized that this room served to tally both the foodstuffs transferred to the Northwest Group for storage and dishes served in the Northeast Group (Figure 9.4). Artifactual evidence—fragments of carved stone, paper-making artifacts, carving tools, and such—from the adjacent residential Room 4 of Str. 13Q-4F suggests that its occupants were scribes (Lamoureux-St-Hilaire 2018b:287–291). These data, along with the instrumental nature of the adjoining passageway, have led me to suggest that this section of the palace was under the purview of an *ajk'uhuun*—a Classic Maya noble title best translated as "worshipper" (Lamoureux-St-Hilaire 2018b:290–291, following Zender 2004: 180–195). This rich context supports the hypothesis that an *ajk'uhuun* was involved—perhaps not in the service of, but in the control of, food served at courtly feasts (Coe and Kerr 1998:94; LeCount 2010:135).

Service

The focal point of the Northeast Courtyard was the massive northern platform and its hieroglyphic staircase, which, at close to 60 m², spanned the courtyard's width, abutting not only Str. 13Q-4G but also Str. 13Q-4B2 to the east and the passageway to the west (Figure 9.4). Retainers leaving the Northwest Group would have exited the passageway onto this stage, since the four-step-tall, 30 m² vast staircase leading to the platform was the only access point to four of its rooms (Rooms 2–5) and to Room 1 of Str. 13Q-4F (Lamoureux-St-Hilaire 2018b:115).

This monumental stage was surrounded by politically charged art (Lamoureux-St-Hilaire 2018b:127–134). Stucco friezes decorated the façades of Strs. 13Q-4B2, -4G, and -4F. The upper step of the staircase, mostly destroyed by looters, featured up to fifteen hieroglyphic monuments—four of which were salvaged from looters' back dirt (Elements 57, 58, 60, and 61). Additionally, the platform's eastern edge created a veranda-like, semi-interior space, featuring a bench with two hieroglyphic monuments in its backrest (Elements 55 and 56). While none of these carved monuments were located in their original context, they told the feats of past La Corona royals and of their overlords, the Kaanul kings (Canuto et al. 2017; Lamoureux-St-Hilaire 2018b; Stuart et al. 2015).

In other words, retainers carrying foodstuffs from the Northwest Group would have stepped onto this political stage for service, granting a definite ideological dimension to the presented food. By serving the meals to hosts and guests alike, the servers involved all feasters in the exercise of royal politics.

Consumption

The aforementioned middens of the Northwest Group document the kinds of food eaten at court. In particular, the middens dated to the Tucán occupation (Middens F and D) included a variety of food-related vessels: small Tinaja Red, Infierno Black, and Pantano Impressed jars (13–18 cm in diameter), which could have been used to serve beverages; large Tinaja Red, Infierno Black, Carmelita Incised, Nanzal Red bowls, dishes, and plates (up to 60 cm in diameter), which could have been used to serve soups, stews, and dry food such as tamales; and a wide variety of smaller Altar Orange, Trapiche Incised, Pabellon Modeled-Carved, Cedro Gadrooned, Provincia Plano-Relief, Caribe Incised, Tumba Black-on-Orange, Poite Incised, Tres Naciones Gray, Chablekal Gray, Chicxulub Incised, and Saxche-Palmar dishes, bowls, *tecomates*, and vases that could have been used for consuming dry foods and beverages, such as cacao-based drinks, stews, atole, tamales, and roasted meat (Figure 9.5; Lamoureux-St-Hilaire 2018b:303–332; also see Beliaev, Davletshin, and Tokovinine 2010; Eppich 2009; Houston, Stuart, and Taube 1989; LeCount 2001; Taube 1989).

Beyond documenting the types of food consumed at court, the fine ceramics—especially those belonging to the Tres Naciones fine gray sphere and to the Altar and Balancan fine orange spheres—tie ninth-century La Corona to an international trade network extending to the Gulf Coast and the Northern Lowlands (Foias and Bishop 2013; Sabloff 1975; Smith 1971). If access to these imported vessels highlights the healthy economy of the La Corona royal court, their handling by guests would certainly have been significant, involving them in the government's foreign network.

In addition to ceramics, abundant faunal data from these middens indicate that meat eaten at court predominantly consisted of deer but also included turkey, peccary, dog, opossum, crocodile, and fish (Fridberg 2018, and personal communication, 2018). Finally, macrobotanical data indicate that maize and fruits such as nance, sapote, and citrus were among the botanical ingredients included in courtly meals (Cagnato 2018; Lamoureux-St-Hilaire 2018b:404–406). While these data document valuable aspects of the diet of the La Corona court, identifying loci of food consumption is harder, since this kind of activity left virtually no primary refuse. Thus, my inferences about eating loci rely on geochemical data, artifacts in related contexts, and architectural evidence.

Geochemical data gathered from stucco surfaces in excavation units in the Northeast Courtyard differed significantly from those within the Northwest Group. While evidence for food preparation and discard abound

Figure 9.5. Photo of a sample of the vessel fragments from the following types found in Midden F: Carmelita Incised (top), two Pantano Impressed: Stamped (middle), Pabellon Modeled-Carved (bottom left), and Altar Orange: Red Slip (bottom right). Photo by the author.

in the ancillary group (Lamoureux-St-Hilaire et al. 2019), a thick overburden resulting from extensive, destructive looting prevented a thorough geoarchaeological study of the Northeast Courtyard (Lamoureux-St-Hilaire 2018b:362–368). Yet concentrations of midlevels of phosphorous and higher levels of potassium in uncovered segments of the Courtyard suggest that food consumption occurred in several of its areas (Figure 9.6; Lamoureux-St-Hilaire 2018b:400–402). Relevant geochemical signatures were found on interior and exterior benches, on the front platform of Str. 13Q-4G, on its staircase, and in the courtyard, fronting Room 2 of Str. 13Q-4B1. While these data do strengthen the idea that food was consumed regularly within the Northeast Group, they cannot distinguish daily meals from feasting events.

Artifactual, geochemical, and architectural data identify distinct areas of the Northeast Courtyard as conducive to both eating and communication, thus supporting the idea that commensality was a central political strategy for the La Corona royal court. The size of the courtyard, coupled with its elevated stage, corresponds to proxemic proportions ideal for "communication of detailed information over small distances" (Moore 1996:796, following Kolata 1993). More precisely, this architectural space could have accommodated groups of distinct sizes and may be subdivided into three categories: a semipublic stage, limited stages, and private settings.

The Northeast Group's semipublic stage was Str. 13Q-4G's front platform, where the upper echelons of the court could have consumed food in front of an audience, with the potential to interact with guests in the courtyard below. Several reconstructible vessels—small and large bowls and jars—were found on this stage and in adjacent rooms, suggesting that meals were consumed there. In addition, several bulky jar necks, seemingly reused as pot stands, were left on the front platform of Str. 13Q-4G. These may have supported round-bottomed jars, which, located under the building's façade, would have efficiently collected rainwater for drinking (Lamoureux-St-Hilaire 2018b:257).

The broad steps fronting the stage could have held dozens of individuals. These steps, which featured hieroglyphic monuments that related the political legacy of La Corona, conferred a political overtone to this setting, where individuals could have engaged in conversation about the artistic background. It remains unclear if and in what position people would have engaged in feasting in the courtyard itself; they could, for example, have been seated on mats or pillows or, alternatively, on wooden furniture. At any rate, the 220 m² courtyard could have accommodated as many as 101

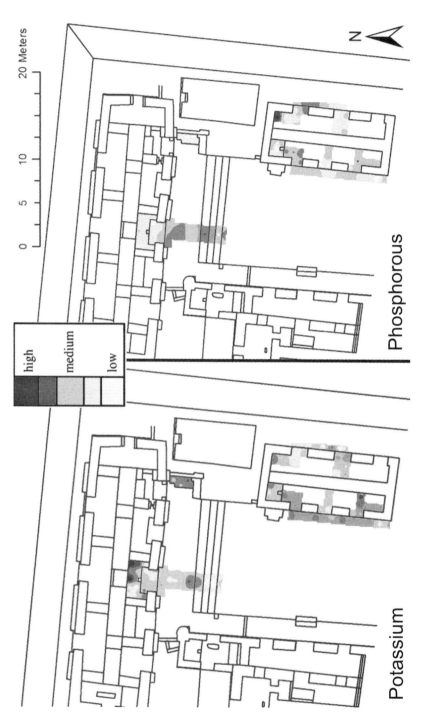

Figure 9.6. Distribution of the relative densities of potassium (left) and phosphorous (right) as reflected by ICP-MS analyses. Map by the author.

to 792 people (Lamoureux-St-Hilaire 2018b:132, following Inomata 2006 and Tsukamoto 2014).

The limited communicational stages of the courtyard were its two exterior benches: one in the veranda, the other located in front of Str. 13Q-4B1. Both benches, occupying the courtyard's east flank, likely featured hieroglyphic panels and were of comparable size (respectively, 2.84 m² and ca. 2.34 m²), comfortably seating two to four people (Lamoureux-St-Hilaire 2018b:127–131, 170–172). Although both benches could have facilitated communication within small groups, their contexts diverged significantly. The veranda bench, built on the Str. 13Q-4G stage, was adjacent to the doorway of this building's small residential Room 2, had walls on three sides, and faced a relatively narrow section of the platform. Meanwhile, the courtyard bench, built in an elaborate masonry style, was located near the courtyard's centerline and faced a potentially larger crowd. Geochemical data from the veranda bench surface suggest that it was used regularly for eating (Lamoureux-St-Hilaire 2018b:384).

Nobles sitting on these two benches could have eaten and conversed while also interacting with interlocutors who moved around them—juxtaposing distinct physical positions, which in turn reified political status. The hieroglyphic panels placed in the backrest of the benches would, once again, have given a political inflection to these interactions. In sum, these exterior benches were ideal for engaging distinct courtiers and vassals in commensal politics, albeit in a less overt fashion than their neighboring semipublic stage.

The third, private setting for commensal politics consisted of the audience rooms in the courtyard, specifically Rooms 3 and 4 of Str. 13Q-4G. Both rooms had communicational functions: they featured broad doorways (averaging 2.06 m) without curtain holders and massive C-shaped benches (respectively, 11 m² and 10 m²), which could each have comfortably accommodated up to eight people. Room 3 was unfortunately severely damaged by looters, but its east section was sufficiently preserved to showcase an unusual feature: a small double niche/window that opened toward the neighboring Room 2 and would have allowed both visual and acoustic contact (Lamoureux-St-Hilaire 2018b:143–144). The layout of Room 4, targeted by two more looters' tunnels, was similar to that of Room 3. Yet a large hieroglyphic panel, Element 59, was placed in the center of the room's back wall, above the bench. The presence of this panel, portraying La Corona ruler Chakaw Nahb Chan dressed as a Kaanul lord (Canuto et al. 2017), and the central location of the room and its prominence have led me to suggest that this was the main throne room of the regal palace (Lamoureux-St-Hilaire 2018b:141–142).

As settings for commensal politics, these rooms provided opportunities to address more private or sensitive matters. Iconographic and epigraphic data (Delvendahl 2010; Miller and Brittenham 2013; Miller and Martin 2004; Schele and Miller 1986) indicate that beyond the royals themselves, guests allowed in these settings were visiting dignitaries or belonged to the upper echelons of local politics. Yet, in accordance with iconographic data, their wide doorways suggest that their occupants could also have engaged with individuals located outside (Lamoureux-St-Hilaire 2018b:111, 505–506). Thus, partial serving vessels found in these rooms, their architectural features, and geochemical data all support the idea that they were used for eating and communication.

These three settings, all conducive to commensality, are situated along an exclusionary or diacritical spectrum: semipublic, limited, and private. Together, they composed a multifaceted space with the potential to host regime-enacting commensal political gatherings ranging from intimate meetings to banquets. In addition, the attached Northwest Group had adequate settings for preparing both small and large meals, which could have been inspected in the passageway structure before being served. Following this, the performance of service, leading attendants onto the politically charged stage, accentuated the value of food. Finally, when refuse and soiled vessels were brought back to the Northwest Group to be cleaned or tossed in middens, they effectively disappeared from the scene.

While these feasts were organized by royals, they prescribed reciprocal obligations in the form of taxes and tribute—a topic documented through both Classic Maya art history (Miller and Martin 2004, for example) and anthropological literature (Dietler 1996, for example). As discussed above, the fruit of royal tithing was necessarily piled in nearby storage facilities, where it would be tallied for later use in the production of food and items at court. In the La Corona palace's Northeast Courtyard, Rooms 1 and 2 of Str. 13Q-4B1 and Rooms 2 and 3 of Str. 13Q-4F are suitable for such functions. Opening directly onto the courtyard, they featured adequate "empty space" for storage furniture, along with administrative benches (Lamoureux-St-Hilaire 2018b:102–110, 171–175).

Institutional gatherings revolving around diacritical feasting filled regal palaces with distinct classes of people who were given a participatory role in the political apparatus while simultaneously reifying royal sovereignty (A. T. Smith 2015:69). With reception areas fully engaged in commensal politics, audience chambers crowded with nobles, stages busy with performances, storehouses and passageways packed with goods and attended by administrators, and ancillary buildings in full use, palaces were at their busiest. Beyond these pragmatic functions, distinct classes of people clad in appropriate regalia and attire interacted by exchanging things and information, thus reifying social and ideological aspects of the political order. Beyond giving their raison d'être to palatial settings, these commensal politics entangled royals and courtiers, simultaneously expressing and fulfilling the regime (Lamoureux-St-Hilaire 2018b:69–70). These events, as a form of communicational technology, were central instruments of power among the Classic Maya.

Discussion

By arranging food-related data and Classic Maya royal feasts within the frame of communication and political networking, I have diverged from most literature on royal courts and palace economies, which generally emphasizes theatrical performances (Inomata 2006; Inomata and Tsukamoto 2014), craft production (Aoyama 2009; McAnany 2010), or the acquisition and preparation of food (Foias 2013; LeCount 2010). Meanwhile, "ancient Maya eating" has mostly been investigated from a dietary perspective, be it from the angle of ceramics (Eppich 2009; Hendon 2002), trace analyses (Hall et al. 1990; Hurst et al. 2002), epigraphy (Beliaev, Davletshin, and Tokovinine 2010; Houston, Stuart, and Taube 1989; Zender 2000), zooarchaeology (Emery 2003; Herrera Flores and Götz 2014), or biological anthropology (Anderson 2010; White et al. 2001). These worthwhile approaches are all fascinating, and by emphasizing the communicational role of feasts, I provide an additional, complementary perspective to better tie ancient Maya foodways and governance together. Several anthropological themes are highlighted by the lens of commensal politics. Below, I explore two broad topics stemming from this approach to food archaeology: the sociopolitical value of feast fare and the risks inherent to commensal politics.

The Sociopolitical Value of Feast Fare

In defining royal-sponsored feasts as a political strategy, I mean that these events were a centripetal force allowing royals to gather allies and vassals at court. Not unlike ideas proposed by Golden and Scherer (2013), I believe these feasts fostered a political community by creating a network of trust. However, only a small segment of society was welcomed in these trust-building events, which essentially allied the royals to nobles and the leaders of "grassroots coalitions of 'like-minded' subjects committed to sociopolitical reproduction" (Smith 2003:155). Thus, royal-sponsored commensal politics did not foster "generalized trust," free of reciprocal expectations across societies (Golden and Scherer 2013:400; Uslaner 2000:574); their very exclusiveness, which barred "non-politicians," created a web of "particularized trust" with tacit reciprocal expectations (Uslaner 2000:573–574).

While these occasions were instrumental in establishing royal sovereignty, they were also a prime opportunity for guests to bolster their own status by acquiring privileged information and regalia, or by simply participating in the supernatural power of their liege (Sahlins 2017a). By stepping inside regal palaces—which embodied divine and international connections—local power brokers participated in divine kingly charisma (Lamoureux-St-Hilaire 2018b:70, 469). This mutual engagement, assembling the regime, coalesced through commensality when allies broke tamal together. Thus, food served at feasts embodied a social contract and, as such, must have been perceived as quintessentially political (Ardren, this volume; Brown and Freiwald, this volume) by guests and hosts alike— a fact epitomized, at La Corona, by the politically charged art decorating the entire Northeast Courtyard of the palace.

One does not need to look to the ancient Maya to observe the communicational and political value of food. Stemming from the idea that every social domain may be examined for its political character (Gramsci, Hoare, and Nowell-Smith 1971), anthropologists and sociologists have expressed the "notion that food is good to communicate" (Jones 2007:8) and that narrative practices during meals yield political agendas that can both empower and diminish distinct commensal agents (Ochs and Taylor 1992). Among American families, for example, meals compose the principal chapters of family dramas (Douglas 1972, 1984), and commensality is instrumental in defining children's competency as family and community members (Ochs and Shohet 2006). At a different level, "entrepreneurial" or "patron-role" feasts have long been argued to be prime political tools for chiefs, big men, or aggrandizers among societies politically less centralized than the Classic Maya (Blanton et al. 1996; Clark and Blake 1994; Dietler 1996; Wiessner 2002) or during earlier periods of Maya prehistory (Brown and Freiwald, this volume). If family meals emphasize household political structures, and if feasting among incipient rulers was an instrumental political tool, then feasts shared among self-asserted politicians (many of whom were undoubtedly related by blood or kin) most definitely expressed the structure of regimes. In this context, cuisine and "inhibition-releasing" substances—such as pulque/*chih* (Brown and Freiwald, this volume; Carter and Matsumoto, this volume; Houston and Stuart 2001; Houston, Stuart, and Taube 2006:120–122; LeCount 2001; Stuart 2005) or chocolate and honey-based fermented beverages or *chab kakaw* (Coe 1994: 140; Hull 2010:241; Vail and Dedrick, this volume)—certainly lubricated the interactions of political agents. In other words, the quality and quantity of feast fare would have been pivotal to the regime's success. Albeit drawing from limited epigraphic evidence (Robicsek and Hales 1981:190), Houston and Stuart (2001:69) describe a Classic Maya logograph for feast, featuring "two stylized faces stuffed with tamales and drink," which, they argue, references generous consumption of "heaps of tamales and bowls of pulque (*chih*) and other savory drinks," which served as "preliminaries" for tribute offerings that "inferiors" offered to their lords.

While royal feasts were occasions to assemble the regime, traditional power brokers—the leaders of communities of production (i.e., the "inferiors")—certainly hosted scaled-down versions of these gatherings for their more restricted political networks. Just as regalia gifted to vassals reinforced their status (Foias 2002, 2013; LeCount and Yaeger 2010; McAnany 2010, 2013; McAnany et al. 2002), the information exchanged and the practices witnessed at royal feasts trickled down to communities of production. Details about the cuisine, its ritualized service, and its architectural context and proclivity for communication were not lost on vassals, who certainly embraced these political practices. Thus, beyond regalia, information and foodways learned at court by vassals and allies were active elements in the assemblage of sovereignty (*sensu* A. T. Smith 2015:6) that entangled Classic Maya political communities. Drawing from comparative literature on premodern complex societies, Graeber and Sahlins (2017) gloss this phenomenon as a broadly universal feature of "stranger kingship," which they label upward nobility,

> whereby the chiefs of satellite areas assume the political statuses, courtly styles, titles, and even genealogies of their superiors in the regional hierarchy . . . the structural effect is a certain "galactic mimesis," insofar as peripheral groups assume the polities and cosmologies of their regional superiors. (Sahlins 2017a:235)

Similarly, Appadurai (1986:21) approaches these events as "tournaments of value" wherein, for example, the elite engage with the royals in consumption, acquiring their customs and tastes (generally of exogenous origins), which they then adapt to local possibilities. Since royal foodways were a pivotal element of commensal politics, Classic Maya processes of "upward nobility" involved emulating royal cuisine, which conferred a key sociopolitical value on royal feasts. Beyond adopting international ceramic styles from the royals—as demonstrated by the wide variety in exotic fine-pasted wares present in the La Corona palace—vassals may have adopted foreign food practices as well, including the use of exotic ingredients (following Dietler 2007:226–227), which were possibly imported and even distributed by the royals. Expectations of feast fare—and its associated privileged knowledge—certainly drew vassals to attend feasts, along with the prospect of acquiring prized regalia despite obligations to offer tithes and sensitive information.

Food-centered, royal-sponsored receptions at La Corona should not be envisioned as "patron-role feasts" aimed at indebting vassals, where "the acceptance of a continually unequal pattern of hospitality symbolically expresses the formalization of unequal relations of status and power, and this acceptance ideologically naturalizes the formalization through repetition of an event that induces sentiments of social debt" (Dietler 1996:97). I believe that to endure for such a long time, these commensal political practices were rather reciprocal, instead resembling what Dietler (1996:98–99) defines as diacritical feasting—events where food quality, not only its quantity, was emphasized (in contradistinction to common fare) and which did not primarily aim at indebting guests but rather at defining "exclusive circles" (Ardren, this volume; Brown and Freiwald, this volume; Fernández Souza, Zimmermann, and Jiménez Álvarez, this volume). In other words, beyond exchanges of regalia-for-tithe, feasts were instruments of soft power held not only to extract rights and privileges from vassals but "to increase the number and loyalty of subjects, as by beneficial or awe-inspiring effects of royal largess, display, and consumption" (Sahlins 2017b:348). Yet these institutional practices—and the expectations they entailed—did not only yield positive outcomes; they also had the potential to be detrimental for anyone involved.

The Risks of Commensal Politics

Many undeniable, pragmatic challenges are associated with the production, acquisition, storage, preparation, and service of feasts (following M. L. Smith 2015). There is now ample evidence that the late Late Classic and Terminal Classic periods were times of environmental stress and food insecurity (Douglas et al. 2015; Iannone 2014). Detrimental climatic events systematically impacted later Classic Maya society and did not necessarily affect the royals less than their subjects, as indicated by settlement abandonment studies showing that the epicenters of polities were often abandoned first (Lamoureux-St-Hilaire et al. 2015; McAnany et al. 2016).

Beyond the production and acquisition of food, its storage represented a clear challenge (M. L. Smith 2015:1218–1220)—once again highlighting the lacunae in our understanding of Classic Maya storage technology (Lamoureux-St-Hilaire 2018b:53–54). Yet the multiproxy data sets from the Northwest Group of the La Corona palace revealed a Classic Maya food storage technique observed in two distinct storehouses (see above). While Str. 13Q-4I revealed artifacts, macrobotanical remains, and geochemical data indicative of the storage and cooking of floral materials, Str. 13Q-4H2 was associated with microliths, microbones, and geochemical data indicative of the storage, butchering, and cooking of faunal products (Lamoureux-St-Hilaire 2018a, 2018b; Lamoureux-St-Hilaire et al. 2019). These mutually exclusive data sets hint at the practice of keeping meat and plant-based foods in distinct storehouses (Lamoureux-St-Hilaire 2018b:409–410; Lamoureux-St-Hilaire et al. 2019). This strategy, which could have prevented cross-contamination and pests, undoubtedly was coupled with other curation methods to minimize risks of spoilage for stored foodstuffs. Since feasts required large amounts of food, storage risk peaked in the days preceding courtly receptions (M. L. Smith 2015:1220–1221). Thus, while the burden of food production was certainly shared with the community's agriculturalists, risk associated with storage and the preparation of feasts was mostly shouldered by royals and their retainers.

Another, more elusive risk associated with commensal politics was the expectations of guests (M. L. Smith 2015). Architectural data from the La Corona palace—its passageway structure and different commensal settings—suggest that the royals minimized risk through quality control and by anticipating distinct groups of guests. Yet the consequences of disappointing feasts could have disrupted the balance in the reciprocal rapport established between the royals and their vassals, with the obvious related snowball effect. For example, if feasts were central in drawing vassals to pay their due and homage, then repetitive, inadequate feasts could have severely hindered royal acquisition of staples (i.e., the efficacy of tithing mechanisms). In addition, communication at feasts likely included the coordination of upcoming events, so that interruption in these, or in their attendance, could have disrupted their occurrence, along with the enactment and materialization of the regime.

While they are inferential, these musings on the pragmatic risks inherent to commensal politics involve basic, logical aspects of the *chaîne opératoire* that binds the links of commensal politics. It is challenging to support empirically the realities associated with this topic; it may very well never be possible. Cross-cultural comparative studies are a promising line of inquiry to study how premodern governments anticipated and prevented risks associated with commensal politics (Beattie 1971; Dirks 1987; Fox 2012; Lamoureux-St-Hilaire 2018b:46–68; Sahlins 2017b; Vale 2001). A certain fact is that the adaptability of key institutions, including commensal political practices, would have been crucial for premodern governments to weather shifts in their geopolitical and ecological environments. By successfully adapting feasting practices and their architectural settings, Classic Maya royal courts could have maintained efficient means of communication within their regime, even as droughts and hegemonic collapses disrupted trade routes and growth cycles. While the La Corona royal court, which endured until ca. 900 CE, exemplifies such a resilient regime, it eventually collapsed, along with its institutional approach to foodways, reflecting the ultimate fragility of political experimentation (McAnany and Lamoureux-St-Hilaire 2017).

Methodological Notes on Food Archaeology

In a recent commentary, Kathryn Twiss (2015) identified key issues with "food archaeology" that can be summarized as (1) problems with the study and integration of distinct types of food-related data sets and (2) definitional inconsistencies regarding concepts of feasts. In this chapter, I endeavored to adequately contextualize and integrate the various data sets I drew from to explore commensal politics. Within space limitations, I organized distinct data sets—architectural and artistic features, macro- and microartifacts, faunal remains, and geochemical data—within their carefully excavated, broader architectural context: the two complementary north groups of the La Corona regal palace. I arranged these data sets along a pragmatic *chaîne opératoire*, following the flow of foodstuffs at court from acquisition to consumption and discard.

This contextualized evidence led me to address Classic Maya commensal politics by focusing on the communicational functions of institutional feasting practices, which I associate with Dietler's (1996) concept of diacritical feasts. Once placed in their rich context, these complementary data sets open a broad window onto Classic Maya royal foodways, allowing me to archaeologically reconstruct governmental practices to a degree comparable to that achieved by combined art historical and epigraphic approaches (Miller and Brittenham 2013; Miller and Martin 2004; Reents-Budet 2001). I hope the results of this exercise contribute to the topic of ancient Maya foodways.

Conclusion

As Twiss (2015:89) states, "Food is an excitingly multifaceted phenomenon." Since food constantly affects every human life, food archaeology has no boundaries. Through its scope, we can study virtually every aspect of ancient societies. When studying both ancient foodways and political practices, we must not assume that people of the past, such as the Classic Maya, had less complex relations with food or simpler political institutions than we do today. Instead, we must continue to ask the right questions and seek answers by adequately combining as many well-contextualized proxies as we can.

It could be argued that the efficacy of a political system is tied to the ability of chief decision makers to delegate. Today, this factor is facilitated by communication technologies like the postal service, the telephone, or the internet—technologies that leave physical (or, at least, traceable) evidence for networks of power, or "assemblages of sovereignty" (A. T. Smith 2015). However, among ancient complex societies lacking such technologies, political tasks were predominantly delegated verbally, a fact that complicates our task as students of ancient political material culture.

While public ceremonies held within the massive plazas of Classic Maya cities were ideal for disseminating aspects of political and religious ideology (Inomata 2006)—and for featuring prominent members of the elite—they offered limited means of political networking. On the other hand, exclusive events taking place in semipublic or private settings within palaces were excellent occasions for connecting distinct classes of politicians (Lamoureux-St-Hilaire 2018b:35–36). Feasting practices, by engaging every member of a political network within the communicational space of palaces, embodied Classic Maya regimes as stages for the "regular operation of an apparatus of governance that defines the terms of association" (A. T. Smith 2015:70). Beyond facilitating material exchanges between vassals and lords through distinct tithing mechanisms, the unifying and satisfying effects of commensal politics enabled networks of communication. Carefully crafted and staged diacritical feasts were thus a key communicational technology used by Classic Maya royals to sustain their regime.

Acknowledgments

I thank Marcello Canuto and Tomás Barrientos for supporting my research as part of the Proyecto Regional Arqueológico La Corona and for contributing to the ideas presented here. Guatemala's Instituto de Arqueología e Historia must also be acknowledged for its continued support for research at La Corona. Some of the research reported here was funded by a National Scientific Foundation Doctoral Dissertation Improvement Grant (NSF Award ID: 1623787, awarded to Canuto and Lamoureux-St-Hilaire) and two Tulane School of Liberal Arts Summer Merit Fellowships. The Dumbarton Oaks Research Library (2017–2018) and the Fonds de recherche du Québec—Société et culture (2014–2016) supported the compilation, synthesis, and writing of the dissertation from which this chapter stems. This chapter was written mostly in the comfortable and peaceful setting of the Boundary End Center. Francisco Estrada-Belli, E. Christian Wells, Clarissa Cagnato, and Diana Fridberg—through their assistance with different lab-based analyses—helped study the excavated material. I would also like to thank Mary Kate Kelly and Sarah Duignan for their comments on an early manuscript. In fact, it was an interview for Sarah Duignan's podcast, *Anthrodish*, that spurred my invitation to join this volume. I am grateful to Traci Ardren for inviting me to contribute to this volume and for her useful comments on an early version of this chapter. Finally, I thank the two anonymous reviewers who helped make this chapter better.

References

Anderson, Eugene N. 2010. "Food and Feasting in the Zona Maya of Quintana Roo." In *Pre-Columbian Foodways: Interdisciplinary Approaches to Food, Culture, and Markets in Ancient Mesoamerica*, ed. John E. Staller and Michael D. Carrasco, 441–465. New York: Springer.

Aoyama, Kazuo. 2009. *Elite Craft Producers, Artists, and Warriors at Aguateca: Lithic Analysis*. Salt Lake City: University of Utah Press.

Appadurai, Arjun. 1986. "Introduction: Commodities and the Politics of Value." In *The Social Life of Things: Commodities in Cultural Perspective*, 3–63. Cambridge: Cambridge University Press.

Beattie, John. 1971. *The Nyoro State*. Oxford: Oxford University Press.

Beliaev, Dmitri, Albert Davletshin, and Alexandre Tokovinine. 2010. "Sweet Cacao and Sour Atole: Mixed Drinks on Classic Maya Ceramic Vases." In *Pre-Columbian Foodways: Interdisciplinary Approaches to Food, Culture, and Markets in Ancient Mesoamerica*, ed. John E. Staller and Michael D. Carrasco, 257–273. New York: Springer.

Blanton, Richard E., Gary M. Feinman, Stephen A. Kowalewski, and Peter N. Peregrine. 1996. "A Dual-Processual Theory for the Evolution of Mesoamerican Civilization." *Current Anthropology* 37:(1)1–14.

Bloch, Marc. 1961. *Feudal Society*. Vol. 2, *Social Classes and Political Organization*. Chicago: University of Chicago Press.

Brown, Donald E. 1991. *Human Universals*. New York: McGraw-Hill.

Cagnato, Clarissa. 2018. "Resultados paleobotánicos de patios y basureros asociados con el Palacio Real de La Corona, Guatemala." In *Proyecto Arqueológico La Corona: Informe final, Temporada 2017*, ed. Tomás Barrientos Q., Marcello A. Canuto, Marissa López, and Eduardo Bustamante, 501–514. Guatemala City: Proyecto Regional Arqueológico La Corona.

Canuto, Marcello A., Tomás Barrientos Q., and Eduardo Bustamante. 2017. "Síntesis y conclusiones de la Temporada de Campo 2016." In *Proyecto Arqueológico La Corona: Informe final, Temporada 2016*, ed. Tomás Barrientos Q., Marcello A. Canuto, and Eduardo Bustamante, 377–385. Guatemala City: Proyecto Regional Arqueológico La Corona.

Canuto, Marcello A., Tomás Barrientos Q., Maxime Lamoureux-St-Hilaire, and Eduardo Bustamante. 2017. "La Casa de los Tronos: El Palacio de La Corona y el gobierno hegemónico de Kaanal." In *III Simposio de Investigaciones Arqueológicas en Guatemala 2016*, ed. Bárbara Arroyo, Luis Méndez Salinas, and Lorena Paiz, 185–198. Guatemala City: Ministerio de Cultura y Deportes, Instituto de Antropología e Historia, Asociación Tikal.

Canuto, Marcello A., and Maxime Lamoureux-St-Hilaire. 2017. "Ancient Political Philosophy and the Maya World: Towards Recognizing Ancient Maya Regimes." Paper presented at Regimes of the Classic Maya: Toward an Archaeology of Political Communities, a Wenner-Gren workshop organized by Marcello Canuto and Maxime Lamoureux-St-Hilaire. New Orleans: Middle American Research Institute.

Clark, John E., and Michael Blake. 1994. "The Power of Prestige: Competitive Generosity and the Emergence of Rank Societies in Lowland Mesoamerica." In *Factional Competition and Political Development in the New World*, ed. Elizabeth M. Brumfiel and John W. Fox, 17–30. Cambridge: Cambridge University Press.

Coe, Michael D., and Justin Kerr. 1998. *The Art of the Maya Scribe*. New York: Harry N. Abrams.

Coe, Sophie D. 1994. *America's First Cuisines*. Austin: University of Texas Press.

Dahlin, Bruce H., Daniel Bair, Tim Beach, Matthew Moriarty, and Richard Terry. 2010. "The Dirt on Food: Ancient Feasts and Markets among the Lowland Maya." In *Pre-Columbian Foodways: Interdisciplinary Approaches to Food, Culture, and Markets in Ancient Mesoamerica*, ed. John E. Staller and Michael D. Carrasco, 191–232. New York: Springer.

Delvendahl, Kai. 2010. "Los conjuntos palaciegos reales de las Tierras Bajas mayas del sur: Una evaluación de los datos arqueológicos e iconográficos." *Estudios de Cultura Maya* 36:87–116.

Dietler, Michael. 1996. "Feasts and Commensal Politics in the Political Economy: Food, Power, and Status in Prehistoric Europe." In *Food and the Status Quest: An Interdisciplinary Perspective*, ed. Polly Wiessner and Wulf Schiefenhövel, 87–125. Oxford: Berghahn.

———. 2007. "Culinary Encounters: Food, Identity, and Colonialism." In *The Archaeology of Food and Identity*, ed. Kathryn C. Twiss, 218–242. Carbondale: Center for Archaeological Investigations; Southern Illinois University Press.

Dietler, Michael, and Brian Hayden. 2001. "Digesting the Feast: Good to Eat, Good to Drink, Good to Think." In *Feasts: Archaeological and Ethnographic Perspectives on Food, Politics, and Power*, ed. Michael Dietler and Brian Hayden, 1–20. Washington, DC: Smithsonian Institution Press.

Dirks, Nicholas B. 1987. *The Hollow Crown: Ethnohistory of an Indian Kingdom*. Cambridge: Cambridge University Press.
Douglas, Mary. 1972. "Deciphering a Meal." *Daedalus* 101(1):61–81.
———. 1984. *Food in the Social Order: Studies of Food and Festivities in Three American Communities*. New York: Russell Sage Foundation.
Douglas, Mary, and Baron Isherwood. 1996. *The World of Goods: Towards an Anthropology of Consumption*. London: Routledge.
Douglas, Peter M. J., Mark Pagani, Marcello A. Canuto, Mark Brenner, David A. Hodell, Timothy I. Eglinton, and Jason H. Curtis. 2015. "Drought, Agricultural Adaptation, and Sociopolitical Collapse in the Maya Lowlands." *Proceedings of the National Academy of Sciences* 112(18):5607–5612.
Emery, Kitty F. 2003. "The Noble Beast: Status and Differential Access to Animals in the Maya World." *World Archaeology* 34(3):498–515.
Eppich, Keith. 2009. "Feast and Sacrifice at El Perú-Waka': The N14-2 Deposit as Dedication." *The PARI Journal* 10(2):1–19.
Foias, Antonia E. 2002. "At the Crossroads: The Economic Basis of Political Power in the Petexbatun Region." In *Ancient Maya Political Economies*, ed. Marilyn A. Masson and David A. Freidel, 223–248. Walnut Creek, CA: Altamira Press.
———. 2013. *Ancient Maya Political Dynamics*. Gainesville: University Press of Florida.
Foias, Antonia E., and Ronald L. Bishop. 2013. *Ceramics, Production, and Exchange in the Petexbatun Region: The Economic Parameters of the Classic Maya Collapse*. Nashville: Vanderbilt University Press.
Fox, Rachel Sarah. 2012. *Feasting Practices and Changes in Greek Society from the Late Bronze Age to Early Iron Age*. BAR International Series 2345. Oxford: Archaeopress.
Fridberg, Diana. 2018. "The Zooarchaeology of La Corona: Sustenance and Symbol." Paper presented at the 83rd Annual Meeting of the Society for American Archaeology. Washington, DC: Society for American Archaeology.
Giddens, Anthony. 1973. *The Class Structure of the Advanced Societies*. London: Hutchison University Library.
Golden, Charles, and Andrew K. Scherer. 2013. "Territory, Trust, Growth, and Collapse in Classic Period Maya Kingdoms." *Current Anthropology* 54(4):397–435.
Graeber, David, and Marshall Sahlins. 2017. "Introduction." In *On Kings*, ed. David Graeber and Marshall Sahlins, 1–22. Chicago: University of Chicago Press.
Gramsci, Antonio, Quintin Hoare, and Geoffrey Nowell-Smith. 1971. *Selections from the Prison Notebooks: Antonio Gramsci*. New York: International Publishers.
Hall, Grant D., Stanley M. Tarka Jr., W. Jeffrey Hurst, David Stuart, and Richard E. W. Adams. 1990. "Cacao Residues in Ancient Maya Vessels from Rio Azul, Guatemala." *American Antiquity* 55(1):138–143.
Halperin, Christina T., and Antonia E. Foias. 2010. "Pottery Politics: Late Classic Maya Palace Production at Motul de San José, Petén, Guatemala." *Journal of Anthropological Archaeology* 29(3):392–411.
———. 2012. "Motul de San José Palace Pottery Production: Reconstruction from Wasters and Debris." In *Motul de San José: Politics, History, and Economy in a Classic Maya Polity*, ed. Antonia E. Foias and Kitty F. Emery, 167–193. Gainesville: University Press of Florida.
Hendon, Julia A. 2002. "Household and State in Pre-Hispanic Maya Society: Gender,

Identity and Practice." *Ancient Maya Gender Identity and Relations*, ed. Lowell S. Gustafson and Amelia M. Trevelyan, 75–92. Santa Barbara, CA: Praeger.

Herrera Flores, David Alejandro, and Christopher Markus Götz. 2014. "La alimentación de los antiguos mayas de la Península de Yucatán: Consideraciones sobre la identidad y la *cuisine* en la época prehispánica." *Estudios de Cultura Maya* 43(43): 69–98.

Houston, Stephen D., and David Stuart. 2001. "Peopling the Classic Maya Court." In *Royal Courts of the Ancient Maya*, Vol. 1, *Theory, Comparison, and Synthesis*, ed. Takeshi Inomata and Stephen D. Houston, 54–83. Boulder: Westview Press.

Houston, Stephen D., David Stuart, and Karl A. Taube. 1989. "Folk Classification of Classic Maya Pottery." *American Anthropologist* 91(3):720–726.

———. 2006. *The Memory of Bones: Body, Being, and Experience among the Classic Maya*. Austin: University of Texas Press.

Hull, Kerry. 2010. "An Epigraphic Analysis of Classic-Period Maya Foodstuffs." In *Pre-Columbian Foodways: Interdisciplinary Approaches to Food, Culture, and Markets in Ancient Mesoamerica*, ed. John E. Staller and Michael D. Carrasco, 235–256. New York: Springer.

Hurst, W. Jeffrey, Stanley M. Tarka Jr., Terry G. Powis, Fred Valdez Jr., and Thomas R. Hester. 2002. "Archaeology: Cacao Usage by the Earliest Maya Civilization." *Nature* 418:289–290.

Iannone, Gyles, ed. 2014. *The Great Maya Droughts in Cultural Context: Case Studies in Resilience and Vulnerability*. Boulder: University Press of Colorado.

Inomata, Takeshi. 2006. "Plazas, Performers, and Spectators: Political Theaters of the Classic Maya." *Current Anthropology* 47(5):805–842.

Inomata, Takeshi, and Kenichiro Tsukamoto. 2014. "Gathering in an Open Space: Introduction to Mesoamerican Plazas." In *Mesoamerican Plazas: Arenas of Community and Power*, ed. Kenichiro Tsukamoto and Takeshi Inomata, 3–16. Tucson: University of Arizona Press.

Jackson, Sarah E. 2013. *Politics of the Maya Court: Hierarchy and Change in the Late Classic Period*. Norman: University Press of Oklahoma.

———. 2015. "Governing Polities: Royal Courts and the Written Landscape of Late Classic Maya Politics." In *Classic Maya Polities of the Southern Lowlands: Integration, Interaction, Dissolution*, ed. Damien B. Marken and James L. Fitzsimmons, 243–262. Boulder: University Press of Colorado.

Jones, Martin. 2007. *Feast: Why Humans Share Food*. New York: Oxford University Press.

Kolata, Alan. 1993. *The Tiwanaku: Portrait of an Andean Civilization*. Cambridge, MA: Blackwell.

Lamoureux-St-Hilaire, Maxime. 2018a. "Estudio económico multifacético de la sección norte del Palacio de La Corona." In *Proyecto Arqueológico La Corona: Informe Final, Temporada 2017*, ed. Marcello Canuto, Tomás Barrientos Q., Marissa López, and Eduardo Bustamante, 479–500. Guatemala City: Proyecto Regional Arqueológico La Corona.

———. 2018b. "Palatial Politics: The Classic Maya Royal Court of La Corona, Guatemala." PhD diss., Tulane University.

Lamoureux-St-Hilaire, Maxime, Marcello A. Canuto, Tomás Barrientos Q., and Eduardo Bustamante. 2020. "Detachment from Power: Sequential Abandonment in the Classic Maya Palace of La Corona, Guatemala." In *Detachment from Place: Beyond an Archaeology of Settlement Abandonment*, ed. Maxime Lamoureux-St-Hilaire and Scott Macrae. Boulder: University Press of Colorado. In press.

Lamoureux-St-Hilaire, Maxime, Marcello A. Canuto, E. Christian Wells, Clarissa Cagnato, and Tomás Barrientos Q. 2019. "Ancillary Economic Activities in a Classic Maya Regal Palace: A Multiproxy Approach." *Geoarchaeology* 34(6):768–782.

Lamoureux-St-Hilaire, Maxime, Scott Macrae, Carmen McCane, Evan Parker, and Gyles Iannone. 2015. "The Last Groups Standing: Living Abandonment at the Ancient Maya Center of Minanha, Belize." *Latin American Antiquity* 26(4):550–569.

LeCount, Lisa J. 1999. "Polychrome Pottery and Political Strategies in Late and Terminal Classic Lowland Maya Society." *Latin American Antiquity* 10(3):239–258.

———. 2001. "Like Water for Chocolate: Feasting and Political Ritual among the Late Classic Maya of Xunantunich, Belize." *American Anthropologist* 103(4):935–953.

———. 2010. "Maya Palace Kitchens: Suprahousehold Food Preparation at the Late and Terminal Classic Site of Xunantunich, Belize." In *Inside Ancient Kitchens: New Directions in the Study of Daily Meals and Feasts*, ed. Elizabeth A. Klarich, 133–160. Boulder: University Press of Colorado.

LeCount, Lisa J., and Jason Yaeger. 2010. "Provincial Politics and Current Models of the Maya State." In *Classic Maya Provincial Politics: Xunantunich and Its Hinterlands*, ed. Lisa J. LeCount and Jason Yaeger, 20–45. Tucson: University of Arizona Press.

Marx, Karl. 1967. *Capital*. 3 vols. New York: New World Paperbacks.

McAnany, Patricia A. 2010. *Ancestral Maya Economies in Archaeological Perspective*. Cambridge: Cambridge University Press.

———. 2013. "Artisans, *Ikatz*, and Statecraft: Provisioning Classic Maya Royal Courts." In *Merchants, Markets, and Exchange in the Pre-Columbian World*, ed. Kenneth G. Hirth and Joanne Pillsbury, 229–254. Washington, DC: Dumbarton Oaks Research Library and Collection.

McAnany, Patricia A., and Maxime Lamoureux-St-Hilaire. 2017. "The Fragility of Political Experimentation from the Perspective of Classic Maya Cities." In *Crisis to Collapse: The Archaeology of Social Breakdown*, ed. Tim Cunningham and Jan Driessen, 305–314. Louvain, Belgium: AEGIS.

McAnany, Patricia A., Jeremy A. Sabloff, Maxime Lamoureux-St-Hilaire, and Gyles Iannone. 2016. "Leaving Classic Maya Cities: Agent-based Modeling and the Dynamics of Diaspora." In *Social Theory in Archaeology and Ancient History: The Present and Future of Counternarratives*, ed. Geoffrey Emberling, 259–288. Cambridge: Cambridge University Press.

McAnany, Patricia A., Ben S. Thomas, Steven Morandi, Polly A. Peterson, and Eleanor Harrison. 2002. "Praise the Ajaw and Pass the Kakaw: Xibun Maya and the Political Economy of Cacao." In *Ancient Maya Political Economies*, ed. Marilyn A. Masson and David A. Freidel, 123–139. Walnut Creek, CA: Altamira Press.

Miller, Mary, and Claudia Brittenham. 2013. *The Spectacle of the Late Maya Court: Reflections on the Murals of Bonampak*. Austin: University of Texas Press.

Miller, Mary, and Simon Martin. 2004. *Courtly Art of the Ancient Maya*. New York: Thames and Hudson.

Moore, Jerry D. 1996. "The Archaeology of Plazas and the Proxemics of Ritual: Three Andean Traditions." *American Anthropologist* 98(4):789–802.

Ochs, Elinor, and Merav Shohet. 2006. "The Cultural Structuring of Mealtime Socialization." *New Directions for Child and Adolescent Development* 111:35–49.

Ochs, Elinor, and Carolyn Taylor. 1992. "Family Narrative as Political Activity." *Discourse & Society* 3(3):301–340.

Reents-Budet, Dorie. 2000. "Feasting among the Classic Maya: Evidence from the Pictorial Ceramics." In *The Maya Vase Book: A Corpus of Rollout Photographs of Maya Vases*, ed. Barbara Kerr and Justin Kerr, 6:1022–1037. New York: Kerr Associates.

———. 2001. "Classic Maya Concepts of the Royal Court: An Analysis of Renderings on Pictorial Ceramics." In *Royal Courts of the Ancient Maya*. Vol. 1, *Theory, Comparison, and Synthesis*, ed. Takeshi Inomata and Stephen D. Houston, 195–236. Boulder: Westview Press.

Restall, Matthew. 2001. "The People of the Patio: Ethnohistorical Evidence of Yucatec Maya Royal Courts." In *Royal Courts of the Ancient Maya*. Vol. 2, *Data and Case Studies*, ed. Takeshi Inomata and Stephen D. Houston, 335–390. Boulder: Westview Press.

Robicsek, Francis, and Donald M. Hales. 1981. *The Maya Book of the Dead: The Ceramic Codex*. Charlottesville: University of Virginia Art Museum.

Sabloff, Jeremy A. 1975. *Excavations at Seibal, Department of Petén, Guatemala*. No. 2, *Ceramics*. Cambridge, MA: Peabody Museum of Archaeology and Ethnology at Harvard University.

Sahlins, Marshall. 2017a. "The Original Political Society." In *On Kings*, ed. David Graeber and Marshall Sahlins, 23–64. Chicago: University of Chicago Press.

———. 2017b. "The Stranger-Kingship of the Mexica." In *On Kings*, ed. David Graeber and Marshall Sahlins, 223–248. Chicago: University of Chicago Press.

Sanders, William T. 1989. "Household, Lineage, and State at Eighth-Century Copan, Honduras." In *The House of the Bacabs, Copán, Honduras*, ed. David Webster, 89–105. Washington, DC: Dumbarton Oaks Research Library and Collection.

Schele, Linda, and Mary E. Miller. 1986. *The Blood of Kings: Dynasty and Ritual in Maya Art*. Fort Worth, TX: Kimbell Art Museum.

Seignobos, Charles. 1902. *The Feudal Régime*. Trans. Earle W. Dow. New York: Henry Holt.

Smith, Adam T. 2003. *The Political Landscape: Constellations of Authority in Early Complex Societies*. Berkeley: University of California Press.

———. 2015. *The Political Machine: Assembling Sovereignty in the Bronze Age Caucasus*. Princeton: Princeton University Press.

Smith, Monica L. 2015. "Feasts and Their Failures." *Journal of Archaeological Method and Theory* 22(4):1215–1237.

Smith, Robert E. 1971. *The Pottery of Mayapan: Including Studies of Ceramic Material from Uxmal, Kabah, and Chichen Itza*. Cambridge, MA: Peabody Museum of Archaeology and Ethnology at Harvard University.

Smyth, Michael P. 2016. "Storage, Tribute, and Political Administration among the Lowland Maya." In *Storage in Ancient Complex Societies: Administration, Organization, and Control*, ed. Linda R. Manzanilla and Mitchell S. Rothman, 251–270. New York: Routledge.

Stuart, David. 2005. *The Inscriptions from Temple XIX at Palenque: A Commentary*. San Francisco: Pre-Columbian Art Research Institute.

Stuart, David, Marcello A. Canuto, Tomás Barrientos Q., and Maxime Lamoureux-St-

Hilaire. 2015. "Preliminary Notes on Two Recently Discovered Inscriptions from La Corona, Guatemala." decipherment.wordpress.com/2015/07/17/preliminary-notes-on-two-recently-discovered-inscriptions-from-la-corona-guatemala.

Taube, Karl A. 1989. "The Maize Tamale in Classic Maya Diet, Epigraphy, and Art." *American Antiquity* 54(1):31–51.

Tokovinine, Alexandre. 2016. "It Is His Image with Pulque: Drinks, Gifts, and Political Networking in Classic Maya Texts and Images." *Ancient Mesoamerica* 27(1):13–29.

Tsukamoto, Kenichiro. 2014. "Multiple Identities on the Plazas: The Classic Maya Center of El Palmar, Mexico." In *Mesoamerican Plazas: Arenas of Community and Power*, ed. Kenichiro Tsukamoto and Takeshi Inomata, 50–69. Tucson: University of Arizona Press.

Twiss, Katheryn C. 2015. "Methodological and Definitional Issues in the Archaeology of Food." In *Commensality: From Everyday Food to Feast*, ed. Susanne Kerner, Cynthia Chou, and Morten Warmind, 89–98. New York: Bloomsbury.

Uslaner, Eric M. 2000. "Producing and Consuming Trust." *Political Science Quarterly* 115(4):569–590.

Vale, Malcolm G. A. 2001. *The Princely Court: Medieval Courts and Culture in North-West Europe, 1270–1380.* New York: Oxford University Press.

Van der Veen, Marijke. 2003. "When Is Food a Luxury?" *World Archaeology* 34(3): 405–427.

Vidal-Lorenzo, Christina, Maria Luisa Vázquez-de-Ágredos-Pascual, and Gaspar Muñoz-Cosme. 2016. "Storage Places in the Maya Area." In *Storage in Ancient Complex Societies: Administration, Organization, and Control*, ed. Linda R. Manzanilla and Mitchell S. Rothman, 271–292. New York: Routledge.

Weber, Max. 1947. *The Theory of Social and Economic Organization.* Trans. and ed. A. M. Henderson and Talcott Parsons. New York: The Free Press.

White, Christine D., David M. Pendergast, Fred J. Longstaffe, and Kimberley R. Law. 2001. "Social Complexity and Food Systems at Altun Ha, Belize: The Isotopic Evidence." *Latin American Antiquity* 12(4):371–393.

Wiessner, Polly. 2002. "The Vines of Complexity: Egalitarian Structures and the Institutionalization of Inequality among the Enga." *Current Anthropology* 43(2): 233–269.

Zender, Marc. 2000. "A Study of Two Uaxactún-Style Tamale Serving Vessels." In *The Maya Vase Book: A Corpus of Rollout Photographs of Maya Vases*, ed. Barbara Kerr and Justin Kerr, 6:1038–1055. New York: Kerr Associates.

———. 2004. "A Study of Classic Maya Priesthood." PhD diss., University of Calgary.

CHAPTER 10

Thinking (and Eating) Chichén Itzá: New Food Technology and Creating the Itzá State at Xuenkal

TRACI ARDREN

Despite the emphasis scholars often place on continuities in the techniques of Maya food preparation from the pre-Columbian period onward, it would be a mistake to think of Maya kitchens as technologically static places unchanged over the centuries. There is ample evidence that cooking technologies evolved during the Classic period, as new foods and tools were introduced through contact and exchange. With those new tools came the specialized knowledge required to use them, a type of knowledge situated within the praxis of specific social identities. This chapter looks at one important development in the technology of food preparation that I argue was closely tied to the reinvention of urban identities at the extraordinary Terminal Classic site of Chichén Itzá and its regional dependents. This instrument was part of not only new food preparation techniques but also new social interactions and shifts in daily practice that accompanied the introduction of new technology. The use of ceramic grater bowls, better known as *molcajetes*, at Chichén Itzá was a culinary innovation that coincided with a number of significant changes in the daily lives of the city's occupants—changes that engendered new social interactions, memories, and identities.

Evidence from Xuenkal, an outlying center brought forcefully within the political and economic sphere of Chichén, shows that these tools played a part in feasting events that acted as rituals of inclusion (Ardren and Alonso Olvera 2017; Ardren et al. 2005). Conspicuous consumption of food and exotic trade goods helped cement new social bonds of obligation and interdependence between the emergent rulers of Chichén and the existing elites at a small nearby center. The new foods that accompanied these experiences added a powerful sensory component to the creation of a new social identity centered in the material culture, architectural spaces, and social dynamics of the Itzá state. Patron-role feasting was designed to legitimize sociopolitical asymmetries and reinforce the membership of local elites in the Itzá state. Nonlocal trade items, a superabundance of materials, and new food technology combine to suggest locals had a new level of access to disposable wealth not seen at Xuenkal in earlier periods.

This chapter illuminates the processes by which the Chichén city-state succeeded during a time in which other Maya populations were in crisis, having largely given up on earlier urban models. The unique success of Chichén rested on a powerful combination of participation in pan-Mesoamerican trade and ritual, which has been well studied, as well as lesser known changes in the daily practices of regional elites who were brought into the political and economic ideology of the Itzá state, and thereafter constituted an essential element of its economic apparatus. For the immense urban settlement of Chichén to be successful, it had to draw local elites into a new way of thinking, a new social imaginary, in which the series of linked pilgrimage centers—of which Chichén was only one—were worth the tremendous sacrifices of land, labor, and resources demonstrated so clearly in the archaeological record of this period. As William Isbell (2000:252) suggests, when we look at the creation and evolution of social imaginaries, we move away from innate or static identities to identities as a process of dialogue, something constructed strategically through practice and interaction. While military force may have been used initially to bring regional centers under the control of Chichén leadership, archaeological evidence shows that daily practices such as new foodways, along with shifts in crafting and ritual, were used to solidify the membership of those local centers into the new urban imaginary of Chichén.

The Problem of Chichén Itzá

The ancient Maya city of Chichén Itzá, a UNESCO World Heritage site since 1986, and the main tourism site in the state of Yucatán, Mexico, has fascinated scholars for centuries (García Solís 2017). It is a large urban center, at least 30 km² in extent, although it was likely much larger in the past, and much of the ancient settlement has been consumed by historic and modern construction (Taube et al. in press). The urban center has monumental architecture that is both more elaborate than what is found at many Classic Maya centers and stylistically similar to well-known features of sites outside the Maya area. Since the dredging of the Great Cenote in the nineteenth century, we have known that the portable material culture of Chichén Itzá was more diverse than that of any other Maya city, with ample amounts of exotic long-distance trade items, such as gold and turquoise, generally not found at other Maya sites (Tozzer 1957). But most importantly, all of these features date to a time when other Maya cities across the lowlands were in decline, occupation and construction in the Southern Lowlands had largely ceased, and the cities of the Northern Lowlands were sparsely occupied by impoverished populations. Thus the "problem" of Chichén is its unique rise to dominance during a time when no other Maya city was capable of anything similar. A secondary problem has always been who lived at the city: Was it populated by local Maya people from the Northern Lowlands, by a mixture of people from across Mesoamerica, or by a ruling group of central Mexicans?

Despite the vast amount of ink that has been spilled describing various aspects of this unusual city, relatively little is known of the mechanisms by which it rose to such power and dominance at the end of the Late Classic (700–900 CE) and beginning of the Terminal Classic (850–1000 CE) periods (Andrews 1990; Cobos 2016). Peter Schmidt's research provided evidence that Chichén was founded in the Late Preclassic period as a small center like many others in the region, and then grew in size during the Late Classic period (Pérez de Heredia 2012; Schmidt 2000, 2003), in concert with regional patterns of development and material culture. We still know very little about why Chichén Itzá became the paramount center of the Terminal Classic period—it was likely not deeply enmeshed in the Late Classic dynastic politics of other nearby primate centers such as Cobá or Uxmal, and thus perhaps it was buffered from many of the impacts of the Late Classic "collapse." However, what is well established is that by as early as the ninth century, the elite (and perhaps a midlevel merchant class) of Chichén participated in long-distance exchange networks that controlled both maritime and overland trade in exotics such as gold but also commodities such as obsidian, salt, and pottery (Andrews et al. 1988; Andrews et al. 1989; Ardren and Lowry 2011; Cobos 2016; Glover et al. 2018). Also well documented is that a distinctive set of ceramic wares was produced and utilized at the site and its regional dependents during this time, and these wares seem to have been deployed emblematically throughout the area in places where Chichén exerted economic and political power (Smith and Bond-Freeman 2017). The Sotuta ceramic complex, as it is known, is a perfect metaphor for the social processes in action at Chichén—it arises from a local tradition but includes a small but significant number of new forms that are better known from other parts of Mesoamerica (Johnson 2015; Robles Castellanos 2006).

William Ringle, Tomás Gallareta Negrón, and George J. Bey III showed how the elite of Chichén participated in a pan-Mesoamerican messianic cult of the avatar Quetzalcoatl, patron of merchants and leaders, that facilitated long-distance exchange networks (Ringle, Gallareta Negrón, and Bey 1998:185). They further suggested that Chichén Itzá was a pilgrimage center in a network of other Terminal Classic–Epiclassic centers such as Cholula, Cacaxtla, and El Tajín—all of which have major shrines that transcend ethnic differences across diverse parts of Mesoamerica (Ringle, Gallareta Negrón, and Bey 1998:185). One result of this messianic cult was the temporary reinvention of urbanism in the Maya area after its thorough rejection by beleaguered citizens across the Maya Lowlands at the end of the Late Classic period, a phenomenon described as the Classic Maya collapse. The leaders of Chichén, in concert with elites from other parts of Mesoamerica who shared participation in the cult of Quetzalcoatl, used military force, economic power, and territorial expansion to build a large urban population at the earlier modest center. Murals at Chichén depict military campaigns of territorial expansion, and research at nearby centers demonstrates a pattern of artifactual replacement associated with violent destruction of elite architecture that has been interpreted as evidence of local absorption into the political and economic sphere of Chichén (Ambrosino, Ardren, and Stanton 2001; Anderson 1998; Ardren et al. 2005; Ardren et al. 2010; Glover et al. 2018; Manahan, Ardren, and Alonso Olvera 2012; Robles Salmerón, Amparo, Stanton, and Magnoni 2011; Smith and Bond-Freeman 2017).

Other than analyses of the military campaigns shown in elite murals and carved stone monuments at the Temple of the Warriors, not enough attention has been paid to exactly how regional elites were absorbed into the political patronage of Chichén, and perhaps into the messianic cult of Quetzalcoatl. The site of Xuenkal has abundant evidence of an occupation by Sotuta pottery–using people in the Terminal Classic period following a decline in fortune at the end of the Late Classic period (Manahan, Ardren, and Alonso Olvera 2012). Xuenkal is located in an area of richer-than-average soils and natural depressions useful for agricultural intensification. Eight seasons of research by the Proyecto Arqueológico Xuenkal, under the direction of Ardren and later Ardren and Manahan, demonstrated a program of new architectural forms, craft intensification, and artifactual shifts in association with the presence of Sotuta pottery in contexts where local Cehpech pottery was also used (Ardren and Alonso Olvera 2017; Manahan, Ardren, and Alonso Olvera 2012:353). I have argued that by looking at regional centers important to the broader economy of Chichén, rather than just at its elite propaganda, we can better see the heterogeneous social processes of state building and power consolidation at work (Ardren, Alonso Olvera, and Manahan 2016; Ardren et al. 2010; Marcus 2012).

In the 1980s, Anthony P. Andrews and colleagues (1989) noted the existence of a network of regional centers that predate the florescence of Chichén Itzá but also have material evidence for a distinctive occupation contemporary with the height of Chichén. These sites, most of which are located on the northern plains between Chichén and its port Isla Cerritos 100 km away on the Gulf of Mexico, share the presence of abundant Sotuta pottery and green obsidian in shoddy architecture visible at ground surface. One of the three largest semiurban centers in this region is Xuenkal, located halfway between Chichén Itzá and Isla Cerritos. Xuenkal was first occupied in the Late Preclassic period and grew to occupy approximately 2.5 km^2 of land that was continuously settled by the Late Classic period. In its early history, Xuenkal participated in northern lowland architectural and artifactual traditions, perhaps best epitomized by nearby Ek Balam, where vaulted masonry palace architecture, elaborate slateware ceramics, and royal iconography were abundant. In concert with patterns documented at other centers surrounding Chichén Itzá, including Ek Balam, Ichmul de Morley, Yula, and Yaxuna, construction of new buildings at Xuenkal slowed at the end of the Late Classic period. However, the Terminal Classic period brought a revival of building and occupation, albeit in a less sophisticated manner, as well as a wealth of new trade items. While there is no evidence for population replacement in the Terminal Classic period, there is distinct support for an infusion of new material wealth not present in previous periods, new levels of intensified craft production, and diminished skills or resources dedicated to architectural construction.

Recent research has disproven models from the last century that argued that the florescence of Chichén Itzá was due to a large-scale invasion from central Mexico (Andrews, Andrews, and Robles Castellanos 2003; Cobos 2007, 2016; Johnson 2015; Kristan-Graham and Wren 2018; Price, Tiesler, and Freiwald 2019; Ringle 1990; Robles Castellanos 2006), although how to describe the actors responsible for the social transformations of the eleventh to twelfth centuries at Chichén remains a matter of debate (Bíró and Pérez de Heredia 2018; Cobos 2016; Kristen-Graham and Wren 2018; Volta and Braswell 2014). Current data indicate that during the Terminal Classic period, a large local Maya population resided at the city and adopted various new cultural attributes as part of a reinvention of urbanism after the fall of southern Maya society. A robust maritime trading economy brought merchants from sites across Mesoamerica connected through the cult of Quetzalcoatl into regular contact with one another, which resulted in a circulation of goods, people, and ideas throughout the region. Simultaneously, a shared religio-political belief system that upheld this economic network is visible in the similar artistic traditions of the Terminal Classic period (also called Epiclassic by some scholars; see Cohodas 1989) at these cities. However, decades of research at Chichén and at sites within its sphere of influence have yet to reveal evidence of large population movements during the Terminal Classic period. No material indications of invasion, conquest, or even population replacement have been found. The archaeological record of Chichén, even at its earliest phase, is largely consistent with other sites in the Northern Maya Lowlands, especially in residential areas where evidence of the sorts of daily habits that often reveal a foreign presence in the archaeological record should be most visible.

The stylistic shift in pottery long associated with the Itzá polity is now understood to be a regional variant of local northern slateware traditions, with the important addition of three new forms (Andrews and Robles Castellanos 1985; Bey 2001; Johnson 2015; Robles Castellanos 2006; Stanton and Gallareta Negrón 2001). All of the slateware complexes share many characteristics, including compositional attributes, vessel forms, and decorative techniques. What sets Sotuta complex materials apart from other slateware complexes, aside from a reliance on a redder clay, is the presence of three forms found elsewhere in Mesoamerica. Grater bowls, ladle-handled censers, and griddles are introduced to the Maya area during the Terminal Classic period at Chichén and its regional dependents as part of the Sotuta complex.

Ringle and colleagues (1998:216) have suggested that ladle-handled censers are part of the ritual incense-burning complex consistently found in association at sites identified to be part of the cult of Quetzalcoatl, including Chichén. The other two new ceramic forms are closely associated with culinary traditions of central Mexico and Oaxaca—grater bowls to aerate vegetables for salsas and griddles for making tortillas. While these new forms are not found in huge numbers throughout central Chichén, they are ubiquitous artifacts wherever later construction took place. Grater bowls were found in the Carnegie-era Monjas and Caracol excavations at Chichén, both structures with late occupations; at the Monjas complex, likely an elite residential area (Brainerd 1958:260); in the 1960 explorations of the Sacred Well by INAH (Pérez de Heredia 1998); and in the 2009 excavations into the Gran Nivelación and Great Ballcourt

(Méndez Cab 2016). Given that there has been very little excavation of domestic structures within central Chichén, this sample of *molcajetes* is likely only those discarded and reutilized in construction fill, with the exception of the Great Well examples, which were likely offerings. Outside Chichén Itzá, grater bowls are one of the most distinctive artifactual markers of a presumed Itzá presence, and they are usually associated with middens and occupational debris, although in at least one context they were found in a ritualized termination assemblage (Ambrosino, Ardren, and Stanton 2001; Smith and Bond-Freeman 2017; Stanton and Gallareta Negrón 2001). They seem to have been the ideal utilitarian form to leave as an emblematic marker of the power and identity of the Itzá state.

Thus, it appears that the Maya population of Chichén Itzá and its regional dependents adopted new foodways as they came to learn how to use new forms of cooking technology with no precedent in the Maya region. These culinary shifts brought locals into a pan-Mesoamerican tradition of food preparation that augmented centuries of local tradition with innovative new tastes and textures. The archaeological contexts where these new forms such as grater bowls are found—modest Terminal Classic constructions on top of earlier elite architecture—suggest that they were in use by elites at regional centers within the Chichén polity. They are often found in great quantities, with patterns of breakage that do not correspond to normal wear but indicate ritualized consumption and disposal. When found in association with feasting debris, it is likely these new ceramic forms were used as part of efforts to absorb regional elites and the resources they controlled into patron-client relationships at the heart of the collective politico-religious ideology of Chichén leadership.

Cuisine is a form of specialized knowledge that creates and cements identities. As Cathy Costin (2004) notes, specialization is as much a social relation as it is an economic one. Obtaining ingredients, preparing complicated recipes, learning how to serve new foods, and talking about such meals are all ways in which social identities circulate and solidify through the material culture of food. Patterned changes in the tools used to prepare food indicate how daily habits shifted and how information about new forms of food preparation spread. Innovations in food-preparation tools can reflect many things—improvements in efficiency, technological developments, or the introduction of new foods into the diet (Crown 2000). Both grater bowls and griddles presented radically new methods of food preparation and would have required instruction in their use that provided opportunities for contingent cultural change. As ubiquitous as the tortilla is throughout modern Mexico, the arrival of griddles (comales) in the Terminal Classic period marked the beginning of Maya consumption of heated corn dough breads—available evidence suggests corn was consumed primarily through steamed and stewed forms (tamales and pozoles) prior to the introduction of the comal (Smith 1971; Taube 1989). Given that gastronomically conservative cultures like the Maya can be slow to adopt radically new forms of familiar foods, a heightened social context may have been the first place foods prepared in *molcajetes* and comales were consumed.

Feasting events can provide the kind of mechanisms through which social imaginaries circulate and strengthen. Following Charles Taylor (2002: 106) and others, I define the social imaginary as "the ways in which people imagine their social existence, how they fit together with others, how things go on between them and their fellows, the expectations that are normally met, and the deeper normative notions and images that underlie these expectations." Given that the population of Chichén Itzá and its surrounding countryside dependents was composed of local Maya people as well as visiting merchants and some possible residents from other parts of Mesoamerica, material culture was a crucial way to reinforce a sense of shared membership. Social events with heightened political or sensory impact created a space for discourse about participation in this pilgrimage center and its network of similar centers across Terminal Classic Mesoamerica. Shared daily practices, such as foodways that combined regional traditions with new food-processing technology and culinary substances, generated a sense of shared membership in a new collective identity. While aggressive campaigns of territorial expansion may have provided the Itzá polity with a massive land base, and dramatic collective rituals may have drawn people to the urban center, changes in daily habits may have been one mechanism to maintain a large population willing to participate in the agenda of the Itzá state.

State Building through Food

As Christine Hastorf (2017:224) has written, "Culinary traditions are active in all practices of identity formation," whether that be at the individual, family, community, or national level. Intangible concepts like "identity" are given tangible, material form in the daily tools used to harvest and prepare food, the specific recipes used to cook a meal, and the rules under which food is served and consumed. Food was identified by Catherine Palmer (1998:181) as one of the three flags of "banal nationalism," or the shared and commonplace habits that enable nations to be reproduced, the means by which we don't forget our national identities. We can see this working from the top down, as in the designation of a "national dish" by emerging elites in postcolonial movements (Appadurai 1988; Pérez Monfort 2004), or from the bottom up, as in the widespread notion that the modern American diet is characterized by fatty, unhealthy food. Although Maya society was never as unified as a modern nation, individual polities reached the level of city-states, and it is clear from shared artifactual and residential patterns that the citizens of many ancient Maya cities had a sense of shared membership in a cultural urban imaginary (Ardren 2015; Magnoni et al. 2014). Iconography created by the elite but visible to large numbers of ancient citizens in the massive plazas of Maya cities communicated an identity based on collective membership in the civic-religious life of their city. This is especially true at Chichén Itzá, where plaza spaces are immense and iconography emphasizes collective activities (Kristan-Graham 2018; Miller 2018; Ringle, Gallareta Negrón, and Bey 1998).

Food studies of cross-cultural encounters highlight the use of foodstuffs to communicate or reinforce ideas of inclusion and exclusion (Hastorf 2017:246). Foods that are at first exotic and unfamiliar gradually can be embraced as part of a culinary tradition, even sometimes evolving to become signature foods closely linked to identity, such as the potato in Ireland or the peanut in the Deep South. There has been less investigation of introduced food technologies, such as preparation techniques and kitchen utensils, although scholars in Latin America have chronicled the influence of modern mechanized tools such as the corn mill or blender on traditional cuisines of indigenous cultures (Ayora-Diaz 2016; Caballero-Arias 2016). A consistent observation is that with new technologies, cooks also adopt the values and tastes of a new culture and adapt these to local needs (Ayora-Diaz 2016:96). The naturalization of new tastes, textures, and techniques happens in a context of everyday practice among friends and family. This can lead to transformations in the social and cultural significance of well-known foods as they pass out of fashion or favor, with newer foodstuffs assuming the role of identity marker.

Ideas are encoded in new foods—depending on historical specificities, new foods may be imposed on a population or they can be the salvation of the hungry. The means by which a new food or cooking technique is shared is also central to the experience and acceptance of the introduced culinary experience, but is the specialized knowledge of how to use this new tool restricted to the elite, or is it shared in communal feasts? Practical forms of knowledge such as cooking techniques are often very fixed to the bodily experience of learning, practicing, and ultimately cooking—they are reproduced in action and observations, often unconsciously, until they become part of the personal characteristics of the cook, and thus part of her social identity (Nikolic 2016:161). Many cooks outside the modern West do not remember learning to cook—so new tools or foods that are introduced and require instruction often generate a heightened social experience in which ideas that have become completely naturalized are opened up for examination and revision.

The new cooking tools that appear at Chichén Itzá and the surrounding region in the Terminal Classic period as part of the Sotuta ceramic complex opened up new ways to prepare vegetables, salsas, and even corn, the "signature food" of the Maya. Grater bowls allowed even maceration and aeration of chiles and other vegetables into sauces, while griddles allowed the cooking of corn masa quickly over high heat. These food-preparation tools are part of a package of new material culture—of which the Sotuta ceramic complex is but one component—that arrived in the Northern Maya Lowlands along with the iconography of Quetzalcoatl and exotic trade items from across Mesoamerica and beyond. In addition to large collective rituals of incorporation that may have solidified elite participation in a revival of the tradition of urbanism, and membership in a militaristic religious cult that served the needs of the state, the cities across Mesoamerica that were linked by shared membership in the cult of Quetzalcoatl and widespread interregional trade also shared a new set of foodways. Fragile new social connections across regions and cultures may have been cemented not only in large public rituals but also in smaller intimate meals, especially meals that utilized familiar ingredients in novel new preparations.

Molcajetes at Xuenkal

Eight years of research across the central core and peripheral areas of Xuenkal documented a shift in settlement patterns during the Terminal Classic period from dispersed residential groups typical of earlier periods across the Northern Lowlands to large nucleated platforms with simple and expedient structures (Manahan, Ardren, and Alonso Olvera 2012). One of these platforms, 8M-1, yielded ample evidence for increased domestic production of shell, lithic, and textile products during the Terminal Classic period (Ardren et al. 2010; Ardren, Alonso Olvera, and Manahan 2016). Other platforms of this style had associated domestic debris with less evidence of intensive crafting but artifacts diagnostic of the Sotuta ceramic complex, Mexican green obsidian, and new long-distance trade items like Plumbate pottery. These structures reutilize older Early and Late Classic architectural platforms as their base, often with little effort made to encase those structures in the usual manner of Maya architectural renovation. Instead, during the tumultuous Terminal Classic period, walls were built simply with a double line of large rectangular boulders, roughly shaped, that supported perishable walls and a thatched roof. The Sotuta constructions at Xuenkal did not have plaster floors, and likely packed-earth surfaces served this purpose. Given that architecture built at Xuenkal only one hundred to two hundred years earlier utilized vaulted ceilings over core-veneer masonry, stuccoed walls, and thick plastered floors, the extremely simple architecture of the Terminal Classic constructions is strikingly less sophisticated and shows either a radical reorientation of resources or, more likely, the loss of local knowledge and skills necessary for architectural construction.

As part of sampling locations with evidence for the Terminal Classic occupation of Xuenkal, I identified two rectangular superstructures (9M-79 and 9M-80) that form an L arrangement upon the western and northern edges of a large basal platform (Str. 9M-78; Figure 10.1). An open central plaza area is bounded by these two rectangular structures, a pyramidal structure (9M-81) on the northeast, and other smaller structures on the east. The southern side of the plaza is open. This plaza group is part of Group J, and is located near the center of the ancient settlement, inside the barricade. Through topographic mapping of the area and three test pits excavated in front of structures 9M-79 and 9M-80 in 2006, we verified the presence of large quantities of Terminal Classic occupational debris within dark soils, a typical indication of midden or domestic rubbish. The variety of ceramic materials, including trade wares, and their relatively fine state of preservation suggested the remains of a high-status residential area. One of the test pits revealed two courses of a basal stairway on the south side of structure 9M-80. Diagnostic materials from the basal platform indicated that it was originally an Early Classic construction with significant Late and Terminal Classic modifications, including the reutilization of well-carved Puuc-style columnettes in the stairway.

The Terminal Classic construction was a set of four small rooms roughly delimited by unworked boulders on the summit of 9M-79 and four rooms on the summit of 9M-80 (Figure 10.2). These walls incorporated some reutilized stone but were primarily made of very simple unmodified boulders. No plaster surfaces were preserved in association with these struc-

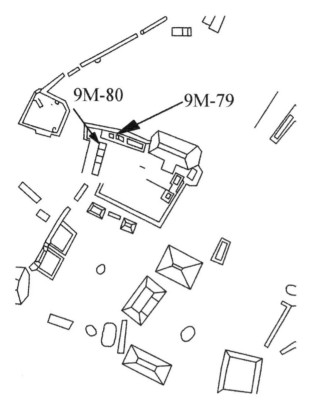

Figure 10.1. Location of Structures 9M-79 and 9M-80 in central Xuenkal. Illustration by Justin P. Lowry, Proyecto Arqueológico Xuenkal.

tures, and very few artifacts were recovered from inside the rooms. But an artifact-rich midden extended along the entire western half of the front of Structure 9M-79 up to where it intersected with Structure 9M-80 to form the corner of the L arrangement.

Analysis of the shallow (no more than 30 cm deep) but extensive (20 m east–west) midden debris from in front of Structures 9M-79 and 9M-80 shows a rich assortment of exotic trade items, food remains, and crafting debris in keeping with materials from other Sotuta structures at the site. The presence of exotic goods such as central Mexican obsidian, Plumbate pottery from Pacific Guatemala, and Fine Orange pottery from Tabasco indicate that the occupants, while living in extremely modest architecture, enjoyed material culture considered an indication of elite contexts during this time (Neff 2001). Other materials include evidence for spinning and possible cloth production at levels higher than necessary for domestic consumption needs (also found elsewhere at the site at this time), lithic and shell-working implements, and new types of food and drink.

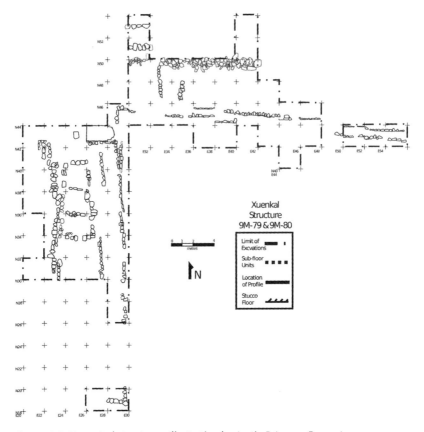

Figure 10.2. Excavated structures. Illustration by Justin P. Lowry, Proyecto Arqueológico Xuenkal.

As in other Terminal Classic contexts across Xuenkal, the exotic trade wares (Tohil Plumbate, Fine Orange) were found mixed with local ceramic material from both the Cehpech and Sotuta spheres, or what Cobos (2007) has called the "late Sotuta phase" (Manahan, Ardren, and Alonso Olvera 2012:347). In earlier work, I have suggested that these two ceramic spheres overlap at Xuenkal and that it is difficult to differentiate certain types, given their very close similarities of form and manufacture (Manahan, Ardren, and Alonso Olvera 2012). Along with others, I argue that this is evidence that the Sotuta ceramic tradition, minus the three new forms discussed above, was a local phenomenon that originates in earlier ceramic traditions (Johnson 2015). Two Accelerator Mass Spectrometry (AMS) dates obtained from deer bone collagen from the midden are consistent with the overlap model of Cehpech and Sotuta ceramic spheres, and date to the first decades of the eleventh century (Ardren and Morehart n.d.). Plumbate and Fine Orange pottery fragments from effigy vessels may have held cacao or other beverages, although residue analyses have not been performed.

Of particular significance to this chapter was the presence of fifty-six grater bowl fragments from various Sotuta sphere types in the midden materials in front of Structures 9M-79 and 9M-80 (Figure 10.3). Grater bowls were one of the most common artifacts recovered, and many of the fragments could be refitted, indicating they were broken in place. They have been identified as Dzitas Slate, Muna Slate, and Balantun Black-on-Slate types, again indicating a contemporaneity and continuity between Cehpech and Sotuta slateware traditions. The grater bowls were lightly used before being discarded in this midden, and samples have been the subject of micro- and macrobotanical analyses (Ardren and Morehart n.d.).

Figure 10.3. *Molcajete* (grater bowl) fragment from Structure 9M-79 midden at Xuenkal. Photograph by the author.

A well-known characteristic of the Terminal Classic material culture associated with Chichén Itzá is a shift to green (rather than gray) obsidian that originates in central Mexico (Andrews, Gallareta Negrón, and Cobos Palma 1989; Braswell 2000; Healan 2007). Throughout the Classic period, lowland Maya centers relied almost entirely on gray obsidian from multiple sources in the Guatemalan highlands. One of the most striking examples of a dramatic shift in economic trade patterns was the introduction of green obsidian to cities in the Maya Lowlands connected to Chichén Itzá. Nearly a third of the obsidian from the midden context at Structures 9M-79 and 9M-80 was from central Mexico (n=16 of 56), and it was found in core, flake, and blade form, the only forms found in this context. All of the obsidian lithic tools showed evidence of unifacial retouching, a characteristic of reuse or reutilization. There was also a great deal of chert blade and flake tools, with evidence of use, as well as stone-polishing tools, pumice stone for sharpening edges, and mano fragments.

Analysis of the shell from this midden by Alejandra Alonso Olvera, utilizing protocols from the Taller de Producción de Concha del Museo del Templo Mayor, also demonstrated the presence of tools related to crafting activities (Alonso Olvera, Ardren, and Manahan 2013). A total of seventy-one shell elements of both bivalves and gastropods were recovered from the midden excavations, with gastropods being more common. The shell originated in the Gulf of Mexico and the Atlantic Ocean, although as at the larger craft production platforms at Xuenkal, Pacific coast species (*Pinctada mazatlanica*) were also present at the 9M-79 and 9M-80 midden. Pacific shell was also found in the excavations at Isla Cerritos, and it must have been one of the many maritime trade goods that moved into the peninsula via the port site and then overland to Xuenkal and eventually Chichén. Utilitarian forms outnumber ornamental forms by 2:1, and shell drills, needles, gouges, and scrapers were all recovered from the midden context (Alonso Olvera, Ardren, and Manahan 2013:13). Ornaments were unfinished small mosaic plates or disks, similar to what was found in greater quantity at the larger craft production platform, Structure 8M-1 (Alonso Olvera 2013; Alonso Olvera, Manahan, and Ardren 2009).

In summary, the materials from this shallow midden along the face of Structures 9M-79 and 9M-80 are consistent with a pattern of other Terminal Classic artifacts closely associated with the large capital of Chichén Itzá. Against the hastily made architecture of Structures 9M-79 and 9M-80, the occupants of Xuenkal left a single-episode trash heap of food remains, crafting tools, and pottery remains, some of them local and some of them exotic trade goods. We have no other elaborate middens like this one from earlier periods at Xuenkal with which to compare, but the assortment of materials here suggests that elite participants, like those who were pressed into intensified craft production at the site (Ardren et al. 2010), were feted generously with local delicacies such as deer, turtle, and black iguana. Iguana was an important food source throughout Mesoamerica, but it is less common in the faunal collections of earlier periods in Yucatán (Rivas Romero et al. 2018:173). The construction fill of Structure 8M-1, a Sotuta-era platform, had a greater diversity of animal food remains than the fill of a Late Classic structure at the site (9M-136), and it appears that Itzá-era dietary patterns at Xuenkal embraced a wider variety of animal foods as well as a wider variety of food textures, preparation techniques, and serving vessels (Rivas Romero et al. 2018). Repeated exposure to new forms of food and new cooking technology likely were some of the more intimate means by which subjugated regional elites were brought into the fold of the new regional power.

Engineering Indebtedness through New Foodways

In a synthesis of many decades of research by archaeologists into the social use of feasting in pre-Industrial-Age societies, Bryan Hayden (2014: 21) states, "[Feasts] are ideal for the creation, reproduction, transformation, and concealment of power relations." Feasts are polysemous, with numerous social outcomes and intentions, but a primary feature of feasting in ancient states was the enhancement of solidarity and social cohesion between social groups. Hayden and others have argued that within agricultural societies in particular, where there is often a perception (or where such a message is conveyed by the state) that resources can be endlessly expanded, competition and escalation of aggrandizer strategies are favored and common (Hayden 2014:18). Feasting can be understood as an extremely effective way to utilize resources to acquire or maintain power, especially in times of social upheaval. Feasts can convert surplus into literally unlimited amounts of social capital in very short periods of time.

Equally important for this case study is the power of feasting events to advance social relations, especially inequalities. The Xuenkal midden context fits the definition of a patron-role feast, designed to legitimize sociopolitical asymmetries, because the material remains indicate their nonlocal origin, and the abundance of materials (relative to local patterns of consumption) suggests access to disposable wealth not seen at Xuenkal in earlier periods (Dietler 2001:82). It is also instructive to think about

Michael Dietler's definition of the diacritical feast, which includes a performative display of ranked difference without the expectation of reciprocal hospitality (Dietler 1990; 2001:85). Again, the nature of the objects discarded in the Xuenkal context suggests that the participants in this feast, who were surely limited in number, given the relatively discrete size of the midden and its location within the center of the monumental core, had access during this particular moment in time to rare objects, tastes, sounds, and perhaps ideas that helped absorb them into the new political economy and ideology emanating from Chichén Itzá. New foods added an additional sensory dimension to these rituals, one to which memory and identity could have been harnessed in powerful ways.

The absence of feasting middens at Chichén Itzá itself also underscores how this event, preserved in the material record of Xuenkal, may not have been reciprocated within the heart of the urban center. Outlying elites who were left to supervise the increased production of crafts and natural resources, as well as the overland trade routes between Chichén and its port, needed to be brought into a sustainable patron-client relationship with the dominant forces at the capital. Feasting events, with their appeal to the senses and potential for pleasurable and unusual experiences that might have included intoxication, music, spectacle, and the invocation of new protective spirits or ancestors, were the perfect tool to engender a change of attitude and cement a sense of obligation. Raymond Firth (1983) called this "indebtedness engineering," and the leaders of Chichén had every reason to invest in the local leaders of regional centers newly under their control. A new regional social identity was cemented in the bellies and minds of the subservient elites responsible for generating the extraordinary levels of surplus needed to sustain the capital.

By analyzing the ways in which the Japaneseness of Japanese pasta is constructed, claimed, and evaluated, Atsuko Ichijo and Ronald Ranta (2016:21) argue that a new food item, in this case pasta, was made into something recognizably Japanese through the accumulative participation of many ordinary people. Everyday and repeated actions of individuals can reinforce dominant ideas of the state, as well as contest those ideas. Food is a central way in which social life is constituted and experienced; ideas encoded in food are circulated among those who share meals or foodways and thus solidified as valid and enduring (despite being highly malleable). Because of the capacity for food to carry symbolic power in relation to group membership, status, and identity, foodways are an excellent window into how individual membership in complex political organisms is created and maintained. The ancient state, like the modern nation, was created by the performance of activities that signaled collective shared membership in the state ideology—daily practices shared by a community of people who did not all know one another personally but who understood that the members of their identity community performed the same daily practices.

Conclusion

The distinctive culture of Terminal Classic–Epiclassic Chichén Itzá, a city larger than any other Maya center at the time and one that kept alive the model of urban settlement after it had been rejected throughout the Southern and much of the Northern Lowlands, has often been examined through the monumental art and architecture of its core. However, the city relied on a huge supporting population under the control of nearby elites, who provided material goods to fuel the economic dominance at the heart of Chichén's legitimization. In addition to regional economic control, Chichén was linked to other likely trading partners across Mesoamerica through a set of shared religious practices and domestic changes. One of the changes in daily practices that impacted individuals within the orbit of Chichén was the introduction of new food-preparation tools, what Michael Dietler (2001:66) has called the "micro-politics of daily life." At Xuenkal, we have evidence of one way in which these new foodways were made into something recognizably Maya. Conspicuous consumption of foods produced in new ceramic forms, along with the disposal of these tools as part of feasting debris in a highly visible location alongside elite residential structures, demonstrates how local elites were brought into a new social identity that emanated from the urban capital. Dietary changes made the political and economic changes associated with the capital more concrete, and such a feast would have provided a highly charged social arena for the performance of state values. In this particular context, we see how Maya people of Xuenkal learned how to be the Itzá, by eating correctly with food made on highly charged objects provided by the new state. The tangible and visceral experience of eating solidified the intangible and charged experience of a new social order. In this way, thinking Chichén was linked undeniably to eating Chichén.

Acknowledgments

I wish to express my appreciation to the following colleagues for the many productive conversations and debates we have had on the nature of Sotuta pottery and the

Itzá state: Alejandra Alonso Olvera, Anthony P. Andrews, George J. Bey III, Rafael Cobos Palma, Lilia Fernández Souza, Tomás Gallareta Negrón, Marcus Noe Pool Cab, Eduardo Pérez de Heredia, William Ringle, Fernando Robles Castellanos, and Travis W. Stanton.

References

Alonso Olvera, Alejandra. 2013. "Economic Strategies of Terminal Classic Households in the Northern Maya Lowlands: Multicrafting and Economic Diversification of a Mid-elite Residential Compound at Xuenkal, Yucatan." PhD diss., University of Calgary, Canada.

Alonso Olvera, Alejandra, Traci Ardren, and T. Kam Manahan. 2013. "Análisis comparativo de la producción y el consumo de artefactos de concha en tres contextos domésticos y sus implicaciones en la economía política y la economía local del sitio arqueológico de Xuenkal en el Clásico Tardío-Terminal." 9th Congreso Internacional de Mayistas, San Francisco de Campeche, Mexico.

Alonso Olvera, Alejandra, T. Kam Manahan, and Traci Ardren. 2009. "La producción de bienes de concha y la economía política de Xuenkal." *Los Investigadores de la Cultura Maya* (Campeche, Mex.: Universidad Autónoma de Campeche) 17(1): 266–283.

Ambrosino, James N., Traci Ardren, and Travis W. Stanton. 2001. "The History of Warfare at Yaxuná." In *Ancient Mesoamerican Warfare*, ed. M. Kathryn Brown and Travis W. Stanton, 109–124. Walnut Creek, CA: Altamira Press.

Anderson, Benedict. 1983. *Imagined Communities: Reflections on the Origin and Spread of Nationalism*. New York: Verso.

Anderson, Patricia K. 1998. "Yula, Yucatan, Mexico: Terminal Classic Maya Ceramic Chronology for the Chichen Itza Area." *Ancient Mesoamerica* 9(1):151–165.

Andrews, Anthony P. 1990. "The Fall of Chichen Itza: A Preliminary Hypothesis." *Latin American Antiquity* 1(3):258–267.

Andrews, Anthony P., E. Wyllys Andrews V, and Fernando Robles Castellanos. 2003. The Northern Maya Collapse and It's Aftermath. *Ancient Mesoamerica* 14:151–156.

Andrews, Anthony P., Frank Asaro, Helen V. Michel, Fred H. Stross, and Pura Cervera Rivero. 1989. "The Obsidian Trade at Isla Cerritos, Yucatán, Mexico." *Journal of Field Archaeology* 16(3):355–362.

Andrews, Anthony P., Tomás Gallareta Negrón, and Rafael Cobos Palma. 1989. "Preliminary Report of the Cupul Survey Project." *Mexicon* 11(5):91–95.

Andrews, Anthony P., Tomás Gallareta Negrón, Fernando Robles Castellanos, Rafael Cobos Palma, and Pura Cervera Rivero. 1988. "Isla Cerritos: An Itzá Trading Port on the North Coast of Yucatán, Mexico." *National Geographic Research* 4(2): 196–207.

Andrews, Anthony P., and Fernando Robles Castellanos. 1985. "Chichen Itza and Coba: An Itza-Maya Standoff in Early Postclassic Yucatan." In *The Lowland Maya Postclassic*, ed. Arlen F. Chase and Prudence M. Rice, 62–72. Austin: University of Texas Press.

Appadurai, Arjun. 1988. "How to Make a National Cuisine: Cookbooks in Contemporary India." *Comparative Studies in Society and History* 30(1):3–24.

Ardren, Traci. 2015. *Social Identities in the Classic Maya Northern Lowlands: Gender, Age, Memory, and Place*. Austin: University of Texas Press.

———, ed. 2017. *Informe técnico (parcial) de la segunda fase de investigación y trabajo de campo (2010)*. Report submitted to the Instituto Nacional de Antropología e Historia, Mexico City, Mexico.

Ardren, Traci, and Alejandra Alonso Olvera. 2017. "Los mayas del Clásico Terminal en Xuenkal: Una población asociada a Chichén Itzá." *Arqueologia Mexicana* 25 (145):53–58.

Ardren, Traci, Alejandra Alonso Olvera, and T. Kam Manahan. 2016. "The Artisans of Terminal Classic Xuenkal, Yucatan, Mexico: Gender and Craft during a Period of Economic Change." In *Gendered Labor in Specialized Economies: Archaeological Perspectives on Male and Female Work*, ed. S. Kelly and T. Ardren, 91–116. Boulder: University Press of Colorado.

Ardren, Traci, Rafael Burgos V., T. Kam Manahan, Sara Dzul G., and José Estrada F. 2005. "Recent Investigations at Xuenkal, Yucatán." *Mexicon* 27(5):92–97.

Ardren, Traci, and Justin P. Lowry. 2011. "The Travels of Maya Merchants in the Ninth and Tenth Centuries AD: Investigations at Xuenkal and the Greater Cupul Province, Yucatan, Mexico." *World Archaeology* 43(3):428–443.

Ardren, Traci, T. Kam Manahan, Julie K. Wesp, and Alejandra Alonso Olvera. 2010. "Cloth Production and Economic Intensification in the Area Surrounding Chichen Itza." *Latin American Antiquity* 21(3):274–289.

Ardren, Traci, and Christopher T. Morehart. N.d. "Microbotanical Remains from Grater Bowls at Xuenkal." Manuscript in preparation for submission to Proceedings of the National Academy of Sciences.

Ayora-Diaz, Steffan, ed. 2016. *Cooking Technology: Transformations in Culinary Practice in Mexico and Latin America*. London: Bloomsbury.

Bey, George J., III 2001. "The Role of Ceramics in the Study of Conflict in Maya Archaeology." In *Ancient Mesoamerican Warfare*, ed. M. Kathryn Brown and Travis W. Stanton, 19–30. Walnut Creek, CA: Altamira Press.

Bíró, Péter, and Eduardo Pérez de Heredia. 2018. "La organización política y el paisaje de Chichén Itzá, Yucatán, México en el período Clásico Terminal (830–930 DC)." *Latin American Antiquity* 29(2):207–221.

Brainerd, George W. 1958. *The Archaeological Ceramics of Yucatan*. University of California Anthropological Records, Vol. 19. Berkeley: University of California Press.

Braswell, Geoffrey E. 2000. "Obsidian Exchange Spheres." In *The Postclassic Mesoamerican World*, ed. Michael E. Smith and Frances F. Berdan, 131–158. Salt Lake City: University of Utah Press.

Caballero-Arias, Hortensia. 2016. "From Bitter Root to Flat Bread: Technology, Food, and Culinary Transformations of Cassava in Venezuelan Amazon." In *Cooking Technology: Transformations in Culinary Practice in Mexico and Latin America*, ed. S. Agor-Diaz, 41–54. Bloomsbury: London.

Cobos, Rafael. 2007. "Multepal or Centralized Kingship? New Evidence on Governmental Organization at Chichén Itzá." In *Twin Tollans: Chichén Itzá, Tula, and the Epiclassic to Early Postclassic Mesoamerican World*, ed. Jeff K. Kowalski and Cynthia Kristan-Graham, 314–343. Cambridge, MA: Harvard University Press.

———. 2016. *Arqueología en Chichén Itzá: Nuevas explicaciones*. Mérida: Ediciones de la Universidad Autónoma de Yucatán.

Cohodas, Marvin. 1989. "The Epiclassic Problem: A Review and Alternative Model." In *Mesoamerica after the Decline of Teotihuacan, AD 700–900*, ed. Richard A. Diehl and Janet Catherine Berlo, 219–240. Washington, DC: Dumbarton Oaks Research Library and Collection.

Costin, Cathy L. 2004. "Craft Economies of Ancient Andean States." In *Archaeological Perspectives on Political Economies*, ed. Gary M. Feinman, Linda M. Nichols, and James M. Skibo, 189–223. Salt Lake City: University of Utah Press.

Crown, Patricia L. 2000. "Women's Role in Changing Cuisine." In *Women and Men in the Prehispanic Southwest*, ed. Patricia L. Crown, 221–266. Santa Fe, NM: School of American Research.

Dietler, Michael. 1990. "Driven by Drink: The Role of Drinking in the Political Economy and the Case of Early Iron Age France." *Journal of Anthropological Archaeology* 9(4):352–406.

———. 2001. "Theorizing the Feast: Rituals of Consumption, Commensal Politics, and Power in African Contexts." In *Feasts: Archaeological and Ethnographic Perspectives on Food, Politics, and Power*, ed. Michael Dietler and Brian Hayden, 65–114. Washington, DC: Smithsonian Institution Press.

Firth, Raymond. 1983. "Magnitudes and Values in Kula Exchange." In *The Kula: New Perspectives on Massim Exchange*, ed. Jerry W. Leach and Edmund Leach, 89–117. Cambridge: Cambridge University Press.

García Solís, Claudia Araceli. 2017. "Archaeology and Tourism: The Performance of Conservation at the World Heritage Site of Chichen Itza." PhD diss., School of Archaeology, La Trobe University.

Glover, Jeffrey B., Zachary X. Hruby, Dominique Rissolo, Joseph W. Ball, Michael D. Glascock, and M. Steven Shackley. 2018. "Interregional Interaction in Terminal Classic Yucatan: Recent Obsidian and Ceramic Data from Vista Alegre, Quintana Roo, Mexico." *Latin American Antiquity* 29(3):475–494.

Hastorf, Christine A. 2017. *The Social Archaeology of Food: Thinking about Eating from Prehistory to the Present*. New York: Cambridge University Press.

Hayden, Brian. 2014. *The Power of Feasts: From Prehistory to the Present*. Cambridge: Cambridge University Press.

Healan, Dan M. 2007. "New Perspectives on Tula's Obsidian Industry and Its Relationship to Chichén Itzá." In *Twin Tollans: Chichén Itzá, Tula, and the Epiclassic to Early Postclassic Mesoamerican World*, ed. Jeff K. Kowalski and Cynthia Kristan-Graham, 429–447. Cambridge, MA: Harvard University Press.

Ichijo, Atsuko, and Ronald Ranta. 2016. *Food, National Identity and Nationalism: From Everyday to Global Politics*. London: Palgrave Macmillan.

Isbell, William H. 2000. "What We Should Be Studying: The 'Imagined Community' and the 'Natural Community.'" In *The Archaeology of Communities: A New World Perspective*, ed. Marcello A. Canuto and Jason Yaeger, 243–266. New York: Routledge.

Johnson, Scott A. J. 2015. "The Roots of Sotuta: Dzitas Slate as a Yucatecan Tradition." *Ancient Mesoamerica* 26(1):113–126.

Kristan-Graham, Cynthia. 2018. "The Least Earth: Curated Landscapes at Chichen Itza." In *Landscapes of the Itza*, ed. L. Wren, C. Kristan-Graham, T. Nygard, and K. Spencer, 226–257. Gainesville: University Press of Florida.

Kristan-Graham, Cynthia, and Linnea Wren. 2018. "Introduction: Looking Backward, Looking Forward at Chichen Itza." In *Landscapes of the Itza*, ed. L. Wren, C. Kristan-Graham, T. Nygard, and K. Spencer, 1–27. Gainesville: University Press of Florida.

Magnoni, Aline, Traci Ardren, Scott Hutson, and Bruce Dahlin. 2014. "The Production of Space and Identity at Classic-Period Chunchucmil, Yucatán, Mexico." In *Making Ancient Cities: Space and Place in Early Urban Societies*, ed. A. Creekmore and K. Fisher, 145–180. Cambridge: Cambridge University Press.

Manahan, T. Kam, Traci Ardren, and Alejandra Alonso Olvera. 2012. "Household Organization and the Dynamics of State Expansion: The Late Classic–Terminal Classic Transformation at Xuenkal, Yucatan, Mexico." *Ancient Mesoamerica* 23(2):345–364.

Marcus, Joyce. 2012. "Yucatan at the Crossroads." In *The Ancient Maya of Mexico: Reinterpreting the Past of the Northern Maya Lowlands*, ed. Geoffrey E. Braswell, 349–372. Bristol, CT: Equinox.

Méndez Cab, Alan Enrique. 2016. "Estudio de las formas cerámicas del Grupo Dzitas de Chichén Itzá." In *Arqueología en Chichén Itzá: Nuevas explicaciones*, ed. Rafael Cobos, 83–96. Mérida: Ediciones de la Universidad Autónoma de Yucatán.

Miller, Virginia E. 2018. "The Castillo-sub at Chichen Itza: A Reconsideration." In *Landscapes of the Itza*, ed. L. Wren, C. Kristan-Graham, T. Nygard, and K. Spencer, 171–197. Gainesville: University Press of Florida.

Neff, Hector. 2001. "Production and Distribution of Plumbate Pottery: Evidence from a Provenance Study of the Paste and Slip Clay Used in a Famous Mesoamerican Tradeware." Report Submitted to FAMSI, famsi.org/reports/98061.

Nikolic, Mona. 2016. "Cooking Techniques as Markers of Identity and Authenticity in Costa Rica's Afro-Caribbean Foodways." In *Cooking Technology: Transformations in Culinary Practice in Mexico and Latin America*, ed. Steffan Ayora-Diaz, 167–180. London: Bloomsbury.

Palmer, Catherine. 1998. "From Theory to Practice: Experiencing the Nation in Everyday Life." *Journal of Material Culture* 3(2):175–199.

Pérez de Heredia, Eduardo. 1998. "Chen K'u: La cerámica del Cenote Sagrado de Chichén Itzá." FAMSI Report 9760. http://www.famsi.org/reports/97061es/97061esPerezdeHeredia01.pdf.

———. 2012. "The Yabnal-Motul Ceramic Complex of the Late Classic Period at Chichen Itza." *Ancient Mesoamerica* 23(2):379–402.

Pérez Monfort, Ricardo. 2004. "El mole como símbolo de la mexicanidad." *Patrimonio Cultural y Turismo Cuadernos* (Mexico City: Consejo Nacional para la Cultura y las Artes) 12:71–86.

Price, T. Douglas, Vera Tiesler, and Carolyn Freiwald. 2019. "Place of Origin of the Sacrificial Victims in the Sacred Cenote, Chichén Itzá, Mexico." *American Journal of Physical Anthropology* 170(1):98–115.

Ringle, William M. 1990. "Who Was Who in Ninth-Century Chichen Itza?" *Ancient Mesoamerica* 1(2):233–243.

Ringle, William M., Tomás Gallareta Negrón, and George J. Bey III. 1998. "The Return of Quetzalcoatl: Evidence for the Spread of a World Religion during the Epiclassic Period." *Ancient Mesoamerica* 9(2):183–232.

Rivas Romero, Javier. 2017. "Análisis zooarqueológico de la fauna vertebrada, Temporadas de Campo 2010–2011, Xuenkal." In *Informe técnico (parcial) de la segunda fase de investigación y Trabajo de Campo (2010)*, ed. Traci Ardren, 134–154. Report submitted to the Instituto Nacional de Antropología e Historia, Mexico City, Mexico.

Rivas Romero, Javier, Christopher Götz, Traci Ardren, Alejandra Alonso, Justin Lowry, and T. Kam Manahan. 2018. "La explotación de recursos faunísticos en el sitio maya yucateco de Xuenkal durante el Clásico Tardío y Terminal." *Mexicon* 40:167–174.

Robles Castellanos, Fernando. 2006. "Las esferas cerámicas Cehpeh y Sotuta del apogeo del Clásico Tardío (730–900 DC) en el norte de la península de Yucatán." In *La producción alfarera en el México Antiguo III*, ed. Beatriz L. Merino C. and Angel García Cook, 281–344. Mexico City: Instituto Nacional de Antropología e Historia.

Robles Salmerón, María Amparo, Travis Stanton, and Aline Magnoni. 2011. "Investigaciones preliminares en el sitio de Ikil, Yucatán." *Estudios de Cultura Maya* 19: 125–140.

Schmidt, Peter. 2000. "Nuevos datos sobre la arqueología e iconografía de Chichén Itzá." *Los Investigadores de la Cultura Maya* (Campeche, Mex.: Universidad Autónoma de Campeche) 8:38–48.

———. 2003. "Siete años entre los itzá: Nuevas excavaciones en Chichén Itzá y sus resultados." In *Escondido en la selva: Arqueología en el norte de Yucatán*, ed. Hans Prem, 53–63. Mexico City: Instituto Nacional de Antropología e Historia and Bonn: University of Bonn.

Smith, J. Gregory, and Tara Bond-Freeman. 2017. "In the Shadow of Quetzalcoatl: How Small Communities in Northern Yucatan Responded to the Chichen Itza Phenomenon." In *Landscapes of the Itza*, ed. L. Wren, C. Kristan-Graham, T. Nygard, and K. Spencer, 138–170. Gainesville: University Press of Florida.

Smith, Robert E. 1971. *The Pottery of Mayapan: Including Studies of Ceramic Material from Uxmal, Kabah, and Chichen Itza*. Papers of the Peabody Museum of Archaeology and Ethnology, Vol. 66. Cambridge, MA: Peabody Museum at Harvard University.

Stanton, Travis W., and Tomás Gallareta Negrón. 2001. "Warfare, Ceramic Economy, and the Itza: A Reconsideration of the Itza Polity in Ancient Yucatan." *Ancient Mesoamerica* 12(2):229–245.

Taube, Karl A. 1989. "The Maize Tamale in Classic Maya Diet, Epigraphy, and Art." *American Antiquity* 54(1):31–51.

Taube, Karl A., José Francisco Osorio León, Francisco Pérez Ruíz, Rocío González de la Mata, and Travis W. Stanton. In press. *Ducks, Monkeys, and Cacao: Recent Investigations at the Initial Series Group, Chichen Itza, Yucatan*. San Francisco: Precolumbia Mesoweb Press.

Taylor, Charles. 2002. "Modern Social Imaginaries." *Public Culture* 14(1):91–124.

Tozzer, Alfred M. 1957. *Chichén Itzá and Its Cenote of Sacrifice*. Memoirs of the Peabody Museum of Archaeology and Ethnology, Vol. 11–12. Cambridge, MA: Peabody Museum at Harvard University.

Volta, Beniamino, and Geoffrey E. Braswell. 2014. "Alternative Narratives and Missing Data: Refining the Chronology of Chichen Itza." In *The Maya and Their Central American Neighbors: Settlement Patterns, Architecture, Hieroglyphic Texts, and Ceramics*, ed. Geoffrey E. Braswell, 356–403. London: Routledge.

CHAPTER 11

Faunal Foods as Indices of Commoner Wealth (or Poverty) in Rural versus Urban Houselots of the Terminal Classic and Postclassic in Northwest Yucatán

MARILYN A. MASSON, TIMOTHY S. HARE,
BRADLEY W. RUSSELL, CARLOS PERAZA LOPE,
AND JESSICA L. CAMPBELL

Zooarchaeologists have long considered whether proprietary privileges contributed to food resource inequalities (Emery 2003; Götz 2011; Hamblin 1984; Masson 1999; Masson and Peraza Lope 2008; Pohl 1985; Reitz and Scarry 1985). While generalizations do not apply to Maya sites across time and space (Masson 2004; Montero-López 2009), it is reasonable to ask to what degree were faunal resources treated as commodities like other foods and craft goods at various points in time and space in the political economies of the region? Patterns of scarce or absent faunal bone also reflect the greater relative importance of plant foods at the household scale (Morell-Hart, this volume).

In this chapter, we consider the meaning of faunal scarcity at humble rural houselots of the Terminal Classic (850–1100 CE) and Postclassic periods (ca. 1100–1500 CE) in the Mayapán vicinity of the northwestern plains physiographic region of the Yucatán Peninsula (Figure 11.1). The study area is defined by a 40 km² settlement zone, centered on the small town center of Tichac (modern Telchaquillo) in Terminal Classic times, and surrounding the large, walled, urban political capital of Mayapán during the Postclassic. Meat-poor rural residents clearly relied more heavily on concoctions of botanical foods cooked in ceramic vessels and such staples as maize, prepared with grinding stones commonly present at dwellings of all periods. Rural foodways for seven of the eight fully excavated rural houselots in this sample differed from those of affluent commoners living in certain neighborhoods within the walled urban city of Mayapán during the Postclassic period. However, the paucity of fauna in most of the rural con-

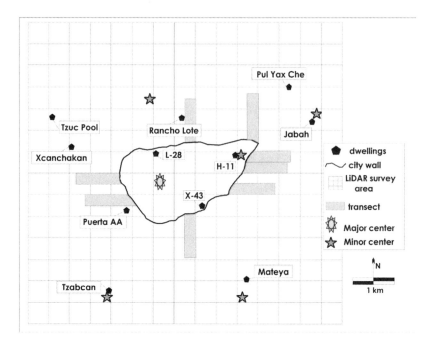

Figure 11.1. Map of the 40 km² LiDAR survey study area showing the locations of fully excavated dwellings mentioned in the text, relative to the Mayapán city wall. Terminal Classic rural dwellings include Pul Yax Che, Tzuc Pool, Mateya, and Tzabcan. Postclassic rural dwellings include Jabah, Rancho Lote, Camino Xcanchakan, and Puerta AA. Postclassic urban dwellings include Structures L-28, H-11, and X-43.

texts reflects a broader pattern of food inequality for poorer households of the study area. One rural houselot accessed faunal resources to the same extent as poorer urban commoners living on the edge of the walled urban settlement. Comparisons to test pit results in the rural and urban zone further buttress the findings from rural, fully excavated contexts, and indicate that faunal resources were accessed differentially among commoners. These results suggest no simple rural-urban or temporal dichotomies with respect to access to faunal foods and other desired commodities. These data also revise a general view, from prior studies, that commoners uniformly tended to be more affluent in the Postclassic period due to enhanced opportunities for commercial exchange (e.g., Masson 2000; Sabloff and Rathje 1975) by highlighting the existence of rural and urban poor. The Terminal Classic houselots in this sample provide a longer-term perspective on relative rural impoverishment.

Status and power regularly affected the distribution of preferred cuts of meat in complex societies and also the overall quantity and diversity of animals obtained (e.g., deFrance 2009, Table 1; Driver 2004; Haller, Feinman, and Nicholas 2006; Lepovsky et al. 1996; Masson 1999; Masson and Peraza Lope 2008, 2013; Pohl 1985). Hunting rights were often restricted by elites in premodern states (e.g., deFrance 2009:127; Jackson and Scott 2003; Pohl 1989:153–154; Teeter and Chase 2004). When scarcity is documented in the archaeological record, how do we determine whether natural resource shortages were to blame or whether have-not households were prevented from accessing wild foods for culturally restrictive reasons? Both factors could have been influential, with the former likely amplifying the latter. In the Contact period (ca. 1502–1540 CE) in Yucatán, immediately following the Postclassic era, Spaniards were impressed with the bountiful quantities of deer—and their apparent tameness (Landa 1941:4; Masson and Peraza Lope 2013:273; Tozzer 1941:186n972). Scarcity at some Postclassic house groups is thus surprising. Elsewhere on the Yucatán Peninsula, Postclassic Maya residential contexts are associated with abundant faunal remains, especially white-tailed deer, brocket deer, peccary, or turkey (Emery 2003; Götz 2007, 2008, 2010, 2011; Götz and Sierra 2011; Götz and Stanton 2013; Hamblin 1984; Masson 2004; Masson and Peraza Lope 2008; Scott 1980, 1982; Shaw and Mangan 1994). Smaller taxa such as iguana, fish, and armadillo and unusual foods such as crocodile and tapir varied in popularity in polities distributed across differentiated ecological zones of the Maya Lowlands; preferences also changed over time (Carr 1996; Hamblin 1984; Masson 2004; Mock 1994). Surely, in a land such as northwest Yucatán, overrun today with iguana, access to such ubiquitous small game would have been nearly impossible for elites to control. Iguana bones are among those most commonly recovered within urban Postclassic Mayapán (Masson and Peraza Lope 2008, Table 2).

Yet in the rural outskirts of Mayapán, few animal bones were recovered (not even those of iguana) at humble Postclassic dwellings and their precursors in the Terminal Classic. This chapter considers whether these parallel data reflect similar or different environmental or political factors. In contrast, faunal bone is more abundant at some commoner houselots of the urban zone of the Postclassic city. Rural farmers, living closer to the field and forest margins, should have enjoyed liberal access to animal foods, and yet, they did not. Pottery vessels, along with grinding stones, represent the primary evidence for preparing, storing, and consuming foods, presumably of a botanical nature, at peripheral or poorer households.

Background

Four factors represent the usual explanatory culprits invoked in explaining faunal abundance or the opposite circumstance, faunal scarcity. The first of these is environmental conditions, especially droughts affecting ecological environments and the availability of animal resources. The second is preservation. The absence of organic remains, such as bones, is potentially due to the weathering in shallow soils or certain soil chemistry conditions. The third is sampling; inadequate sample sizes or lack of parity in sampling of specific types of contexts can lead to a failure to recover objects such as faunal bone. The fourth factor is social. Obtaining or consuming animal resources may be a privilege controlled by elites. Other factors, such as ethnicity and related food aversions, may account for discrepancies, but these are unlikely within a single study area such as the Mayapán vicinity where other indicators of ethnic social distinctions are rare or exhibited only for elites (Masson and Peraza Lope 2010, 2013).

Shortages

Many years ago, Marilyn Masson (1993:261) addressed the problem of Terminal Classic animal bone scarcity in northeastern Belize, suggesting that the ninth-century droughts and high human population levels resulted in a paucity of game. Newer data reveal catastrophic droughts during the eleventh century as well (Kennett et al. 2012). Subsequent to the Terminal Classic, paleoenvironmental studies revealed the return of high forest environments to the area in the Postclassic (e.g., Turner and Sabloff 2012), when human population levels gradually rebounded. At Laguna de On (Belize), a small hinterland village, animal bone was plentiful in Postclassic contexts. This correlation led Masson to infer that animal resources thrived in the reforested habitat of the Postclassic period. Animal bones at Laguna de On include deer, crocodile, and tapir (a species known to thrive in high forest) and a range of other diverse, smaller animals (Masson 1993, Table 21; 2004). In contrast, Terminal Classic era faunal bone at Laguna de On and nearby sites in the area was so scarce that a salted catfish export industry developed at coastal locations in Belize, such as Northern River Lagoon, to provision the interior (Masson 2004; Mock 1994). The argument for scarcity of faunal resources during the Terminal Classic gained little traction for many years but is now more accepted (Emery 2007), particularly following increased documentation of Terminal Classic era droughts in the Southern as well as Northern Lowlands (Douglas et al.

2015; Gill 2001; Hodell, Curtis, and Brenner 1995; Hoggarth et al. 2016; Kennett et al. 2012). Acknowledging the importance of environmental impacts to faunal resources in certain populous areas of the Terminal Classic Lowlands does not deny that in some more thinly populated regions, environmental pressures were insignificant (Emery, Wright, and Schwarcz 2000; Wright 2006).

Taphonomy

Factor number two, taphonomic preservation, is irrelevant for this study for several reasons. Where human bone preserves, animal bone does also. Late and Terminal Classic Maya sites in this region frequently have human remains (Tiesler et al. 2010) along with faunal bones (Götz 2008, 2011; Götz and Stanton 2013). Similarly, Terminal Classic and Postclassic contexts investigated by Masson (1993) at Laguna de On, Belize, also had human bone; both contexts were in shallow soils, but only the Postclassic era deposits had faunal bone. Urban Mayapán, the settlement zone within the city's 9.1 km circumferential wall, is riddled with human burials and other mortuary deposits (Serafin 2010, 2020; Smith 1962), and faunal bone is richly concentrated in middens and other houselot spaces excavated in contexts across the city. In the study area, sixty-one test pits yielded faunal remains, and thirty-seven of these contexts had fifty or more bones per cubic meter. Full horizontal excavations of three ordinary houses within the city wall (urban zone) yielded faunal bone densities (per cubic meter) ranging from 3.1 to 12.9, and commoner crafting houses had more, ranging from 80.3 to 174.8 per cubic meter. Mayapán's rural houses are, like many of their urban counterparts, partly visible at the surface, with shallow depths like those of ordinary houses near the interior edges of the walled city. These urban houses near the edge of the city had artifact assemblages that suggest their inhabitants were poorer, engaged in less diverse economic activities, and built their houses later compared to commoners located in the more densely settled, longer-lived neighborhoods of the city (Masson and Peraza Lope 2014a). Given these parallels, there is no reason to infer that preservation was poorer in the rural area than in the urban zone. Two rural Terminal Classic occupations of houses of the eight evaluated in this chapter had preserved burials, despite the lack of faunal bone for this period. We can rule out uneven bone preservation as a factor in this study.

Sampling

Initial feedback that we received on this study asked whether differential sampling accounted for a relative absence of fauna in the rural contexts compared to urban Mayapán, but this is unlikely. Although middens are denser, deeper, and more extensive in the tightly occupied downtown Mayapán, toward the outskirts of the inner walled city, where settlement density is lighter and room existed for expansion, houselots are nonetheless tightly bounded by *albarrada* walls (large limestone boulder walls that delimit the area of residential spaces). An extensive test pit sampling program across the city revealed that household trash was discarded in and around dwellings, and within or just outside of these houselot walls. Urban dwellings near the city wall replicate the concentrated features and debris of the crowded downtown area but at a more modest scale. Test pits in open spaces between houselots, by comparison, had sparser debris. At Mayapán's urban houselots, animal bones are scattered across the floors of structure interiors or patio spaces, in addition to their recovery in midden deposits. For example, urban commoner house I-55 had from 17 to 189 bones recovered within 2 × 2 m excavation units that sampled interior and patio spaces; most grid squares across this horizontally excavated dwelling also yielded faunal bone, although more was found in middens. At a poorer urban house, H-11, bones recovered from 2 × 2 m grid squares in interior or patio spaces ranged from 10 to 84 bones per unit. Horizontal excavation methods were replicated in the urban and rural zones, with samples from interior dwelling and patio spaces, as well as potential refuse zones to the sides and rear of the dwellings and along the edges of houselot boundary walls. For all rural and urban dwellings, excavations sampled at least 19 cubic meters. Sampling methods in the rural zone would have at least recovered some bone, rather than none at all, as is the case for seven of eight dwellings.

Proprietary Use

Gastropolitics resulted in preferential animal use at numerous sites across the Maya Lowlands. Leslie Shaw (1991) recognized the use of dogs for festive events in the town center of Colha, Belize, during the Late Preclassic period. Dogs were also reserved as a ceremonial food at Mayapán (Masson and Peraza Lope 2013, Table 6) and at Cozumel (Hamblin 1984: 113). Monumental centers also generally reveal greater access to faunal resources, as measured by quantity, quality, or diversity, at public buildings where elites sponsored events (Emery 2003; Masson and Peraza Lope 2008; Pohl 1985). It is noteworthy that where Late/Terminal Classic animal bone exists in northern Yucatán, it is from higher-status contexts (Götz 2007, 2008, 2011). Bone tools are also common in northern Yucatán during this period (Ardren 2002). When resources were scarce, as for deer on the island of Cozumel, animal bones suitable for toolmaking, such as antlers and metapodials, were valuable imported commodities (Carr 1996). Deer skulls were especially valued at Mayapán, with restricted distributions, and they are conspicuously scarce relative to postcranial remains (Masson and Peraza Lope 2008:176). Isotopic bone chemistry studies suggest that some Maya sites obtained deer from well beyond their local catchment areas in Belize (Freiwald 2010; Thornton 2011; Yaeger and Freiwald 2009), presumably through trade.

Mayapán's monumental center exhibits greater faunal diversity than its residential zone, attesting to the consumption of exotic animal products such as felines and tapir (Masson and Peraza Lope 2008). The distribution of preferred cuts benefited higher-status members of society even at small sites such as Laguna de On (Masson 1999). Contact period accounts (Landa 1941:92, 106, 141, 158) and the Maya codices (Götz 2007; Tozzer and Allen 1910:289–290) reveal that choice cuts of meat were presented at ritual occasions as gifts brought to, and consumed at, important ritual events. Yet deer meat, including all body parts, is widely distributed across urban Mayapán. At monumental center buildings, animals were brought to ritual localities in their entirety and butchered and cooked onsite (Masson and Peraza Lope 2013). Frequently at Mayapán, full-sized subadult deer (animals reaching adult size, but with unfused long bone ends) are present in such high proportions that we have suggested animal husbandry as an important industry for the city (Masson and Peraza Lope 2008:176–178). After Mayapán fell, its former governors, the Cocom, withheld "game and fruit" in a trade embargo with the coastal Ah Kin Chel polity, with whom they were accustomed to trading for fish and salt (Landa 1941:40). This passage attests to food trade, including deer. White-tailed and brocket deer, along with many other animals, presumably would have roamed the forests and fields between the Postclassic cities and towns of the peninsula, and some were raised in captivity (Masson and Peraza Lope 2008), along with turkeys. How then, could rural families toiling in support of the city fail to access these food sources?

A hierarchy of taxa seems to have existed at the Postclassic site of Laguna de On (and for Postclassic Colha), with larger game exhibiting preferential distribution compared to certain smaller animals such as armadillo (Masson 1999). Even if access to larger game animals was subject to sumptuary rules, rural residents should have opportunistically been able to obtain coatimundi, small birds, iguana, cenote fish, gophers, and other small taxa still consumed by villagers in northern Yucatán today. A total of 46,771 bones have been identified to taxa from Mayapán's site center (1996–2004 excavations), with an additional 33,149 from the residential zone (2002–2009). The most abundant remains are those of white-tailed deer, brocket deer, peccary, turkey, and iguana. Twenty-one species of fish, and lesser proportions of small mammals, including ringtail (*Bassariscus astutus*, a mammal of the raccoon family), porcupine, rabbit, gopher, other rodents, foxes, grison, felines, coati, agouti, manatee, tapir, opossum, and armadillo, along with crocodile, turtle, frogs, and snakes, were also identified (Masson and Peraza Lope 2008, Tables 1–3).

A Word about Demography

The argument for resource scarcity does not rest solely on the effects of climate change. It is part of a more complex equation involving variables of human demand and environmental capacities. Universal explanations for the collapse of Classic period Maya society do not fit for every set of city-states and their subject towns, and the record sometimes shows longer-term resilience and recovery during or following periodic shortages of the Classic and Postclassic periods (Demarest, Rice, and Rice 2004; McAnany and Yoffee 2009). The length and frequency of the ninth-century droughts, on the other hand, tipped the balance for southern polities. Peripheral kingdoms that tied their political and economic fortunes to hubs in the central Petén would have experienced profound collateral damage (Gill 2001; Turner and Sabloff 2012).

It is unclear whether settlement studies are currently refined enough to quantify the effects of population pressure on resources heading into the ninth and tenth centuries. Demographic purists require temporal control well beyond the grasp of the average regional archaeological project, but surveys of the northern Yucatán generally find that populations peaked during the Terminal Classic period. This population zenith included urban and countryside zones (Hanson 2008; Hixson 2011; Houck 2004; Johnson 2000; Smith 2000). In an area of 40 km² around Mayapán, Terminal Classic houses were dispersed with such regularity that each was within sight of another dwelling in all directions. This sprawl was associated with the small town center of the Late/Terminal Classic period, Tichac (modern

Telchaquillo), a Rank IV center in the regional system (Garza Tarazona de González and Kurjack Bacso 1980). Postclassic settlement was also considerable, if dispersed, outside of the city wall and expanded Mayapán's urban population by around 30 percent (Russell 2008).

Thus, the relatively continuous countryside settlement of Terminal Classic date is characteristic of large tracts across the northwest plains, including the Mayapán environs. Dispersed, regular housing and cultivated landscapes created an anthropogenically managed countryside. Options for trading food during shortages may have been curtailed by significantly high populations. Exceptionally high populations in the Terminal Classic period would have contributed to predation pressure on animal populations and, presumably, their increased value in exchange. A final drought of eighty years in length (1020–1100 CE) would have been far more difficult to endure than shorter, yet devastating rainfall shortages before and after this period (Hoggarth et al. 2016, 2017; Kennett et al. 2012, Figure 2). Beyond the study area, Postclassic settlement levels are lower than Terminal Classic ones in rural zones between town centers, according to the results of surveys referred to previously. Nonetheless, the Mayapán polity experienced its own series of droughts, famines, and correlating unrest that resulted in large-scale flight and nearly collapsed the polity during the fourteenth century, but for a brief respite and recovery just after 1400 CE (Masson and Peraza Lope 2014b). Droughts and famine also had disastrous consequences in the late sixteenth and seventeenth centuries (Hoggarth et al. 2017; Masson and Peraza Lope 2014b, Table 8.1; Quezada 2014).

Despite the Terminal Classic and Postclassic rural faunal scarcities discussed here, animal foods were available to residents of regional centers, as indicated by Christopher Götz's research (2007, 2008, 2011; Götz and Stanton 2013). Thus, faunal resources existed, but rural families did not access them. Rural households were poorer than their urban counterparts, with fewer options for provisioning themselves with game and fowl via hunting or via the marketplace. Why? Were tribute obligations so heavy and costs so high that animal foods were priced beyond the means of farming families? Were animal resources demanded among tax payments imposed on farmers? Were sumptuary laws in effect, and were these tied to climate-related shortages? Did such factors work in combination?

Contrary to the prevailing rural pattern in our sample, the precocious rural Postclassic houselot (residential group) of Jabah differs from the other rural dwellings in a variety of ways, and the greater relative affluence of its residents correlates with the recovery of animal bones at this

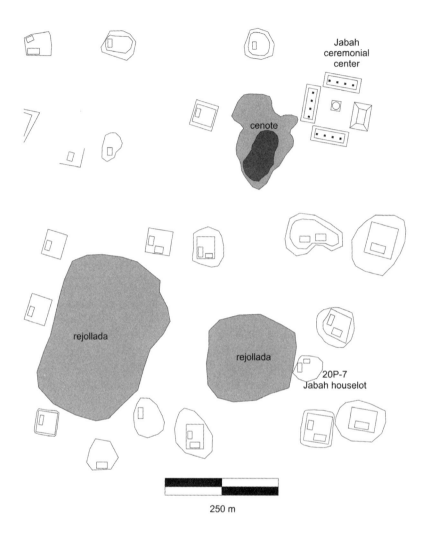

Figure 11.2. Map showing the location of the Jabah minor monumental center, cenote, and Jabah houselot (20P-7) discussed in the text. This houselot's architecture and platform is modest compared to adjacent commoner architecture in terms of platform elevation and construction fill. Note the two *rejolladas* (depressions) to the immediate west of the houselot, which are of the sort that served as moisture traps and agrarian features in the region.

context. This exception reminds us that even in rural zones, the fates of families were variable and affected by historical contingencies or social advantages tied to geographic location. The Jabah houselot and those to which it is compared are described in greater detail in the section below.

Urban and Rural Houses Sampled at Mayapán

In 2013, the authors of this chapter, in collaboration with the National Center for Airborne Laser Mapping (NCALM), conducted a LiDAR survey and ground-checking program of a 40 km² area representing the near periphery of Mayapán, focusing on settlement outside of the city walls (see Figure 11.1). Our prior research in the urban zone provided a robust view of relatively affluent commoner life, especially for nonelite house groups engaged in surplus crafting (Masson and Peraza Lope 2014a, Masson et al. 2016). Most households, irrespective of occupation, possessed nonlocal trade goods. Other "ordinary" (nonsurplus crafter) houselots provide helpful comparisons, perhaps representing the residences of full-time cultivators; they were less affluent than contexts engaged in surplus crafting. However, this prior work lacked a rural perspective. How did wealth compare between residents living within and outside of the wall? Were there parallels in agrarian lifeways before (Terminal Classic) and after the rise of the Postclassic capital?

The LiDAR survey indicated a continuous distribution of dwellings across the entire 40 km² area (Hare, Masson, and Russell 2014). Particularly populous were Terminal Classic and Postclassic era populations. In 2015, we returned to horizontally excavate a sample of peripheral dwellings, including four Terminal Classic and four Postclassic contexts (see Figure 11.1). Most of these dwellings were probably occupied by farming families, given the lack of evidence for occupational specialization, which for crafting, is easily recognized by surface deposits of debris within urban Mayapán (Masson and Peraza Lope 2014a; Masson et al. 2016). From Bradley Russell's (2008) prior survey transect and test pitting program (see Figure 11.1), we knew that material densities tended to be low outside the city wall and that evidence for surplus crafting was not found in this zone.

The Terminal Classic and Postclassic dwellings discussed in this chapter are referred to as rural, but that term has different meanings for the settings of each. The Terminal Classic houses were in the periphery of a Rank IV town (Telchaquillo/Tichac), some 30 km from the nearest Rank

III center at Yaxcopoíl, according to the Garza and Kurjack regional survey (1980). These Terminal Classic houselots were both rural and remote from the largest political capitals of their day (Uxmal, Chichén Itzá). In contrast, the Postclassic dwellings lay within a thirty-minute walk of the largest political capital of the Lowlands at this time.

The results of these houselot excavations revealed three general findings (Masson et al. 2020). First, variability in rural wealth is evident from the quantity of overall possessions as well as the diversity of trade goods present (e.g., Smith 1987). Second, considerable occupational duration characterizes most rural dwellings in our sample, with two exceptions among the sample of eight. Third, all rural commoners were dependent on regional trade for goods deemed essential to daily life. They did not make their own pottery and obtained household vessels through exchange. They were not economically autonomous.

The Jabah domestic group (20P-7) that is the focus of this chapter was part of a rural sample of eight horizontally excavated houses in 2015. This group was built on the smallest platform and exhibited the least elaborate architecture within a settlement cluster of houselots located 250 meters to the south of a minor Postclassic era monumental center and cenote (see Figures 11.1, 11.2). The dwelling is located at the edge of a large depression (*rejollada*) of the sort identified as important moisture traps for agrarian activities in the region (Kepecs and Boucher 1996; Munro-Stasiuk et al. 2014), and for this reason, the Jabah houselot was thought to be a good candidate to represent a humble farmer's dwelling (Figure 11.2). Both the center and the cenote to the north of this group bear the local name of Jabah; they served as the nucleus of a satellite community located 1,500 meters to the northeast of the city wall of the urban Postclassic capital of Mayapán (Figure 11.1).

Figure 11.1 illustrates the locations of eight rural houselots discussed in this chapter, as well as fully excavated commoner houses within the urban zone of Postclassic Mayapán that represent the most appropriate comparisons due to their relatively undifferentiated activities, size, and complexity. Maps illustrate the features of eight rural houselots and three urban houselots in Figures 11.3 and 11.4. These residential contexts vary in terms of the number of dwellings per group (one or two) and the number of outbuildings, but all are within the size range of humble commoner dwellings defined for a large sample from urban Mayapán, for which most nonelite houses were from 20 to 80 m^2 (Masson, Hare, and Peraza Lope 2014:239, Figure 5.19). Seven of eight of the principal houses per group shown in Figures 11.3 and 11.4 range from 25 to 50 m^2 in size, except for

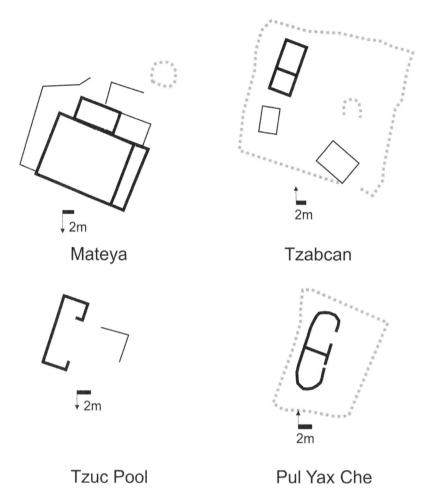

Figure 11.3. Rural Terminal Classic house group maps in the study sample. Maps drafted by Pedro Delgado Kú and Luis Flores Cobá.

Mateya (which is larger), but this dwelling lacks other correlates of status such as architectural elaboration associated with elite dwellings.

Wealth comparisons indicate that two dwelling groups, one of Terminal Classic (Mateya) and one of Postclassic date (Jabah), were located within 250–500 m of minor centers in the peripheral zone. These contexts exhibit greater nonceramic artifact diversity and quantities (Masson et al. 2020). Rural dwellings, compared to urban Mayapán crafters, were relatively poor, but for some artifact quantities, they are similar to ordinary (noncrafter) urban houselots located near the edge of the interior part of

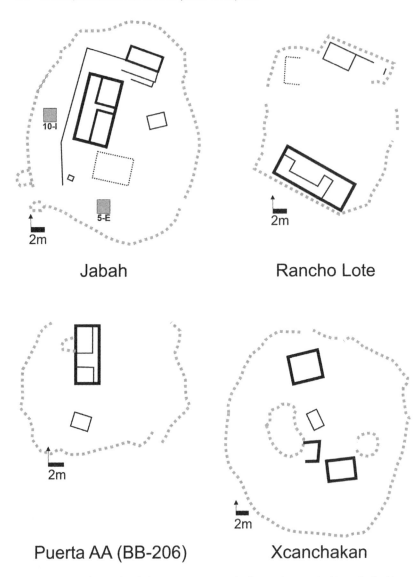

Figure 11.4. Rural Postclassic house group maps in the study sample. Maps drafted by Pedro Delgado Kú and Luis Flores Cobá.

the city wall (Figure 11.5). It is important to note that many residents (irrespective of location) engaged in low-level manufacturing of ornaments and other nonceramic goods, even when they were not explicitly engaged in surplus production (Masson et al. 2016). Part-time activities commonly complemented major household work pursuits such as agriculture, but do not seem to have contributed significant income in residential groups that generated little surplus.

The question of occupational duration and intensity is an important one. In the Puuc region, rural dwellings are inferred to have been seasonally occupied by farmers (Dunning 2004:105), a factor that would result in fewer material remains than for houses lived in year-round by full family contingents. In the Mayapán study area, dwellings are located on sizable modified hill platforms. These represent natural knolls that were enlarged and shaped into rectangular form by the addition of tons of stone fill, retaining walls, and houselot boundary walls. However, variation exists in the size and elaboration of such platforms, as is visible for the Jabah houselot (Figure 11.2). This level of investment does not seem likely for

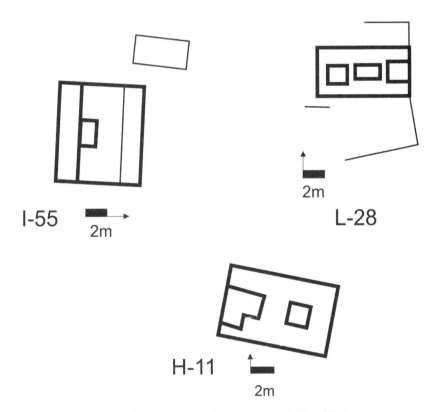

Figure 11.5. Urban Postclassic commoner houses. Houses L-28 and H-11 are located at the edge of the urban zone near the city wall as shown in Figure 11.1 and had generalized domestic assemblages, while I-55 had evidence of surplus craft production. Drawing by Marilyn A. Masson.

seasonal dwellings. Two dwellings had burials, suggesting year-round occupation or a fuller range of ordinary domestic events (including death and burial) at these contexts. Artifact assemblages from our sample are also diverse in terms of function and raw material and replicate the inventory ranges expected for typical dwellings, beyond expectations for ephemeral seasonal features.

Lesser quantities of material do not suggest that rural farmers were autonomous. Peasants and other agriculturalists of premodern states, long idealized as self-sufficient, have proven to be a heterogeneous class of people linked to regional economies in varying, sometimes complex ways (Masson and Peraza Lope 2004; Robin 2013; Sheets 2000; Wolf 1982). The rural residents in our study area at the Mayapán sample acquired most of their tools or raw materials for making them via regional exchange. Most obvious are ceramic vessels—for both periods—with ranges in slips and forms present that are common at sites elsewhere in the region. There is no evidence for rural pottery manufacture, unlike urban Mayapán, where potters' house groups exhibit exceptionally high densities of ceramic sherds and specific artifacts or features related to production, such as molds or caches of raw materials (Delgado et al. 2020; Masson et al. 2016). All eight rural dwellings tested had obsidian, with the Postclassic Jabah house exhibiting quantities comparable to or exceeding levels of ordinary (noncrafting) houses within urban Mayapán. Three Postclassic and three Terminal Classic houses also had modest quantities of marine shell debris, derived from the peninsular coasts; but once again, Jabah was the houselot with quantities comparable to ordinary houses in the urban zone (Masson et al. 2020, Table 5.1). All eight rural houses also used chert/chalcedonies of regional but nonlocal origin; three of the Postclassic houses had densities near or beyond those of ordinary urban houses at Mayapán. These nonfaunal data reveal that rural dwellers engaged in trade networks within and beyond northern Yucatán (Masson et al. 2020).

The most logical explanation for modest rural houselot artifact densities—in relative terms as compared to urban crafter houselots—is that agricultural work generally did not yield surplus quantities that would have permitted the acquisition of greater quantities of possessions and valuables (Masson et al. 2020). It is revealing that this relative austerity is also observed among urban noncrafter contexts and suggests that cultivators, whether they were living within or beyond the city wall, had poor options for accumulating wealth. It is possible that the labor burden of agricultural production, including quantities due in tribute, afforded farmers less time for other pursuits.

It is not known whether environmental constraints, heavy tribute burdens, or a combination of these were to blame. We are mindful that Doug Kennett and colleagues (2012) identified a precipitous drought of eighty years in duration during the eleventh century CE that would have severely impacted the populous countryside residents in our study area at this time. The fourteenth century was also a time of repeated environmental challenges for Mayapán (Masson and Peraza Lope 2014b), but the well-watered thirteenth century was associated with prosperity and growth. Currently, we do not possess absolute dates for Postclassic rural houselots. Should such dates reveal that peripheral occupation dates to the fourteenth rather than the thirteenth century, environmental factors would loom conspicuously as contributors to countryside wealth suppression.

Faunal Bone Quantities

Despite parallel excavation and sampling procedures in the urban and rural excavations of dwellings, only seventy-eight faunal bones were collected at one of the eight dwellings. The single house (Jabah) with fauna was of Postclassic date, not far from a Postclassic era minor center. Given the agrarian advantages of *rejolladas* (Kepecs and Boucher 1996; Munro-Stasiuk et al. 2014) and the dwelling's modest features, we anticipated it to be representative of a commoner rural Postclassic house. Instead, it was by far the most affluent and diversified residence of the eight tested, suggesting an urban effect experienced by outlying residents within a settlement cluster associated with a minor center. The other three Postclassic houses, Puerta AA, Camino Xcanchakan, and Rancho Lote, had fewer artifacts overall, and no faunal bone was recovered.

Comparing the density of faunal bone is a valid metric for this study for three reasons. First, little difference exists in the relative importance of specific animals in faunal assemblages across the site's residential zone (Masson and Peraza Lope 2008, 2013) or for the samples discussed in this chapter. Bone weight was not recorded, because deer and turkey formed the greatest proportion (relative to fewer small taxa) of most samples. Second, no evidence exists for differences in taphonomic effects or bone processing that would affect fragmentation and representation tallied by bone counts. Third, measures such as MNI (minimum number of individuals) are not helpful, given that the MNI equals one for small samples such as Jabah and other contexts compared in this chapter (Masson and Peraza Lope 2013).

Table 11.1. Postclassic faunal bone densities from full horizontal excavations at Jabah and four Postclassic houselots within Mayapán's city wall (labeled as "urban" in the table below). Surplus crafting commoner houselots (such as I-55a and Q-176) were generally more affluent compared to H-11 and L-28.

Fully excavated structures	N faunal bone/cu m	Context type
Rural Jabah (20P7)	2.7	Rural commoner dwelling, outside city wall near minor center
Urban L-28	4.2	Commoner dwelling, not a surplus crafter, near/inside city wall
Urban H-11	13.0	Commoner dwelling, not a surplus crafter, near/inside city wall, near minor center
Urban I-55a	77.7	Commoner dwelling, surplus crafter near minor center within city wall
Urban Q-176	161	Commoner dwelling, surplus crafter, downtown Mayapán

Jabah yielded an overall density of 2.7 bones per cubic meter of excavation. Comparisons are provided in Table 11.1 to two fully excavated, ordinary (noncrafting) houses within the city wall, L-28 and H-11, that also had low faunal densities (4.2 and 13.0). Other fully excavated urban commoner (surplus crafter) dwellings at Mayapán had greater amounts of bone, for example, I-55a (77.7) and Q-176 (161.0). The Jabah house is a standout in the rural zone, but its occupants accessed fewer animal resources than its urban contemporaries.

Middens, as refuse zones, should yield higher densities than fully excavated dwellings, as the latter include samples of broader expanses of space where little debris was discarded (interior rooms, walls, house platform rubble). Two midden units at the Jabah house, indicated by gray (2 × 2 m) squares in Figure 11.4, have animal bone densities per cubic meter that are higher than for the overall house (13.8 and 42.8/cu m for units 5-E and 10-I) and compare more favorably to urban commoner results.

More robust comparisons are offered in Figures 11.6–11.9, which graphically display the number of bones from test pits across the Postclassic walled urban zone and rural contexts outside the city wall (from Russell 2008). These test pits specifically targeted household refuse zones often identifiable as concentrations of debris on the surface. Figures 11.6–11.7 include only units where faunal bone was recovered; Figures 11.8–11.9 include sixty-one units where no bone was present. Figure 11.6 illustrates lower-density contexts with fewer than one hundred faunal bones/cu m, and Jabah (shown in black) falls within the middle of this range. Other rural (outside the wall) contexts, shown as striped bars, also exhibit low faunal densities greater than or less than those of Jabah, as do a number of commoner houselots (gray bars) within the urban zone. These data indicate that Jabah is not anomalous for the study area. Thirty-one contexts graphed in Figure 11.7 yielded more than one hundred bones/cu m, with the highest value at 1,697/cu m; all but one of these contexts are of Postclassic date. One Terminal Classic context is labeled "G-48 rural" on the x-axis of the graph.

Elite structures (dotted bars) fall within this higher-density range (Figure 11.7), as well as some urban commoner contexts and two rural dwellings (G-48 and H-40a, striped bars). These latter two rural dwellings were located just outside the city wall, but close to important clusters of diverse activity, including city gates and nearby public architectural facilities. These data indicate that simple urban-rural dichotomies do not neatly correlate with faunal densities in the study area. Graphing the number of bones according to interval categories (Figure 11.8) reveals that faunal bone was often absent in test pit contexts across the greater Mayapán vicinity for the Terminal Classic and Postclassic periods (61 contexts). This finding places the absence of fauna at seven of eight fully excavated rural dwellings in greater perspective, that is, they are indicative of a broader pattern. Twenty-four test pit contexts had from 1 to 50 bones/cu m, twelve had from 50 to 200/cu m, eighteen had from 200 to 750/cu m, and seven had from 750 to 1,697/cu m. Access to faunal resources was not guaranteed for residents of the study area. These data are illustrated spatially in Figure 11.9 for both periods. Most of the contexts without fauna are located in the rural zone outside the city wall (56 of 61 contexts with no fauna).

Of the seven fully excavated rural contexts from which no faunal bone was recovered, we would most expect the Postclassic Rancho Lote dwelling to have had animal remains, as well as Puerta AA. Both are closer to the city wall than Jabah (Figure 11.1) and were located near routes into and out of the city's gates. They also exhibit typical Postclassic Mayapán architectural styles (Smith 1962), with rectangular houses and interior benches, and their residents might have emulated other aspects of urban commoner lifeways. In contrast, the Postclassic Camino Xcanchakan house differs from the standard urban house form in exhibiting an unusual pair of small square dwellings that lack interior benches. However, house form

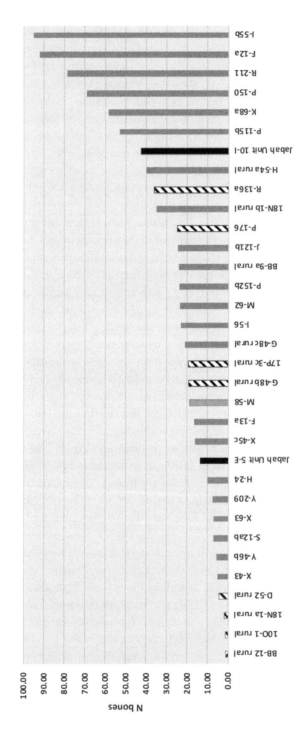

Figure 11.6. Frequency distributions of test pit contexts with fewer than one hundred bones/cu m, from refuse zones of urban and rural Mayapán (Terminal Classic and Postclassic periods). Midden unit results from Jabah are indicated by black bars, and other rural contexts (outside the city wall) are marked with striped bars.

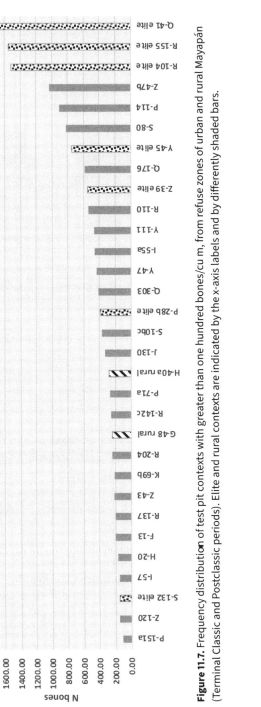

Figure 11.7. Frequency distribution of test pit contexts with greater than one hundred bones/cu m, from refuse zones of urban and rural Mayapán (Terminal Classic and Postclassic periods). Elite and rural contexts are indicated by the x-axis labels and by differently shaded bars.

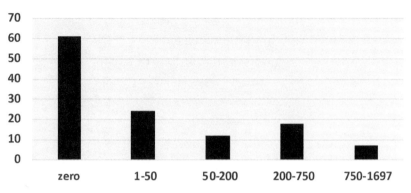

Figure 11.8. Interval distribution of N bones/cu m for a sample of test pits in or near residential groups of 122 contexts within and outside the city walls of Mayapán (includes Terminal Classic and Postclassic periods). The large number of test units without faunal bone indicates that poorer contexts often lacked faunal material in the study area. A minor proportion (N=10) of the zero value contexts represent test pits in randomly selected locations between, rather than within or next to, house groups (less dense deposits).

does not correlate with the presence or absence of faunal bones at these Postclassic rural sites.

Faunal Bone Diversity

How did specific animal consumption at Jabah compare with that of Postclassic era residents within the city? Percentages of identified bone reveal interesting patterns. Jabah's faunal assemblage has a greater relative proportion of white-tailed deer (as much as 76% when large deer-sized long bone fragments are included with bones identified to species) compared to fully excavated commoner houses in the urban zone (31%–48% deer bone and deer-sized mammal bone fragments). Generally equivalent quantities of peccary (0.7%–2.0%) and brocket deer (1.5%–2.8%) are found at Jabah and urban commoner (noncrafter) contexts. Fish bone percentages are also comparably low (0.5%–3.8%). Jabah differs in the quantity and diversity of small mammal bones present, but these were minor foods in the overall Mayapán diet. Iguana is infrequent at Jabah (2.8%), although this taxon varies considerably at commoner houselots (5.8%–36.5%) within the urban zone (Masson and Peraza Lope 2008).

Conspicuously absent at Jabah are wild or domesticated turkey bones, regularly found across most urban contexts at Postclassic Mayapán (Phillips et al. 2017; Pollock and Ray 1957). Ongoing research by Lori Phillips and colleagues (2017) is distinguishing the proportions of wild and domesticated turkeys at the site; their results will likely help nuance the sociospatial patterns of turkey use at the city. Turkey and large bird long bone fragments (almost certainly also representing turkey) made up from 9.5 percent to 33.5 percent of the combined identified faunal assemblage of fully excavated Postclassic urban houselots. Although turkey was widely distributed within the city, it may have had greater commercial value, given that downtown urban houses or those next to outlying elite groups (Q-176, Q-39, Q-40a, H-11) had higher proportions of turkey (22.5%–33.5%) than other contexts (I-55, L-28, X-43) where turkey bones formed 8.5 percent to 9.5 percent. Of the downtown houses, two of the three (Q-39, Q-40a) were most closely spatially affiliated with elites, and thus do not represent typical urban commoner dwellings.

Ceramic Densities, Occupational Duration, Foodways

Factors important for evaluating densities include occupational duration and intensity. Ceramic sherd quantities reflect these measures indirectly. Table 11.2 provides sherd densities per cubic meter of excavation for contexts compared in this chapter. The Postclassic sherd density at Jabah (133 sherds/cu m) is low, compared to the density of an affluent urban commoner crafter house I-55 (528). It is also lower than the ordinary (noncrafter) urban house H-11 (241), but it is greater than another modest urban house, located near the city wall, L-28 (88.7). Both the Jabah and I-55 dwellings revealed evidence for longer-term occupation, with multiple construction phases and at least one outbuilding (see Figures 11.3, 11.4), but Jabah's Postclassic occupation may have been briefer than that of I-55 and more analogous to houses built within and near the city wall toward the end of Mayapán's occupation (Masson, Hare, and Peraza Lope 2014:210). Jabah and L-28 also share similar low faunal densities in contrast to other fully excavated urban dwellings in our sample.

Lower Postclassic sherd densities are found at rural houses Puerta AA (33/cu m), Rancho Lote (68/cu m), and Camino Xcanchakan (27/cu m). These densities are less than the Jabah value (133/cu m). Rancho Lote, Puerta AA, and Camino Xcanchakan ceramic densities correlate with other metrics that suggest relatively lower levels of affluence for these rural commoners (Masson et al. 2020). While lower densities sometimes signal shorter occupations, residents of Rancho Lote and Camino Xcanchakan

Table 11.2. Sherd density (N/cu m) Rural Houses, Terminal Classic and Postclassic (fully excavated sample). Locations indicated on Figure 11.1.

	Volume	Terminal Classic sherds	Postclassic sherds	Terminal Classic sherd density	Postclassic sherd density
RURAL HOUSES					
Jabah	28.5	2,654	3,798	93	133
Xcanchakan	29.7	26	807	1	27
Rancho Lote	19.1	34	1,301	2	68
BB-206	22.8	19	743	1	33
Mateya	26.6	4,787	487	180	18
Pul Yax Che	19.9	508	3	25.5	0
Tzuc Pool	22.8	6,052	214	265	9
Tzabcan	21.6	3,179	201	147	9
URBAN HOUSES					
I-55	47.3		24,965		528
H-11	35.8		8,633		241
L-28	30.4		2,696		89
X-43	18.6		1,527		82

Note: Sherds tallied for the Terminal Classic exclude low numbers of sherds of enduring pottery types dated to the Late/Terminal Classic. Densities were calculated to include the Late/Terminal Classic sherds (not shown here), but results were nearly identical. There were 133 sherds in total of Late/Terminal Classic age, compared to 17,259 for the Terminal Classic (all 8 rural houses). A total of 25,957 sherds were recovered and analyzed for all periods from this sample. Also note that a significant Terminal Classic occupation existed in the Jabah vicinity, though not analyzed in this chapter, as sherds were mostly from architectural fill. Urban Mayapán houses listed are those not associated with pottery, figurine, or censer manufacture (for which sherd densities are higher due to production activities).

were in place long enough to construct additional houses and outbuildings; Puerto AA also has a single, but modest, outbuilding. Excavations at Jabah reveal significant development of the residential group. It exhibits the most architectural features of the four Postclassic rural houselots, with a second dwelling and multiple special purpose ancillary buildings (small round storage or pen enclosures, a square storage structure, and a possible shrine). Such segmentation of social space is one indicator of residential complexity and longevity (Kent 1990:137).

Among the four Terminal Classic rural dwellings, two, Tzabcan and Mateya, had nonresidential ancillary structures. Terminal Classic houselots Pul Yax Che and Tzuc Pool consisted of a single dwelling with no ancillary structures. They are candidates for the most ephemeral occupations of the sample. Ancillary structures likely reflect agricultural storage facilities or, sometimes, apiaries (Freidel and Sabloff 1984:11; Russell 2008:377, 579). The regular occurrence of these features in our rural sample suggests a primary focus on agricultural production.

Terminal Classic sherd densities (see Table 11.2) reveal that of the four houselots of this period, three exceed the quantities at Jabah, with ratios of sherds/cu m of 180, 265, and 147. One case of this period has fewer sherds (Pul Yax Che, with 25.5). The paucity of nonceramic materials at Pul Yax Che and its lack of outbuildings point to a shorter-term occupation. Three Terminal Classic families thus generated greater quantities of ceramic debris compared to their rural Postclassic counterparts at Rancho Lote, Puerta AA, and Camino Xcanchakan; their values also exceed the quantities at Jabah (although not as greatly as for the other three rural Postclassic contexts). Two of the Terminal Classic rural densities (ranging from 180 to 265/cu m) are comparable to that of an urban (commoner, surplus crafting) Postclassic house, I-55 (225/cu m).

The sherd density results can be considered more deeply with calculations of the minimum number of vessels (MNV) per cubic meter of excavation. MNVs correct for potential differences related to varying vessel sizes (and the number of fragments they generate) in the two time periods. By this measure, Jabah retains its exceptional status in the rural sample, with at least 5.9 vessels/cu m. The next three highest results are observed at Terminal Classic dwellings, Mateya with 4.2/cu m, Tzuc Pool with 4.0/cu m, and Tzabcan with 2.4/cu m. Lower results ranging from 1.3 to 1.6/cu m characterize the briefly occupied Terminal Classic Pul Yax Che dwelling, and two Postclassic houses (Puerta AA, Rancho Lote). The lowest MNV density is at Postclassic Camino Xcanchakan (0.9/cu m). Except for Jabah, two Terminal Classic dwellings have over twice the minimum numbers of vessels as the remaining Postclassic rural sample. By this measure, the Jabah, Mateya, and Tzuc Pool localities hosted more ceramic-using activities than the other five rural contexts. Values at two humble urban Postclassic commoner residences are similarly low, with 4.7 MNV/cu m at house L-28 and 1.7 MNV/cu m at house X-43. All of the results summarized above, however, pale in comparison to the value of 32.8 MNV/cu m at the more affluent commoner (surplus crafter) urban house of I-55. In summary, MNVs for some rural houselots are on par with ordinary, more modest urban contexts but are of low density compared to wealthier urban groups.

What might ceramic vessel densities suggest with respect to foodway differences between residential groups? The eight assemblages studied here all possessed ollas, basins, and dishes used for a wide variety of food and water storage, preparation, and serving. *Cazuelas* (basins) were more important for the Terminal Classic contexts (forming 13%–26% of the sherd samples), compared to Postclassic contexts (2%–7%). Also, bowls are present (5%–7%) at three Terminal Classic houselots but are absent at the other rural contexts. These differences attest to greater form and functional diversity in pottery-related cuisine for the Terminal Classic set of houselots. The basins are probably related to the preparation of large pots of food, gruel, pozole, or other shared concoctions of botanical foods. Future studies of skeletal isotopes within and beyond the study area may help refine these preliminary observations (e.g., Kennett et al. 2016).

Discussion

In summary, Jabah is the only rural house, of the eight investigated, with faunal bone; its proportions of taxa generally resemble those of poorer urban houselots, except for the surprising absence of turkey and the presence of white-tailed deer in quantities beyond the norm. We attribute the exclusive presence of faunal bone at Jabah to benefits its residents must have garnered from living in proximity to a sizable minor ceremonial group. Other commoner dwellings near Jabah exhibit more precocious architectural investments than the excavated dwelling 20P-7, suggesting that these families enjoyed greater affluence (see Figure 11.4). Artifact frequencies and classes reveal that Jabah's residents mimicked urban contexts in additional ways, and these behaviors differentiate 20P-7 from the remaining rural sample (Masson et al. 2020). They performed small-scale crafting but generated little or no surplus. They made some ritually important items, as suggested by a figurine (or censer) mold. In terms of wealth, the occupants of this house possessed obsidian, as well as a copper object, as did some ordinary residents of urban Mayapán (Paris 2008). Jabah householders and their ordinary contemporaries living within the city wall likely committed a significant proportion of their time to farming, an activity that itself can represent a specialization, with options for diversification in terms of crops cultivated (e.g., Chase et al. 2014; Fedick 2010, 2020; Sheets et al. 2012; Wyatt 2020).

The absence of fauna at the other rural dwellings represents a surprising result compared to Postclassic residential contexts elsewhere on the peninsula, implying that animal resources were not generally available to everyone living near the city. An argument has been presented for husbandry of deer and turkey within the urban zone (Masson and Peraza Lope 2008), and if this were true, then control and commodification of faunal resources via husbandry and animal product exchange would likely have resulted in regulations or other restrictions concerning access. There is no evidence that Jabah's occupants consumed husbanded deer or engaged in this practice, as butchered subadult bones are not present in the sample. Most deer bones from this context represent lower limbs, suggesting suboptimal cuts of meat. The exclusive presence of adult deer at Jabah may indicate that they were obtained through hunting, but it is difficult to explain why this option was not exercised by other households in our rural sample.

Animal resources were restricted in the rural zone for both periods considered in this study, perhaps due to depletion from demographic and climatic factors and a concordant rise in their value. Countryside inhabitants obtained regional pottery and other essentials not locally available in the Mayapán area. Yet such exchanges did not involve meat or fowl, at least for seven of the eight houselots discussed here. Full depletion of animal resources did not occur during the Terminal Classic, given that residents of major centers supplemented their diets with faunal foods (Götz 2007, 2008, 2011). This contrasting pattern to our rural sample suggests that animal resources were restricted through tributary demands, sumptuary laws, or some other institutional imposition (Götz 2011).

The downtown urban zone of Mayapán was full of animals, tended, butchered, and consumed; faunal bone is regularly recovered in modest quantities from some, but not all, ordinary houses. Walking through the cityscape would have filled the senses with sights, smells, sounds, and residues of animal use, bone debris and tools, hide, meat, humans hustling to provide their tended creatures with food and water, dogs barking, peccaries grunting, turkeys calling, iguanas scurrying, and droppings littering the streets and houselots. But farther out, near the city wall and at the field and forest margin beyond the wall where animal life should have thrived, the scene was more quiet, except in hot spots like Jabah. To what degree did the city co-opt key aspects of the forest ecology and re-create it within its walls, even as a populous periphery transformed a forest environment into an agrarian one? This process represents an important implication of our findings. The city, for reasons not yet fully known, did not share this animal bounty with those who likely grew much of the plant food staples on which it depended.

An alternative explanation lingers, awaiting better radiocarbon dating of the Postclassic rural houselots. If these residential groups were built after 1300 CE, residents may have lived during a period of serial environmental shortages that culminated in hunger and unrest. If so, their shortages may have derived from environmental triggers similar to those of the Terminal Classic houselots. In this scenario, the rural Postclassic houselots in our sample were settled later than those within the city wall. Does the abundant faunal bone of urban houselots date primarily to the prosperous thirteenth century? Within the city wall, some families ceremoniously abandoned their dwellings in the 1300s, and a number of monumental buildings were also shut down with rites of termination prior to 1400 CE (Masson and Peraza Lope 2014b; Peraza Lope and Masson 2014). Drought, famine, and political unrest led to significant outmigration from Mayapán in the fourteenth century, prior to a brief recovery in the early fifteenth century.

Emerging results from the countryside around Mayapán suggest that agriculturalists in this zone subsisted primarily on plant foods, much of which they likely would have cultivated themselves, when rainfall permitted. With the exception of those in Jabah, rural residents had a diet lacking in animal resources that stands in contrast to that of significant numbers of Postclassic urban residents who accessed meat and fowl on at least a semiregular basis (Kennett et al. 2016; Masson and Peraza Lope 2008, 2013). Faunal scarcity is also observed in the urban zone among poorer Postclassic contexts (see Figures 11.6, 11.8, 11.9), revealing this condition as a correlate of variation in status and means rather than a simple reflection of time period or rural-urban location. Elsewhere in the Maya area, local diets also varied considerably in terms of reliance on plant foods and meat, with some populations or individuals approaching a vegetarian diet (Gerry 1993; Reed 1999), as Carolyn Freiwald observes (2010: 399). She, along with Erin Thornton (2011), also notes that deer were sometimes a traded commodity that originated from nonlocal settings, and that differences in deer diets attest to a range of possible procurement strategies (including husbandry) and a mosaic of local ecological settings.

Conclusion

Although certain Postclassic contexts at urban Mayapán and hinterland sites such as Laguna de On and Colha, Belize, are associated with abundant faunal remains, they are scarce in rural contexts of this period around Mayapán (Masson 1999, 2004). Terminal Classic faunal scarcity of the

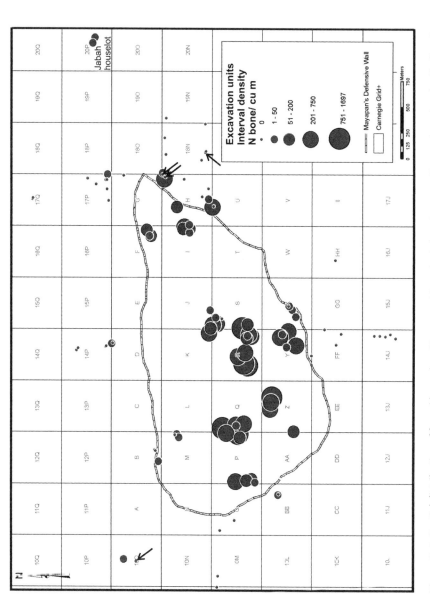

Figure 11.9. Spatial distribution of faunal bone densities per cubic meter intervals across the greater urban (walled) and rural Mayapán vicinity, a visual representation of data displayed in Figure 11.8. Almost all contexts are of Postclassic date, except for Terminal Classic contexts indicated by arrows.

study area, on the other hand, parallels patterns at smaller sites in Belize (Masson 2004). For both periods, more highly ranked regional centers did acquire animal resources, and Postclassic commoners living within Mayapán or in distant northeastern Belize seemed to obtain them in significant quantities. These findings suggest that animals were variably commodified, valued, and folded into exchange economies. The results also point to wealth differentials within the commoner class for Postclassic Mayapán to an extent not previously documented, which are also supported by analysis of artifact assemblages for rural and urban Mayapán. These findings support a growing body of literature concerning inequality among Maya commoners (Hutson 2016; Masson and Peraza Lope 2004, 2014a; Yaeger and Robin 2004).

In this chapter, we argue that taphonomic variables do not account for the paucity of animal remains in the rural contexts studied, given that Postclassic era fauna preserves well within the city (and earlier at Terminal Classic sites such as Chichén Itzá), and that the houselots were extensively sampled in a manner equivalent to that of their urban Mayapán counterparts. The recovery of bone at Jabah also suggests we do not face a preservation problem. Furthermore, human bone was also preserved within burials at two rural contexts in the sample. Jabah's faunal and artifact assemblage stands apart from those of the other seven rural houselots and underscores differences in commoner wealth, even for the rural sector.

Faunal diversity and quantity varies within urban Mayapán, with large quantities of diverse taxa recovered from elite and public buildings and a more limited range of animals found in commoner urban houselots. Periodic droughts are known to have plagued northern Yucatán from 1000 CE forward, and these would have aggravated conditions amenable to thriving local animal populations. Periods of scarcity would have contributed to the increased value of animal products. Farmers in the rural zone near Mayapán (except for Jabah) were among the poorest families documented thus far, and this pattern held through time from the Terminal Classic to the Postclassic. Rural impoverishment is not explained in these cases by relative isolation. Families were not self-sufficient, given the relatively abundant ceramic quantities of both periods, and the fact that pottery vessels were obtained through regional trade networks. These houselots also obtained tools or raw materials through trade for small-scale artifact manufacture from nonlocal sources.

Despite these findings, it is difficult to believe that rural farmers did not take advantage of opportunities to secure forest animals or those inhabiting milpa fields (or fallow fields). Furthermore, it seems unlikely that regulations or market prices could have fully suppressed such acquisition. More data are needed from rural samples to compare with the findings reported here.

Acknowledgments

This research derives from a long-term, collaborative investigation of Mayapán and its environs with my codirectors: Carlos Peraza Lope (Centro INAH-Yucatán), Timothy S. Hare (Morehead State University), and Bradley W. Russell (College of St. Rose), along with field directors, authors, and analysts Pedro Delgado Kú, Bárbara Escamilla Ojeda, Wilberth Cruz Alvarado, and Luis Flores Cobá. Special thanks are due to Jessica Campbell for her help identifying the Jabah fauna from the 2015 season. This research was funded by the National Science Foundation (NSF-BCS-1406233).

References

Ardren, Traci. 2002. "Death Became Her: Images of Female Power from Yaxuna Burials." In *Ancient Maya Women*, ed. Traci Ardren, 68–88. Walnut Creek, CA: Altamira Press.

Carr, H. Sorayya. 1996. "Precolumbian Maya Exploitation and Management of Deer Populations." In *The Managed Mosaic: Ancient Maya Agriculture and Resource Use*, ed. Scott L. Fedick, 251–261. Salt Lake City: University of Utah Press.

Chase, Arlen F., Lisa J. Lucero, Vernon L. Scarborough, Diane Z. Chase, Rafael Cobos, Nicholas P. Dunning, Scott L. Fedick, Vilma Fialko, Joel D. Gunn, Michelle Hegmon, Gyles Iannone, David L. Lentz, Rodrigo Liendo, Keith Prufer, Jeremy A. Sabloff, Joseph A. Tainter, Fred Valdez Jr, and Sander E. van der Leeuw. 2014. "Tropical Landscapes and the Ancient Maya: Diversity in Time and Space." In *The Resilience and Vulnerability of Ancient Landscapes: Transforming Maya Archaeology through IHOPE*, ed. Arlen F. Chase and Vernon L. Scarborough. Special issue of *Archaeological Papers of the American Anthropological Association* 24:11–29.

deFrance, Susan D. 2009. "Zooarchaeology in Complex Societies: Political Economy, Status, and Ideology." *Journal of Archaeological Research* 17(2):105–168.

Delgado Kú, Pedro C., Bárbara del C. Ojeda Escamilla, Marilyn A. Masson, Carlos Peraza Lope, and Douglas J. Kennett. 2020. "Commoner and Elite Houses Investigated at Mayapán, Yucatán." In *Settlement, Economy, and Society at a Postclassic Maya City: Mayapán, Yucatán, Mexico*, ed. Marilyn A. Masson, Timothy S. Hare, Carlos Peraza Lope, and Bradley W. Russell (in press). Pittsburgh: Center for Comparative Archaeology, Department of Anthropology, University of Pittsburgh.

Demarest, Arthur A., Prudence M. Rice, and Don S. Rice, eds. 2004. *The Terminal Classic in the Maya Lowlands: Collapse, Transition, and Transformation*. Boulder: University Press of Colorado.

Douglas, Peter M. J., Mark Pagani, Marcello A. Canuto, Mark Brenner, David A. Hodell, Timothy I. Eglinton, and Jason H. Curtis. 2015. "Drought, Agricultural Adaptation, and Sociopolitical Collapse in the Maya Lowlands." *Proceedings of the National Academy of Sciences* 112(18):5607–5612.

Driver, Jonathan C. 2004. "Food, Status, and Formation Processes: A Case Study from Medieval England." In *Behaviour Behind Bones: The Zooarchaeology of Ritual, Religion, Status, and Identity*, ed. Sharyn Jones O'Day, Wim Van Neer, and Anton Ervynck, 244–251. Oxford: Oxbow Books.

Dunning, Nicholas P. 2004. "Down on the Farm: Classic Maya 'Homesteads' as 'Farmsteads.'" In *Ancient Maya Commoners*, ed. Jon C. Lohse and Fred Valdez Jr., 97–116. Austin: University of Texas Press.

Emery, Kitty F., Lori E. Wright, and Henry Schwarcz. 2000. "Isotopic Analysis of Ancient Deer Bone: Biotic Stability in Collapse Period Maya Land-use." *Journal of Archaeological Science* 27(6):537–550.

———. 2003. "The Noble Beast: Status and Differential Access to Animals in the Maya World." *World Archaeology* 34(3):498–515.

———. 2007. "Assessing the Impact of Ancient Maya Animal Use." *Journal for Nature Conservation* 15(3):184–195.

Fedick, Scott L. 2010. "The Maya Forest: Destroyed or Cultivated by the Ancient Maya?" *Proceedings of the National Academy of Science* 107(3):953–954.

———. 2020. "Maya Cornucopia: Indigenous Food Plants of the Maya Lowlands." In *Nuts and Bolts of the Real "Business" of Maya Exchange*, ed. Marilyn A. Masson, David A. Freidel, and Arthur A. Demarest, 224–237. Gainesville: University Press of Florida.

Freidel, David A., and Jeremy A. Sabloff. 1984. *Cozumel: Late Maya Settlement Patterns*. New York: Academic Press.

Freiwald, Carolyn. 2010. "Dietary Diversity in the Upper Belize River Valley: A Zooarchaeological and Isotopic Perspective." In *Precolumbian Foodways: Interdisciplinary Approaches to Food, Culture, and Markets in Ancient Mesoamerica*, ed. John E. Staller and Michael D. Carrasco, 399–420. New York: Springer.

Garza Tarazona de González, Silvia, and Edward B. Kurjack Bacso. 1980. *Atlas arqueológico del Estado de Yucatán*. 2 vols. Mexico City: Instituto Nacional de Antropología e Historia, Centro Regional del Sureste.

Gerry, John P. 1993. "Diet and Status among the Classic Maya: An Isotopic Perspective." PhD diss., Department of Anthropology, Harvard University.

Gill, Richardson B. 2001. *The Great Maya Droughts: Water, Life, and Death*. Reprint ed. Albuquerque: University of New Mexico Press.

Götz, Christopher Markus. 2007. "El aprovechamiento de animales vertebrados en Chichén Itzá, Yucatán: Uso alimenticio y ritual." In *Chichén Itzá: Nuevas interpretaciones históricas*, ed. Alexander Voss and Andreas Koechert, 51–74. Colección Americana. Hanover, Germany: Verlag für Ethnologie.

———. 2008. "Coastal and Inland Patterns of Faunal Exploitation in the Prehispanic Northern Maya Lowlands." *Quaternary International* 191(1):154–169.

———. 2010. "Appendix I: The Faunal Materials from Yaxuná, Yucatán, Mexico." In *Archaeological Investigations at Yaxuná, 1986–1996: Results of the Selz Foundation Yaxuna Project*, by Travis W. Stanton, David A. Freidel, Charles K. Suhler, Traci Ardren, James N. Ambrosino, Justine M. Shaw, and Sharon Bennett, 265–283. BAR International Series 2056. Oxford: Archaeopress.

———. 2011. "Diferencias socioeconómicas en el uso de animales vertebrados en las tierras bajas mayas del norte." In *Vida cotidiana de los antiguos mayas del norte de la*

Península de Yucatán, ed. Rafael Cobos and Lilia Fernández Souza, 45–68. Mérida, Mex.: Universidad Autónoma de Yucatán.

Götz, Christopher M., and Thelma Sierra Sosa. 2011. "La arqueofauna de Xcambó, Yucatán, México." *Antípoda: Revista de Antropología y Arqueología* 13(July):119–145.

Götz, Christopher M., and Travis W. Stanton. 2013. "The Use of Animals by the Pre-Hispanic Maya of the Northern Lowlands." In *The Archaeology of Mesoamerican Animals*, ed. Christopher M. Götz and Kitty F. Emery, 191–232. Atlanta, GA: Lockwood Press.

Haller, Mikael J., Gary M. Feinman, and Linda M. Nicholas. 2006. "Socioeconomic Inequality and Differential Access to Faunal Resources at El Palmillo, Oaxaca, Mexico." *Ancient Mesoamerica* 17(1):39–55.

Hamblin, Nancy L. 1984. *Animal Use by the Cozumel Maya*. Tucson: University of Arizona Press.

Hanson, Craig. 2008. "The Late Mesoamerican Village." PhD diss., Tulane University. Ann Arbor: University Microfilms.

Hare, Timothy S., Marilyn A. Masson, and Bradley W. Russell. 2014. "High-Density LiDAR Mapping of the Ancient City of Mayapán." *Remote Sensing* 6:9064–9085.

Hixson, David R. 2011. "Settlement Patterns and Communication Routes of the Western Maya Wetlands: An Archaeological and Remote-Sensing Survey, Chunchucmil." PhD diss., Tulane University. Ann Arbor: University Microfilms.

Hodell, David A., Jason H. Curtis, and Mark Brenner. 1995. "Possible Role of Climate in the Collapse of Classic Maya Civilization." *Nature* 375(6530):391–394.

Hoggarth, Julie A., Sebastian F. M. Breitenbach, Brendan J. Culleton, Claire E. Ebert, Marilyn A. Masson, and Douglas J. Kennett. 2016. "The Political Collapse of Chichén Itzá in Climatic and Cultural Context." *Global and Planetary Change* 138: 25–42.

Hoggarth, Julie A., Matthew Restall, James W. Wood, and Douglas J. Kennett. 2017. "Drought and Its Demographic Effects in the Maya Lowlands." *Current Anthropology* 58(1):82–113.

Houck, Charles W., Jr. 2004. "The Rural Survey of Ek Balam, Yucatán, Mexico." PhD diss., Department of Anthropology, Tulane University. Ann Arbor: ProQuest/UMI.

Hutson, Scott R. 2016. *The Ancient Urban Maya: Neighborhoods, Inequality, and Built Form*. Gainesville: University Press of Florida.

Jackson, H. Edwin, and Susan L. Scott. 2003. "Patterns of Elite Faunal Utilization at Moundville, Alabama." *American Antiquity* 63(3):552–572.

Johnson, James Gregory. 2000. "The Chichen Itza–Ek Balam Transect Project: An Intersite Perspective on the Political Organization of the Ancient Maya." PhD diss., Dept. of Anthropology, University of Pittsburgh. Ann Arbor, MI: University Microfilms.

Kennett, Douglas J., Sebastian F. M. Breitenbach, Valorie V. Aquino, Yemane Asmerom, Jaime Awe, James U. L. Baldini, Patrick Bartlein, Brendan J. Culleton, Claire Ebert, Christopher Jazwa, Martha J. Macri, Norbert Marwan, Victor Polyak, Keith M. Prufer, Harriet E. Ridley, Harald Sodemann, Bruce Winterhalder, and Gerald H. Haug. 2012. "Development and Disintegration of Maya Political Systems in Response to Climate Change." *Science* 338(6108):788–791.

Kennett, Douglas J., Marilyn A. Masson, Stanley Serafin, Brendan J. Culleton, and Carlos Peraza Lope. 2016. "War and Food Production at the Postclassic Maya City of Mayapán." In *The Archaeology of Food and Warfare: Food Insecurity in Prehistory*, ed. Amber M. VanDerwarker and Gregory D. Wilson, 161–192. New York: Springer.

Kent, Susan, ed. 1990. *Domestic Architecture and the Use of Space: An Interdisciplinary Cross-Cultural Study*. New York: Cambridge University Press.

Kepecs, Susan, and Sylviane Boucher. 1996. "The Pre-Hispanic Cultivation of Rejolladas and Stone-Lands: New Evidence from Northeast Yucatan." In *The Managed Mosaic: Ancient Maya Agriculture and Resource Use*, ed. Scott Fedick, 69–91. Salt Lake City: University of Utah Press.

Landa, Diego de. 1941. *Landa's Relación de las cosas de Yucatán*. Trans. Alfred Tozzer. Papers of the Peabody Museum of American Archaeology and Ethnology, Vol. 18. Cambridge, MA: Peabody Museum at Harvard University.

Lepofsky, Dana L., Karla D. Kusmer, Brian Hayden, and Kenneth P. Lertzman. 1996. "Reconstructing Prehistoric Socioeconomies from Paleoethnobotanical and Zooarchaeological Data: An Example from the British Columbia Plateau." *Journal of Ethnobiology* 16(1):31–62.

Masson, Marilyn A. 1993. "Changes in Maya Community Organization from the Classic to Postclassic Periods: A View from Laguna de On, Belize." PhD diss., Department of Anthropology, University of Texas at Austin.

———. 1999. "The Manipulation of 'Staple' and 'Status' Faunas at Postclassic Maya Communities." *World Archaeology* 31:93–120.

———. 2000. *In the Realm of Nachan Kan: Postclassic Maya Archaeology at Laguna de On, Belize*. Boulder: University Press of Colorado.

———. 2004. "Fauna Exploitation from the Preclassic to the Postclassic Periods at Four Maya Settlements in Northern Belize." In *Maya Zooarchaeology: New Directions in Method and Theory*, ed. Kitty F. Emery, 97–124. Los Angeles: Cotsen Institute of Archaeology at UCLA.

Masson, Marilyn A., Timothy S. Hare, and Carlos Peraza Lope. 2014. "The Social Mosaic." In *Kukulcan's Realm: Urban Life at Ancient Mayapán*, by Marilyn A. Masson and Carlos Peraza Lope, 193–268. Boulder: University Press of Colorado.

Masson, Marilyn A., Timothy S. Hare, Carlos Peraza Lope, Bárbara C. Escamilla Ojeda, Elizabeth H. Paris, Betsy Kohut, Bradley W. Russell, and Wilberth Cruz Alvarado. "Household Craft Production in the Prehispanic Urban Setting of Mayapán, Yucatan, Mexico 2016." *Journal of Archaeological Research* 24(3):229–274.

Masson, Marilyn A., and Carlos Peraza Lope. 2004. "Commoners in Postclassic Maya Society: Social versus Economic Class Constructs." In *Ancient Maya Commoners*, ed. Jon C. Lohse and Fred Valdez, 197–224. Austin: University of Texas Press.

———. 2008. "Animal Use at the Postclassic Maya Center of Mayapan." *Quaternary International* 191(1):170–183.

———. 2010. "Evidence for Maya-Mexican Interaction in the Archaeological Record of Mayapan." In *Astronomers, Scribes, and Priests: Intellectual Interchange between the Northern Maya Lowlands and Highland Mexico in the Late Postclassic Period*, ed. Gabrielle Vail and Christine Hernandez, 77–114. Washington, DC: Dumbarton Oaks Research Library and Collection.

———. 2013. "Animal Consumption at the Monumental Center of Mayapán." In *The*

Archaeology of Mesoamerican Animals, ed. Christopher M. Götz and Kitty F. Emery, 233–280. Atlanta, GA: Lockwood Press.

———. 2014a. "The Economic Foundations." In *Kukulcan's Realm: Urban Life at Ancient Mayapán*, by Marilyn A. Masson and Carlos Peraza Lope, 269–424. Boulder: University Press of Colorado.

———. 2014b. "Militarism, Misery, and Collapse." In *Kukulcan's Realm: Urban Life at Ancient Mayapán*, by Marilyn A. Masson and Carlos Peraza Lope, 521–540. Boulder: University Press of Colorado.

Masson, Marilyn A., Carlos Peraza Lope, Timothy S. Hare, Bradley W. Russell, Pedro Delgado Kú, Bárbara Escamilla Ojeda, and Luis Flores Cobá. 2020 (in press). "Rural Economies at Agrarian Houselots before and after the Rise of Urban Mayapán." In *Nuts and Bolts of the Real "Business" of Ancient Maya Economic Exchange*, ed. Marilyn A. Masson, David A. Freidel, and Arthur A. Demarest, 80–97. Gainesville: University Press of Florida.

McAnany, Patricia A., and Norman Yoffee, eds. 2009. *Questioning Collapse: Human Resilience, Ecological Vulnerability, and the Aftermath of Empire*. Cambridge: Cambridge University Press.

Mock, Shirley B. 1994. "The Northern River Lagoon Site (NRL): Late to Terminal Classic Maya Settlement, Saltmaking, and Survival on the Northern Belize Coast." PhD diss., Department of Anthropology, University of Texas at Austin.

Montero-López, Coral. 2009. "Sacrifice and Feasting among the Classic Maya Elite and the Importance of the White-tailed Deer: Is There a Regional Pattern?" *Journal of Historical and European Studies* 2:53–68.

Munro-Stasiuk, Mandy J., T. Kam Manahan, Trent Stockton, and Traci Ardren. 2014. "Spatial and Physical Characteristics of Rejolladas in Northern Yucatán, Mexico: Implications for Ancient Maya Agriculture and Settlement Patterns." *Geoarchaeology* 29(2):156–172.

Paris, Elizabeth H. 2008. "Metallurgy, Mayapan and the Postclassic Mesoamerican World System." *Ancient Mesoamerica* 19(1):43–66.

Peraza Lope, Carlos, and Marilyn A. Masson. 2014. "An Outlying Temple, Hall, and Elite Residence." In *Kukulcan's Realm: Urban Life at Ancient Mayapán*, by Marilyn A. Masson and Carlos Peraza Lope, 105–148. Boulder: University Press of Colorado.

Phillips, Lori, Erin Thornton, Kitty Emery, and Carlos Peraza Lope. 2017. "Let's Talk Turkey: Turkey Use and Management at Postclassic Mayapán." Paper presented at the 81st Annual Meeting of the Society for American Archaeology, Vancouver, B.C.

Pohl, Mary D. 1985. "The Privileges of Maya Elites: Prehistoric Vertebrate Fauna from Seibal." In *Prehistoric Lowland Maya Environment and Subsistence Economy*, ed. Mary D. Pohl, 133–143. Papers of the Peabody Museum of Archaeology and Ethnology, Vol. 77. Cambridge, MA: Peabody Museum at Harvard University.

———. 1989. "Ethnozoology of the Maya: Faunal Remains from Five Sites in the Petén, Guatemala." In *Excavations at Seibal, Department of Petén, Guatemala*, ed. J. A. Graham, G. Tourtellot III, Mary D. Pohl, and G. R. Willey, 142–174. Memoirs of the Peabody Museum of Archaeology and Ethnology, Vol. 17, No. 3. Cambridge, MA: Peabody Museum at Harvard University.

Pollock, Harry E. D., and Clayton E. Ray. 1957. "Notes on Vertebrate Animal Remains from Mayapan." *Current Reports* 41:633–656. Washington, DC: Carnegie Institution of Washington, Department of Archaeology.

Quezada, Sergio. 2014. *Maya Lords and Lordship: The Formation of Colonial Society in Yucatán, 1350–1600*. Norman: University of Oklahoma Press.

Reed, David M. 1999. "Cuisine from Hun-Nal-Ye." In *Reconstructing Ancient Maya Diet*, ed. Christine D. White, 183–196. Salt Lake City: University of Utah Press.

Reitz, Elizabeth, and C. Margaret Scarry. 1985. *Reconstructing Historic Subsistence with an Example from Sixteenth-Century Spanish Florida*. Special Publication Series No. 3. Ann Arbor, MI: Society for Historical Archaeology.

Robin, Cynthia. 2013. "Peopling the Past: New Perspectives on the Ancient Maya." *Proceedings of the National Academy of Sciences* 98(1):18–21.

Russell, Bradley W. 2008. "Postclassic Maya Settlement on the Rural-Urban Fringe of Mayapán, Yucatán, Mexico." PhD diss., Department of Anthropology, State University of New York at Albany—SUNY. Available online at: mayapanperiphery.net/downloads.html.

Sabloff, Jeremy A., and William L. Rathje. 1975. "The Rise of a Maya Merchant Class." *Scientific American* 233:72–82.

Scott, Robert F., IV. 1980. "Further Comments on Faunal Analysis and Ancient Subsistence Activities at Colha." In *The Colha Project, Second Season, 1980 Interim Report*, ed. Thomas R. Hester, Jack D. Eaton, and Harry J. Shafer, 281–288. San Antonio, TX: Center for Archaeological Research, and Venice: Centro Studi e Ricerche Ligabue.

———. 1982. "Notes on Continuing Faunal Analysis for the Site of Colha, Belize: Data from the Early Postclassic." In *Archaeology at Colha, Belize: The 1981 Interim Report*, ed. Thomas R. Hester, Harry J. Shafer, and Jack D. Eaton, 203–207. San Antonio, TX: Center for Archaeological Research, and Venice: Centro Studi e Ricerche Ligabue.

Serafin, Stanley. 2010. "Bioarchaeological Investigation of Violence at Mayapan." PhD diss., Department of Anthropology, Tulane University.

———. 2020. "A Bioarchaeological Perspective on Diet, Health, and Lifestyle at Mayapán." In *Settlement, Economy, and Society at Mayapán, Yucatan, Mexico*, ed. Marilyn A. Masson, Timothy S. Hare, Carlos Peraza Lope, and Bradley W. Russell (in press). Pittsburgh, PA: Center for Comparative Archaeology, Department of Anthropology, University of Pittsburgh.

Shaw, Leslie C. 1991. "The Articulation of Social Inequality and Faunal Resource Use in the Preclassic Community of Colha, Northern Belize." PhD diss., University of Massachusetts Amherst. Available online via ProQuest.

Shaw, Leslie C., and Patricia H. Mangan. 1994. "Faunal Analysis of an Early Postclassic Midden, Operation 2032, Colha, Belize." In *Continuing Archaeology at Colha, Belize*, ed. Thomas R. Hester, Harry J. Shafer, and Jack D. Eaton, 69–78. Studies in Archaeology No. 16. Austin: Texas Archaeological Research Laboratory.

Sheets, Payson. 2000. "Provisioning the Ceren Household: The Vertical Economy, Village Economy, and Household Economy in the Southeast Maya Periphery." *Ancient Mesoamerica* 11(2):217–230.

Sheets, Payson, David Lentz, Dolores Piperno, and John Jones. 2012. "Ancient

Manioc Agriculture South of the Ceren Village, El Salvador." *Latin American Antiquity* 23(3):259–281.
Smith, A. Ledyard. 1962. "Residential and Associated Structures at Mayapán." In *Mayapan, Yucatan, Mexico*, ed. Harry E. D. Pollock, Ralph L. Roys, Tatiana Proskouriakoff, and A. Ledyard Smith, 165–320. CIW Publication No. 619. Washington, DC: Carnegie Institution of Washington,
Smith, James Gregory. 2000. "The Chichén Itzá–Ek Balam Transect Project: An Intersite Perspective on the Political Organization of the Ancient Maya." PhD diss., University of Pittsburgh. Ann Arbor: University Microfilms.
Smith, Michael E. 1987. "Household Possessions and Wealth in Agrarian States: Implications for Archaeology." *Journal of Anthropological Archaeology* 6(4):297–335.
Teeter, Wendy G., and Arlen F. Chase. 2004. "Adding Flesh to Bones: Using Zooarchaeology Research to Answer the Big-Picture Questions." *Archaeofauna* 13:155–172.
Thornton, Erin Kennedy. 2011. "Reconstructing Ancient Maya Animal Trade through Strontium Isotope ($^{87}Sr/^{86}Sr$) Analysis." *Journal of Archaeological Science* 38(12): 3254–3263.
Tiesler, Vera, Andrea Cucina, T. Kam Manahan, T. Douglas Price, Traci Ardren, and James H. Burton. 2010. "A Taphonomic Approach to Late Classic Maya Mortuary Practices at Xuenkal, Yucatán, Mexico." *Journal of Field Archaeology* 35(4): 365–379.
Tozzer, Alfred M. 1941. "Notes." In *Relación de las cosas de Yucatan*, ed. and trans. A. M. Tozzer. Papers of the Peabody Museum of American Archaeology and Ethnology, Vol. 18. Cambridge, MA: Peabody Museum at Harvard University.
Tozzer, Alfred M., and Glover M. Allen. 1910. *Animal Figures in the Maya Codices*. Papers of the Peabody Museum of American Archaeology and Ethnology, Vol. 4, No. 2. Cambridge, MA: Peabody Museum at Harvard University.
Turner, Billie L., II, and Jeremy A. Sabloff. 2012. "Classic Period Collapse of the Central Maya Lowlands: Insights about Human-Environment Relationships for Sustainability." *Proceedings of the National Academy of Sciences* 109(35):13908–13914.
Wolf, Eric R. 1982. *Europe and the People without History*. Berkeley: University of California Press.
Wright, Lori E. 2006. *Diet, Health, and Status among the Pasión Maya: A Reappraisal of the Collapse*. Vanderbilt Institute of Mesoamerican Archaeology Series, Vol. 2. Nashville: Vanderbilt University Press.
Wyatt, Andrew. 2020 (in press). "Gardens of the Maya." In *Nuts and Bolts of the Real "Business" of Maya Exchange*, ed. Marilyn A. Masson, David A. Freidel, and Arthur A. Demarest, 187–209. Gainesville: University Press of Florida.
Yaeger, Jason, and Carolyn Freiwald. 2009. "Complex Ecologies: Human and Animal Responses to Ancient Landscape Change in Central Belize." *Research Reports in Belizean Archaeology* 6:83–91.
Yaeger, Jason, and Cynthia Robin. 2004. "Heterogenous Hinterlands: The Social and Political Organization of Commoner Settlements near Xunantunich, Belize." In *Ancient Maya Commoners*, ed. Jon C. Lohse and Fred Valdez Jr., 147–174. Austin: University of Texas Press.

CHAPTER 12

Human-Deity Relationships Conveyed through *Balche'* Rituals and Resource Procurement

GABRIELLE VAIL AND MAIA DEDRICK

Contemporary Maya speakers associate animal and plant resources with the locations where they originate (i.e., those that come from the forest, or *monte*; those grown in the milpa; and those associated with the house-lot, or *solar*), each of which has different properties. Interaction with these distinct resource zones depends, in many cases, on gender and serves to establish unique relationships between the people who work together to make use of the resources they contain. Likewise, those who exploit the different resource zones also enter into relationships with the various deities that control access to them.

This chapter examines the use of both wild and domesticated animals and several different plant resources that form part of ritual meals prepared in payment to the deities. The ceremonies that we focus on are the *u hanli kab'* (dinner of the bees) among the Yucatec Maya and the ceremony for renewing the god pots among the Lacandón. The two share key features, which include preparing special foods and also using the ritual beverage *balche'* for the payment to the deity protectors. Honey is an essential ingredient for both types of offerings.

By engaging in the acts of everyday life (hunting, agricultural pursuits, and food preparation), Maya people become obligated to the deities, who serve as protectors of different types of animals and other resources, such as community lands and *monte*, caves and other sinkholes, the products of the milpa, and more. We consider what contemporary Maya rituals and those described in ethnohistoric sources can help us understand about human-deity relationships in the Postclassic Maya codices, in particular those related to beekeeping and harvest rituals. We also examine how these associations shape relationships between family members, ritual specialists, and other members of Maya communities who participate in the preparation and consumption of the ritual meal offered to the deities.

Understanding the Relationships Entailed in Food Offerings

This chapter mobilizes perspectives of ontological archaeology to provide insights into the relationships between humans and deities in the preparation and performance of offerings as documented in the Maya codices. We consider in particular the food and drink offerings that involve honey, such as *balche'*, and ritual activities related to beekeeping and honey harvesting. Our ontological approach draws on posthumanist and materialist scholarship to bridge the human/nonhuman divide (e.g., Alberti 2016; Harrison-Buck and Hendon 2018; Hutson 2010; Watts 2013). This perspective emphasizes relationality, in which one being cannot exist without the next, and humans participate with plants, animals, gods, and other beings as they cofacilitate everyday life (see also Morell-Hart, this volume). In several instances, we refer to this way of being as a web of existence, but it could also be called a "meshwork," a term that Timothy Ingold (2011:63–64) has used to describe "entangled lines of life, growth and movement," in which action "emerges from the interplay of forces conducted along [its] lines" (see also Ingold 2007:80).

One facet of an ontological perspective is that it acknowledges the existence of distinct realities—worlds within worlds, which together constitute a "pluriverse" (Blaser 2009; Blaser and de la Cadena 2018; Escobar 2008). Scholars engaging with the ontological approach point out that, traditionally, anthropologists have reduced distinct realities, or ways of being, to epistemologies, or ways of knowing, thus trivializing the differences between the world's peoples (Latour 1993). For the purposes of this chapter, such a theoretical approach provides us with the freedom to attempt to articulate the relationships between humans and other-than-humans enacted in rituals and conourishment activities recorded in the codices, without judging such ideas based on a modernist ontology that reifies divisions between nature and culture, as well as humans and nonhumans. In this chapter, we describe relationships between people, gods, and animals, and instances in which people become gods, based on accounts documented in ethnohistoric, ethnographic, and epigraphic works.

In Mesoamerica and more broadly, ontological archaeology follows the lead of scholarship that accepts indigenous knowledge and motives for ritual activity as described by practitioners, without seeking to rationalize them from an outsider's perspective. Such approaches can be attributed, first and foremost, to indigenous scholars and those who have worked closely, and in some cases collaboratively, with indigenous peoples. In Yucatán, for example, Juan Castillo Cocom tells us that the Yucatec Maya term *iknal* refers to one's "embodied and disembodied quality of 'being present' as the *context* and *product* of relationships," a concept well suited to discussions of relational ontologies and one that we embrace (Castillo Cocom, Rodríguez, and Ashenbrener 2017:65). Unfortunately, indigenous scholars such as Castillo Cocom, who resist the urge to make universalizing claims, rarely receive well-deserved citations and attributions for ideas generated when taking an ontological approach (Todd 2016).

The considerations of ontological archaeology apply to questions of food and identity in the Maya-speaking area, where human food procurement required, and still necessitates, relationships with deities of the natural world (e.g., Brown and Emery 2008). As previously mentioned, each animal and plant can be found in a particular web of belonging that involves a dynamic set of deities. As humans seek to use animals and plants for their own ends, they engage in petitions to and persuasion of the deities, seeking both protection for themselves, their families, and their animals and permission to benefit from the gifts of the gods through reciprocal offerings. Relationships with the gods associated with the natural world often require mediation on the part of ritual specialists, who maintain critical temporal knowledge regarding the most auspicious days on which to make appropriate offerings to each deity, which may also include music, song, and performance; missteps may be dangerous. In performing their role, pre-Hispanic ritual specialists would have consulted codices, where we find relevant details recorded.

As we discuss below, a scene from the Madrid Codex appears to demonstrate that bees inhabit the Maya world thanks to the deities who brought them into being shortly after the creation of the four world quarters. Humans who wish to interact with bees in ways such as harvesting honey must not only respect the bees but also engage with the bees' protector deities. Such deities take the form of large bees and include the principal bee, the *noh yum kab'*, and other bee deities of various categories. Humans therefore do not own bees, but care for them in the name of a particular deity (Jong 1999).

After presenting an overview regarding the classification of animals, human space, and labor, we discuss ethnographic and historical information concerning rituals involving the use of honey, as well as those related to bees more generally, to help illustrate the role that human-deity relationships played in the procurement of food and the patterning of daily life. These details then help us draw relevant observations about *balche'* and bee ceremonies represented in the Postclassic codices from the northern Maya region.

Animal Classification

All of the animals exploited by Yucatec Maya communities fall into two broad categories—the *ba'alche' k'aax* (animals of the forest) and the *alak'* (domesticated animals). The wild animals fall into six different groups, which include the *alak'* of the gods, the social insects, the animals that walk on the forest floor, the snakes, the birds, and the butterflies. Interestingly, the *alak'* of the gods include several game species (including deer, peccary, and agouti), but not others (such as armadillos and wild turkeys). Domesticated animals of indigenous origin include the domesticated turkey (*tso'*) and the stingless bee species *Melipona beecheii* (*xunan kab'* or *kolel kab'*), as well as the dog and the Muscovy duck (Jong 1999:134–135).

Animals falling into each of these categories are protected by deities known as *ah kanulob*, who are their rightful owners as well as protectors. They allow people to hunt or domesticate their animals as long as they are respectful and do not take more than they need. In return for this concession, humans must repay the deities for their gifts, through the performance of a ceremony meant to redeem or exchange, termed *loh* (Jong 1999:137, 139).

Different types of *loh* are performed by hunters, agriculturalists, and beekeepers, and others are done to protect the *solar* more broadly. Our interest is in the *loh* performed by beekeepers in recompense for a successful harvest, which is known as *u hanli kab'*, or "dinner of the bees." The ceremony is similar in most respects to that performed for a successful maize harvest, the *u hanli kol*, or "dinner of the *milpa*" (Jong 1999:153–154).

Yucatec Maya Ethnographic Information: The Organization of Community Space and Labor

In this section, we include information about apiculture from communities across the Yucatán Peninsula and neighboring areas today but focus on activities depicted in a detailed ethnographic study of beekeeping in

Tepich, Quintana Roo (Jong 1999). When we refer to Yucatán throughout this section, we mean the northern portion of the Yucatán Peninsula, broadly within the current Mexican states of Campeche, Yucatán, and Quintana Roo.

In Tepich, and more generally in communities across the peninsula today, the world outside the home is divided into domestic space, which includes the *solar* where women engage in many of their daily activities, including gardening, and the milpa, a field thinned of trees and planted with a variety of staple and complementary crops, maize being primary among them. Interspersed with actively cultivated milpa fields are previous fields in various stages of regrowth, from low brush to high and mature forests more than fifty years old. Within this patchwork of land use, older forests tend to be farther from town, while more frequently cultivated land can be found near town, where it is more convenient to access. Once land has been left fallow for thirty years, it is considered *ka'anal k'aax*, or high forest, where "wild" or undomesticated but encouraged resources are sought (Flores and Ucan Ek 1983; González-Cruz, García-Frapolli, and Casas 2015).

The *solar* includes the family's home; the kitchen; the crib where the maize is stored after harvesting (which may also be used for domestic rituals); various workspaces; enclosures for any domesticated animals kept, such as pigs or chickens; the thatched structure housing the stingless bees (*Melipona beecheii*, or *xunan kab'*), if kept; and a family garden with fruit trees (Jong 1999:211). In the majority of communities in Yucatán, women care for the living beings (human, animal, and plant) that inhabit the houselot, except for the stingless bees and the deities who protect the domestic animals, which men primarily oversee (Jong 1999:215).

Jong (1999:214) notes that in the community of Tepich, several households related through the patrilineal line may contribute to labor in the *solar*, even though each household may otherwise be economically independent. Within the *solar*, the men of the families build and maintain structures that house bees at a distance of at least twenty meters from living and kitchen areas. Men or women may own and inherit the logs containing the hives (Restall 1997:113–116; Thompson 1999), but in Tepich, the *xunan kab'* receive care only from men (Jong 1999:217). Their care involves cleansing/purification rituals, the harvest of the honey three or four times a year, and the performance of the appropriate rituals to pay the deity protectors for the honey that has been taken (Jong 1999: Chap. 5). Men also do whatever construction is needed within the *solar* for the well-being of animals and bees (e.g., build pens for the animals and construct an A-frame structure to house the bees' logs; Jong 1999:215). The hive owner must arrange for a *loh* ceremony following the construction of a new house for the bees (Jong 1999:167).

Women in Tepich are prohibited from participating in the harvesting of honey, although it is given to them immediately afterward for straining and storing (Jong 1999:180; see also Redfield and Villa Rojas 1934: 69; Weaver and Weaver 1981:5). Following the process of extracting the honey, beekeepers will clean the inside of the log hive with water and leaves from the *chakah* tree (*Bursera simaruba*), which must be gathered prior to opening the hives (Jong 1999:178; see also Weaver and Weaver 1981). *Chakah* is said to have a cooling influence, which is important after the "heat" (*k'inam*) generated by the activities associated with harvesting. One of the reasons women are not involved in harvesting honey is that pregnant and menstruating women are believed to have an abundance of *k'inam*, a quality also shared with honey, an excess of which can be dangerous for the bees (Jong 1999:196–197; Redfield and Villa Rojas 1934).

Women are responsible for most of the day-to-day domestic tasks in the *solar* (cooking, caring for children, raising the hens and pigs, and caring for the gardens). They are not confined to this space, however, but also venture out to obtain items such as firewood (and sometimes water), and at times help their husbands or male relatives in the milpa (Jong 1999:217). Beginning at around age eight, girls work alongside their mothers, helping with the tasks as they can, as do boys with their fathers. Jong (1999:217–218) notes that in Tepich, women establish relationships outside their own *solares* primarily by distributing food to other households when needed, and by preparing the special ritual foods offered to the deities during ceremonies. While the latter is most often done at home, on certain occasions foods are prepared at the site of the ceremony or in a nearby house. When this occurs, the altar serves to demarcate gender-specific activity areas, which can only be crossed by the ritual specialist, or *hmen*, who may work in either space.

The *hmen* serves as a mediator between the world of the gods and that of its human inhabitants. This role is invariably filled by a man, usually one who has trained with a well-established *hmen* and is generally an elder of the community. The *hmen* directs the preparation of ritual offerings (food, drink, incense, tobacco, etc.), prepares the altar, consecrates the offerings, intones the prayers, invites the deities to the feast, and ensures that everything has been carried out properly. He acts on behalf of the ritual sponsor, the sponsor's family, and the other participants (Jong 1999:182–184, 225–227).

Relationships between the participants in the ceremony, human and deity alike, are enacted during the course of preparing, consecrating and offering, and consuming the foods designated for the *ah kanulob* deity protectors, as well as the other deities who must receive payment for their favors. Throughout this extended process, men and women maintain separate spaces in which they spend time conversing and building rapport. This can be seen as an extension of their division across the landscape during the activities of daily life, such as when women work in the houselot and men work in the fields. However, as Robin (2006) has pointed out, such daily activities often merge as people of all identities gather together or coordinate to complete a necessary larger task or cross by one another as they gather equipment. It is difficult to know what the norms were in the Postclassic period, despite written accounts specifying that women—except for those past the age of childbearing—were excluded from most rituals. Data from the codices suggest that the gender boundaries were not always as rigidly maintained as Spanish chroniclers were led to believe (Vail and Stone 2002).

Of the offerings prepared for rituals, perhaps the most diagnostic is *balche'*, an alcoholic drink made from the bark of the *balche'* tree, honey from the stingless bee *Melipona beecheii*, and "virgin" water (*suhuy ha'*). Ethnohistoric sources describing life in sixteenth-century Yucatán mention *balche'* as a key component of all rituals and, we suggest, a marker of Yucatec ethnic identity. This is further suggested by its significance in the Postclassic Maya codices.

Pre-Hispanic sources call attention to the importance of honey in Postclassic Yucatec Maya culture, as suggested by the twenty-eight almanacs that constitute the beekeeping section of the Madrid Codex (which makes up over 10% of the codex as a whole; Vail 1994). In addition to its ritual uses, honey had medicinal properties that were well known to the pre-Hispanic inhabitants of Yucatán, and curers and midwives used it to treat a variety of conditions. It played an especially significant role for women prior to and following childbirth (González-Acereto, Quezada-Euán, and Medina-Medina 2006:234; Osado 1933; Redfield and Villa Rojas 1934; Roys 1931; Yurrita Obiols and Vásquez 2013:233–234). Additionally, Maya farmers were aware of the importance of bees in pollinating a variety of plants grown in the milpa and in the *monte*, and this is likely another of the reasons stingless bees were kept by farming families and played such a seminal role in indigenous cosmologies. *Balche'* (both the bark itself and the drink made from it) was also believed to be efficacious for various ailments, and its consumption was a sign of participation in community-based rituals that were integral for defining those who could claim long-term ties to communities in the peninsula (see Chuchiak 2003).

Balche' Rituals in Ethnohistoric Accounts

Balche' today is first and foremost a libation of the gods (Jong 1999; McGee 1990). Its consumption by humans results from the need to petition or thank the deities for particular acts. What we believe to be *balche'* rituals are depicted in the Late Postclassic Maya codices and likely on some Classic period Maya vessels, but our best source of information about them comes from ethnohistoric and ethnographic descriptions. Little research has been done to date to identify *balche'* ceremonies in the archaeological record, although preliminary work to identify honey by its chemical composition has been undertaken (Bianco, Alexander, and Rayson 2017). A growing body of literature documents archaeological evidence for pre-Hispanic beekeeping practices across the Maya area (Batún Alpuche 2009; Paris et al. 2018; Źrałka et al. 2018), and contemporary efforts to revitalize the cultivation of native bees in Maya communities are on the rise (González-Acereto, Quezada-Euán, and Medina-Medina 2006; Pat Fernández et al. 2018).

Both indigenous-language documents and accounts written by Spanish chroniclers highlight the importance of *balche'* in ritual and communal life in Yucatán in the years following the Spanish Conquest. A passage from the Yucatec *Book of Chilam Balam of Chumayel*, recorded in written form during the eighteenth century, notes: "This is the *balche'* ceremony . . . We, the rulers spread in many separate parts, we worship them, the true gods" (cited in Chuchiak 2003:137).

Spanish civil and ecclesiastical authorities found the devotion to *balche'* drinking, and its association with idolatrous practices (i.e., offerings to images of the Maya gods), so odious that "in order to avoid such great sins, they prohibited the drinking of *balche'*" (*Relación de Nabalam, Tahcabo and Cozumel* 1579). To support this prohibition, Spanish authorities also cut down *balche'* trees when seen on someone's land (Don Agustín Francisco de Echano, *juez provisor* of the Diocese of Yucatán, 1765; cited in Chuchiak 2003). Despite these prohibitions, however, celebrations of the clandestine rituals continued unabated, although they required more planning and preparation, since the ingredients became increasingly hard to find.

Colonial Accounts of *Balche'* Preparation

Diego de Landa, writing around 1566, provides a great deal of information about the flora and fauna of Yucatán, focusing especially on that which people used as food, in medicines, and for construction materials. Of *balche'*, he writes: "I will speak first of the wine that the Indians esteem so highly, and therefore plant them [the *balche'* tree] in all their enclosures or around their houses. It is an ugly tree, producing nothing but its roots, and its wine by using honey and water" (Landa 1978 [ca. 1566]:104). Elsewhere, he notes that their wine is made of honey, water, and "the root of a certain tree they grow for this purpose" (Landa 1978 [ca. 1566]:35). Landa and others were mistaken in noting that the root is used in making the *balche'* drink; as Bruman (2000) notes, it is the bark.

The three principal ingredients of *balche'*—the bark of the *balche'* tree (*Lonchocarpus punctatus*), fresh honey, and water from sacred underground sources, such as cenotes (sinkholes) or caves—were all associated with uncultivated lands known as the *monte*. Although the *balche'* tree could also grow in the *solar*, or domestic space, Spanish prohibitions and the felling of such trees led people to seek out its bark in the forest. Moreover, although most families had hives in their *solares*, *balche'* makers preferred honey from wild bees, as well as water from pristine sources (Chuchiak 2003). Foraging parties, financed principally by members of the elite class, sought both *balche'* bark and wild honey from frontier areas beyond Spanish control. Such was the importance of *balche'* bark that elites maintained the trees in milpa plots far removed from the towns, where they could remain hidden, and a special class of official developed to buy and trade in this illicit material. Several towns became known for having stores of the bark, and in some instances, the beverage itself was sold (Chuchiak 2003: 143nn20 and 21).

A description from 1579, written by Giraldo Díaz de Alpuche, a Spanish official of the town of Dzonot, describes the process of making the drink: "They made it in several large wooden containers like large casks, and they added to the mixture from twenty to thirty and even fifty *arrobas* of water and they cooked and boiled it there for two days" (Chuchiak 2003:144, citing de la Garza et al. 1983, 2:84–85). As the quote indicates, the ingredients for the *balche'* drink were gathered and left to ferment in large wooden vats, or canoes, within someone's milpa or *solar* in preparation for a ceremony in which they would be ritually fed to the gods. Once fermented, the *balche'* drink was carried by those assisting with the ceremony to the location of the ritual in large gourds or wooden containers.

These descriptions tell us that in pre-Hispanic times, *balche'* trees may have been present in both houselots and the forest—existing within both spaces, they may have transcended internal divisions of community space. On the other hand, men likely sought out honey from wild bees in groups similar to hunting parties, and this search may have entailed extended periods of time in the woods. During such trips, men would have taught their sons to recognize different plant and insect species, and surely participated in expedient hunting as opportunities arose (but see Masson et al., this volume, regarding possible prohibitions on expedient hunting in the environs of Mayapán).

Balche' Rituals in Colonial Period Yucatán

Landa describes the use of *balche'* in two different contexts—public rituals at which sacrifices (offerings) are made and to which everyone contributes, and private ceremonies sponsored by an individual who bears the expense. His discussion focuses on the public rituals; like the examples discussed below, they include a ceremonial component led by a ritual specialist, which is undertaken by the leading men of the town—those whom Landa terms the "chiefs" and the "priests" (Landa 1978 [ca. 1566]:70). The location of the "public" component of the ritual varies according to what it is, but it often takes place either in the courtyard of a temple or at one of the four entrances to the town, or it alternates between them. Landa notes that for the temple ceremonies, the men participated without the women (although elderly women were admitted to perform dances); he notes, however, that "women were admitted to festivals held in other places" (Landa 1978 [ca. 1566]:70). (For a discussion of feasting in a *Preclassic* community, see Brown and Freiwald, this volume.)

Landa makes little mention of the types of offerings of food and drink that participants made to the deities, although he does mention the general feasting that occurred after the ceremony concluded: "After this burning of the incense, all ate the gifts and presents, and the wine went about until they became very drunk" (Landa 1978 [ca. 1566]:71). *Balche'* (Landa's "wine") is an exception, however; Landa notes its use in most of the monthly festivals (i.e., those taking place during each of the eighteen divisions of the Maya *haab'*, or year), some of which were limited to practitioners of certain professions (whereas others were celebrated by the community as a whole). Two that especially stand out are those for the months of Tzek and Yaxk'in. The sponsor of the Tzek festival hosted the event in his house and invited all those who kept bees for their honey.

During the festival, the participants presented numerous offerings to the deities, especially to the four Chaakob (Rain Deities), to whom "they gave four platters with balls of incense in the middle of each, and painted on the rims with figures of honey, to bring abundance of which was the purpose of the ceremony" (Landa 1978 [ca. 1566]:73). Landa notes that the ceremony concluded with the drinking of wine, for which the hive owners provided abundant stores of honey.

Yaxk'in saw preparations for an initiation ceremony that took place during the following month (Mol). An elderly woman dressed in a feathered cape presided; to assure that they would grow up to be fine craftsmen in the trades of their parents, she gave each of the boys and girls assembled nine blows on their knuckles. The ceremony concluded, unsurprisingly, with a feast, or what Landa calls "a fine drinking affair." Of this, he remarks, "[W]e must not believe that the devout old woman was allowed to become so drunk as to lose the feathers of her robe on the road" (Landa 1978 [ca. 1566]:75). From this, we must conclude that elderly women—at least those performing ritual roles—were permitted to drink *balche'* on occasion. Although not further specified by Landa, this passage brings to mind the elderly "sorceresses" Landa discusses, who played the role of midwives, healers, and "godparents" for a particular community.

Chuchiak (2003:145) pieces together a more detailed account of *balche'* offerings from a number of Colonial period documents, finding that a ritual specialist, or *ah k'in*, conducted *balche'* ceremonies, which a sponsor—generally a member of the elite class—financed. The *ah k'in* directed participants (all male, according to Chuchiak's sources) in constructing an altar, where they placed stone and clay images of the deities on leaves of the *habin* tree (*Piscidia piscipula*). They hung gourds containing *balche'* from the altar, and around this they built a wooden enclosure that served as the sacred space for the performance of the ritual (Chuchiak 2003:145). The four-sided ritual space and the combination of nine and thirteen gourds—ritual numbers that scholars link to the underworld and celestial realm, respectively—served to re-create the Maya cosmos.

Following this, the *ah k'in* offered *balche'* directly to the gods by pouring it onto the lips of the deity images. Next, he offered four gourds of *balche'*, one to each of the world directions, and then drank a fifth gourd to symbolize the central space (Chuchiak 2003:147). The remaining participants were then free to drink their gourds of *balche'* and partake of the ritual foods, although this took place based on their social rank or political position, meaning that those of the highest rank received their *balche'* first, followed by members of the farming class. This pattern continued until all of the *balche'* had been drunk and the participants were inebriated (Chuchiak 2003:147). At the conclusion of the ritual, the selection of the host or sponsor for the next ceremony occurred. Although costly, this was considered a prestigious position that allowed the individual chosen to develop important social ties and gain political power.

Reference to the ethnohistoric sources suggests several important facets about the social relationships enacted through *balche'* rituals. Elites organized and paid for them, and they may also have controlled access to the materials necessary for making the drink. Certainly, the order in which participants drank *balche'* reinforced hierarchies. The rituals occasioned reciprocal relationships between elites in the community as the obligation to hold the ceremony rotated through them, and they fulfilled their obligations to feed the deities in return for the deities feeding them. Elites also cemented the loyalty of the agricultural class by means of such rituals, and men bonded more generally through their participation in the ceremonies, as did women who socialized as they fulfilled their own obligations in the form of ceremonial preparations. The consumption of *balche'* was also believed to have curative effects, and participation in the ceremony served to bring members of the community together for a common purpose (Chuchiak 2003:147). Chuchiak (2003) notes that, on occasion, the need for community cohesion overrode the restrictions on women participating, and Landa reports that elderly women were at times involved in dances and drinking (Landa 1978 [ca. 1566]).

Contemporary *Balche'* Rituals

Balche' continues to form a key component of rituals in Yucatec Maya communities today, as well as among the Lacandón, along with the maize drink *saka'* (often sweetened with honey), ritual "breads," and tobacco. To get a better sense of how these rituals illustrate human-deity relationships, we focus first on the ceremony for renewing the god pots in the Lacandón Maya community of Naja' (located in the rainforest of Chiapas, Mexico), and then discuss the *u hanli kab'* ceremony in Tepich, Quintana Roo.

As was the case in the Colonial period, in Yucatán today individuals sponsor the *balche'* rituals and provide the bulk of the materials (consumable and otherwise); they also hire a ritual specialist to oversee the ceremony. This specialist, called the *hmen*, intones the prayers and ensures adherence to the proper order of events (Love and Peraza Castillo 1984). Among the Lacandón, the sponsor and his sons or sons-in-law are responsible for preparing the *balche'*, whereas his wives prepare the ceremonial foods in a special cooking hut used solely for preparing ritual foods.

Lacandón *Balche'* Ceremonies

The Lacandón ceremony for renewing the god pots provides a close analogue to rituals practiced prior to Spanish contact documented in colonial sources, although the lack of a ritual hierarchy (i.e., a priesthood) suggests some very significant differences. The ritual itself took place in the god house, a structure that had many functions, including storing the god pots and other ritual paraphernalia when not in use (see Davis 1978:59, Figure 8, for the layout). A god pot was a vessel modeled with the features of a particular deity. It was uninhabited until activated ceremonially by the burning of incense, at which time the god would come to temporarily reside in his god pot to receive the prayers and offerings of the supplicants. The principal Lacandón deities include Äkinchob, the god of the milpa; Äkna', the moon goddess; Hachäkyum, the solar deity and creator of humans; Ixchel, the goddess of pregnancy and childbirth; K'ak', god of fire and war; Kisin, lord of death; Mensäbäk, god of rain; and Sukunkyum, lord of the underworld (McGee 1990:62–63, Table 6.1). *Balche'* ceremonies are primarily undertaken as a payment for favors already given, but they may also be performed to "bribe" certain deities, such as the Rain Deities (*ha'anak'uh*), to provide more favorable weather conditions (Davis 1978:106).

The Lacandón from the community of Naja' prepare *balche'* for a number of different ceremonial occasions. R. Jon McGee witnessed a *balche'* ceremony in the early 1980s, in which the ritual participants prepared the beverage using ten large jarfuls of water, carried in a clay jar with a representation of the god of *balche'* (Bol or Bor) modeled on the side; five liters of honey (although sugar cane or granulated sugar could be substituted); and an unspecified number of strips of *balche'* bark. The ceremony's sponsor, aided by one of his sons or sons-in-law, collected the ingredients and transported them to the *balche' chem* (a hollow tree in the shape of a canoe), where they mixed them together, covered them with palm and banana leaves to protect them from contamination, and left them to ferment for a period of twelve to twenty-four hours (McGee 1991).

Based on her residence with the Lacandón in the 1970s, Virginia Dale Davis notes that one of the community elders generally sponsors the *balche'* ritual and decides whether it is important to make a new *balche' chem* prior to the ceremony. These logs used to make the "canoes" are approximately twenty feet long and two feet in diameter and are made of mahogany (*caoba*; *Swietenia macrophylla*) or another durable wood such as *k'uh che'* (*cedro*; *Cedrela odorata*). This is the first of a number of cooperative acts undertaken in preparing the *balche'* drink. Only married men with pregnant wives, or those who stop to watch, are required to help hew the new *balche' chem* or contribute to making the drink. These same men also help drag it from the forest, where it is constructed, to the lake, where it is towed to the opposite shore and then dragged into position near the god house (Davis 1978:85–86). Women do not participate in making the *balche' chem* or *balche'* drink, except for the sponsor's wives, provided they are not pregnant. Women whose husbands are involved may watch the *balche'* drink being made. This process may last as long as three days and begins with those making the drink cutting and beating branches of the *balche'* tree to loosen the bark, which is peeled off and dried (Davis 1978:87). It is then treated in a manner similar to that described in the ethnohistoric sources.

Before offering *balche'* to the gods, the sponsor or his appointee leads two chants that are said to prevent hangovers. These are required when offering *balche'* (and other items) as payment to the gods (Davis 1978: 88). The ceremonial sponsor consecrates the *balche'* with the participation of the men in the community. This takes place in the middle of the night, and involves a chant, sometimes preceded by a flute version of the melody. It serves to transform the foamy, fermenting liquid into a "supernaturally efficacious substance" (Davis 1978:89). Women are prohibited from watching the consecration, which would negate its effectiveness.

The deities selected to receive offerings are fed through their god pots with a couple of drops of *balche'* placed on their mouths. When the gods receive the *balche'*, they consume its essence (*pishan*), which is the opposite of how it tastes to humans; in other words, the earthly version should be weak so that it is strong when the gods consume it. The making of *balche'* is overseen by the god Bor, who tracks the progress of the mixture as it ferments. The ceremonial sponsor chooses someone to assume Bor's responsibilities in the earthly realm, and this man oversees each aspect of the process, from collecting the ingredients to mixing them, intoning the chants, pouring the beverage, and so forth (Davis 1978:106). In this sense, Bor and the person filling his role at Naja' enter into a unique relationship for the duration of the ceremony.

The consumption of *balche'* is also linked to one's relationship to the deity world. Only those men and women who have made their *mekchur* payment to the gods—a presentation of offerings in a ceremonial setting following a child's survival into adulthood—are eligible. While both men and women participate in *balche'* consumption, it is an activity primarily meant to bind the men of the community through their shared participation in the ritual, and to ensure that their obligations to the deities have been met. Indeed, all men residing in the community are expected to join in the ritual activities taking place in the god house (Davis 1978: 106–107). Women, on the other hand, are excluded from the primary site of the ritual (the god house), but they gather in the ceremonial cooking house of the sponsor's wife, where they are brought one or two cupfuls of *balche'* by their husbands.

Like the god pots, the jug in which *balche'* is served is anthropomorphic. Although it is named for Bor (the god of alcoholic beverages), the jug used in the largest god house at Naja' was manufactured by the Rain Deity, Mensäbäk (Davis 1978:113). The current and previous owners therefore have a kin relationship with the Rain Deity.

Another edible offering made during the ritual is cacao, used to flavor the *balche'* or maize drink. It is prepared at the direction of the sponsor's wife, who uses a traditional stone mano and metate to grind the roasted cacao beans, to which she adds a type of grass that makes the cacao beverage foam. This part of the process takes place in the god house, one of the few times when a woman is permitted to enter it (the other is during the ritual instruction of her daughters, which takes place during the *mekchur* payment). The sponsor's principal wife prepares the cacao with the help of her younger female relatives, much as the wife of the principal celestial deity teaches the younger women the skills needed to froth cacao offered to the principal god, K'akoch (Davis 1978:213–214).

Each of the edible offerings—except for the *balche'*—is prepared by women (the sponsor's wife and her daughters/daughters-in-law) within the ceremonial cookhouse. Davis (1978:61) notes that women used to sing as they made the ceremonial food; this let the gods know that offerings were being prepared and they would soon be summoned. A number of inedible offerings, prepared by the men, are also presented during the *balche'* ceremony, including copal incense, rubber figures, and headbands (Davis 1978:76). These are transformed when received by the gods—the incense into food and the rubber figures into servants (McGee 1990:91).

Davis (1978:106) notes that although generally no longer practiced, the men participating in the *balche'* ritual once played musical instruments (rattles, flutes, and drums) as part of the ceremony, both to highlight different stages of the ritual and as a form of entertainment. Storytelling and singing were also important components of the ceremony. The pre-

Hispanic sources suggest that these types of performances were another facet of human-deity interactions. Indeed, specific deities, such as K'ayum among the Lacandón, were the patrons of music and song, and certain individuals developed special relationships with them (McGee 1990:62).

The Lacandón example differs from the ethnohistoric examples recorded in Yucatán in a number of respects. First of all, there is no ritual specialist present among the Lacandón, although the sponsor and sponsor's wife seem to fill that role. And though this may depend on the perspectives of those recording the ritual processes, the wives seem to play a more central role in the ritual, and their status in terms of whether or not they are pregnant influences their husbands' and their own participation in various elements of the ceremony. While women cannot watch the consecration of the *balche'*, they can enter into the god house to prepare the cacao, and they prepare the ceremonial foods in a designated cookhouse, occasionally singing, and certainly building social ties. As was the case with the rituals previously described, the gods inhabit physical materials — in this case the god pots. Somewhat distinctly, one god (Bor) plays a role in the ceremony through the enactment of one of the ritual participants, who thereby achieves an intimate relationship with that deity. This closely corresponds to representations that we see in the codices and fits well with our ontological perspective; it may not have been noted by Spaniards recording rituals during the Colonial period due to limitations they faced in understanding the rituals.

Making New God Pots

God pots may be shared with one's father or father-in-law, and typically number between five and seventeen per household (Davis 1978:73). Both male and female deities are represented and are distinguished by the patterning on their clothing (Davis 1978:72). When constructing one's god pots, the owner selects those deities that he believes will provide the most help in response to his supplications (Davis 1978:74). These are "crafted as a corporeal replica of the god to whom it is dedicated. Five cacao beans are placed in the bowl of the new god pot to represent the heart (*pishan*), lungs (*sat'ot'*), liver (*tamen*), stomach (*tsukir*), and diaphragm" (Davis 1978:75). Moreover, the heads are given anthropomorphic features; the body serves as the chest, and the bottom as the feet.

In communities such as Naja', the manufacture of new god pots involves the performance of a god pot renewal ceremony, held approximately every four years. The manufacturing process, undertaken in a temporary shelter outside the community, takes approximately three months to complete. Those involved in making the new god pots also construct small pots used for making offerings and a god pot with arms for the wife of the caretaker of the underworld (Äknah).

Once the new god pots are completed, a ceremony is held to present them. This involves burning copal in the god pot dedicated to Äknah in the early morning, followed by the burning of a large rubber figure in the same god pot, which takes place in the area outside the god house. This signals to the deities that they should descend from the celestial realm to inhabit their new god pots. It is accompanied by a song, during which the owners awaken the new god pots by striking them with beads that were acquired originally from the gods, who are credited with making them (Davis 1978:75, 77).

At the end of the ceremony, the Äknah god pot and the small offering pots are taken to a sacred cave to be left as offerings, as are the god pots that are being retired (those full of copal). Those responsible for their ritual deposition cover the offerings with palm leaves and burn incense to them (Davis 1978:76).

The new god pots, like those made previously, are intended to stave off illness and death, which is accomplished by supplicating and feeding ("paying") the deities for cures. In this way, they serve as intercessors between the world of humans and that of the gods and establish a relationship of reciprocity between the two. This is mirrored in the upperworld by the actions of the deities there, who call on the principal god K'akoch by supplicating their god pots, and ask him not to destroy their way of existence and to keep them from growing old (Davis 1978:77).

Balche' Ceremonies in Yucatán

In contrast to those of the Lacandón, indigenous deities supplicated in Tepich, Quintana Roo, are primarily limited to the deity protectors of the land, the community, and the animals; the directional Rain Deities (Chaakob); and the principal Rain Deity, Kun K'uh (Jong 1999). Of the several rituals in which *balche'* is offered as payment to the gods in Yucatec Maya communities, we focus on the *u hanli kab'*, or dinner of the bees, of which honey is one of the principal components.

In celebrating the *u hanli kab'*, the ceremonial sponsor selects a *hmen* to oversee the ceremony. The *hmen*'s first responsibility is to prepare *balche'*. The process involved is similar to that described in the previous section.

The *balche'* must be ready before the other offerings are made so that it can be used to sanctify, or consecrate, the other ritual offerings, which include special breads (*xnohwahob*), a corn gruel (*saka'*), a chicken broth (*k'ol*), a porridge (*xnabal*), the *hostias* (hosts), and the "bees." The "bees" are made from a mixture of cornmeal and honey from the *xunan kab'*, and are placed in two cleaned calabash (*Crescentia cujete*) gourds that are later left in the structure housing the beehives (Jong 1999:183).

With the exception of the *balche'*, the wife of the sponsor prepares the other ritual food items and receives assistance from the other female members of the *solar*. The main ingredients of the ritual foods include maize, which is used to prepare the *saka'*, the *xnabal*, the *xnohwahob*, and the *hostias*; chickens; *xunan kab* honey (used in the "bees" and the *hostias*, as well as the *balche'*); and squash seeds (Jong 1999:183). The sacred meal is composed, therefore, of foods resulting from both male and female labor (the former including maize, squash, and honey, and the latter, chickens). Prior to the introduction of European animals, turkeys would have been used instead of chickens. It is interesting to note, however, that the word for wild turkey (*kutz*) appears in the codical texts referencing faunal offerings, rather than that for domesticated turkey (*tso'*). Additionally, other species of game animals, including deer, turtle, and fish, were also important ritual offerings depicted in almanacs in the Dresden and Madrid codices (V. Bricker 1989; Vail and Hernández 2013). This suggests that during the Postclassic period, men may have been solely responsible for procuring the foods prepared as offerings to the deities—something that is no longer the case today. In so doing, they acquired obligations to the *ah kanulob* of both the forest and of the *solar*.

To prepare the ritual meal described above, women in Tepich grind maize for the *saka'* and the various breads and prepare the breads for cooking—a task in which the *hmen* participates so as to make sure that they are done to the deities' specifications. Prior to baking the *xnohwahob* (thick corn tortillas), they are decorated in a particular fashion, which can include adding patterns of crosses or dots. The *hmen* then fills the indentations in the tortillas with *balche'* and pepitas (ground squash seeds), using a scoop made from a *habin* leaf. The *hostias*—a mixture of *xunan kab'* honey and cornmeal—are also decorated like the *xnohwahob* and "consecrated" with *balche'* and pepitas to make them fit for the deities who receive the offering (Jong 1999:183–184).

While the women prepare the tortillas, the men dig the pit for the earth oven, or *pib'*, lay a layer of logs across it and a layer of stones on top of that, and then burn the logs. Once the logs have burned sufficiently, the stones collapse into the pit. This is the signal to place the chickens and various breads into the *pib'*, cover them with palm leaves and earth, and leave them overnight. The next day, before removing the baked offerings, the *hmen* sprinkles *balche'* over the *pib'* to sanctify them.

To celebrate the *u hanli kab'* in an appropriate manner, the *hmen* must prepare a space that allows interaction between the deities and their human hosts. For the Lacandón, this is provided by the god house, whereas Yucatec communities have no such permanent structure. Therefore, while the food cooks, the *hmen* builds an altar in front of the structure housing the bees in the *solar* on which to place the offerings to the deities. It must be constructed to certain specifications to meet the deities' expectations: it is square in shape to mirror the quadripartite world, and has two arches composed of *habin* leaves and twine to signify the sky. The *hmen* covers the table with *habin* leaves that form a surface fit for receiving the offerings for the deities. He then places a cross, his divining crystal, the hosts, *xnabal*, and *balche'* in a row running down the center of the table. The other offerings (the *saka'*, *xnohwah*, and calabashes with *k'ol*) are placed on either side, with six offerings on one side of the table and seven on the other (Jong 1999:184).

From the center of the arched branches, the *hmen* hangs a calabash of *saka'*, another with broth (*k'ol*), and one of the large tortillas with a cross and arc design. These are placed at the hole to the sky, where the deities are said to descend to receive the offerings. Beneath the altar, also at the center, the *hmen* places a tin containing resins (*chal*) harvested from the beehives, which is used as an incense to attract the deities. Additionally, two candles on the altar are lit for the gods who come to partake of the offerings. The "bees," an offering made of cornmeal and honey, are placed on a log in the apiary (Jong 1999:184).

Following the invitation to the gods to join the meal, the *hmen* divides the food and beverages among the ceremonial participants (all men), and the sponsor chooses someone to take the *k'ol* to the women and children, who are gathered in the kitchen area of the *solar* (Jong 1999: Prologue; Love and Peraza Castillo 1984:264). In this way, the entire family and extrafamily group of participants joins in sharing the ritual meal and in fulfilling their obligations to the deities who allowed them to harvest the honey and wax from the *xunan kab'* hives for ritual and personal use.

In this context, the *hmen* once again plays his critical role as mediator between humans and the gods. Bees exist in the ceremony not only through their contributions of honey but also in the little figures of cornmeal and honey occupying the beehives nearby. Women prepare the foods and men cook them. Men eat the foods and drink the *balche'*, while women and children receive the foods deemed ritually appropriate.

Pre-Hispanic *Balche'* Rituals: Evidence from the Codices

The Maya codices depict a number of ceremonies in honor of the deities, including a dozen or more dedicated to the deity owners of the stingless bees. In light of the descriptions of the *u hanli kab'* ritual in Tepich and the Lacandón *balche'* ceremonies, we draw conclusions about the activities and rituals enacted, as well as the relationships they suggest between human and deity participants and between human actors.

What may be a Postclassic version of the *u hanli kab'* ritual is depicted on page 106a of the Madrid Codex (Figure 12.1), where the creator deity Itzamna appears in the role of the ritual specialist, as indicated by his headdress (termed a "miter" by Landa) and the serpent scepter he holds for sprinkling *balche'*. The *ha'* glyph in his other hand (signifying "water" or "liquid" more generally) likely represents *balche'*, and he stands adjacent to a thatched structure containing beehives (in this instance, only one is shown, with a bee emerging from it). A vessel with glyphs representing maize foods and an iguana offering indicates the types of foods prepared for the ritual, and the four directional glyphs surrounding the picture symbolize a ritual circuit around the hives, similar to that described for the *balche'* ceremony in ethnohistoric sources.

The fact that the *hmen* is portrayed by Itzamna suggests that this was the principal deity invoked in the ritual payment, of which we see only a simplified set of offerings (perhaps a type of broth or porridge prepared with iguana, as well as some of the *xnohwahob*). The image may imply that the *hmen* became the god Itzamna during the ritual, much as the sponsor's assistant in the god pot ceremony became the god Bor. If the ethnographic data provide useful guidelines, then women of the family sponsoring the ritual prepared the offerings of iguana and tortillas, which men cooked in a *pib'* (e.g., Jong 1999). Although the altar is not pictured, the depiction of Itzamna adjacent to the thatched structure housing the bees' hives suggests it would have been present next to the hives, as in the *u hanli kab'* ceremony celebrated at Tepich.

In performing the ritual, the *hmen* not only offers payment to Itzamna in recompense for the honey harvest (perhaps that depicted in the first frame of the almanac on Madrid Codex pages 103c–104c [Figure 12.2],

Figure 12.1. Creator Deity Itzamna performing what is likely an *u hanli kab'* ceremony in front of a thatched structure housing a beehive, on Madrid Codex page 106a. After Brasseur de Bourbourg (1869–1870).

which shows Itzamna having just finished harvesting honey from the hive). He is named as the bees' owner in the text (*u kab' itzamna*, "Itzamna's bees"). Similarly, he is named as the owner of the bees that have recently been established in a new colony on Madrid 103c, frame 1 (*och yotoch u kab' itzamna*, "Itzamna's bees enter their house"). In a cognate scene on Madrid 105c–106c, offerings are given to mark the establishment of Itzamna's bees in their home. These include a (wild?) turkey and rubber incense that is being burned in a brazier. As we have seen in reference to the Lacandón, incense is one of the items fed to the gods, and rubber figures are burned to them. It is of particular interest that it is rubber incense (*k'ik'*), rather than copal (*pom*), that is the principal incense offering to the deities in the beekeeping almanacs of the codex. Although its significance is not clear, it may have been offered as a substitute for blood (also called *k'ik'*). Among the Lacandón of Naja', red paint is a substitute for blood offerings.

In the other almanacs that depict offerings as part of the establishment of new hives, the Maize Deity also receives iguana offerings (as did Itzamna for the *u hanli kab'*), and the death god's offerings consist of fire and bones (see Madrid Codex 103c, frame 2; 104c–105c, frame 2). This is also the case on Madrid 103b–106b, frame 3, in an almanac that seems to be associated with harvesting honey from the hives (Figure 12.3). If this is what was intended, then it may be a shorthand version of the *u hanli kab'* ritual depicted on Madrid 106a. In the almanac on 103b–106b, the offerings and associated ceremonial dates are included for thirteen different deity owners. Only the first five are pictured, however; the others are simply mentioned in the text caption. Offerings are segregated into those given to celestial/upperworld deities (including *xnohwahob* and animals such as turtles, turkey, and deer), and those given to underworld/death deities (including fire, bones, skulls, and disembodied eyeballs).

We find this intriguing for what it reveals about human-deity relationships: similar to the case of the Lacandón, each of the deities associated with the natural world played a role in human food-procurement pursuits and required acknowledgment in the form of prayers and offerings of comestible items. The latter varied in form based on the deity's primary associations and abode, and the human actors who incurred the obligations were required to know the appropriate form of offering in each situation (depending on which deity was involved and the day in the sacred calendar on which the ritual occurred). For this, they engaged the services of a ritual specialist (*hmen*), who used codices to record what the numbers and types of offerings should be.

Human-deity relationships are also determined by the associations and

Figure 12.2. Harvesting honey from the hive, on Madrid Codex pages 103c–104c. After Brasseur de Bourbourg (1869–1870).

Figure 12.3. Ritual offerings made during the honey harvest, on Madrid Codex pages 103b–106b. After Brasseur de Bourbourg (1869–1870).

prognostications linked to particular actions and actors on specified dates in the ritual calendar, or *tzolk'in*. For example, on auspicious dates associated with the upperworld deities, prognostications include "abundance of food," "feasting," and "goodness." These examples illustrate the reciprocity that takes place in human-deity interactions when humans fulfill their ritual obligations to the deities. On the other hand, rituals performed on inauspicious days associated with the underworld deities have negative repercussions and can lead to illness or death or to other bad omens.

The almanac on Madrid 103b–106b (described above; see Figure 12.3) differs from the others in this section of the codex in that it highlights three ritually significant dates—Kib' (wax), Kab'an (honey, bee), and Etz'nab' (flint/flint knife). This may express the duration of the ceremony in each instance (three days), the first being when the honey and wax are extracted and the *balche'* made, the second when the ritual offerings are made, and the third when other ritual events (such as bloodletting?) were undertaken. It is clear from the other almanacs throughout this section of the codex that Kab'an days were those preferred for activities involving the bees, especially harvesting the honey, introducing bees to new hives, and performing rituals of payment to the deities. It is not always the case that the activities take place on Kab'an days, however. Honey extraction also takes place on 13 K'an and 13 Ik', for example. Both are days with generally positive associations in the *tzolk'in*, however (the glyph naming K'an is also used for foods made from maize, and Ik' has the meaning of "wind, breath" and "life").

On Madrid 109a (Figure 12.4), we see what may be the descent of the bee deities to receive the essence of the offerings. In this respect, it is of interest that the offerings depicted in the first frame include the glyphic collocation for abundance (*yax-k'an*) in a vessel (perhaps suggesting an abundant harvest or an abundance of the food offering intended), and rubber incense in an *incensario*, which is also shown in the third frame, although this is substantially eroded. Itzamna's bees are said to produce abundantly in the caption to the first frame, and the third frame may specify that the Maize Deity's bees produced abundantly. The almanac begins on the day 10 Kab'an in the ritual calendar, an appropriate time for offerings to Itzamna.

Another almanac that varies from the others in this section occurs on Madrid 110a (Figure 12.5). Its calendric and hieroglyphic texts are, unfortunately, substantially eroded, but its four frames provide valuable information on how the pre-Hispanic Maya of Yucatán perceived stingless bees and their cosmological significance. What is portrayed is a quadripartite

Figure 12.4. Deities imbibing the essence of offerings made, on Madrid Codex page 109a. After Brasseur de Bourbourg (1869–1870).

Figure 12.5. Bees associated with the four world quarters, marked by the world trees on Madrid Codex page 110a. After Brasseur de Bourbourg (1869–1870).

mapping of space, represented by four different types of trees or vegetation (a cacao tree in the first frame, what may be a ceiba in the second, a spiny plant—perhaps an agave—in the third, and an unidentified plant—possibly tobacco—in the fourth). A bee is shown descending to each, with what appears to be the avian form of Itzamna (the "Principal Bird Deity") perched on the ceiba tree in the second frame. We interpret this almanac as showing the establishment of the present world, attributed to the Bakab deities in the *Book of Chilam Balam of Chumayel*, who plant trees in the four world quarters to separate the earth from the sky (Knowlton 2010:65). The inclusion of bees in the four scenes indicates that they were likewise part of this creation, offered to the human inhabitants as a source of precious substances, much like the plants on which they perched. This, then, provides a mythological basis for the relationships linking humans, deities, and stingless bees up to the ethnographic present.

Balche' would undoubtedly have been a component of many of the other ritual scenes in the codices, although it is not easy to recognize, since it has not been identified epigraphically. It may be the case, however, that it was called *ha'*, as among the Lacandón, with various modifying adjectives. If this proves to be true, then it had a widespread distribution in the screenfold books.

It may be referenced in the caption to the first frame of the almanac on Dresden Codex pages 32a–35a (Figure 12.6), for example. On the right side of the picture, Chaak is shown holding an offering of tortillas sweetened with honey. He stands facing a seated deity, who is named as the god of the year, or *haab'*. The text specifies that the version of Chaak pictured here is the red, or eastern, Chaak. He is associated with the phrase *chak ha'* ("great water," possibly signifying *balche'*) and with a collocation meaning "feast," modified by the phrase *k'ul*, or "sacred." Below the seated deity is a reference to *chak waah*, "great tortillas," likely similar to the *xnohwahob* described for the *u hanli kab'* in Tepich. Although the ceremonial context remains unclear, the payment of food offerings to the deities to reinforce the reciprocal relationship is clearly portrayed.

A later scene in the same almanac shows what is likely *balche'* fermenting in a pot (the vessel is marked by *kab'* glyphs, suggesting that honey is a principal ingredient). A number of other offerings are present (a deer haunch, tortillas, incense), as well as three skulls in a vessel, recalling some of the offerings made to the underworld deities in the almanacs dedicated to the stingless bees. The figure named in the caption, who is also pictured in the scene, is the Rain Deity Chaak, who wears a mantle decorated with footprints and is seated on a platform (described as a road in the text),

Figure 12.6. Ritual offerings involving honey on Dresden Codex pages 32a–35a, including tortillas sweetened with honey (frame 1) and *balche'* fermenting in a vessel (frame 4). After Förstemann (1880).

also marked with footprints. Research undertaken by Victoria and Harvey Bricker (1992) suggests that this serves to mark the halfway point of the solar year, or *haab'*, corresponding to the start of the month Yax.

According to Landa's account, the month Yax was associated with the renovation of the temple in honor of the Chaakob (Landa 1978 [ca. 1566]), a fact that assumes importance in light of the almanac's previous frame, which shows a deity seated within a temple with an offering, and a Chaak lying on top of it. Offerings pictured include deer and turtle meat in tortillas and perhaps a type of porridge. Landa's description goes on to note that the festival celebrated in Yax also involved the renovation of the "terra-cotta idols" and the braziers associated with them (Landa 1978 [ca. 1566]), a description that sounds very much like the Lacandón ceremony for renewing the god pots. It may be this that is highlighted in this almanac.

Of further interest in relation to Davis's discussion of *balche'* rituals among the Lacandón is that the frame occurring just prior to that showing Chaak on top of the temple involves a sacrificial ritual (the Maize Deity has been decapitated). This is likely to signify a harvest ritual, which in Yucatán follows the same structure as the *u hanli kab'*. Offerings of tortillas and incense are pictured, as would be expected, and the four deities depicted (the quadripartite Pawahtuns, or Bakabs) play various musical instruments, similar to those described as originally forming part of ritual offerings to the deities in Lacandón ceremonies. Other codical scenes also point to the importance of music and song in ceremonial contexts involving interactions with deities.

Almanacs such as this make it clear that the feasts prepared in payment to the gods involved not just comestibles but also music, song, and performance. It was only through highly scripted, socially enacted rituals that human-deity relationships could be negotiated and a balance achieved.

Human-God-Bee Relationships Inferred for the Past

As we have shown, humans living in the Maya area during pre-Hispanic times, and in Yucatán in particular, could not just go about the business of procuring food for their families in what today might be called a secular way. No step in the food system could be accomplished without supplication to the gods: not planting the fields, establishing a new beehive, constructing a bee home, or harvesting goods from field and forest. One of these actions necessitated another—as gods initially supplied bees and plants to the world, and in fact owned nonhuman actors such as bees, they could not be ignored as humans reaped the benefits of their production. Similarly, in the process of cementing ties with the deities, humans engaged with bees, food, ritual plants (such as the *habin* tree), and game animals, as well as with one another. Gods could express dissatisfaction with humans through negative outcomes meted out on the plants and animals associated with them, as well as through direct interference with human well-being.

Among humans, we see that women and men maintained separate spaces for activities that enabled rituals to occur, with notable exceptions, including the ability of the *hmen* and elderly women to work across such divides. While at times only men, select elderly women, and gods may have consumed *balche'*, eventually all engaged in eating the ceremonial foods with ingredients consisting primarily of honey, maize, squash seeds, and game animals. These food items represent the labor of men, women, gods, and bees, from locations in the *solar*, the milpa, and the *monte*. The altars further integrated space and the four world quarters invoked during a successful ritual. Humans commemorated the webs of being involved in spaces across the community on a daily basis as they acquired, prepared, and ate foods, but also on the ritual occasions described in this chapter, accompanied by music, song, and performance, and even transformation into other beings across these categorical divides, as humans became gods, for example.

Time itself became an actor as well, seen especially in the prognostications of the *tzolk'in*, and we can detect scribes' preoccupation with tracking auspicious and unfavorable days in the innumerable calendrical calculations found in the Madrid Codex. The moving parts involved in any ritual compelled support from specialists who could help ensure that relationships would not face uncertainty due to failures in planning. The specialist could also confirm the effectiveness of ritual meal preparation and consecration. Meanwhile, hefty provisions required sponsors from the ranks of elites who could bear the cost on behalf of their extended families, while expecting the favor to be returned. A sponsor cemented relationships between people of varying social and gender identities and allowed the powerful to maintain their favor with the gods, sustaining high outputs of honey, maize, and other plant and animal products granted them.

Conclusions

In this chapter, we have provided epigraphic, ethnohistoric, and ethnographic accounts of rituals incorporating *balche'* and related to beekeeping. Ceremonies such as these emphasize the importance of webs of relationship between deities, humans, animals, and plants in accessing food. People—women and men, rich and poor, old and young—reinforced their complex social identities through the roles they played as they prepared for and performed rituals.

References

Alberti, Benjamin. 2016. "Archaeologies of Ontology." *Annual Review of Anthropology* 45:163–179.

Batún Alpuche, Adolfo Iván. 2009. "Agrarian Production and Intensification at a Postclassic Maya Community, Buena Vista, Cozumel, Mexico." PhD diss., University of Florida.

Bianco, Briana, Rani Alexander, and Gary Rayson. 2017. "Beekeeping Practices in Modern and Ancient Yucatán: Going from the Known to the Unknown." In *The Value of Things: Prehistoric to Contemporary Commodities in the Maya Region*, ed. Jennifer P. Mathews and Thomas H. Guderjan, 87–103. Tucson: University of Arizona Press.

Blaser, Mario. 2009. "The Threat of the Yrmo: The Political Ontology of a Sustainable Hunting Program." *American Anthropologist* 111(1):10–20.

Blaser, Mario, and Marisol de la Cadena. 2018. "Pluriverse: Proposals for a World of Many Worlds." In *A World of Many Worlds*, ed. Marisol de la Cadena and Mario Blaser, 1–22. Durham, NC: Duke University Press.

Brasseur de Bourbourg, Charles É. 1869–1870. *Manuscrit Troano: Études sur le système graphique et la langue des Mayas*. Paris: Imprimerie impériale.

Bricker, Victoria R. 1989. "Faunal Offerings in the Maya Codices." In *Sixth Palenque Round Table, 1986*, ed. Merle Greene Robertson (General Editor) and Virginia M. Fields (Volume Editor), 285–292. Norman: University of Oklahoma Press.

Bricker, Victoria R., and Harvey M. Bricker. 1992. "A Method for Cross-Dating Almanacs with Tables in the Dresden Codex." In *The Sky in Mayan Literature*, ed. Anthony F. Aveni, 43–86. New York: Oxford University Press.

Brown, Linda A., and Kitty F. Emery. 2008. "Negotiations with the Animate Forest: Hunting Shrines in the Guatemalan Highlands." *Journal of Archaeological Method and Theory* 15(4):300–337.

Bruman, Henry J. 2000. *Alcohol in Ancient Mexico*. Salt Lake City: University of Utah Press.

Castillo Cocom, Juan, Timoteo Rodríguez, and McCale Ashenbrener. 2017. "Ethnoexodus: Escaping Mayaland." In *"The Only True People": Linking Maya Identities Past and Present*, ed. Bethany J. Beyyette and Lisa J. LeCount, 47–71. Boulder: University Press of Colorado.

Chuchiak, John. 2003. "'It Is Their Drinking That Hinders Them': Balché and the Use of Ritual Intoxicants among the Colonial Yucatec Maya, 1550–1780." *Estudios de Cultura Maya* 24:137–171.

Colección de documentos inéditos relativos al descubrimiento, conquista y colonización de las antiguas posesiones españoles de ultramar. 1579. Published in de la Garza et al. 1983.

Davis, Virginia D. 1978. "Ritual of the Northern Lacandon Maya." PhD diss., Tulane University.

de la Garza, Mercedes, Ana Luisa Izquierdo, María del Carmen León, and Tolita Figueroa, eds. 1983. *Relaciones histórico-geográficas de la gobernación de Yucatán*, vol. 2. Mexico City: Universidad Nacional Autónoma de México.

Escobar, Arturo. 2008. *Territories of Difference: Place, Movements, Life, Redes.* Durham, NC: Duke University Press.

Flores, José Salvador, and E. Ucan Ek. 1983. *Nombres usados por los mayas para designar a la vegetación.* Cuadernos de Divulgación 10. Xalapa, Veracruz, Mexico: INIREB.

Förstemann, Ernst. 1880. *Die Maya Handschrift der Königlichen öffentlichen Bibliothek zu Dresden.* Mit 74 Tafeln in Chromo-Lightdruck. Lichtdruckeret, Leipzig: Verlag der A. Naumannschen.

González-Acereto, J. A., José Javier G. Quezada-Euán, and Luis A. Medina-Medina. 2006. "New Perspectives for Stingless Beekeeping in the Yucatan: Results of an Integral Program to Rescue and Promote the Activity." *Journal of Apicultural Research* 45(4):234–239.

González-Cruz, Gabriela, Eduardo García-Frapolli, and Alejandra Casas. 2015. "Responding to Disturbances: Lessons from a Mayan Socio-Ecological System." *International Journal of the Commons* 9(2):831–850.

Harrison-Buck, Eleanor, and Julia A. Hendon. 2018. "An Introduction to Relational Personhood and Other-Than-Human Agency in Archaeology." In *Relational Identities and Other-Than-Human Agency in Archaeology*, ed. Eleanor Harrison-Buck and Julia A. Hendon, 3–28. Boulder: University Press of Colorado.

Hutson, Scott R. 2010. *Dwelling, Identity, and the Maya: Relational Archaeology at Chunchucmil.* Lanham, MD: Altamira Press.

Ingold, Timothy. 2007. *Lines: A Brief History.* London: Routledge.

———. 2011. *Being Alive: Essays on Movement, Knowledge and Description.* London: Routledge.

Jong, Harriet J. de. 1999. "The Land of Corn and Honey: The Keeping of Stingless Bees (Meliponiculture) in the Ethno-Ecological Environment of Yucatan (Mexico) and El Salvador." PhD diss., Universiteit Utrecht, Netherlands.

Knowlton, Timothy. 2010. *Maya Creation Myths: Words and Worlds of the Chilam Balam.* Boulder: University Press of Colorado.

Landa, Diego de. 1978 [ca. 1566]. *Yucatan Before and After the Conquest* (translation of *Relación de las cosas de Yucatán*). Trans. William Gates. New York: Dover.

Latour, Bruno. 1993. *We Have Never Been Modern.* Cambridge, MA: Harvard University Press.

Love, Bruce, and Eduardo Peraza Castillo. 1984. "Wahil Kol: A Yucatec Maya Agricultural Ceremony." *Estudios de Cultura Maya* 15:251–305.

McGee, R. Jon. 1990. *Life, Ritual, and Religion among the Lacandon Maya.* Belmont, CA: Wadsworth.

———. 1991. "The *Balche'* Ritual of the Lacandon Maya." *Estudios de Cultura Maya* 18:439–457.
Osado, Ricardo ("El Judío"). 1933 [1700s]. "Medicina doméstica." Manuscript in the Ayer Collection (1844), Newberry Library, Chicago.
Paris, Elizabeth H., Carlos Peraza Lope, Marilyn A. Masson, Pedro C. Delgado Kú, and Bárbara C. Escamilla Ojeda. 2018. "The Organization of Stingless Beekeeping (Meliponiculture) at Mayapán, Yucatan, Mexico." *Journal of Anthropological Archaeology* 52:1–22.
Pat Fernández, Lucio Alberto, Francisco Anguebes Franceschi, Juan Manuel Pat Fernández, Pablo Hernández Bahena, and Rodimiro Ramos Reyes. 2018. "Condición y perspectivas de la meliponicultura en comunidades mayas de la reserva de la biósfera Los Petenes, Campeche, México." *Estudios de Cultura Maya* 52:227–254.
Redfield, Robert, and Alfonso Villa Rojas. 1934. *Chan Kom: A Maya Village*. Washington, DC: Carnegie Institution of Washington.
Relación de Nabalam, Tahcabo and Cozumel. 1579. Published in de la Garza et al. 1983.
Restall, Matthew. 1997. *The Maya World: Yucatec Culture and Society, 1550–1850*. Stanford, CA: Stanford University Press.
Robin, Cynthia. 2006. "Gender, Farming, and Long-Term Change: Maya Historical and Archaeological Perspectives." *Current Anthropology* 47(3):409–433.
Roys, Ralph L. 1931. *The Ethno-Botany of the Maya*. New Orleans: Middle American Research Institute, Tulane University.
Thompson, Philip C. 1999. *Tekanto, a Maya Town in Colonial Yucatán*. New Orleans, LA: Middle American Research Institute, Tulane University.
Todd, Zoe. 2016. "An Indigenous Feminist's Take on the Ontological Turn: 'Ontology' Is Just Another Word for Colonialism." *Journal of Historical Sociology* 29(1):4–22.
Vail, Gabrielle. 1994. "A Commentary on the Bee Almanacs in Codex Madrid." In *Códices y documentos sobre México: Primer simposio*, ed. Constanza Vega Sosa, 37–68. Mexico City: Instituto Nacional de Antropología e Historia.
Vail, Gabrielle, and Christine Hernández. 2013. "Maya Hieroglyphic Codices Database." Available at mayacodices.org.
Vail, Gabrielle, and Andrea Stone. 2002. "Representations of Women in Postclassic and Colonial Maya Literature and Art." In *Ancient Maya Women*, ed. Traci Ardren, 203–228. Walnut Creek, CA: Altamira Press.
Watts, Christopher, ed. 2013. *Relational Archaeologies: Humans, Animals, Things*. London: Routledge.
Weaver, Nevin, and Elizabeth C. Weaver. 1981. "Beekeeping with the Stingless Bee *Melipona beecheii*, by the Yucatecan Maya." *Bee World* 62(1):7–19.
Yurrita Obiols, Carmen Lucía, and Mabel Vásquez. 2013. "Stingless Bees of Guatemala." In *Pot-Honey: A Legacy of Stingless Bees*, ed. Patricia Vit, Silvia R. M. Pedro, David Roubik, 99–111. New York: Springer.
Źrałka, Jarosław, Christophe Helmke, Laura Sotelo, and Wiesław Koszkul. 2018. "The Discovery of a Beehive and the Identification of Apiaries among the Ancient Maya." *Latin American Antiquity* 29(3):514–531.

CHAPTER 13

Conclusion: In Maya Food Studies, Who Is Maya? What Is Food?

JEFFREY M. PILCHER

The ancient Maya have enthralled the modern imagination in an increasingly sensorial fashion. During the nineteenth-century age of industry, outsiders first glimpsed ghostly visions of a lost civilization through the travel accounts of John Lloyd Stephens (1841) as illustrated by the classic lithographs of Frederick Catherwood. Beginning with the mid-twentieth-century deciphering of glyphs by Tatiana Proskouriakoff (1963), the Maya acquired a voice to speak of the lineages of dead kings. Now, *Her Cup for Sweet Cacao* conveys the tastes and smells of the Maya to twenty-first-century readers with a growing interest in food. As these chapters show, cracking the Maya culinary code holds enormous promise for expanding our knowledge of diverse gender, status, and ethnic identities within this remarkable ancient world.

Archaeologists and historians, with their shared concern for change over time, have followed broadly similar paths toward the study of food. Scholars in both disciplines first approached food for what it could say about seemingly more important topics; thus, diet and subsistence served as measures of standards of living and of the rise and fall of societies over the *longue durée* (Braudel 1979; Flannery 1982; Haviland 1967; Lentz 1991; Pohl 1994; Rotberg and Rabb 1985; Steckel and Rose 2002; White 1999; Wright 2006). An awareness of culinary cultures as worthwhile subjects took off around 1990, beginning among Mayanists with the analysis of epigraphic and ethnographic sources and as part of the New Cultural History's interest in formerly overlooked texts such as cookbooks (Belasco 1989; Coe 1994; Flandrin and Montanari 1999; Gabaccia 1998; Pilcher 1998; Pyburn 1989; Taube 1989). Research has flourished in both fields since the turn of the century with increasingly sophisticated approaches to sensory analysis, social distinction, identity formation, and historical memory (Freedman 2008; Hastorf 2017; Joyce and Henderson 2007; MacDonald 2008; Norton 2008; Rappaport 2017; Rath 2010; Staller and Carrasco 2010; Stross 2011; Wilk 2006).

Although the contributors to this volume speak to important debates within the field of archaeology, what impressed me most from a food studies perspective was the many ways that foods helped construct social identities within the Maya world. Clearly there was no single Maya cuisine, just as we can no longer speak of modern-day Mexican, Italian, or Chinese national cuisines as anything other than ideological constructs (King 2019; Pilcher 1998; Scarpellini 2015; Wilk 1999). In a similar fashion, food studies scholars have gone a long way toward disaggregating the influences of gender, ethnicity, and class among, for example, African American foods that were once lumped together under the controversial label of "soul food" (Opie 2008; Tompkins 2012; Wallach 2019; Williams-Forson 2006). In deconstructing Maya cuisine, the contributors to this volume make innovative use of such important new food studies approaches as embodied practice, mobility studies, and deconstructing edibility.

More than half of the chapters in this volume mention some form of ritual consumption in their titles, which is hardly surprising, given the centrality of feasting in recent archaeological research (Bray 2003a; Dietler and Hayden 2001; Jones 2007). But scholarly attention to performance extends beyond ceremonial commensality to include diverse expressions of "embodied practice," as performance studies scholars broadly define their subject (Taylor 2003; Worthen 2004). For example, James McCann (2009) has reconstructed the repertoires and improvisations that served to record, convey, and transform cooking skills historically in Africa in the absence of formal cookbooks. The authors herein have been particularly adept at locating the materializations of cooking and eating performances, as well as the meanings and memories they once conveyed, in abandoned spaces and cluttered middens.

Temples, palaces, and courtyards, through their architectural design and ornamentation, leave the most obvious evidence of feasting in the archaeological record, although even here, careful interpretation is needed to discern the social meanings of commensality. M. Kathryn Brown and Carolyn Freiwald (this volume) ground this collection in the Preclassic period by noting that the modest platforms on which the distinctive Mesoamerican truncated pyramids were later built started out as spaces for communal feasting. The debris supporting this conclusion also provides a helpful reminder to the field of food studies, which congratulates itself on the breadth of its vision from "farm to fork" but too often ignores the inevitable waste at the end of (and indeed all along) the commodity chain. Based on an analysis of food remains and ritual artifacts, Brown and Freiwald argue that although these feasts were "potlucks" to which community members contributed, they were not gatherings of equals but rather held "subtle ritual and political dimensions that created the possibility for social positioning and provided opportunities for key participants to gain status and create debts that could lead to their political advantage." Their discussion of a small-scale, early polity contrasts with Maxime Lamoureux-St-Hilaire's account (this volume) of mature Maya kingship at La Corona. This Late Classic Versailles proclaimed the ruler's grandeur to subjects and visitors through a progression of theatrical spaces, from vast public courtyards to intimate throne rooms. Elaborately carved benches served both to stage the ritual consumption of tamales and chocolate and, through glyphs and scenes painted on the backrests, to interpret the political meaning of these feasts as tribute or largesse, all to the accompaniment of musicians and dancers. The chapter also explores the risks involved in hosting such feasts, including environmental stress, food spoilage, and disappointed guests. Thus, whereas Brown and Freiwald point out the latent inequalities of the intimate potluck, Lamoureux-St-Hilaire emphasizes the perils to the powerful of a banquet gone awry.

Feasting played a vital role in maintaining the spiritual realm as well as political life among the ancient Maya. Jon Spenard, Terry G. Powis, Adam King, and Nilesh Gaikwad (this volume) examine the ritual consumption of beverages within caves. Although subterranean grottos have not received the archaeological attention given to pyramids, plazas, and ballcourts, they were nevertheless valued throughout Mesoamerica as critical sites of contact between humans and the supernatural world. Spenard and his coauthors reveal not only the types of beverages that were consumed, including cacao and alcoholic beverages, but also symbolic inversions of the usual associations between ritual spaces and elite males. Both caves and cacao were gendered female among the Maya, and commoners as well as elites likely conducted ceremonies within these extensive underground spaces. Meanwhile, Gabrielle Vail and Maia Dedrick (this volume) map the ritual geography around *balche'*, a honey-based alcoholic beverage, whose consumption patterns corresponded to the four cardinal directions of the Maya cosmos, while also revealing an appreciation of the ecological importance of bees in pollinating crops. Vail and Dedrick likewise pay attention to the gendering of *balche'* rituals; although men and at times respected older women monopolized temple ceremonies, women participated in rituals elsewhere and prepared food offerings.

All of the chapters in this collection offer insights into the embodied practices of Maya cooking, but two in particular examine regional cuisines in a holistic fashion with an eye toward various forms of integration and differentiation. Lilia Fernández Souza, Mario Zimmermann, and Socorro del Pilar Jiménez Álvarez (this volume) use the foodways of a Late Classic settlement in Yucatán to illuminate a social hierarchy comprising not only elites and commoners but also a range of intermediate groups. Households were ranked first by access to raw materials, including domesticated and hunted animals, fields, gardens, orchards, beehives, and even water from private cenotes (sinkholes). Culinary equipment afforded another way of displaying status through delicate serving dishes and specialized tools and appliances such as storage containers, grinding stones, and cutting implements. The greatest sign of status (among the ancient Maya and still today) was the ability to command the labor of others, whether gangs of men working in the fields or cadres of women grinding corn and wrapping tamales. Fernández and her collaborators found a remarkable variation between high- and low-status households. Although fancy imported metates and obsidian blades are unsurprising in elite kitchens, the complete absence of grinding stones among the very poor is quite astonishing. Did humble women grind their metates literally to dust or carry them off when moving house, while more affluent neighbors bought new ones? Perhaps this indicates a Classic-era version of street foods, which are as much a response to inadequate housing as to any popular desire for alfresco dining. Whatever the case, food clearly materialized social hierarchies not only through unequal access to nutrients but also through tastes and performances of status.

Julia Hendon (this volume) complements the Yucatecan example by showing that food could alternately exacerbate social stratification or help prevent the emergence of such hierarchies. As case studies, she examines the highland Copán valley of western Honduras, which had been incorporated into the Maya world and its political culture of kingship by the fifth century CE, and the Lower Ulúa valley on the northern Honduran coast, which stood apart as a politically decentralized and ethnically diverse frontier, as in some ways it remains to the present. Although inhabitants of the two regions had broadly similar access to ingredients, their differing culinary preferences were expressed through the tastes and refinements of "sauces, fillings, and flavoring elements . . . that reflected local identities, created distinction, and fostered commensal relations." Hendon also reminds us of the culinary performances that attach meaning to foods such as cacao: "Served in tall, finely made and decorated drinking vessels, the liquid would be whipped or poured from a height to produce a frothy, foaming head on the surface of the liquid that seems to have been the quintessence of elegance and was highly valued." Personal identities could also be formed through the labor of food preparation, as Nicholas Carter and Mallory Matsumoto (this volume) illustrate with the example of a woman denoted by hieroglyphs as the "tamale person," although we cannot know if that was how she thought of herself. Hendon's comparative study clearly indicates that local performances of cooking and eating were made possible by and gained meaning within broader networks of travel, trade, and tradition.

To examine such networks, the emerging field of mobility studies offers methodologies that can be as useful for the ancient Maya as for modern globalization. Mobility studies is premised on the notion that although the movements of people, goods, and ideas are often studied in isolation — for example, by migration history, international economics, and media studies — they are in fact connected and can only be understood in relationship to one another. Elizabeth Zanoni (2018) demonstrated the value of such an approach for examining the transatlantic invention of Italian-American cuisine. Often dismissed as bastardized products of assimilation, pasta, cheese, and wine manufactured by migrants in the Americas substituted for expensive Italian imports, thereby satisfying the migrants' desire for familiar foods while allowing them to remit money to family at home. Mobility studies often focuses on three basic variables: the mode of travel, whether merchant ship, pilgrim's trail, or military campaign; the scale of movement, ranging from global to regional and local; and the exceptions to mobility, or the barriers that impede some types of movement but not others. For example, the Columbian exchange of maize to Europe, without the accompanying movement of people (indigenous cooks) and ideas (the alkaline-processing technology nixtamal), contributed to widespread outbreaks of the dietary-deficiency disease pellagra (Pilcher 2012).

Mobility studies often evokes images of jet airplanes and global travelers — or their Classic-era equivalent, Maya chocolate on the Ancestral Pueblos' "turquoise trail" (Crown and Hurst 2009) — but this scholarly framework can also provide insights at more localized scales as well. Marilyn Masson's discussion (this volume) of unequal meat distribution in Terminal Classic and Postclassic Mayapán nicely illuminates how urban gravitational fields can affect the movements of people and commodities. Of course, there is nothing new in cities attracting wealth, but what was more striking was the lack of animal remains in the homes of rural dwellers who should have had access to small game in fields and forests. This finding is all the more significant when extended from the Classic to the Postclassic, as declining human populations might have eased the environmental stresses that contributed to resource inequality. Nevertheless, although highly prized deer meat was widely distributed across the city of Mayapán, poor farmers apparently could not even provide themselves with an iguana. Compounding the riddle, at least one family outside the city wall had access to meat at a comparable level to artisan households within Mayapán. Masson suggests a variety of possible explanations for these rural-urban disparities, including commodity markets, tribute demands, and sumptuary laws. But everyday patterns of mobility could also influence meat consumption, albeit in ways that may be difficult to discern in the archaeological record. Communal feasting outside the home could help ameliorate inequalities, while the preparation and consumption of hunted or trapped animals by men directly in the fields could exacerbate inequalities within the family.

Among the many foods of Mesoamerica, cacao surely had the most extensive commodity trade, reaching as far north as present-day New Mexico. The epigraphical sources examined by Nicholas Carter and Mallory Matsumoto (this volume) reveal a great deal about the tastes and meanings of cacao, which was "variously described as 'new' (*ach*), 'ripe' (*k'an*), 'sweet' (*tzah*), or flavored with a variety of additives including 'honey' (*kab'* or *chab'*), 'lima bean' (*ib'*), 'cherry' (*suutz*), and possibly 'chili' (*ich*)." Moreover, a mural at Piedras Negras situates cacao at the ceremonial heart of a royal reception of visitors. The authors suggest that the ancient Maya may even have had a sense of terroir, identifying and valuing cacao based on its regional origins. Regardless of whether Maya connoisseurs sought to distinguish Soconusco from Belize cacaos in blind tastings, Julia Hendon clearly shows that origins mattered in the meanings attached to cacao. Although a local crop in the Lower Ulúa valley, produced and consumed by ordinary folk, it was an imported commodity at Copán, used by elites to participate in a pan-Maya culture of kingship and to differentiate themselves from their subjects. Nevertheless, the cultivar-commodity dichotomy does not explain the full range of cacao's meanings or the greater or lesser degrees of social distinction derived from it, even among the cases surveyed in this volume (cf. Fernández Souza, Zimmermann, and Jiménez Álvarez; Spenard et al.).

The circulation of recipes and culinary equipment could be as significant as commodity exchange in ancient Mesoamerica. Traci Ardren (this volume) makes a compelling case that *molcajetes* (grater bowls or mortars) and comales (earthenware griddles), introduced from central Mexico during the Terminal Classic, provided a critical element of elite identity at Chichén Itzá. A "city like no other," this Yucatecan metropolis arose as other Maya urban centers were declining, and it shared monumental architecture, a luxury trade, and a messianic cult with distant Cholula and El Tajín. Scholars no longer believe that Chichén was founded by invaders from central Mexico, but they still struggle to explain how the city maintained its hegemonic regional grip as commoners elsewhere rejected elite tribute demands. By examining novel cooking utensils in a subject town as well as at the city's ceremonial center, Ardren shows how feasting helped foster shared Itzá identities. Similar examples of culinary soft power range from the standardized Inka kitchenware used to distribute food and reinforce imperial ideology across the Andes (Bray 2003b) to McDonald's Cold War–era burger-and-fry evangelism (Watson 1997). Botanical analysis of the foods prepared in these appliances holds great promise for understanding regional culinary exchanges and transformations during this critical period in Mesoamerican history. With comales came the skills of making tortillas, which, as Vail and her coauthors note, were prized enough to serve as offerings to the bee gods. *Molcajetes*, by contrast, make a curious choice for feasting precisely because they are generally less efficient for large-scale food production than metates, for example, in grinding chile and seeds for making large quantities of mole, a central Mexican festival dish that has never gained particular favor among the Maya. The presence of *molcajetes* in ceremonial centers rather than in detached kitchen sites suggests that they may have been used for intimate dinner parties among the elite rather than grand banquets, rather like the tableside guacamole presentations in upscale Mexican restaurants. (Celebrity chefs may soon rediscover tableside "guacamole à la Chichén Itzá" as the next big trend in the "pre-Hispanic menus" of *la nueva cocina mexicana* [nouvelle Mexican cuisine].)

The high status assigned to *molcajetes* and comales at Chichén Itzá contrasts with the more ambivalent attitudes toward another culinary novelty introduced from central Mexico, pulque. This alcoholic beverage, fermented from the sap of the agave (century plant), has been dated to classic Teotihuacán and spread widely across Mesoamerica. Although a valuable dietary supplement, pulque was associated in the Aztec Empire with the fearsome gods of drunkenness, Four Hundred Rabbits, and was banned from consumption by commoners (Bruman 2000; Correa-Ascencio et al. 2014; Taylor 1979). The introduction of pulque to the Maya world seems to have not been well documented yet, but the Late Classic epigraphic references discussed by Carter and Matsumoto (this volume) indicate the fascination and dread that this beverage inspired among the Maya as well. Depictions of pulque consumption, by way of enemas to heighten its psychoactive properties, suggest that the goal was to achieve otherworldly visions rather than to enhance sociability in drinking together. The few known narratives likewise refer to ceremonial occasions such as making offerings, impersonating gods, or dedicating structures. At times, Maya glyphs record kings consuming pulque, although that was not necessarily a positive thing. In China, the last emperor of Shang is remembered for drinking so much that he lost the Mandate of Heaven and was overthrown by the Zhou (Sterckx 2015). Unlike the Aztec rulers who banned consumption by commoners, the Maya elite seem to have provided the pulque to their subordinates, or at least preferred to be depicted in that fashion. As Native Americans discovered with the arrival of European distilled liquor, exotic foods can prove dangerously alluring.

The example of pulque points to a third important line of research, pursued here and in food studies more generally, which seeks to question the focus of the entire field. Shanti Morell-Hart (this volume) frames the issue quite bluntly: "When it comes to ancient Maya foods, we cannot even take edibility for granted." By exploring the boundaries of what is considered to be food, we can see more clearly the ways that social meanings are constructed around it. Although evolutionary psychologists may well be correct in attributing humans' remarkable taste memory to the foragers' need to distinguish safe foods from toxins (the "omnivore's paradox"), it may be more useful to examine how these mental tools have been repurposed in a cultural fashion to distinguish insiders from outsiders. The visceral unease arising from foods that are perceived as dangerous has often been reflexively associated with people who eat such foods, making them appear less than human (Fischler 1980; Long 2004; Rohel 2017; Tompkins 2012). Another socially constructed boundary has arisen at times between food and medicine. Although the Chinese, for example, consider food to be crucial to health (Chang 1977), Western societies increasingly separated the two categories beginning in the early modern period (Flandrin 1999). Nevertheless, even in Europe and North America, the boundaries inevitably blur, as Sidney Mintz (1985) noted in his discussion of sugar as a "drug food." Alcohol may likewise be considered as food—a glass of wine with dinner—or as a drug—as in late-night binge drinking (Wilson 2005). Finally, social rules govern the constitution of a proper meal; Audrey Richards (1939) observed agrarian societies in which people did not feel that they had eaten without a culturally significant starch. By contrast, Mary Douglas (1972) defined middle-class, Anglo-American meals of the mid-twentieth century by the formula meat plus two side dishes.

The central place of maize in diet and culture was seemingly universal among the Maya, and indeed throughout Mesoamerica. Fernández Souza, Zimmermann, and Jiménez Álvarez (this volume) observe the connection between the "symbolism of divine rulership and the expression of Maya rulers as an embodiment of the Maize Deity." Lamoureux-St-Hilaire (this volume) likewise cites logographs that indicate feasting with "two stylized faces stuffed with tamales and drink." Spenard and his collaborators (this volume) specify further that maize was gendered male, perhaps in part because it favored sunshine, unlike cacao, which was considered female and grew in the shade. Maize could be prepared in diverse ways, including in tamales, tortillas, pozoles (stews), and atoles (smoothies), but the first step in most any recipe was to prepare nixtamal by simmering the maize with an alkaline limestone, a method dating back among the lowland Maya to the Preclassic period (Cheetham 2010). Carter and Matsumoto (this volume) describe "two key benefits [of nixtamalization]: reduction of the labor required to grind maize, by breaking down the kernel's durable external pericarp or shell; and enhanced nutrition, by releasing niacin and amino acids inherent in the maize and contributing additional calcium from the lime." From a modern, functionalist perspective, we can see that nixtamal technology allowed societies to prosper and spread across Mesoamerica as well as the eastern woodlands of North America, where it was called hominy. Why women adopted this recipe in the first place, without knowledge of amino acids or B vitamins, remains a mystery, although one that may be addressed by following Shanti Morell-Hart's suggestion that "the emergence of key staple crops such as maize, beans, and squash was tied more closely to their flavors than to their caloric content." Perhaps early Maya women began adding limestone to their cooking pots because of the rich umami flavors that it imparted to the maize, never imagining that great civilizations would one day rise from their serendipitous culinary experiment.

Apart from the ubiquitous nixtamalized maize, all other components of the Maya diet seem to have been "ethnic foods" that varied with local tastes. Julia Hendon (this volume) shows that even such fundamental Mesoamerican ingredients as beans, a valuable source of protein, and chile peppers, a widely prized condiment, might be absent from regional cuisines. Hendon also reminds us that cooks can prepare the same ingredients in distinctive ways to assert local identities. And, of course, what outsiders might assume to be completely identical foods can provoke intense rivalries; think of *gallo pinto* (black beans and rice in Nicaragua and Costa Rica), arepas (maize patties in Colombia and Venezuela), and tamales (steamed maize dumplings throughout Mesoamerica and the Caribbean basin). Petra Cunningham-Smith, Ashley E. Sharpe, Arianne Boileau, Erin Kennedy Thornton, and Kitty F. Emery (this volume) survey another revealing culinary boundary in their discussion of Maya dog breeding and consumption. They show that although dogs were clearly eaten, tremendous variability occurred in the ways they were consumed and in the meanings they were assigned. Faunal analyses suggest that dogs provided an important nutritional source in early societies, but over time the Maya became more selective in their consumption. In some places, dogs became valued commodities in long-distance trade, while in others, they seem to have disappeared almost entirely from the menu. The authors note that they were a "'sometime food' eaten with the full cognizance of the symbolic meaning of the dog beyond its nutritional value" as "participants in specific ceremonies, hunters, companions (in life and death), healers, and symbols. These combine with the dog's role as food to expand the definition of 'food uses.'"

The cases examined in this book also help us problematize what exactly we mean by eating. The Spanish conquistadors found many New World practices to be profoundly at odds with their expectations of a proper meal. The natives drank alcohol in a binge fashion for its spiritual properties rather than in measured cups to enhance sociability; worse still, they often consumed it by way of enemas. The mastication of tobacco among the Maya and of coca in the Andes was another method of ingesting substances that violated European standards because it was spit out rather than swallowed. Yet another indigenous practice for consuming tobacco was described with astonishment as "drinking smoke" (Schivelbusch 1993:97). These are all efficient methods for consuming substances that stimulate or restore the body, which is perhaps the most basic meaning of the concept of eating, and Europeans eventually reconciled themselves to each, in one way or another. Nevertheless, they illustrate the ways that eating practices, as well as the foods themselves, provide a means for societies to differentiate themselves from supposedly uncivilized others.

One final socially constructed boundary illuminated by the authors serves to divide humans from nonhuman entities. Mesoamerican deities were famously fluid in their identities, often donning the masks of others to assume their character and powers, and Maya rulers likewise regularly impersonated gods in rituals. Taking an ontological perspective on Maya beekeeping, Vail and Dedrick explore the relationships between humans, gods, and animals. To harvest honey successfully, humans not only had to respect the bees themselves but also offer sacrifices to the animals' supernatural protectors, who took the form of giant bees. In a similar fashion, Morell-Hart adopts a posthumanist approach to explore the ways that plants could socialize humans to encourage their transplantation and propagation and through their incorporation into human bodies. Indeed, the Maya famously believed that their flesh was maize.

The emerging field of Maya food studies holds enormous promise for answering long-standing questions about the rise and fall of civilizations, for example, through the invention of nixtamal and feasting at Chichén Itzá. Moreover, attention to food can help frame new research agendas about what it meant to be Maya in terms of gendered cooking and eating and experiments with ethnic foods. By examining embodied practices around food production and consumption, diverse forms of circulation, and the very boundaries of edibility and humanity, these chapters also expand the limits of archaeology and food studies. Nevertheless, the authors say a great deal about communal feasting but far less about everyday home cooking, although Brown and Freiwald note the intimate connection between the two. Likewise, while the contributors discuss the importance of sensory analysis of Maya foodways, even more could be done to show the relationships between taste as physical experience and as social distinction. With continued research along these lines, future surveys of the Maya world will be able to give cooks and farmers the attention they deserve—on a level with priests and kings.

References

Belasco, Warren. 1989. *Appetite for Change: How the Counterculture Took on the Food Industry.* New York: Pantheon Books.
Braudel, Fernand. 1979. *The Structures of Everyday Life: The Limits of the Possible.* Vol. 1 of *Civilization and Capitalism, 15th–18th Century.* Trans. Siân Reynolds. New York: Harper and Row.
Bray, Tamara L., ed. 2003a. *The Archaeology and Politics of Food and Feasting in Early States and Empires.* New York: Kluwer Academic/Plenum.
———. 2003b. "Inka Pottery as Culinary Equipment: Food, Feasting, and Gender in Imperial State Design." *Latin American Antiquity* 14(1):3–28.
Bruman, Henry J. 2000. *Alcohol in Ancient Mexico.* Salt Lake City: University of Utah Press.
Chang, K. C., ed. 1977. *Food in Chinese Culture: Anthropological and Historical Perspectives.* New Haven: Yale University Press.
Cheetham, David. 2010. "Corn, Colanders, and Cooking: Early Maize Processing in the Maya Lowlands and Its Implications." In *Pre-Columbian Foodways: Interdisciplinary Approaches to Food, Culture, and Markets in Ancient Mesoamerica,* ed. John E. Staller and Michael D. Carrasco, 345–368. New York: Springer.

Coe, Sophie D. 1994. *America's First Cuisines.* Austin: University of Texas Press.
Correa-Ascencio, Marisol, Ian G. Robertson, Oralia Cabrera-Cortés, Rubén Cabrera-Castro, and Richard P. Evershed. 2014. "Pulque Production from Fermented Agave Sap as a Dietary Supplement in Prehispanic Mesoamerica." *Proceedings of the National Academy of Sciences* 111(39):14223–14228.
Crown, Patricia L., and W. Jeffrey Hurst. 2009. "Evidence of Cacao Use in the Prehispanic American Southwest." *Proceedings of the National Academy of Sciences* 106(7):2110–2113.
Dietler, Michael, and Brian Hayden, eds. 2001. *Feasts: Archaeological and Ethnographic Perspectives on Food, Politics, and Power.* Washington, DC: Smithsonian Institution Press.
Douglas, Mary. 1972. "Deciphering a Meal." *Daedalus* 101(1):61–81.
Fischler, Claude. 1980. "Food Habits, Social Change, and the Nature/Culture Dilemma." *Social Science Information* 19(6):937–953.
Flandrin, Jean-Louis. 1999. "Dietary Choices and Culinary Technique, 1500–1800." In *Food: A Culinary History from Antiquity to the Present*, ed. Jean-Louis Flandrin and Massimo Montanari; trans. Albert Sonnenfeld, 403–417. New York: Columbia University Press.
Flandrin, Jean-Louis, and Massimo Montanari, eds. 1999. *Food: A Culinary History.* Trans. Albert Sonnenfeld. New York: Columbia University Press.
Flannery, Kent V., ed. 1982. *Maya Subsistence: Studies in Memory of Dennis E. Puleston.* New York: Academic Press.
Freedman, Paul. 2008. *Out of the East: Spices and the Medieval Imagination.* New Haven: Yale University Press.
Gabaccia, Donna R. 1998. *We Are What We Eat: Ethnic Food and the Making of Americans.* Cambridge, MA: Harvard University Press.
Hastorf, Christine A. 2017. *The Social Archaeology of Food: Thinking about Eating from Prehistory to the Present.* New York: Cambridge University Press.
Haviland, William A. 1967. "Stature at Tikal, Guatemala: Implications for Ancient Maya Demography and Social Organization." *American Antiquity* 32(3):316–325.
Jones, Martin. 2007. *Feast: Why Humans Share Food.* New York: Oxford University Press.
Joyce, Rosemary A., and John S. Henderson. 2007. "From Feasting to Cuisine: Implications of Archaeological Research in an Early Honduran Village." *American Anthropologist* 109(4):642–653.
King, Michelle T., ed. 2019. *Culinary Nationalism in Asia.* London: Bloomsbury.
Lentz, David L. 1991. "Maya Diets of the Rich and Poor: Paleoethnobotanical Evidence from Copan." *Latin American Antiquity* 2(3):269–287.
Long, Lucy M., ed. 2004. *Culinary Tourism.* Lexington: University Press of Kentucky.
MacDonald, Nathan. 2008. *Not Bread Alone: The Uses of Food in the Old Testament.* New York: Oxford University Press.
McCann, James. 2009. *Stirring the Pot: A History of African Cuisine.* Athens: Ohio University Press.
Mintz, Sidney W. 1985. *Sweetness and Power: The Place of Sugar in Modern History.* New York: Viking Penguin.
Norton, Marcy. 2008. *Sacred Gifts, Profane Pleasures: A History of Tobacco and Chocolate in the Atlantic World.* Ithaca, NY: Cornell University Press.

Opie, Fredrick Douglass. 2008. *Hogs and Hominy: Soul Food from Africa to America*. New York: Columbia University Press.
Pilcher, Jeffrey M. 1998. *¡Que vivan los tamales! Food and the Making of Mexican Identity*. Albuquerque: University of New Mexico Press.
———. 2012. *Planet Taco: A Global History of Mexican Food*. New York: Oxford University Press.
Pohl, Mary Deland. 1994. "The Economics and Politics of Maya Meat Eating." In *The Economic Anthropology of the State*, ed. Elizabeth M. Brumfiel, 119–148. Lanham, MD: University Press of America.
Proskouriakoff, Tatiana. 1963. *Historical Data in the Inscriptions of Yaxchilan*. Mexico City: Centro de Estudios Mayas.
Pyburn, K. Anne. 1989. "Maya Cuisine: Hearths and the Lowland Economy." In *Prehistoric Maya Economies of Belize*, ed. Patricia A. McAnany and Barry L. Isaac, 325–344. Greenwich, CT: JAI Press.
Rappaport, Erika Diane. 2017. *A Thirst for Empire: How Tea Shaped the Modern World*. Princeton: Princeton University Press.
Rath, Eric C. 2010. *Food and Fantasy in Early Modern Japan*. Berkeley: University of California Press.
Richards, Audrey I. 1939. *Land, Labour and Diet in Northern Rhodesia: An Economic Study of the Bemba Tribe*. London: Oxford University Press.
Rohel, Jaclyn, ed. 2017. *Genealogies of Edibility in Global Culture*. A special issue of *Global Food History* 3(2).
Rotberg, Robert I., and Theodore K. Rabb, eds. 1985. *Hunger and History: The Impact of Changing Food Production and Consumption Patterns on Society*. New York: Cambridge University Press.
Scarpellini, Emanuela. 2015. *Food and Foodways in Italy from 1861 to the Present*. London: Palgrave Macmillan.
Schivelbusch, Wolfgang. 1993. *Tastes of Paradise: A Social History of Spices, Stimulants, and Intoxicants*. Trans. David Jacobson. New York: Vintage Books.
Staller, John E., and Michael D. Carrasco, eds. 2010. *Pre-Columbian Foodways: Interdisciplinary Approaches to Food, Culture, and Markets in Ancient Mesoamerica*. New York: Springer.
Steckel, Richard H., and Jerome C. Rose, eds. 2002. *The Backbone of History: Health and Nutrition in the Western Hemisphere*. Cambridge: Cambridge University Press.
Stephens, John Lloyd. 1841. *Incidents of Travel in Central America, Chiapas, and Yucatan*. 2 vols. New York: Harper and Brothers.
Sterckx, Roel. 2015. "Alcohol and Historiography in Early China." *Global Food History* 1(1):13–32.
Stross, Brian. 2011. "Food, Foam and Fermentation in Mesoamerica: Bubbles and the Sacred State of Inebriation." *Food, Culture, and Society* 14(4):477–501.
Taube, Karl A. 1989. "The Maize Tamale in Classic Maya Diet, Epigraphy, and Art." *American Antiquity* 54(1):31–51.
Taylor, Diana. 2003. *The Archive and the Repertoire: Performing Cultural Memory in the Americas*. Durham, NC: Duke University Press.
Taylor, William B. 1979. *Drinking, Homicide, and Rebellion in Colonial Mexican Villages*. Stanford, CA: Stanford University Press.

Tompkins, Kyla Wazana. 2012. *Racial Indigestion: Eating Bodies in the Nineteenth Century*. New York: New York University Press.
Wallach, Jennifer Jensen. 2019. *Every Nation Has Its Dish: Black Bodies and Black Food in Twentieth-Century America*. Chapel Hill: University of North Carolina Press.
Watson, James L., ed. 1997. *Golden Arches East: McDonald's in East Asia*. Stanford, CA: Stanford University Press.
White, Christine D., ed. 1999. *Reconstructing Ancient Maya Diet*. Salt Lake City: University of Utah Press.
Wilk, Richard R. 1999. "'Real Belizean Food': Building Local Identity in the Transnational Caribbean." *American Anthropologist* 101(2):244–255.
———. 2006. *Home Cooking in the Global Village: Caribbean Food from Buccaneers to Ecotourists*. London: Berg.
Williams-Forson, Psyche A. 2006. *Building Houses Out of Chicken Legs: Black Women, Food, and Power*. Chapel Hill: University of North Carolina Press.
Wilson, Thomas M., ed. 2005. *Drinking Cultures: Alcohol and Identity*. Oxford: Berg.
Worthen, W. B. 2004. "Disciplines of the Text: Sites of Performance." In *The Performance Studies Reader*, ed. Henry Bial, 10–25. New York: Routledge.
Wright, Lori E. 2006. *Diet, Health, and Status among the Pasión Maya: A Reappraisal of the Collapse*. Nashville: Vanderbilt University Press.
Zanoni, Elizabeth. 2018. *Migrant Marketplaces: Food and Italians in North and South America*. Urbana: University of Illinois Press.

Index

Acanceh, 94
addiction to food, 4
agency, 2, 3, 131
agriculture, 3, 5, 6, 9, 12, 142, 310–313
Aguateca, 176, 178
Altun Ha, 193
ancestors, 32, 47, 52, 100, 190, 222, 290
Andrews, Anthony P., 8, 278
Appadurai, Arjun, 4, 138, 189, 262
apprenticeship, 2, 5
authenticity, 6
Aztecs, 11, 70, 107, 372, 373; marketplaces of, 11

Balankanche Cave, 52
balche' (honey-wine), 7, 18, 68, 74, 101, 105, 138, 334–363, 368
ballcourts and ballgame, 29, 94, 223, 227, 234, 235, 368
bees and beekeeping, 18, 102, 128, 130, 334–363, 369, 375
Belize River valley, 27, 28, 48–74
Blackman Eddy, 16, 27–42
burials, 55, 56, 138, 161, 173, 177, 224, 225, 234, 301, 312; in caves, 55
burning and burned deposits, 54, 175, 221, 230

cacao (chocolate), 5, 7, 9, 26, 33, 61, 68, 71–74, 76, 89, 92, 94–96, 98, 105, 106–114, 127–129, 132, 133, 135, 141, 143, 146, 191–193, 204, 211, 221, 230, 232–234, 254, 262, 287, 349, 359, 368, 369, 370, 371, 374
Cacaxtla, 277
Cahal Pech, 27, 37, 173
Calakmul, 11, 70, 88, 90, 104, 146, 167; Chiik Nahb murals at, 11, 70, 88, 95, 96, 98, 100
Campo Dos, 227, 234
Cancuén, 72, 163, 180
Caracol, 177, 193
Carnegie Institution of Washington, 7, 279
Carrasco, Michael D., 10
Castillo Cocom, Juan, 336
Catherwood, Frederick, 366
caves, 47–77, 162, 334; and ritual, 47–77
Ceibal, 161, 163, 167, 177
ceramic figurines, 31, 75, 94, 95, 226, 235, 322
ceramic serving vessels, 14, 27, 33, 35, 48, 87, 108, 188, 194, 201, 202, 227, 231, 235, 251, 254, 259, 287, 289, 322, 369
Cerro Palenque, 227, 234
Cerros, 31, 161, 180
Chau Hiix, 193
Chichén Itzá, 18, 192, 211, 274–291, 308, 372, 375

children, 3, 72, 146, 234, 261, 339, 352, 353; and learning, 3, 135; sacrifice of, 106
Chinikihá, 180
Cholula, 277, 372
Cobá, 276
codices, 18, 89, 94, 95, 100, 161, 190, 303, 334–337, 340, 341, 349, 351, 353–361; Dresden Codex, 90, 93, 95, 96, 190, 191, 211; Madrid Codex, 95, 190, 336, 340, 354, 355–361
Coe, Michael D. 9, 87, 110
Coe, Sophie D., 9
Colha, 138, 161, 302
commensality, 17, 137, 142, 219–220, 233, 243, 246, 248, 250, 251, 256, 258–261, 263–266, 367
Copán, 17, 88, 95, 104, 108, 136, 139, 145, 219–236, 371
Cozumel, 9, 163, 176, 302, 303
Cuello, 161, 162
Currusté, 235

Datura, 68, 74–76, 104, 139
deer, 8, 36, 37–40, 56, 61, 92–95, 124, 177–179, 191, 202, 203, 211, 221, 228, 234, 254, 286, 289, 299, 303, 304, 313, 318, 322, 323, 324, 337, 351, 355, 359, 361, 371; husbandry of, 303, 323, 324
dietary inequality, 1, 191, 211, 221, 224, 297–327, 369, 370, 371
Dos Pilas, 106, 176
Dresden Codex. *See* codices
drought, 265, 300, 304, 305, 326
Dzibilchaltun, 167, 211

E-Group, 29, 31
Ek Balam, 167, 278
El Tajín, 277, 372
El Zotz, 110, 112
embodied practice, 367
enemas, 57, 75, 104, 106, 373
epigraphy, 10, 16, 87–115, 253, 260, 370–372; epigraphic captions on food, 11, 95, 98, 143; epigraphic references to food, 10, 47, 71

ethnographic analogy, 6, 52, 70, 72, 337–341, 345–353

faunal remains. *See* zooarchaeology
feasting, 2, 5, 6, 7, 13, 18, 25–42, 137–138, 142, 163, 181, 189, 190, 212, 219, 233, 236, 243, 246, 249, 259–261, 263, 265, 274, 281, 289, 291, 357, 367, 368, 375; diacritical, 246, 259, 263, 265, 290; patron–role, 275, 289; potluck-style, 26, 28, 41, 190, 368; and rise of social complexity, 25; royal courts and, 243; and spatial component of, 5, 28, 133
Freidel, David, 1

Garber, James F., 30
gardens, 3, 6, 128, 191, 338, 369; at Joya de Cerén, 11
GMOs, 4; and GMO drift, 4
God L, 99, 100, 144
Graff, Sarah, 2, 3

Hamblin, Nancy, 8
Haraway, Donna, 131
Hastorf, Christine, 3, 10, 26, 143, 144, 189, 281
hmen (shaman), 71, 74, 339, 345, 350–353, 355, 362
Holmul, 110, 252
Holtzman, Jon D., 13
honey, 18, 101, 105, 135, 138, 192, 221, 262, 334–363
honey-wine. *See balche'*
house societies, 222, 224, 232, 234

Ichmul de Morley, 278
identity formation, 2, 10, 189, 274, 280, 366, 367
Ingold, Timothy, 335
Isla Cerritos, 278, 288
isotope studies, 10, 12, 17, 38, 39, 144, 163, 193, 233, 234, 303; of animals, 38, 39, 163; of human bones, 10, 144, 233, 234
Ixtutz, 109, 113
Izapa, 51

jade (and greenstone), 31, 127, 189, 198, 204, 210, 211
Joya de Cerén, 11, 139, 190, 232; gardens at, 11

Kabah, 201, 212
Kaminaljuyu, 163, 181
kitchens, 5, 6, 12, 18, 135, 146, 161, 193, 199, 200, 201, 212, 230, 244, 246, 248, 251, 274, 282, 338, 352, 369, 372

Lacandón, 52, 75, 334, 346–350, 352–355
La Corona, 17, 104, 243–266, 368
Lagartero, 162, 163, 180
Laguna de On, 300, 301, 303
Lamanai, 176, 177, 193
Landa, Bishop Diego de, 7, 100, 126, 138, 162, 163, 173, 190–192, 211, 342–344
Lentz, David L., 9, 143
LiDAR survey, 298, 307
Lower Ulúa valley, 17, 107, 219–236, 369, 371

Madrid Codex. *See* codices
Maize Deity, 1, 5, 31, 71, 97, 99, 100, 104, 110, 189, 190, 354, 357, 361, 374
markets, 3, 11, 70, 88, 100, 127, 128, 130, 147, 179, 305, 327, 371
Mayapán, 18, 163, 167, 192, 297–327, 343, 370
McLuhan, Marshall, 125, 142
memory, 2, 3, 10, 11–14, 144, 290, 367, 373; and memory work, 2, 12
metates (grinding stones), 96, 135, 141, 195, 198–202, 211, 231, 248, 369, 372
midden, 10, 34, 36, 161, 179, 202, 203, 212, 244, 246, 251, 254, 255, 259, 280, 284–290, 301, 302, 314, 316, 367
Middle American Research Institute, 7–8
Mintz, Sidney, 220, 373

Mixtec, 52
mobility studies, 18, 367, 370
molcajetes (grater bowls), 274–291, 371
Motul de San José, 106, 113, 179

Naj Tunich, 105–106
Naranjo, 111–113
national cuisine, 4, 281, 282
nixtamalization, 7, 99, 110, 135, 204, 370, 374, 376

Olmec, 1, 74, 99
Oxkintok, 88

Pacbitun, 16, 38, 47–72, 193
palace diet, 99, 193
palaces, 6, 11, 13, 16, 88, 99, 176, 193, 195, 200, 201, 211, 212, 243, 244, 246–248, 250, 251, 254–260, 261, 263, 264, 278, 367; feasting rooms of, 6, 201, 254–260, 264; kitchens of, 244, 251
Palenque, 71, 110
paleoethnobotany, 9, 10, 16, 35, 48, 124–150, 228, 251, 254, 289
pathologies (nutritional), 10
Peirce, Charles Saunders, 125, 145
petroglyph, 55
pib' and *pibil* (underground oven), 7, 135, 179, 351–352, 353
Piedras Negras, 95, 107, 127, 129, 134, 139, 148, 193, 371
Pilcher, Jeffrey, 18
Pohl, Mary, 8, 228
Pollan, Michael, 130
Popol Vuh, 1, 100, 147, 162
praxis, daily, 2, 274
Proskouriakoff, Tatiana, 366
pulque, 16, 95, 96, 101–106, 114, 147, 262, 372, 373

Quetzalcoatl, 277, 279, 283
Quiriguá, 51

Rain Deity (Chaak, Tlaloc), 51–52, 106, 190, 344, 346, 348–350, 359
residue analyses, 16, 48, 49, 60, 61, 62,

66, 68, 72, 74, 76, 77, 108, 124, 125, 127, 129, 138, 148, 197, 199, 201, 202, 204–208, 228, 229, 232, 251, 256, 287, 323
Río Amarillo, 126, 129, 134, 148
Río Azul, 93, 108, 110, 112, 113, 138
ritual, 2, 3, 8, 13, 14, 25–33, 35, 40, 41, 47–77, 89, 100, 101, 104, 106, 114, 124, 127, 130, 138, 144, 147, 148, 161–163, 166, 172–182, 199, 212, 213, 223, 227, 229, 230, 235, 250, 275, 279, 280, 283, 303, 334–363, 367, 368; in caves, 47–77, 101, 368; and fauna, 8, 161, 162, 163, 166, 172–182, 229; and food use, 3, 8, 13, 18, 25–27, 30–32, 41, 100, 104, 106, 114, 124, 250, 303, 334–363, 367; funerary, 14, 55; of inclusion, 5, 265, 274, 290; plant use in, 48, 230; and rain, 51
Reilly, F. Kent, 1
Roys, Ralph L., 7

sacbe, 49, 73
salicylic acid, 62, 68–71
salt, 8, 95, 98, 124, 135, 276, 303
San Bartolo, 88
San Diego, Yucatán, 75
shells: freshwater, 37; marine, 31, 33, 36, 38, 41, 49, 94, 227, 283, 285, 288, 312
shortages, of food, 4, 12, 126, 264
signature foods, 4, 189, 211, 283
Sihó, 17, 188–213
social imaginary, 12, 15, 275, 281, 282
Staller, John E., 10
starch grain analyses, 17, 48, 124, 127, 129, 146, 188, 202, 204, 229, 231
Stephens, John Lloyd, 7, 366
storage facilities, 17, 114, 135, 146, 148, 195, 198, 201, 207, 230, 244, 246, 248, 251, 252, 259, 263, 264, 320, 321, 322, 369

Tabi, 94
tamales, 11, 15, 28, 40, 92, 95, 96, 99, 100, 135, 137, 138, 139, 141, 143, 146, 148, 212, 231, 235, 254, 262, 281, 368, 369, 370, 374
technology, of cooking, 2, 10, 274–291, 371
Tepich, 338, 339, 345, 349, 353, 359
Tikal, 91, 134, 163, 167, 193
T'isil, 129, 134, 148
tobacco, 70, 74, 104, 139, 143, 144, 230, 235, 339, 345, 359, 375
Tolok, 37, 38
Tonina, 93, 94
trade, 6, 8, 124, 275, 279, 308, 312; and long-distance items, 31, 33, 124, 128, 275, 276, 284; maritime, 278; in salt, 8
tribute, 6, 100, 246, 248, 259, 305, 311–313, 371
Tulum, 89
turkey, 37, 93, 95, 191, 202, 203, 211, 212, 221, 254, 299, 304, 313, 318, 319, 322, 323, 337, 351, 354, 355

Uxmal, 7, 276, 308

vanilla, 74, 129, 132

warfare, 51, 94, 148, 277
Weismantel, Mary, 125, 146, 147
White, Christine D., 10
Wing, Elizabeth S., 8
women, and culinary labor, 1, 2, 96, 233, 339, 369

Xcalumkin, 147
Xuenkal, 18, 274–291
Xultun, 90, 91, 110, 112, 167
Xunantunich, 38, 251

Yaxchilán, 92
Yaxcopoíl, 308
Yaxuna, 278
Yula, 278

Zanoni, Elizabeth, 370
zooarchaeology, 8, 9, 16, 17, 27, 34, 36, 161–182, 192–193, 202–203, 228, 254, 260, 297–327, 375